JONATHAN M. KATZ

# GANGSTERS OF CAPITALISM

**SMEDLEY BUTLER,**
THE MARINES, AND THE MAKING AND
BREAKING OF AMERICA'S EMPIRE

ST. MARTIN'S GRIFFIN
NEW YORK

Published in the United States by St. Martin's Griffin, an imprint of St. Martin's Publishing Group

GANGSTERS OF CAPITALISM. Copyright © 2021 by Jonathan M. Katz. All rights reserved. Printed in the United States of America. For information, address St. Martin's Publishing Group, 120 Broadway, New York, NY 10271.

www.stmartins.com

Map by Mapping Specialists Ltd.

The Library of Congress has cataloged the hardcover edition as follows:

Names: Katz, Jonathan M., author.
Title: Gangsters of capitalism : Smedley Butler, the Marines, and the making and breaking of America's empire / Jonathan M. Katz.
Other titles: Smedley Butler, the Marines, and the making and breaking of America's empire
Description: First edition. | New York : St. Martin's Press, 2022. | Includes bibliographical references and index. |
Identifiers: LCCN 2021036722 | ISBN 9781250135582 (hardcover) | ISBN 9781250135605 (ebook)
Subjects: LCSH: Butler, Smedley D. (Smedley Darlington), 1881–1940. | Generals—United States—Biography. | United States. Marine Corps—Officers—Biography. | United States. Marine Corps—History—History—20th century. | United States—History, Military—21st century. | Imperialism. | Pacifists—Pennsylvania—Biography. | Quakers—Pennsylvania—Philadelphia—Biography.
Classification: LCC VE25.B88 K38 2022 | DDC 973.91/6—dc23
LC record available at https://lccn.loc.gov/2021036722

ISBN 978-1-250-13559-9 (trade paperback)

Our books may be purchased in bulk for promotional, educational, or business use. Please contact your local bookseller or the Macmillan Corporate and Premium Sales Department at 1-800-221-7945, extension 5442, or by email at MacmillanSpecialMarkets@macmillan.com.

First St. Martin's Griffin Edition: 2023

10  9  8  7  6  5  4  3  2

# Additional Praise for *Gangsters of Capitalism*

"A sensational read."

—Mike Duncan, *New York Times* bestselling author and host of the podcast *Revolutions*

"Engaging . . . The long-dead Marine also serves as Katz's Virgil, leading him on a journey around the world and through the inferno of empire's afterlife." —*The New Republic*

"A real page-turner." —Noam Chomsky

"A perfect marriage of author and subject." —Emily Tamkin, *The New Statesman*

"I can't praise it enough. Compelling, readable, and profound." —Jamelle Bouie

"May well be the most intrepid biography you will ever read." —Ben Fountain, author of the National Book Award finalist *Billy Lynn's Long Halftime Walk*

"A taut, unnerving account . . . Katz thoughtfully reckons with empire's true cost." —Daniel Immerwahr, author of *How to Hide an Empire*

"A bracing, necessary read for our times." —Jon Lee Anderson, author of *Che: A Revolutionary Life*

"Katz writes really beautifully about very ugly things. I couldn't recommend this book more highly." —Spencer Ackerman, author of *Reign of Terror*

"Searing . . . An eye-opening portrait of American hubris." —*Publishers Weekly*

"Katz's realism may shock many readers, but they would be well served to join him in pulling back the curtain, tipping over the jugs of institutional Kool-Aid, and taking a long, cold, hard look in the proverbial mirror." —*Task & Purpose*

"A fantastic book." —Rachel Maddow

"Really remarkable . . . [Katz] takes it to the next level." —Clint Smith, winner of the National Book Critics Circle Award for *How the Word Is Passed*

## ALSO BY JONATHAN M. KATZ

*The Big Truck That Went By*

*For Claire, for everything*

*The one who deals the blow forgets.*
*The one who carries the scar remembers.*
—Haitian proverb

# CONTENTS

*(Nine pages of photos appear between pages 224 and 225.)*

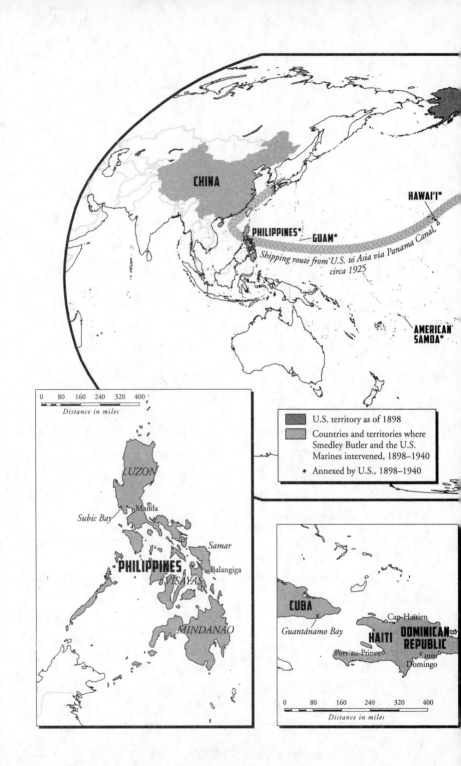

CHINA

HAWAI'I*

PHILIPPINES* — GUAM*

*Shipping route from U.S. to Asia via Panama Canal, circa 1925*

AMERICAN SAMOA*

U.S. territory as of 1898

Countries and territories where Smedley Butler and the U.S. Marines intervened, 1898–1940

* Annexed by U.S., 1898–1940

0  80  160  240  320  400
*Distance in miles*

*LUZON*

*Subic Bay*    Manila

*Samar*

**PHILIPPINES**    Balangiga

*VISAYAS*

*MINDANAO*

CUBA

Cap-Haïtien

*Guantánamo Bay*    HAITI    DOMINICAN REPUBLIC

Port-au-Prince    Santo Domingo

0  80  160  240  320  400
*Distance in miles*

UNITED STATES OF AMERICA
(MAINLAND)

FRANCE

CUBA

HAITI
DOMINICAN REPUBLIC
PUERTO RICO*

MEXICO

U.S. VIRGIN ISLANDS*

HONDURAS
NICARAGUA

PANAMA      COLOMBIA

MEXICO

BELIZE

GUATEMALA

HONDURAS

La Ceiba

EL SALVADOR

NICARAGUA

Corinto
Managua
Granada

Bluefields

COSTA RICA

Panama Canal

Colón

PANAMA

Panama City

COLOMBIA

0    80   160   240   320   400
Distance in miles

Map by Mapping Specialists Ltd.

# PROLOGUE

The bankers' men were back. Smedley Butler sized up the one doing all the talking—the bond salesman in the tailored suit. The visitor was sitting in the vaulted main hallway the Butlers used as a living room, his cannonball-shaped head framed by the retired general's old command flags, medals, swords, and assorted tropical bric-a-brac. Two mammoth red satin umbrellas, given to Butler by villagers on his last overseas mission, to China, swayed gently overhead atop their fifteen-foot poles.

The bond salesman, one Gerald C. MacGuire, represented himself as a member of the American Legion, a veterans' organization founded at the end of the Great War. He was trying to persuade Butler to come to the next Legion convention, in Chicago, to give a speech denouncing President Franklin Delano Roosevelt—specifically his recent decision to take the dollar off the gold standard. Butler, the salesman said, would travel in secret with a few hundred legionnaire friends. Once they were at the convention, they would spread out around the assembly and start a chant to demand that Butler be given the floor.

What rank-and-file veteran could afford a five-day trip to Chicago in the middle of the Great Depression, Butler wondered. MacGuire replied it would all be taken care of: train tickets, hotels, everything.

"How do you get the money to do that?" the general asked.[1]

"Oh, we have friends," MacGuire responded. Then he opened a bank book showing $42,000 in deposits—worth over $850,000 nearly a century later.

Butler was accustomed to people asking him for favors. It was the price of fame. For thirty-three years and four months he had been in active service as a United States Marine, a veteran of nearly every overseas conflict dating back to the war against Spain in 1898.[2] Respected by his peers, beloved by his men, he was known throughout the country as "The Fighting Hell-Devil Marine," "Old Gimlet Eye," "The Leatherneck's Friend," and the famous "Fighting Quaker" of the Devil Dogs. Bestselling books had been written about him. Hollywood adored him. President Roosevelt's cousin, the late Theodore himself, was said to have called Butler "the ideal American soldier."[3] Over the course of his career, he had received the Army and Navy Distinguished Service Medals, the French Ordre de l'Étoile Noire, and, in the distinction that would ensure his place in the Marine Corps pantheon, the Medal of Honor—twice.

But most who asked for an audience at the general's converted farmhouse in Newtown Square, a suburb off Philadelphia's Main Line, did not carry thick bankbooks, as the bond salesman did. Nor did they pull up in his dirt driveway in a chauffeured Packard limousine. Butler wanted to know more. Asking around in the days that followed, he learned MacGuire had been a Navy man in the World War, and had suffered a skull fracture at sea in 1918—off the exact spot on the coast of France where Butler had been stationed. That explained the ties to the American Legion, if little else.

Over the following weeks, MacGuire continued the courtship. In Newark, where Butler was attending the reunion of a National Guard division, MacGuire showed up at his hotel room and tossed a wad of cash on the bed—$18,000, he said.

"You put that money away before someone walks in here," Butler barked. Then he asked where all the money was coming from. MacGuire told the general he was working for several wealthy backers. One of them was Robert Sterling Clark—an heir to the Singer sewing machine fortune, whom Butler had known as a lieutenant in China during the Boxer Rebellion decades earlier. Another was MacGuire's boss, the well-connected financier Grayson M.-P. Murphy, who had close ties with the nation's most powerful bank, J. P. Morgan & Co., and Wall Street's most influential law firm, Sullivan & Cromwell.[4] Clark himself paid a visit to the Newtown Square house soon after, hinting broadly that he would cover the Butlers' mortgage if the Marine played ball.

The dates of the American Legion convention came and went. Butler did not go. But then, a few months later, in early 1934, Butler received a postcard from MacGuire. It was sent from the French Riviera, where the bond salesman had just arrived after visiting Fascist Italy. About two months later, Butler received another postcard, this time from Germany. The Reichstag fire had happened a year earlier. Hitler was now chancellor, on his way to becoming führer. MacGuire said he was having "a wonderful time" in Berlin.

In August 1934, MacGuire called Butler from Philadelphia and asked to meet. Butler suggested an abandoned café at the back of the lobby of the Bellevue-Stratford Hotel.

"The time has come to get the soldiers together," MacGuire said.

"Yes," Butler replied. "I think so, too."

He had no idea what they were talking about. He just wanted the salesman to keep talking until the outlines of what he was really after became clear.

First MacGuire excitedly recounted all he had seen in Europe. In Fascist Italy and Nazi Germany, he'd learned that Mussolini and Hitler were able to stay in power because they kept soldiers on their payrolls in various ways. "But that setup would not suit us at all. The soldiers of America would not like that," the businessman opined.

But in France, MacGuire had "found just exactly the organization we're going to have." Called the Croix de Feu, or Fiery Cross, it was like a more militant version of the American Legion: an association of French World War veterans and paramilitaries organized under the populist authoritarian Col. François de La Rocque. On February 6, 1934—six weeks before MacGuire arrived—thousands of members of the Croix de Feu had taken part in a riot of mainly far-right and fascist groups that had tried to storm the French legislature. The insurrection was stopped by police; at least fifteen people, mostly rioters, were killed. But in the aftermath, France's center-left prime minister had been forced to resign in favor of a conservative.

MacGuire had attended a meeting of the Croix de Feu in Paris. It was the sort of "super-organization" he believed Americans could get behind—especially with a beloved war hero like Butler at the helm.

Then he made his proposal: The Marine would lead half a million veterans in a march on Washington, blending the Croix de Feu's assault on the French legislature with the March on Rome that had put Mussolini's Fascisti in power in Italy a decade earlier. They would be financed and armed by some of the most powerful corporations in America—including

DuPont, the nation's biggest manufacturer of explosives and synthetic materials.[5]

The purpose of the coup was to stop Roosevelt's New Deal, the president's program to end the Great Depression, which one of the millionaire du Pont brothers had deemed "nothing more or less than the Socialistic doctrine called by another name."[6] Butler's veteran army, MacGuire explained, would pressure the president to appoint a new secretary of state, or "secretary of general affairs," who would take on the executive powers of government. If Roosevelt went along with this, he would be allowed to remain as a figurehead, like the king of Italy. Otherwise, he would be forced to resign, placing the new super-secretary in the White House.

Smedley Butler knew a coup when he smelled one. He had been in many himself. He had overthrown governments and protected "friendly" client ones around the world on behalf of some of the same U.S. bankers, lawyers, and businessmen who were apparently trying to enlist his help.

It had been largely on their behalf that Butler and his Marines trained and helped put into power the Hitlers and Mussolinis of Latin America: dictators like the Dominican Republic's Rafael Trujillo and Nicaragua's soon-to-be leader, Anastasio Somoza, who would employ violent repression and their U.S.-created militaries to protect American investments and their own power. MacGuire's easy dismissal of electoral democracy recalled the disdain for other republics past U.S. presidents had shown. The resulting interference in other countries' affairs had been prodded on and aided by moneyed interests like J. P. Morgan; MacGuire's boss, Grayson Murphy; and their globetrotting lawyer friends at Sullivan & Cromwell.

In other words, Butler knew these people. He knew the world they traveled in. He had made a life in the overlapping seams of capital and empire, and he knew that the subversion of democracy by force had turned out to be a required part of the job he had chosen. "I spent most of my time being a high-class muscle man for big business, for Wall Street and for the bankers," Butler would write a year later. "In short, I was a racketeer for capitalism."[7]

And Butler knew another thing that most Americans didn't: how much they would suffer if anyone did to their democracy what he had done to so many others across the globe.

"Now, about this super-organization," MacGuire asked the general. "Would you be interested in heading it?"

"I am interested in it, but I do not know about heading it," Butler told the bond salesman, as he resolved to report everything he had learned to Congress. "I am very greatly interested in it, because you know, Jerry, my interest is, my one hobby is, maintaining a democracy. If you get these five hundred thousand soldiers advocating anything smelling of fascism, I am going to get five hundred thousand more and lick the hell out of you, and we will have a real war right at home."

Eight decades after he publicly revealed his conversations about what became known as the Business Plot, Smedley Butler is no longer a household name. A few history buffs—and a not-inconsiderable number of conspiracy theory enthusiasts—remember him for his whistleblowing of the alleged fascist coup. Another repository of his memory is kept among modern-day Marines, who learn one detail of his life in boot camp—the two Medals of Honor—and to sing his name along with those of his legendary Marine contemporaries, Dan Daly and Lewis "Chesty" Puller, in a running cadence about devotion to the Corps: "It was good for Smedley Butler / And it's good enough for me."

I first encountered the other side of Butler's legacy in Haiti, after I moved there to be the correspondent for the Associated Press. To Haitians, Butler is no hero. He is remembered by scholars there as the most *mechan*—corrupt or evil—of the Marines. He helped lead the U.S. invasion of that republic in 1915 and played a singular role in setting up an occupation that lasted nearly two decades. Most notoriously, Butler instigated a system of forced labor, the *corvée,* in which Haitians were required to build hundreds of miles of roads for no pay, and were killed or jailed if they did not comply. Haitians saw it for what it was: a form of slavery, enraging a people whose ancestors had freed themselves from enslavement and French colonialism over a century before.

Such facts do not make a dent in the mainstream narrative of U.S. history. Most Americans prefer to think of ourselves as plucky heroes: the rebels who topple the empire, not the storm troopers running its battle stations. U.S. textbooks—and more importantly the novels, video games, monuments, tourist sites, and blockbuster films where most people encounter versions of American history—are more often about the Civil War or World War II, the struggles most easily framed in moral certitudes of right and wrong, and in which those fighting under the U.S. flag had the strongest claims to being on the side of good.

"Imperialism," on the other hand, is a foreign-sounding word. It brings· up images, if it brings any at all, of redcoats terrorizing Boston, or perhaps British officials in linen suits sipping gin and tonics in Bombay. The idea that the United States, a country founded in rebellion against empire, could have colonized and conquered other peoples seems anathema to everything we are taught America stands for.

And it is. It was no coincidence that thousands of young men like Smedley Butler were convinced to sign up for America's first overseas war of empire on the promise of ending Spanish tyranny and imperialism in Cuba. Brought up as a Quaker on Philadelphia's Main Line, Butler held on to principles of equality and fairness throughout his life, even as he fought to install and defend despotic regimes all over the world. That tension—between the ideal of the United States as a leading champion of democracy on the one hand and a leading destroyer of democracy on the other—remains the often unacknowledged fault line running through American politics today.

For some past leaders, there was never a tension at all. When the U.S. seized its first inhabited overseas colonies in 1898, some proudly wore the label. "I am, as I expected I would be, a pretty good imperialist," Theodore Roosevelt mused to a British friend while on safari in East Africa in 1910.[8]

But as the costs of full-on annexation became clear, and control through influence and subterfuge became the modus operandi of U.S. empire, American leaders reverted seamlessly back to republican rhetoric. They could do so because, as Sven Lindqvist has written of colonialism in all its forms, "the men representing civilization out in the colonies were 'invisible' not only in the sense that their guns killed at a distance, but also in that no one at home really knew what they were doing." (Though it should not be forgotten that the United States still has five wholly owned colonies today in Puerto Rico, the U.S. Virgin Islands, Guam, American Samoa, and the Northern Mariana Islands, along with a plethora of largely uninhabited smaller islands and atolls.)[9]

The denial deepened during the Cold War. In 1955, the historian William Appleman Williams wrote, "One of the central themes of American historiography is that there is no American Empire."[10] It was essential for the conflict against the Soviet Union—"the Evil Empire," as Ronald Reagan would call it—to heighten the supposed contrasts: *they* overthrew governments, *we* defended legitimate ones; *they* were expansionist, *we* went abroad only in defense of freedom.

Even capitalism was played down as a motivation during those years. In early drafts of his 1947 speech announcing a policy of "containing" Soviet expansion, President Harry S. Truman stressed the economic imperatives of keeping countries in the U.S. orbit, particularly those essential for access to oil in the Middle East. But that sounded too base—"like an investment prospectus," Truman complained—so his team scrapped it for rhetoric more likely to persuade Congress to throw money at foreign wars. In his final draft, Truman proclaimed that "it must be the policy of the United States to support free peoples who are resisting attempted subjugation by armed minorities or by outside pressure."[11]

As long as the United States seemed eternally ascendant, it was easy to tell ourselves as Americans that the global dominance of U.S. capital and the unparalleled reach of the U.S. military had been coincidences, or fate; that America's rise as a cultural and economic superpower was just natural—a galaxy of individual choices, freely made, by a planet hungry for an endless supply of Marvel superheroes and the perfect salty crunch of McDonald's fries.

But the illusion is fading. The myth of American invulnerability was shattered by the September 11, 2001, attacks. The attempt to recover a sense of dominance resulted in the catastrophic "forever wars" launched and, as of this writing, still burning at various levels in Afghanistan, Iraq, Libya, Syria, Somalia, and elsewhere. The deaths of well over half a million Americans in the coronavirus pandemic, and our seeming inability to halt or contend with the threats of climate change, are further reminders that being the richest and most powerful empire on Earth has its limits, and we can neither accumulate nor consume our way out of a fragile and interconnected world.

I experienced the gulf between the promise and realities of American power most acutely during my years living in Haiti, particularly in the aftermath of the catastrophic 2010 earthquake. I watched with horror and frustration as my neighbors waited in vain for the promised U.S.-led efforts to rescue and rebuild. Instead my country deployed thousands of armed troops to keep people from migrating, while shuffling around billions of dollars in Haiti's name. Precious little was ever put into people's hands on the ground. Despite an upwelling of sympathy from millions of Americans, those in business and government ended up channeling their energies into the worst of our historical patterns, treating Haiti's disaster as an opportunity to make profits and execute political schemes, treating Haitian lives and priorities as largely irrelevant.[12]

As I looked through history to find the origins of the patterns of self-dealing and imperiousness that mark so much of American policy, I kept running into the Quaker Marine with the funny name. Smedley Butler's military career started in the place where the United States' overseas empire truly began, and the place that continues to symbolize the most egregious abuses of American power: Guantánamo Bay. His last overseas deployment, in China from 1927 to 1929, gave him a front-row seat to both the start of the civil war between the Communists and the Nationalists and the slowly materializing Japanese invasion that would ultimately open World War II.

In the years between, Butler blazed a path for U.S. empire across the world, helping seize the Philippines and the land for the Panama Canal, and invading and helping plunder Honduras, Nicaragua, Haiti, the Dominican Republic, Mexico, and more. Butler was also a pioneer of the militarization of police: first spearheading the creation of client police forces across Latin America (known in most Spanish-speaking countries as the Guardia Nacional and in Haiti as the Gendarmerie), then introducing those tactics to U.S. cities during a two-year stint running the Philadelphia police during Prohibition.

Yet Butler would spend the last decade of his life trying to keep the forces of tyranny and violence he had unleashed abroad from consuming the country he loved. He watched the rise of fascism in Europe with alarm. Perhaps he intuited at some elemental level the observation that would be voiced decades later by the Pan-Africanist political philosopher Frantz Fanon: "What is fascism but colonialism in the heart of a traditionally colonialist country?"[13] He would spend his last stores of energy in antiwar speeches and anti-imperialist tracts. In 1935, Butler published a short book about the collusion between business and the armed forces called *War Is a Racket*. The warnings in that thin volume would be refined and amplified years later by his fellow general, turned president, Dwight Eisenhower, whose speechwriters would dub it the military-industrial complex.

Late in 1935, Butler would go further, declaring in a series of articles for a radical magazine: "Only the United Kingdom has beaten our record for square miles of territory acquired by military conquest. Our exploits against the American Indian, against the Filipinos, the Mexicans, and against Spain are on a par with the campaigns of Genghis Khan, the Japanese in Manchuria and the African attack of Mussolini."[14]

Butler was not just throwing stones. In that article, he repeatedly called himself a racketeer—a gangster—and enumerated his crimes:

> I helped make Mexico and especially Tampico safe for American oil interests in 1914. I helped make Haiti and Cuba a decent place for the National City Bank boys to collect revenues in. I helped in the raping of half a dozen Central American republics for the benefit of Wall Street. . . . I helped purify Nicaragua for the international banking house of Brown Brothers in 1909–12. I brought light to the Dominican Republic for American sugar interests in 1916. I helped make Honduras "right" for American fruit companies in 1903. In China in 1927 I helped see to it that Standard Oil went its way unmolested.
>
> During those years, I had, as the boys in the back room would say, a swell racket. I was rewarded with honors, medals, promotion. Looking back on it, I feel I might have given Al Capone a few hints. The best he could do was operate in three city districts. We Marines operated on three continents.[15]

Butler was telling a messier story than the ones Americans like to hear about ourselves. There is no *Saving Private Ryan* about the U.S. conquest of the Philippines. The Library of the Marine Corps at Quantico keeps Butler's antiwar tract hidden away from the handful of books about Butler and his Marine contemporaries' lives—shelving a few copies of *War Is a Racket* with other critical texts, including a thin volume of writings by Karl Marx.

But we ignore the past at our peril. Americans may not recognize the events Butler referred to in his confession, but America's imperial history is well remembered in the places we invaded and conquered—where leaders and elites use it and shape it to their own ends. Nowhere is more poised to use its colonial past to its future advantage than China, once a moribund kingdom in which U.S. forces, twice led by Butler, intervened at will in the early twentieth century. As a rising People's Republic embarks on its own imperial project across Asia, Africa, and Latin America, Chinese officials use their self-story of "national humiliation" to position themselves as an antidote to American control, finding willing audiences in countries grappling with their own histories of subjugation by the United States.

The dangers are greater at home. As a candidate and then as president, Donald Trump preyed on American anxieties by combining the worst excesses of those early-twentieth-century imperial chestnuts—militarism, white supremacy, and the cult of manhood—with a newer fantasy: that Americans could reclaim our sense of safety and supremacy by disengaging from the world we made; by literally building walls along our border and making the countries we conquered pay for them.

To those who did not know or ignored America's imperial history, it could seem that Trump was an alien force ("this is not who we are," as the liberal saying goes), or that the implosion of his presidency has made it safe to slip back into comfortable amnesias. But the movement Trump built—a movement that stormed the Capitol, tried to overturn an election, and as I write these words still dreams of reinstalling him by force—is too firmly rooted in America's past to be dislodged without substantial effort. It is a product of the greed, bigotry, and denialism that were woven into the structure of U.S. global supremacy from the beginning—forces that now threaten to break apart not only the empire but the society that birthed it.

The story of the making of America's global empire is at once more sweeping and smaller than one might expect. It involves forgotten wars against martial artists and criminal syndicates, marvels of engineering and human endurance, and zombies. (You read that correctly.) But the circle of people who were involved throughout was claustrophobically small. Names like Roosevelt, Alfred Thayer Mahan, Herbert Hoover, Roger Farnham, and the law firm of Sullivan & Cromwell pop up again and again. Their interests meanwhile were furthered and protected by an astoundingly tight coterie of Marines, including Dan Daly, John Lejeune, Littleton Waller, and, most of all, Smedley Darlington Butler.

No individual embodied this story more than Butler. His contradictions are America's. He helped create them; he fought, unsuccessfully, to resolve them. Butler was blind to many things. He never understood the ways that racism drove the policies that sent him into war and shaped the way he thought and acted when he got there. (The racist language he and his contemporaries threw around in conversation and their letters was often shocking; fair warning.) He died without ever fully reconciling his deepest contradictions, leaving them to scatter kaleidoscopically across the edges of communal memory: the decorated hero, the conspiracy whistleblower, the *mechan* imperialist, the rogue critic.

How did a venerated veteran turn into a crusader against war? When did the armed vanguard of the banks decide he had been a "racketeer for capitalism"? And why, in a nation founded on promises of democracy and liberty, have so many cast their lot with authoritarianism—both in Butler's time and ours? These are not simple questions, I learned. To answer them, I had to immerse myself not only in Butler's life and writings, but also in the places where he fought, whose complex stories are intertwined with our own.

As I did so, I thought about the work of the great Haitian scholar Michel-Rolph Trouillot, who wrote that "any historical narrative is a particular bundle of silences"—of events downplayed or forgotten, of perspectives excluded from the archives. "One 'silences' a fact or an individual," Trouillot wrote, "as a silencer silences a gun."[16] In order to tell the full story of the people and forces that made America's empire, and how the debts they incurred are now coming due, I realized I had to lace up my hiking shoes and follow the trail the Marines blazed. It turned out to be a five-year journey that took me all over the world. But the story would have to start where it began and ended for Butler, in his hometown of Philadelphia.

# ONE

## PHILADELPHIA

As far as I know, the world's only public monument to Smedley Butler is a modest plaque inside Philadelphia's city hall. I paid it a visit one sunny afternoon. The behemoth municipal complex rises up from the middle of the boulevard, its limestone-and-granite tower soaring 548 feet into the sky. At the top stands a far more famous monument to one of Butler's fellow Quakers: William Penn, the founder of the city and of the state that bears his family name.

Penn arrived in America in 1682, dreaming of freedom and profits. Many of his fellow first settlers of Pennsylvania were also Quakers, as members of the Religious Society of Friends are still known. They were fleeing religious persecution in England. Most threatening to the empire was the Quakers' "Peace Testimony," in which the faithful pledge to abstain from "all outward wars and strife and fightings with outward weapons, for any end or under any pretence whatsoever." Thousands of Friends were imprisoned for refusing to serve in the military or swear an oath to the king. Hundreds died in the king's jails.

Penn promised his American colonists the right to substantial religious freedom and self-government by an elected assembly. He also asked them to respect the rights of the native Lenape peoples, whose ancestors had lived on the land he was colonizing for thousands of years.

But Penn was also a craven businessman. He had sold off half a million acres of Lenape territory before he even opened talks with the tribal elders, and enslaved multiple Africans on his estate. "Though I desire to extend religious freedom, yet I want some recompense for my trouble," Penn wrote. His settlers broke his promise to respect the Lenape almost immediately.[1]

This was the tension at the heart of the city Penn founded, the place he named Philadelphia—"place of fraternal love" in ancient Greek—and of the country whose independence was proclaimed in its statehouse in 1776. Conceived on ideals of peace, justice, and brotherhood, it would be built on conquest and exploitation.

The thirty-seven-foot-tall bronze statue of Penn was installed atop the city hall tower in 1894. His broad-brimmed Quaker hat was the highest point downtown for nearly a century.

The simpler bronze plaque to Smedley Butler is hidden inside the entrance, fifty stories below. It commemorates neither his years of conquest nor his subsequent pursuit of peace, but a stint fighting Philadelphia's gangsters when he briefly led the city's police department in the 1920s. The inscription reads:

> *He enforced the law impartially*
> *He defended it courageously*
> *He proved incorruptible*

By the nineteenth century, Philadelphians had grown restless. Their city was perfectly positioned as a terminus for railroads to haul settlers and troops across the continent, and to bring resources and money back the other way. Through the former Lenape lands west of the Schuylkill River, the Pennsylvania state government built a transportation corridor dubbed the "Main Line of Public Works."

Railroad barons built summer mansions along the Main Line tracks. As the inner city swelled with immigrants and formerly enslaved people in the years after the Civil War, the bosses set up commuter service so they, and the bankers and lawyers who worked for them, could live in their suburban homes full-time. In 1884, a few families set up a private high school on the grounds of a Quaker college to educate the new crop of wealthy white boys growing up on the Main Line. They called it the Haverford College Grammar School.

One of the school's students in 1898 was Smedley Butler. He was the oldest son of a prominent Quaker family in the nearby town of West Chester. His father, Thomas S. Butler, was the district's congressman. But the real money and power belonged to the family of his mother, the former Maud Mary Darlington. The Darlington name was all over West Chester's streets, civic buildings, and banks. Thomas owed his congressional office to Maud's father, Smedley Darlington—one of his predecessors in the seat, and the boy's namesake.

Smedley Butler was scrawny but scrappy. At sixteen years old, he loved baseball, football, and his classmates' attention. The only classes he liked were public speaking and Latin, where the teacher offered dramatic re-tellings of ancient naval battles. ("He could so imitate a storm raging on the sea around the Roman galleys," Butler would later recall.)[2] His father, Thomas, expected the boy to follow him into law. Acting might have been a better career choice, but Smedley was not conventionally handsome. Thomas had saddled him with the signature Butler nose, a protruding hawk's beak that dominated his young face. The rest of his features were pure Maud: puffy steel-blue eyes, sandy reddish hair, and a wily resting smirk.

In early 1898, Thomas began bringing home stories from Washing-ton about a brewing political crisis with Spain. One of the old Iberian empire's last remaining colonies, Cuba, was in revolt. Cuban exiles and their scattered allies among the U.S. elite were trying to push Congress to intervene.

In late January, President William McKinley dispatched the USS *Maine,* one of the Navy's first two steel battleships, to protect American business interests and lives.

Then, on February 17, the *Philadelphia Inquirer* dropped on the But-lers' doorstep with startling news. The *Maine* had exploded in Havana Harbor. At least 258 American sailors and Marines were dead. Smedley pictured their lifeless faces, floating in the burning bay.

For an upper-class couple like Maud and Thomas, the *Maine* disaster was a blow to America's nascent global ambitions. For a distracted teen-ager, it offered something even more consuming: a mystery. No one knew what had caused the explosion. For weeks, newspapers ramped up spec-ulation, offering competing theories. Joseph Pulitzer's New York *World* quoted an American doctor who claimed to have overheard Spaniards in Havana making threats against the *Maine* before it blew. Not to be outdone, William Randolph Hearst's *New York Journal* claimed, without evidence, DESTRUCTION OF THE WAR SHIP MAINE WAS THE WORK OF AN ENEMY. The media mogul offered an astounding $50,000 cash reward (over $1.5 million today) for "exclusive evidence that will convict the person, persons or government criminally responsible."[3]

No evidence was found. On March 21, a U.S. naval court of inquiry announced that the destruction looked consistent with an outside explosion—possibly by a floating mine. But even the court had to admit that it could not fix responsibility for the destruction of the ship "upon any person or persons."[4]

But by then, Smedley, like millions of other Americans, knew exactly whom to blame. In their attempts to push the United States into the fight for Cuban independence, the war caucus had spent years selling stories of Spanish cruelty. One Spanish colonial governor in particular, Don Valeriano Weyler y Nicolau, had become a villain at American dinner tables for killing noncombatants, burning homes and farms, and his forces' taste for rape and torture.

"Butcher" Weyler's most notorious innovation was aimed at starving the insurgency of public support. He had ordered hundreds of thousands of Cuban civilians rounded up into squalid garrison towns, behind barbed wire and guarded by soldiers with machine guns. The Spanish called it *reconcentración*. U.S. newspapers translated it into a newly coined term: concentration camps.[5]

Photographs circulated of grown men reduced to living skeletons and visitors sitting atop mountains of *reconcentrado* bones. In a typical article, the *New York Times* reported that forty Cuban men, women, and children had tried to evade capture in a cave in Matanzas Province, only to have the Spanish soldiers set fire to the caverns and shoot those who ran outside gasping for air.[6]

Such stories hit close to home for Philadelphia Quakers raised on accounts of their ancestors' torture and imprisonment without trial. A Quaker newspaper, the *Friends' Intelligencer and Journal,* featured the eyewitness reports of Clara Barton—the founder of the American Red Cross, who was in Cuba to distribute food and medical aid to the camps—describing her volunteers' battles with "filth and death."[7] As winter turned to spring in 1898, the Friends establishment continued condemning Spanish brutality in Cuba while characteristically protesting the American march to war.

But the boys at the Haverford School were not interested in such nuances. When Congress declared war, they gathered around the bonfires singing "We'll Hang Governor Weyler to a Sour Apple Tree" and stripped the yellow from the maroon in their school's colors so it would look less like the Spanish flag.[8]

Schoolyard rallies weren't enough for Maud Butler's oldest son. "I clenched my fists when I thought of those poor Cuban devils being starved and murdered by the beastly Spanish tyrants," Butler later said. "I was determined to shoulder a rifle and help free little Cuba."[9]

There were several obstacles to overcome before he could join the cause. The first was his age—two years below the minimum. An attempt to sneak off and convince the local Army unit to take him ended with the commander telling him to "run along home."[10]

Then there was his father. Thomas Butler had joined nearly all of his Republican colleagues in voting for the war, but he wasn't about to see his eldest child go off and die in a Caribbean ditch.

Thorniest of all were the Quakers. Neither of his parents were devout, but they had passed on many of their sect's values to their son. His whole life, Smedley would address his loved ones in the Quaker plain style: using "thee" and "thou," always signing letters to Maud "thy affectionate son." Although both of Smedley's grandfathers had fought for the Union in the Civil War, that had been considered a special case by some Friends, whose opposition to war was matched only by their hatred of slavery.

It was Maud who broke through the barriers. She understood, more than anyone, what going to war meant to her son. Had the world been different, she likely would have gone to fight Spain herself.

To Thomas, she suggested letting Smedley start at a junior officer's rank: a benefit available to the rich and politically connected at the time, and one that might serve to keep him in training longer and out of the hottest fights.

To the West Chester Quaker meeting, she made her position plain: expel Smedley and the Darlington family fortune goes with him.

The solution to the age problem turned out to be the easiest of all. On a Monday morning in April before dawn, Smedley snuck out again. This time, his mother was with him. While Thomas slept, Maud and her teenage son walked the half mile to the West Chester train station. Nearly six hours and two trains later, they arrived at the Marine Barracks in Washington, D.C. Maud waited outside as her son lied about his age to the colonel commandant.[11] He surely did not care. The Marines needed all the bodies they could get.

Butler left the Haverford School before graduation to begin training. He was thrilled at the first sight of the sergeant major who led his instruction: a towering spit-and-polish Scotsman who had fought under Sir Horatio Kitchener in the recent British colonial conquest of the Sudan.[12] But as the days unfolded, Smedley realized where he really was: a holding pen for daddy's boys. One of Butler's fellow recruits was George Reid, nephew of a high-ranking Marine Corps officer with the same name. Another was Robert Francis Wynne, the son of a prominent New York journalist—a pretty boy with short hair pomaded and parted down the middle. (For reasons lost to time, the boot campers decided to call him "Pete.")

The sergeant major drilled the boy recruits on what were considered essential officers' skills, like memorizing regulations and organizing dress parades.

In the meantime, Lt. Col. Robert W. Huntington's new Marine battalion deployed to Cuba without them. At night, Smedley, Pete, and George would hunker down with the newspaper, devouring the updates from the correspondents on the beach where the Marines had landed: Guantánamo Bay.

The junior officers' deployment orders finally arrived the day after the Fourth of July 1898. Maud made sure she and Thomas were at New York Harbor to see their son off. She wore her best blue-and-white silk dress with the big balloon sleeves. Smedley watched her standing on the dock until she'd vanished into the horizon.[13]

# TWO

## GUANTÁNAMO

It would take Butler five days to reach Guantánamo by ship. A century later, there were faster ways to get there. On a humid Monday before dawn, I joined the check-in line in a little-used concourse at Fort Lauderdale–Hollywood International Airport, taking my place behind the paunchy contractors, human-rights monitors in natural fibers, and yawning young veterans with jet-black tattoos. The triweekly charter flight was operated by a cargo carrier with a fleet of ancient Embraer regional jets that smelled, for some reason, like ammonia. The ticketing website assured us we were going "to Guantanamo Bay . . . & Back Again."

The most direct route would have been to fly directly over Cuba's Sierra Cristal mountains to the naval station perched on the island's southeastern shore. But the Cuban government does not allow U.S. aircraft to go that way—threatening to shoot down any plane that uses its airspace to reach a base Fidel Castro once called a "dagger plunged into the heart of Cuban soil."[1] Instead our pilot traced a route over the Bahamas, loping southeast until I spotted the peaks of my former home in Haiti. Then he slashed back west over the white-capped waves of the Windward Passage. As I leaned forward to snap a picture of Cuba's emerald coast, I was nearly jolted out of my seat by what felt like a dead stop in midair. The pilot executed a hard-right turn, then dove. The cabin rattled like a cage as we careened sharply toward a tiny landing strip cut into the bay's leeward edge. We thudded down and skidded to a halt just as the dark blue sea came back into view.

Stepping onto the runway, I was blinded by sunlight. A U.S. sailor with a clipboard ordered me to remove my sunglasses and hat. The only languages I heard as we crammed into seats on the gray fifty-foot utility boat that would take us to the main part of the base were English and a smattering of Arabic from the lawyers and translators. There was nothing other than the heat to indicate we were in Cuba. We shoved off across the turquoise bay, the Stars and Stripes fluttering from the stern.

It had taken a lot of effort to get this far. Naval Station Guantanamo Bay is an active installation.[2] There are strategic airfields; Navy, Coast Guard, and of course Marine detachments; and a naval hospital. It is also, more notably, home to the most notorious prison camp in the world—a place where inmates are denied their basic rights and kept outside the boundaries of any system of law. It had taken a year of phone calls and emails to convince the Defense Department that I was not coming primarily to investigate the condition of the detainees.

I disembarked nearly at the same spot where Smedley Butler first set foot on foreign soil over a century before. Chief Mass Communication Specialist Monique Meeks, the Navy public affairs officer assigned to me, was waiting at the dock. With a volley of cheerful questions about my trip, she ushered me into a white Ford pickup.

The main drag, Sherman Avenue, looked like a suburb in central Florida. We passed a supermarket/department store running a sale on North Face jackets and an outdoor movie theater. There was the famous "Gitmo" McDonald's, where news photographers love to take pictures of Ronald McDonald waving past the concertina wire. Past that were the residential neighborhoods: condo complexes with identical plastic playgrounds on every cul-de-sac. The combined elementary, middle, and high school was up the road.

"So you're here looking for the general. What was it again?" Meeks asked as we sat down for lunch at a make-your-own-burrito place.

"Smedley Butler."

"Right." She smiled at the name. Butler had not left anywhere near as much of a direct legacy at Guantánamo as he did in the places he went after. He arrived as an unremarkable sixteen-year-old recruit, weeks after the major battles had been fought. But this was nonetheless a vital site in the story of the United States' rise as a global hegemon, and in Butler's life personally. Guantánamo Bay was not only the first place he was deployed, but the first place U.S. forces landed in the 1898 war that displaced Cuba's incipient democracy—the invasion that kicked off the United States' scramble for empire. This installation was America's oldest overseas base, a symbol of everything one generation of leaders dreamed the United States could be, and now the embodiment of what it had become.

The public affairs office had made a list of the historical sites I could see. "If you're interested in seeing the fence line, let me know. Have to check with the Marines," Meeks said, as she dipped a chip into her salsa.

I decided to press my luck. I knew there was little chance of seeing the prison camps. But I asked if we could go by the former site of Camp X-Ray—the cellblock used to house the first prisoners brought from Afghanistan in 2002. The site was no longer in use. The captives held there had long since been released, died, or moved to better-guarded and more-hidden places. I thought maybe an abandoned site wouldn't be off-limits.

Meeks was friendly and professional, but any journalist trying to visit the base was suspect in the era of the prison camp, and doubly so in the age of Donald Trump. She said she'd look into it.

New arrivals had long been drawn to the inviting harbor on Cuba's southeastern shore. Waves of island-hopping peoples who first settled the Caribbean prized the bay, guarded by two curled fingers of land a mile and a half apart. Inside is a coastline pocked with sheltering nooks, fringes of wild mangrove, and high hills carpeted with sawgrass and cactus. They fished its plentiful schools of snapper, jacks, and parrotfish, and hunted iguanas and small alligators in its hills. The last of the native peoples who lived there, the Taíno, gave it the name it still bears today: Guantánamo, "land between rivers."

Christopher Columbus first dropped anchor in the bay in 1494. Arriving from the neighboring island he called Hispaniola, he rowed to shore, stole some fish off a barbecue a terrified group of Taíno had left behind, and claimed all of Cuba for his employers in Spain.[3]

During the European wars for domination of the Atlantic that followed, Guantánamo remained a strategic prize. In 1741, the British vice admiral Edward Vernon captured the bay and renamed it Cumberland Harbour. Vernon's crew was full of sailors from Britain's North American colonies who wrote home encouraging their friends and relatives to rush down to the bay—"now or never for a plantation on the island of Cuba." Disease and local resistance ended the brief occupation. But one of

Vernon's crewmen, Lawrence Washington, was so inspired by the voyage that he named his new Virginia plantation after its commander. Washington died soon after; the plantation—Mount Vernon—ended up in the hands of his half brother George.[4]

The people of the country Washington helped found would not give up their hunger for the island, nor its valuable eastern harbor. When Thomas Jefferson left the White House in 1809, he wrote his successor, James Madison, to suggest the places he should annex next: Florida, Canada, and Cuba. With them, the author of the Declaration of Independence wrote, "we should have such an empire for liberty as she has never surveyed since the creation."[5]

The idea especially appealed to the next generations of enslavers, who saw Cuba as a location for one or more potential slave states that could give them a permanent hold on Congress and the Electoral College. In 1851, a group of Americans followed a Venezuelan-born merchant, Narciso López, in an attempt to overthrow the Spanish colonial government in Cuba. (The practice of carrying out a private invasion was known at the time as "filibustering.") When the plotters were discovered and executed in Havana, whites rioted in New Orleans to demand the U.S. annex Cuba anyway. López had tried to recruit Senator Jefferson Davis and Robert E. Lee, then a U.S. Army major, to lead his mission. Both declined. But Davis kept pushing to annex Cuba as the next president's secretary of war.[6]

Ironically, the future secessionists' efforts were undone by racism: several presidents balked at trying to purchase Cuba for fear of absorbing, as President Millard Fillmore had put it, "a population of a different national stock, speaking a different language."[7]

Even as Spain lost all its Latin American territories on the mainland, it kept its hold on *la siempre fiel isla*—the ever-faithful island—by maintaining good relations with the Cuban elites, who used their slave plantations to fill the empire's tax coffers. But eventually the liberal ideas of equality and self-government—and Africans' quests for freedom that had sparked revolutions in nearby Haiti and elsewhere across the Americas—stirred discontent in Cuba as well. In 1868, a plantation owner named Carlos Manuel de Céspedes gathered his enslaved workers at his sugar mill in eastern Cuba, declared them all free, and asked them to join him in revolution. War raged for ten years, until the Spanish managed to exploit enough racial, class, and regional divisions in Cuban society to crush the rebellion.[8] But even a series of reforms, including the abolition of slavery, did not quell Cubans' hunger for independence.

The United States was emerging from its own civil war at the time. Destructive as that conflict had been, it rechanneled the profits of a prewar economy built on Black labor, cotton, continental expansion, and the financing of all three into an industrial boom. That boom had in turn been fueled by new waves of immigration, wartime leaps in technology, and resources taken from the conquest of even more Native American lands.

The new wealth changed the way Americans ate. Until then, their diets had consisted mostly of things that could be grown or wouldn't spoil at home: pork, usually salted or smoked, mashed up corn, and easily stored vegetables like turnips, pumpkins, and beans.[9] With more money, tastier food could be imported. The most popular import was sugar. From 1866 to the turn of the twentieth century, U.S. national sugar consumption skyrocketed from roughly half a ton to 2.66 million tons per year.[10] Manufacturers depended on sugar for canning. Mothers put it in their children's porridge. Brewers used it for beer. And by far the largest supply of sugar—nearly equal to all other sources, foreign and domestic combined—came from Cuba.[11]

The island in turn became dependent on the U.S. market. Cuban and American capitalists poured money and labor into sugar production, letting other industries wither away. When, in 1894, Congress raised tariffs on Spain's colonies, the island's economy reeled.

A year later, an exiled Cuban journalist, poet, and activist named José Martí took advantage of the economic unrest. Martí had spent years in the United States raising money and weapons from Cuban émigrés. In April 1895, Martí landed his rebel force near Guantánamo and launched a new war.

Martí's revolution offered a new generation of Americans a chance to revisit the idea of making Cuba part of their "empire for liberty." The war caucus was led by the thirty-seven-year-old Theodore Roosevelt, who at the time was New York City's police commissioner. The scion of a wealthy Manhattan family of manufacturers and landowners, and a Harvard-trained historian and popular writer in his own right, Roosevelt believed the

United States was the future power of the world. He also believed it was the duty of the white race, particularly the "English-speaking peoples," to "spread into" and make productive the "world's waste spaces."[12] When McKinley won the presidency in 1896, Roosevelt finagled an appointment as assistant secretary of the Navy and started pushing for war with Spain.

McKinley was not interested in Cuba. His full attention was on acting, in his campaign's words, as an "advance agent for prosperity"—which in practice meant as a servant of America's new class of multimillionaires. He was particularly loyal to a group of businessmen who had paid off his crippling debts from an 1893 depression, then bankrolled his way to the White House. Those backers were nervous about plunging into a costly overseas war. Moreover, the power to declare war still rested firmly in Congress— where any bill depended on the support of former Confederates, who, stripped of their slave economy, no longer had as much use for Cuba.

To sell the case for war, expansionists and Cuban exiles organized junkets to publicize the horrors of Spanish rule. Many Americans were especially moved by the story of Martha Thurston, a U.S. senator's wife who died of a heart attack on an aid mission to "Butcher" Weyler's concentration camps.

In an impassioned floor speech, Senator John Thurston declared it his wife's dying wish to free Cuba and its people. As if speaking directly to McKinley's donors, he promised war would literally pay dividends: "War with Spain would increase the business and the earnings of every American railroad. It would increase the output of every American factory, it would stimulate every branch of industry and domestic commerce, it would greatly increase the demand for American labor, and in the end every certificate that represented a share of an American business enterprise would be worth more money than it is worth today."[13]

On April 11, 1898, with the inconclusive results of the inquiry into the *Maine* disaster in hand, McKinley asked Congress for a declaration of war. To win the last holdouts, the legislators added a last-minute amendment sponsored by Senator Henry Teller of Colorado promising not to formally annex the island.

Sanctioned by their government, Americans were swept up in the righteousness of their cause. Teddy Roosevelt resigned his administration post and volunteered to organize an Army cavalry unit. Even a middling student at a Quaker boys' school on Philadelphia's Main Line could see himself as the vanguard of an international crusade.

In a letter written three years earlier, the revolutionary Martí had warned this day would come. Before dying in his very first battle, he told a friend in Mexico that, if the Cubans did not win their independence quickly, the United States would invade, and that from there a U.S. empire would grow. "My duty, as I understand it and have the spirit to realize it, is to prevent, through Cuba's independence, the United States extending itself across . . . the lands of our America," Martí wrote. "I lived inside the monster and I know its guts."[14]

Second Lt. Smedley D. Butler arrived off Santiago de Cuba on July 10, 1898. His first sight of a foreign country was a palm beach littered with burned-out ships. He thought their splayed hulls looked like the ribcages of slaughtered animals.

Butler had little time to get his bearings before he, Pete Wynne, and George Reid were ushered off their transport onto a smaller ship called the *Vesuvius*.[15] The long dynamite cruiser was shaped like a knife, with three fifteen-inch pneumatic guns that rose through the deck like trumpets, still cooling from battle the night before. It took off with a jolt. For two hours, Smedley grabbed the railing, closed his eyes, and tried not to throw up.

At Guantánamo Bay, the recruits' orders were to report to the commander of the Marine battalion, Colonel Huntington, whose exploits in Cuba they had been reading about in their training barracks for weeks. But when Smedley, Pete, and George stepped onto the rickety dock in their dress blue uniforms, the colonel was nowhere to be found. All the recruits got were snickers and derisive glances from the enlisted men. Most had arrived at Guantánamo with the initial invasion force exactly one month earlier. They had been through a lot in that time.

At first, in the hours after the battalion's June arrival, its position had seemed secure. The Spanish garrison had already fled heavy bombardment from the U.S. warships in the bay. But at eight o'clock that first night, a picket sounded the alarm. "The steady tramp of men and the noise of rolling stones down the mountain side indicated the approach of the enemy," an aide recorded in the battalion diary.[16]

The ambush began at dusk the second day. Spanish Mauser bullets fell like rain. When the shooting stopped, the acting sergeant major and the battalion's only competent surgeon were dead. A patrol found two sentries under a tree. Their bodies looked as if they had been butchered with a hatchet.[17]

Colonel Huntington was an experienced commander. He'd started as a young Union soldier in the first land battle of the Civil War, Bull Run, thirty-seven years earlier. Since then, he'd commanded a legation guard in Japan, protected U.S. property during a civil war in the Colombian state of Panama, and survived a South Pacific typhoon. Throughout his career, the Marines had remained an undersized, underfunded rump of the Navy. With America's first overseas war, the government finally needed the one tiny branch that had experience putting men with guns on ships. But everything about the mission had been hasty and improvised. Huntington's aging fellow officers had rounded up every young white body they could find—mostly working-class men from across the Northeast. Most had no fighting experience outside a bar.

Terrified by how his Marines had fared in their first taste of combat, Huntington rushed a message to his senior officer, Commander Bowman Hendry McCalla on the flagship USS *Marblehead*, asking for permission to retreat.

"You were put there to hold the hill and you'll stay there. If you are killed, I'll come out and get your dead body," the commander replied.[18]

That hill, McCalla knew, was key. If the Marines could hold the coast, the Navy could control Guantánamo Bay as a point to anchor, refuel, and resupply. Its ships could then secure the landing zone thirty miles down the coast at Daiquirí Beach, where the main Army expeditionary force was to arrive in two weeks for the attack on Santiago de Cuba.

If they failed, the Spanish could neutralize the bay, and possibly win the war.

America's expansionist dreams might have ended right there were it not for the next party to arrive: eighty-two allied soldiers of the Cuban Regimento Guantánamo under the command of their colonel, Enrique Thomas y Thomas. Most had been born in slavery. All were experienced insurgents—*mambises,* they were called in Cuba—hardened in some cases by three decades of fighting for their freedom.

They also knew the area. Thomas, whose orders were to find the *yan-quis* and ensure their survival on the beachhead, asked for a meeting with McCalla aboard the *Marblehead*. "Comandante," Thomas said, "I prom-ise you that if within three days from this moment the situation has not improved, it will be because not one Cuban [of my regiment] remains alive."[19]

The Cuban colonel then gave the Americans a history-changing piece of intelligence: the reason Guantánamo Bay was so sparsely populated—why they had found nothing but a bombed-out garrison and abandoned fishing village when they arrived—was that it had few sources of fresh water. The Spanish were only able to remain in the area because of a single well still in their possession, in a nearby valley called Cuzco. If the allies destroyed it, Spain would be forced to retreat.

On the morning of June 14, a joint force of mambises and Marines had headed to the Cuzco Valley under the Cuban's command. The Americans were supervised by Capt. George F. Elliott, a pipe-smoking fifty-one-year-old Marine from Greene County, Alabama. It was only a two-mile hike, but a fierce morning sun was baking the hills. Woody cactuses and saw-grass slashed the men's legs. Before long, some of the poorly trained and dehydrated Marines began to falter.

As the allies mounted the humpback ridge overlooking the valley, they broke into three columns. When the first column reached the crest of the ridge, a Cuban captain fired a single shot and the battle began.

The Spaniards, highly visible in their white uniforms, took cover un-der thickets of sea grape and fired back. Shouting "¡Viva Cuba Libre!," the mambises charged. Two were immediately killed. But the charge kept the Spanish off the hillside. The second column of Cubans and Americans reached the front of the hill and opened fire.

Suddenly, a shell cracked out of the sky and exploded beside them. The Americans and Cubans dove for cover.

McCalla had dispatched the USS *Dolphin,* a steel-clad gunboat pow-ered by sails and coal, to bombard the area in support of the ground force. But the sailors had mistaken the second allied column for their enemies. The Americans were shooting at themselves.

Elliott ordered a signalman to call off the ship. But the message didn't get through. Shells were getting closer by the second. Sgt. John Henry

Quick, an aptly named twenty-seven-year-old from West Virginia, raced to the top of the hill, where he knew he would be visible to both ship and enemy. Fixing a polka dot handkerchief to a stick, Quick used an old Civil War–era signal code called "wig-wag" to carefully spell out the ship's name—a confirmation of his identity. The signalman on the *Dolphin* confirmed, and the ship's six-pounder guns and revolving cannon quieted. Then Quick signaled again, this time communicating the correct range coordinates.[20]

Shells exploded in the sea grape thicket. The Spanish scattered for their lives. Some ran directly into Enrique Thomas's third column and were mowed down. For five hours, the allies hunted down stragglers.

That evening, the Americans and Cubans destroyed the well and burned the Spanish *comandancia*. Four hundred and four years of Spanish rule in Guantánamo were over. Some Marines stuck a pole into the ground, and Lt. Herbert Draper hoisted the Stars and Stripes. Pvt. Frank Keeler recorded the moment in his diary: "Three times, three cheers went up from the battalion, and from all the ships in the harbor came back an answering echo . . . 'The Flag up, and up to stay.'"[21]

Today the Cuzco Valley lies inside a weapons storage area, off-limits even to most naval station personnel. As a result, it's uncannily well preserved.

On a sunbaked morning, Chief Meeks drove me there in the white pickup truck. The small-town bustle of the main base fell away as we crunched into the green hills along a fine gravel road. In the middle of the valley, amid woody cactuses, there was what looked like a broken well with a stone foundation and yellow brick sides, covered loosely with rotted wood beams. A few feet away lay a mound of broken red brick.

After a few minutes poking around the high weeds, Meeks found a path and started hiking up the ridge. Despite a loose rock the size of a cantaloupe careening into my shin, I managed to scramble after her to the top. The view was magnificent. We were 350 feet above the sea. The Atlantic stretched to the horizon. To our left was the next razorback ridge. Beyond it, just out of sight, was the main complex of the prison camp.

Standing there, Meeks recounted the version of the story that's been passed down by generations of the U.S. military: "Huntington dispatched two companies with the support of the *Dolphin*. But then the *Dolphin* started firing on the Marines!" Meeks pointed with her sunglasses to the edge of the green ridge, where Sergeant Quick had stood. "The Spanish were coming up after him. He got the *Dolphin* to take them out." She mimicked the sound of a gun.

But that framing of the story leaves out a crucial detail: the Cubans. Not only was destroying the well the Cuban colonel's idea, the mission was carried out under his command. Captain Elliott, the future Marine Corps commandant who supervised the Americans, affirmed that at least 10 percent of his force abandoned the fight because of heatstroke. Thomas courteously credited the Americans as "brave and patriotic" but noted that "the climate has told on them." In the battle's decisive moments, the allies found themselves in hand-to-hand combat in the razor-sharp grass, a style of fighting at which the more experienced mambises excelled.

Without the Cuban fighters' intervention, it seems likely Spain would have kept the well, the bay, and maybe the island. Guantánamo today might be known as a Caribbean Mallorca. Or, if the Cubans had not come to save the Marines, maybe they would have simply won the war on their own, in which case Guantánamo Bay would still be in their hands. Instead, all three nations' stories went in radically different directions.

The American reimagining of the Battle of Cuzco Well began immediately. Captain Elliott had pressed Stephen Crane—the celebrated author of *The Red Badge of Courage* who'd come to Guantánamo as a correspondent for Joseph Pulitzer's New York *World*—into service as an aide at Cuzco Well. Crane's dispatch from the battle recast Sergeant Quick as a latter-day version of the hero of his Civil War novel, who at the climax also weathers enemy fire while holding a flag.

Crane relegated the Cubans to nameless extras: a "hard-bitten, undersized lot, most of them negroes," whose "animal-like babble" (otherwise known as Spanish) was just another noise on the battlefield. When he revised the story for his memoirs, he wrote the Cubans out almost completely.[22]

Those were essentially the versions of the story of the Battle of Cuzco Well that Smedley Butler, Pete Wynne, and George Reid stayed up reading at night in the Marine Barracks in Washington. "[The Marines] had hit some stiff fighting, and the papers had been filled with details of their fine conduct," was all Butler remembered of the stories decades later.[23]

Those who'd gone to Cuba with the idea that they were going to save people who looked like José Martí—a fair-skinned son of Spanish immigrants—were shocked to learn that most of the Cuban army and 40 percent of its officers were Black. Once the U.S. Army arrived, they also found themselves relying on segregated Black units, such as the "Buffalo Soldiers" of the Tenth Cavalry, who landed with Gen. William Shafter's V Corps at Daiquiri Beach on June 22.

White American troops "showed less contempt for the white-skinned Spanish enemy before them than for the blacks battling alongside them," the historian Adriane Lentz-Smith has written.[24] After Roosevelt's spotty record in the July battles for Santiago (among other things, his "Rough Riders" could not bring their horses), the future president burnished his reputation by repeatedly telling a story about pulling a gun on Black U.S. soldiers he thought were fleeing the Battle of San Juan Hill—only to be informed by an aide at the last second that they were restocking rations behind the lines. Roosevelt knew white readers would get the joke: that it was natural to assume Black soldiers were cowards. Yet Roosevelt knew the truth—that the Buffalo Soldiers had played a critical role in the charge that would make him a national celebrity.*

As the war neared its end, the dismissal of Black soldiers on all sides hardened into a conviction that Cubans were a "mongrel" race unfit for self-rule.[25] In the late summer of 1898, the *New York Times* interviewed a white U.S. Army major whose unit was accused of cowardice. He tried to shift blame to his Cuban allies, calling them the "dirtiest, laziest, most worthless lot of niggers it has ever been my lot to encounter" and "an absolute hindrance to us at all times." But, the American officer concluded,

---

* Among those awarded the Medal of Honor for the battle was the Tenth Cavalry's Sgt. Maj. Edward L. Baker Jr., the grandfather of famed jazz saxophonist Dexter Gordon.

"We didn't go to Cuba to fight for the Cubans anyway. We went there to avenge the *Maine* and I think we succeeded."[26]

When the commandant in Washington had informed Butler, Pete Wynne, and George Reid that they were to join Huntington's now-famous battalion in July 1898, Smedley's mind had raced with excitement and dread. "I had done so much talking about this war that there was no way out of it," he later recalled.[27]

Now he was at Guantánamo and still could not find the colonel he was supposed to report to. Following directions at the docks, the three friends climbed the hill that housed the main cluster of tents, which the Marines called Camp McCalla. By the time they reached the top, they were drenched with sweat through their blue wool dress uniforms. But all they found were a group of old men with matted beards lazing on boxes and canvas chairs. These men were wearing undershirts and pieces of khaki uniforms the recruits had not seen before. Orderlies, Butler assumed. He asked one of them for directions to the lieutenant colonel. The old man arched an eyebrow. "Going to help him win the war are you?" he asked. The others laughed.

Furious, Pete Wynne ordered the old man to stand in the presence of officers. This made the other old men laugh so hard one of them fell off the box he'd been sitting on.

Just as Butler was about to start yelling too, a private came up, saluted the man in the canvas chair, and called him "Colonel." Huntington nodded back.

Things only got worse from there. Smedley learned that the man who'd laughed himself off the box was his new captain, Mancil C. Goodrell. The bearded, ramrod Ohioan towered over Smedley's skinny, five-foot-eight frame. He handed him one of the new linen khaki uniforms, better suited for the heat, then motioned for the recruit to follow. Butler picked up the little tin trunk containing everything he'd brought to Cuba: some shirts, underwear, a sewing bag, an extra pair of shoes, and a Bible. Then he followed the captain to his first post, a salt marsh on the edge of camp.

As second lieutenant, Butler should have been in charge of the picket.

But the men barely regarded him, having already taken their positions for the night. Goodrell patted Butler on the head and left him in the hands of a sergeant. The lower-ranking officer laid out Smedley's bedroll under a bush, then went back to the line.

As night settled in, Butler watched the moonlit leaves above him. The air was thick as steam. Fat mosquitoes pelted his arms and back. Suddenly, a rifle cracked. His body jerked involuntarily, bracing for the bullet. But the only noises he heard next were the heaving of his own breath and his hands shaking against the bedding. All he wanted was to go home to his mother. He stayed awake until Goodrell returned at dawn.[28]

Looking back across a storied battlefield career, it might seem strange that Butler would carry with him a memory of that single sleepless night. But he would never forget the fear and isolation he felt on his first night at war, just when it seemed he had finally arrived.

In truth, it wasn't the enemy Butler should have feared that night. Seven times as many U.S. troops died from illness as from battle wounds in the war—mostly typhoid, as well as malaria and yellow fever.[29] Officers tried to control the epidemics with strict hygiene, but they were woefully ill-informed about what measures to take. They had mostly ignored the work of Cuban scientist Carlos Finlay, who theorized two decades earlier that yellow fever was transmitted by mosquitoes. It would not be until after the war, in 1900, that Maj. Walter Reed, a U.S. Army physician and namesake of the future military hospital, would go to Cuba and prove Finlay's theory to the military's satisfaction—a breakthrough that would pay dividends in tropical operations to come.

Butler was not spared in the meantime. A few weeks into his deployment at Guantánamo, he was knocked down with a raging fever, the first of countless bouts with tropical disease he would face in his career. Captain Goodrell visited him regularly in his sickbed. "He came and read to me and rubbed my hot head and did me innumerable little kindnesses," Butler recalled.[30]

It isn't clear why the fifty-four-year-old veteran took such a shine to the sandy-haired recruit. Maybe he identified with him, having joined the military as a teenager in the Civil War. Or maybe Goodrell had been ordered to look after a useful congressman's son.

Whatever his motivation, the attention created an indelible bond. After Butler recovered, Goodrell took him on hikes beyond the perimeter of the camp, where he imparted life lessons. He taught the young officer to always look out for his enlisted men: "If you will insist on carrying but the canteen of a single man, your company will move."[31]

Another time, on a two-man patrol through the moonlit cactus hills into enemy territory, Goodrell remarked that it seemed like a good night for an ambush. Seeing the teenager was properly spooked, Goodrell subjected him to a terrifying tale about being the sole survivor of such an attack during the Civil War. It was a good story. It might have even been true. Butler took the implicit message and carried it with him for the rest of his life: never show fear, especially in front of another Marine.

The perimeter that Butler and Goodrell patrolled in 1898 differs only slightly from the limits of the naval station today. The line is still guarded by Marines. One balmy afternoon, Meeks and I were escorted out to the base's far edge by Sgt. Tanner Bullock. As we raced down the desert road, I spotted two layers of fencing. One was made of chain link topped with coiled barbed wire. Beyond that ran a line of high nets strung between wooden poles.

"Whiskey Echo Five Bravo," Bullock rattled into his radio. "Two pax. Heading for end zone."

Our destination was Marine Observation Post 31. The installation itself is unremarkable: a low-slung concrete building painted in forest-green camouflage and an olive-drab watchtower, marked on its Cuba-facing sides with American flags. What sets it apart is its job: overseeing the North East Gate, the main door between the United States' oldest overseas base and the Republic of Cuba.

For more than half the twentieth century, Cubans and Americans crossed freely back and forth through that gate. The adjacent city of Caimanera was a famous "liberty town" where servicemen got loaded and stumbled in and out of bordellos. In turn, many Cubans held jobs as drivers, janitors, and waiters on the base. In the days when Cuba was a U.S. tourists' playground, Gitmo was known as a low-pressure post of tropical sunsets and carnivals sponsored by Bacardi rum.

The arrangement had its roots in the aftermath of 1898, when Mc-Kinley's secretary of war, Elihu Root, drafted a law laying out conditions for a partial withdrawal of U.S. troops. Stuffed into an appropriations bill by the powerful senator Orville Platt, the law said the U.S. could invade Cuba again whenever it wanted and barred future Cuban governments from making treaties with other powers. It also required Cuba to "sell or lease to the United States lands necessary for coaling or naval stations"—namely, Guantánamo Bay.

With that, U.S. corporations and banks—including J. P. Morgan & Co., Sullivan & Cromwell, and the powerful United Fruit Company—gained control of Cuban sugar, tobacco, railroads, mining, and utilities.[32] Whenever their control or profits were threatened, they sent the Marines from Guantánamo. In 1912, for instance, the Marines crushed an uprising by Black Cuban war veterans demanding equal rights. Such invasions and occupations were a constant source of humiliation for a people who had spent thirty years fighting for independence. "I don't think they even respected their own mothers. They would approach the houses, see a pretty woman in the window or in the doorway, go up to her, and say, 'Fucky, fucky, Margarita,' and in they would go," Esteban Mesa Montejo, an Afro-Cuban veteran of the independence war, told an interviewer in the 1960s.[33]

The Platt Amendment was repealed as a part of a general softening of the U.S. imperial presence in Latin America in 1934. But its replacement law maintained the U.S. right to keep Guantánamo forever—affirming it could leave the bay whenever it wanted but providing no provision by which Cuba could terminate the lease.[34]

U.S. control over Cuba's government remained similarly intact. In the 1950s, Cuba was run by Fulgencio Batista, a Cuban army sergeant who had seized power in a coup. Under his rule, the per-capita value of U.S. investments in Cuba was three times more than its investments in the rest of Latin America combined.[35] In exchange, the United States looked the other way at Batista's repressive violence and his constant short-circuiting of democracy.

The bond between Batista and Washington created an unassailable link in many Cubans' minds between capitalism, dictatorship, and the United States. Some looked back to José Martí and the independence war for inspiration. Fidel Castro, a lawyer who tried to run for congress in an election Batista canceled, had grown up on a farm less than sixty miles from Guantánamo Bay. Castro's absentee father was a former Spanish soldier who fought against the Cubans and Americans, then made a tidy fortune as a tenant sugar plantation manager for United Fruit.[36]

In 1953, Castro was arrested for leading an attack on a government barracks in Santiago. At his trial, he mocked Batista with an allusion to Martí's last letter, calling the dictator a *"monstruum horrendum"* who "doesn't even have guts."[37] From exile, Castro launched a revolution by further emulating Martí: procuring a yacht, filling it with fighters and weapons, and sailing for eastern Cuba.

As Castro's guerrillas fought their way through the mountains, the U.S. funneled firebombs to Batista's troops from Guantánamo Bay. After the dictator fled into exile on New Year's Day 1959, Castro declared he had completed the work of the mambises: "This time . . . the revolution will be consummated. It will not be like the War of 1895, when the Americans arrived and made themselves masters of the country." Castro's new government nationalized U.S. subsidiaries, including his father's former landlords at United Fruit.[38]

Nothing mocked Castro's vision of total independence more than the naval station in his childhood backyard. But all he could do was symbolically refuse to cash America's monthly rent checks of $4,085. (Castro claimed to keep them in a desk drawer.)[39]

In 1960, the U.S. imposed a crippling embargo on Cuba after Castro nationalized two U.S. oil refineries that refused to process Soviet petroleum.[40] In 1961, the naval station took part in a thwarted coup attempt at the Bay of Pigs. A year later, the discovery of Soviet missiles in Cuba nearly provoked a nuclear war, prompting the temporary evacuation of all civilians from Guantánamo Bay.

After a Cuban soldier was shot to death near the fence line in 1964—by a Marine, Castro said—the Cuban leader took a page from Enrique Thomas and tried cutting off the base's water supply. The U.S. commander built desalination plants.[41] Sergeant Bullock proudly showed me the cut water pipe near the Marine guard post, preserved as a symbol of the severed ties.

The empire and its recalcitrant client state built opposing guard posts on opposite sides of the naval station's perimeter. They dug trenches, planted cactuses, and buried tens of thousands of land mines. When Cubans threw rocks at the observation posts, the Americans built the high net fences. The Cubans put up floodlights to blind the American sentries. The Marines responded by building a giant reflector disc bearing the Corps seal: the Eagle, Globe, and Anchor.

I climbed the observation tower with Sergeant Bullock and looked over the fence into the no-man's-land, where thousands of rusting land mines were still buried under the brush. On one side was a totalitarian Communist state, dedicated to thumbing its nose at U.S. imperialism while ensuring complete domination over its own people. On the other was the forty-five-square-mile base, the birthplace of America's overseas empire, now surrounded by hostile territory.

The North East Gate was essentially sealed. The last remaining Cuban workers either quit or moved permanently to the American side. Those still living on the installation are retired now, in a convalescent home on one of the base town's cul-de-sacs. They are the last of a generation of Cubans who remember a time when Guantánamo Bay represented, even to a few, something different than it does today.

The public relations office turned down my request to visit Camp X-Ray. "It's slated for demolition, and there's a lot of debris. We wouldn't want you getting hurt," Meeks explained, with a bit of a wink.

I did get a view of the empty cages of the former Camp Iguana, where children as young as thirteen were once held.[42] And I was given a brief, distant glimpse of the warrens of barbed wire that marked the security check to the main prison camp, as Meeks watched closely to make sure I didn't sneak a photo. But mostly, I had to rely on inference to suss out when I was close to something or someone with ties to the prison. An increase in "No Photography" signs was one telltale clue. I also learned that those currently assigned to prison duty removed their Velcro name patches from their uniforms, so detainees couldn't identify them.

The insistence on hiding any trace of the detention center seemed to go beyond a mere need for security. Only forty people were imprisoned at the base when I visited, out of a high-water mark of roughly 780. It was not hard to keep them out of sight. Tramping through the weeds at the former Camp X-Ray would have likely revealed little about what had gone on there, much less in the interrogation rooms where prior detainees have reported they were isolated, shackled for hours, and forced to urinate on the floor. The most extreme torture is believed to have been done far from Guantánamo entirely, in "black sites" in Afghanistan and friendly client states such as Thailand, Saudi Arabia, and Morocco.[43] So what was my government so intent on hiding?

On my last night on the base, as I walked down an unlit winding road to my assigned quarters, I thought about someone I used to know. James Foley and I went to the same journalism school, a few years apart. After he graduated, we'd struck up a friendship over text and email. In 2012, he vanished while covering Syria's civil war. Years went by without news. Then in August 2014, my phone buzzed with Jim's name. But it wasn't a text from him. A video titled "A Message to America" had been released by the radical jihadist group calling itself the Islamic State in Iraq and al-Sham. While a masked man loomed over him, Jim recited a message denouncing the latest round of U.S. bombing in Iraq. His last recorded words were, "I guess, all in all, I wish I wasn't an American." Then the man cut off his head.[44]

For his execution, Jim's killers dressed him in a safety-orange jumpsuit, the radioactive hue of hunting vests and traffic cones. We all knew what it symbolized: it was the color of the jumpsuits at Guantánamo Bay. A Spanish journalist held with Jim wrote that ISIS had modeled its whole underground gulag on the secret American prison system exemplified by Guantánamo. Captives were handcuffed and blindfolded, stripped naked, waterboarded, and subjected to mock executions.[45] By dressing an American journalist in Guantánamo's color—a uniform some of his captors had been forced to wear—ISIS believed it was justifying his murder and showing America's moral bankruptcy, while recruiting others to their cause.

It was that strange, terrible quality, that unending symbolic power, that ran like a live wire through Guantánamo's history. The features that made the bay a plaything of European empires also made it the target for America's first overseas invasion. Its resulting status—not quite Cuba, not quite the United States—provided the legal justification for George W. Bush's administration to argue the prison there would not be subject to any nation's laws. The erasing and dehumanization of nonwhites and foreigners that marked the bay's first days in American hands would echo through the wars of empire to come.

When the first blindfolded, shackled detainees touched down on the airstrip in 2002—guards shouting in their ears, "You are now the property of the U.S. Marine Corps!"—Guantánamo completed its journey from landform to base to symbol.[46] Its name became mythic, a black hole into which Americans could imagine their enemies simply disappeared; an expression of the strength of the most powerful nation in the world, to be seen and feared by all, consequences be damned. It was the silence that guards that myth, it seemed, that my minders were charged with protecting above all.

Butler's last weeks at Guantánamo were a flurry of activity. Cruisers steamed out of the bay to sink enemy ships and shell batteries along the coastline. On July 21, 1898, the USS *Massachusetts* left with three thousand soldiers to conquer Puerto Rico. News came in that U.S. forces had also landed in the Spanish colonies of the Philippines and Guam. For days, rumors flew that the Marines were headed to a final, desperate scrap for Cuba.

On August 5, the battalion was ordered aboard the USS *Resolute*. "I am writing this in a little hot stateroom so thee must not expect a very lengthy epistle," Smedley wrote his mother. "Word has just come that we are going to the Isle of Pines and that we will not get off tomorrow. I don't know where we will land and I guess nobody else does either."[47]

They never reached the Isle of Pines.[48] The *Resolute* ran into battle along the way at Manzanillo, a last Spanish redoubt and a key port on Cuba's southern coast. Mambises attacked by land. The *Resolute* and five other ships supported them by sea. The ship's guns deafened Smedley as they convulsed the deck. Finally, the orders came: Marines ashore at dawn.

All night, Butler steeled his nerves for his first combat. He thought of his mother. He thought of his mission. He tried to remember his training from Captain Goodrell.

Finally, the sun broke over the Sierra Maestra mountains, and a ship pulled alongside to deliver the news: Spain had signed an armistice. Butler had not come to help win the war after all, at least not by firing a gun. He could not know that U.S. military rule over Cuba would continue, nor that a new epoch of world history had just begun. All he knew was that, for the moment, he and the Marines were going home.

# THREE

**B**utler returned from Cuba feeling like a hero. As his transport steamed into Portsmouth, New Hampshire, in August 1898, fishermen swarmed and cheered the homecoming Marines from their boats. After a few weeks in mass quarantine, Butler paraded with the battalion through a throng of fifteen thousand strong, screaming themselves hoarse for the conquerors of Guantánamo.

Philadelphia newspapers covered Butler's arrival home in West Chester. Maud and Thomas tried to coax him into staying and finishing school. But Smedley felt like a warrior now, a man who'd seen and done too much to go back to books and baseball. Next time, he quietly hoped, he might even get to see combat.

Like most of his countrymen, Smedley assumed the war was over. Spain had surrendered. Cuba was, as far as Americans cared to know, free. But across the world's biggest ocean, hasty decisions and outsized ambitions had plunged the United States into its first Asian quagmire.

Before heading to Cuba, while still assistant secretary of the Navy, Roosevelt had ordered Commodore George Dewey to gather his U.S. Asiatic Squadron in Hong Kong and, if war broke out, attack the Spanish fleet in the nearby Philippines. On May 1, 1898—six days after the United States declared war on Spain—Dewey did just that. The sneak attack was unexpectedly successful—perhaps catastrophically so. In just over six hours, Dewey's little squadron had captured, burned, or sunk nearly the entire Spanish Pacific fleet in Manila Bay.[1]

The victory "opened a vista of possibilities," as McKinley's chief naval adviser, Capt. Alfred Thayer Mahan, put it. For three years, revolutionaries on Luzon, the biggest and most populous island in the Philippines, had been engaged in a revolution to overthrow Spanish rule. Some U.S.

officials imagined an alliance with a coequal Philippine Republic, which might be willing to lease the Americans a port or two.[2]

The more hard-core expansionists saw a bigger opportunity. Earlier that decade, in 1893, a University of Wisconsin historian named Frederick Jackson Turner had proposed a theory to explain both the astounding post–Civil War U.S. prosperity and a growing sense of unease. An economic depression had been brewing at the time. Miners and railroad and factory workers were going on strike for better wages, only to be crushed with deadly violence by police, private security, and the National Guard. Some were turning to socialism or anarchism, emerging philosophies that saw hierarchy and class oppression at the root of the suffering of the poor.

Turner offered an alternative thesis that was more appealing to America's governing elites. For centuries, he noted, Americans had flocked west across an ever-moving frontier in search of what Turner called "free land." Turner imagined that this frontier—the "meeting point between savagery and civilization"—was a "magic fountain of youth" that had built a national character of free enterprise, independence, and individualism. But in 1892, the superintendent of the U.S. Census had announced that white settlers now claimed so much land in North America that there could "hardly be said to be a frontier line" at all.[3]

The implications of Turner's "Frontier Thesis" were alarming: if the frontier made America great, its vanishing portended doom. Expansion's end would mean not just a dwindling of resources to extract and Native American lands to steal, speculate, and build on. It might mean the end of American capitalism itself.

But suddenly in 1898, thanks to Dewey's victory in Manila Bay, a new source of "free land" beckoned in the Philippines: Seven thousand fertile islands, tantalizingly stretching almost the exact length of the west coast of the continental United States. An American East Indies. And a chance to fulfill the ultimate aspiration of merchants and kings since the days of Marco Polo: a direct route to China.

Seizing the islands was legal, from a U.S. standpoint. Senator Teller's amendment to the declaration of war against Spain had only outlawed the annexation of Cuba. It said nothing about other Spanish territories. U.S. forces had seized Puerto Rico; the arrival of a single Navy cruiser was

all it took to capture Guam. McKinley also used the cover of war to annex Hawai'i, a formerly independent kingdom overthrown by U.S. sugar
planters in a private coup five years earlier, as well as part of Samoa and
the Wake Island atoll. With the addition of the Philippines, that would all
add up to a network of coaling stations that would at last allow American
merchant and warships to travel from the coast of California directly to
the Far East—without ever having to rely on another power's ports.[4]

But the Philippines would be the most daunting link in that chain.
The archipelago was home to more than seven million people. They spoke
a hundred languages and dialects and had a dizzying array of religions
and cultures, including a Roman Catholic majority on Luzon and large
and historically independent Muslim populations in the southern islands.

Many Filipinos were also ready to continue fighting for their independence. The nationalists on Luzon, mostly ethnic Tagalogs, had battled
the powerful Spanish army to a stalemate by 1898. When the Americans
declared war on Spain, the president of the First Philippine Republic,
Emilio Aguinaldo, raced to a secret meeting with the U.S. consul in Singapore. As Aguinaldo understood him, the consul promised the United
States would honor Filipino independence if he would join forces against
their common enemy, Spain.[5]

Aguinaldo's cabinet fiercely debated the offer. Some of his advisers
believed Dewey's Asiatic Squadron might play the role for them that the
Marquis de Lafayette and the French fleet had played for George Washington's forces in the American Revolution. Others feared they would
simply be trading one imperial master for another.[6]

The deciding moment came when one of Aguinaldo's most trusted advisers argued that the United States' principles of self-government—and
its founding creed, "that all men are created equal"—would never allow
the North American giant to become a colonial power. To underscore this
faith, Aguinaldo and his cabinet quoted Jefferson's Declaration of Independence in their own ("that these Philippine Islands are, and of right
ought to be, free and independent"). And they adopted "the colors blue,
red, and white . . . of the flag of the United States of North America" for
the new Philippine national banner, as another "manifestation of our profound gratitude toward this great nation for its selfless protection."[7]

They miscalculated. Many Americans did believe in a version of those principles; they'd inspired thousands of young men like Smedley Butler to volunteer for a war against "the beastly Spanish tyrants" in the first place. But there was no consensus that those principles ought to be extended to everyone. As many American thinkers and officials saw it, most people on their own continent did not deserve full rights, much less bronze-skinned islanders on a distant archipelago. Senator Teller himself pronounced on the Senate floor: "The doctrine that the consent of the governed is essential in a republican government has many exceptions. . . . We exclude the alien, we exclude the ignorant and vicious, we exclude women and infants—rightfully."[8]

In fact, it had been even more extreme authoritarian racism that came closest to preventing the annexation. Senator Benjamin Tillman—a one-eyed ex-Confederate who'd overseen a surge in lynching as governor of South Carolina and called for exterminating Black people who did not submit to white rule—warned that annexing the Philippines would mean "another million and a half of negroes, ten million Malays, Negritos, Japanese, and Chinese, to say nothing of the hundreds of thousands of mongrels of Spanish blood" joining the republic. (Tillman bragged in the same speech about having stripped Black people of their right to vote in South Carolina's new state constitution, one of the pioneering documents of Jim Crow.)[9]

"Pitchfork Ben" Tillman, as he was known, was absurdly racist, the kind of hissing Lost Causer who made Roosevelt's circle sound humane by comparison. But the aims of the supposedly more genteel Northerners were no less bloodthirsty. In a speech to a Boston Republican club in 1898, four days before Dewey's attack on Manila Bay, Senator Albert J. Beveridge of Indiana, a close Roosevelt ally, had declared that "the Philippines are logically our first target," and if, "as a part of the Almighty's infinite plan," that meant "the disappearance of debased civilizations and decaying races before the higher civilization of the nobler and more virile types of man"—then so be it.[10]

For Roosevelt and his allies, these ideas meshed seamlessly with the notions of good government and conservation that inspired them elsewhere to create food safety laws and the first national parks.[11] Rudyard

Kipling, the bard of British imperialism, spun the idea into a catchphrase in his new poem "The White Man's Burden"—which he dedicated in a forgotten subtitle to "The United States and the Philippine Islands."

This debate was taking place in a time of compromise, since dubbed the Redemption Era, in which white Northerners and white Southerners healed the divisions of the Civil War by tolerating the reestablishment of white supremacy through both legislation and violence, while focusing on their own prosperity. "Foreclosing black citizenship seemed a small price to pay for reunion between North and South, and between Northern capital and Southern capitalists," Adriane Lentz-Smith has written. War was central to this project.[12]

In the Philippines and the other newly seized territories, the compromise found between the racist isolationists and the racist expansionists was blessedly simple: the Philippines and other new colonies would fall under U.S. control, but their peoples would have no rights under the Constitution.

The Supreme Court sanctioned the idea. The justices—seven of whom had just upheld domestic segregation in *Plessy v. Ferguson*—found in 1901 that, though Puerto Rico was not a "foreign country," it was "foreign to the United States in a domestic sense"—"inhabited by alien races" who could not be governed "according to Anglo-Saxon principles." Over the following years, similar findings would be applied to the Philippines, Guam, and what would soon be called American Samoa. Just as *Plessy* had allowed the racial division of the continental United States, the so-called Insular Cases split the new imperial United States into "'practically two national governments,' one bound by the Bill of Rights, the other not," the historian Daniel Immerwahr has written.[13]

On August 13, 1898, the Spanish helped the Americans stage a mock battle in Manila, surrendering the capital to the United States before Aguinaldo's army could enter.[14] (The Spanish generals preferred to leave the islands to a white-ruled nation rather than admit defeat to native Malays.) When the Filipinos protested that the Americans were reneging on their deal, the State Department denied knowing anything about its consul's promises in Singapore.

McKinley sealed the betrayal with a $20 million payment to Spain in exchange for international recognition of U.S. rule over the Philippines.

He then issued a proclamation to all the peoples of the archipelago, promising the United States had come "not as invaders or conquerors, but as friends" on a mission of "benevolent assimilation."[15]

Relations on Luzon fell apart. "Where these sassy niggers used to greet us daily with a pleasant smile and a *Benhos Dias, Amigo,* they now pass by with menacing looks," a First California Regiment soldier wrote home in January 1899.[16] (In that early stage of building a new white identity politics, that soldier's only frame of racial reference was apparently the European/African split, as expressed by the language's basest racial slur.)

"All this never would have occurred," a Black American soldier wrote anonymously to a Wisconsin newspaper, "if the army of occupation would have treated [the Filipinos] as people."[17]

The Army set up outposts to prevent attacks from their former allies. On February 4, 1899, a panicking twenty-three-year-old private in a unit from Lincoln, Nebraska, fired on a group of Filipino soldiers near a reservoir on the outskirts of Manila, and the new war began.

Though the Americans outgunned their adversaries, it soon became clear that the state volunteer units that made up the bulk of the U.S. Army—already stretched thin from fighting in Cuba—were not up to the task of winning a war against Filipinos fighting on their own turf, for their own homes. Congress began debating whether to increase the size of the standing federal army, a step many Americans had long opposed.

In the meantime, the federal government deployed the reinforcements they already had direct control over: the Marine infantry. In April 1899, Butler accepted a commission as a first lieutenant of Marines and boarded a cross-country train to San Francisco, bound for the archipelago.

W hile I was packing for my trip to the Philippines to search for the Marines' legacy there, my phone buzzed with a news alert: "Gunshots and explosions heard at a mall, casino and hotel complex near Manila's international airport."

I'd known already that the islands were mired in two overlapping crises. One was a slow-burning campaign of repression focused on small towns and Manila's slums. Officially dubbed Operation Double Barrel— better known as the "War on Drugs"—it was in practice a green light for police and allied gangs to murder the poor with impunity. From 2016 to 2018, between five thousand and twenty thousand people were killed.[18]

The other was a more literal war on the southern island of Mindanao, where Muslim separatists in the city of Marawi had sworn allegiance to the Islamic State. With the support of foreign advisers from the United States, Russia, and China, the Philippine military was pounding the jewel of Maranao culture into rubble.[19]

The two crises had one thing in common: the country's president, Rodrigo Duterte. The lapsed Catholic mayor of the largest city on Mindanao, Duterte had won a surprise election in 2016 and quickly become known internationally for his bombast: cursing President Obama and the pope, bragging about killing three men while he was mayor, and mocking his own daughter's disclosure of having been raped.[20] Duterte openly aligned himself with figures from the brutal Marcos dictatorship, which had ruled the Philippines from 1965 to 1986, and oversaw the murder of thousands of Filipinos and the torture of tens of thousands more while enjoying the robust support of the United States.

It seemed at first that the casino attack was blowback from the war in Marawi, especially after ISIS's Syria-based propaganda network claimed responsibility. But Philippine national police quickly issued a statement rejecting ISIS's claim, identifying the attacker as an out-of-work casino employee trying to pay off his debts.[21] Adding to the confusion, the police issued warnings that more terrorist attacks in Manila were imminent. Figuring out what was going on in the Philippines, I realized, would not be easy.

To help me navigate this place, I arranged to work with a fixer—a translator and guide who specializes in helping foreign reporters. Rica Concepcion was a veteran journalist herself, who had years of experience covering her country and had crisscrossed Asia as a documentary producer until her partner and co-filmmaker passed away. It was a testament to our countries' disparities of wealth and power, that a highly regarded Filipino journalist could make more working for a visiting American than she could with an outlet at home.

Rica burned through war stories as fast and deliberately as she did her cigarettes. By the time we met, guiding foreigners through the War on Drugs had become her full-time job. She and her Formula 1–ready driver,

Manny, would pound coffee and nicotine all night, waiting for a call to race to the latest "crime scene," which in Duterte's upside-down world was a place where the police had just killed someone. They called it "the night shift."

"I was glad when you called," she told me as Manny jockeyed through traffic on our first afternoon together. "You work during the day."

For our first outing, we toured the capital. In the century since the first U.S. invasion, Manila had become massive beyond reckoning. More than twenty million people live there, packed into what is now the capital of a nation of more than one hundred million. Traffic is atrocious. Drivers jockey for position on the elevated highway that arcs around the city like a coiled spine, past fashion billboards and pulsating waterfalls of LED lights.

After finding an exit ramp off the elevated highway, Manny raced down a narrow corridor of market stalls, smoothly avoiding a slow-moving jeepney—one of the city's ubiquitous psychedelic-colored public buses, built in the style of old U.S. troop transports. Eventually we hit a wall of traffic even Manny couldn't break through.

"I have to tell you, now that you're here, it will be hard to find Filipinos who know the American War," Rica said as we waited to move.

"Oh?" I replied.

She nodded. "People here don't ask questions about the past."

I'd heard such warnings before. The Filipino historian Vicente Rafael calls this the result of the "manufacturing of amnesia," a product of decades under U.S. colonial educators and elites who, as he told me, "gave up and collaborated and benefited from American rule."

Still, that seemed to be changing, if slowly. Duterte had broken with his predecessors by routinely and publicly bringing up the violent history of U.S. colonization in the islands. Like many would-be autocrats, he had no use for the courtesies that democrats need to placate their electoral bases. In July 2017, he responded to U.S. congressional criticism of his human rights record by sniping: "I will start with your past sins. I will produce—from your archives—the photographs that you took of the people you murdered here in the Philippines. . . . You're investigating me and the internal affairs of my country? I'm investigating you."[22]

Some signs of colonization were still right on the surface. There was Taft Avenue, named for William Howard Taft, the U.S. president and

later chief justice of the Supreme Court who rose to fame as the first civilian governor-general of the Philippines. The street runs parallel to the
thoroughfare that fronts Manila Bay, named Roxas for the first post-
independence Filipino president, though many locals still call it by its
older name: Dewey Boulevard. To my left washed the steel-gray waters
where Spain's Pacific empire met its end at the guns of Dewey's squadron.
To my right was a Kentucky Fried Chicken.

We passed the imposing U.S. embassy and stopped by the Manila
Hotel—the California-mission-style jewel of urban designer Daniel
Burnham's partially realized "Manila Plan." Gen. Douglas MacArthur
had lived there when he was field marshal of the Philippine Army in the
years before World War II. (His father, Arthur C. MacArthur Jr., was yet
another U.S. colonial governor-general of the islands, from 1900 to 1901.)

Past the dense concrete warrens of the central city, we climbed the leafy
parkway of McKinley Road toward the city's new financial center, the
neighborhood of Makati. Rising ahead were glass-and-steel towers where
Filipinos ply their English skills into jobs as call center agents for Veri-
zon, IBM, Citibank, Aetna, and other companies. It was evening, and the
lights were coming on. Because their clients were in the United States, the
call centers worked American hours, up to twelve time zones away.

As we concluded the tour and wound back toward my guesthouse,
Rica told me about her experience shooting a documentary in Laos. She
had visited Long Tieng, a high limestone valley that housed a CIA airfield during the secret U.S. war there in the 1960s and 1970s.[23] When the
Americans retreated from Southeast Asia after the fall of Saigon, Long
Tieng went from to being a thriving secret city of tens of thousands to
a husk of a town. Twenty years later, Rica met abandoned lovers who'd
raised servicemen's children and Hmong street hustlers who greeted her
with an American-style "Hey, man!"

"The Americans trained people there and then they abandoned them,"
Rica recalled. She said it reminded her of the Philippines.

Butler's regiment arrived in Manila Bay on May 23, 1899. They were
posted on the opposite side of the bay from the city, at the tip of a
double-pronged peninsula the Tagalogs called Kawit, the name for a kind

of fishhook it resembles. The Spanish called it Cavite. For centuries, an old Spanish naval base there had guarded the mighty galleons that carried Chinese silk and spices to Spain's colonies in the New World and brought gold and silver back the other way—a trading system that had once made the Spanish empire the envy of its rivals. With Spain's surrender, the base, and the bay, belonged to the United States.

To Butler's unending frustration, that position kept him out of the fight at first. An Army unit at the base of the peninsula held off the closest enemy fighters. Adding insult to injury, they were Pennsylvania Volunteers—a sister unit to the one that had rejected him on account of his age a year before. He had nothing to do but drill and watch Filipino fishermen trolling on wooden platforms, surrounded by the protruding masts of the Spanish battle cruisers Dewey's squadron had sunk. The closest thing to action the Marines saw in their first few months was running out to watch the Navy's ships fire at the Filipinos on the opposing shore.

"I want Papa to go to the President, or somebody who has authority, and request that I be ordered for duty with one of the regiments up at the front," Butler, now eighteen, wrote Maud in a frantic scrawl in August 1899. "If you have any ambition for me to make a name for myself please have this done."[24] He was so upset he forgot to use his Quaker "thees" and "thys."

For about as long as there have been boys, there have been dreams of becoming men on the battlefield. At that moment, however, American society was becoming particularly obsessed with manhood. The United States was transforming from a country of manual laborers into one where people rode machines to office jobs. Electricity and plumbing would soon mean less chopping and hauling at home. The Civil War generation was retiring, taking tales of courage and honor with them. Women were campaigning for, and in a few states had already won, the right to vote. As the historian Kristin L. Hoganson has argued, male leaders feared that all these trends portended national feminization and ruin. "War, they believed, would return the nation to a political order in which strong men governed and homebound women proved their patriotism by raising heroic sons."[25]

Roosevelt had made the case for war's powers of potency at an all-male Republican social club in Chicago in April 1899. Standing before battle-worn U.S. flags from Gettysburg and San Juan Hill, the soon-to-be vice president preached "the doctrine of the strenuous life"—a call for men and boys to show "those virile qualities necessary to win." Roosevelt lauded British rule over India and Egypt for having "trained up generations of men." A healthy state depended on rigid gender roles, he said. "When men fear work or fear righteous war, when women fear motherhood, they tremble on the brink of doom; and well it is that they should vanish from the earth."

Opportunity lay in the Philippines. "The guns that thundered off Manila and Santiago left us echoes of glory, but they also left us a legacy of duty," Roosevelt boomed. If American men did not root out the "savage anarchy" of Filipino self-rule, "some stronger, manlier power would have to step in and do the work." Roosevelt then turned to the conclusion that would define his career, and in many ways the coming decade:

> The twentieth century looms before us big with the fate of many nations. If we stand idly by, if we seek merely swollen, slothful ease and ignoble peace, if we shrink from the hard contests where men must win at hazard of their lives and at the risk of all they hold dear, then the bolder and stronger peoples will pass us by, and will win for themselves the domination of the world.[26]

While the applause echoed in the Hamilton Club, Butler was already on the way to the Philippines. But Roosevelt might as well have been speaking directly to him. Manhood was the quality Smedley craved most. He wanted the stature of his Scottish drill instructor, the confidence of Captain Goodrell, the courage under fire of Sergeant Quick. Above all, he wanted to prove he was not just a congressman's son.

"At the end of thy latest letter thee enjoined me to be a good man and a good soldier," Butler wrote his mother. "Now any fool can be a good man if he tries hard enough but not every man will make a good soldier, so I will devote my energies towards the latter and the former will follow I think." ("My precious Smedley," Maud wrote in response, "I never read such a good letter in my life . . . thee surpasses thyself in everything that is good and wonderful.")[27]

Butler's desire to prove his manhood burned so hot that it blinded him to the moment when a war he'd joined to free peoples from imperialism became a war to subdue a colony.

U.S. officials were hell-bent on capturing the Philippine president, Aguinaldo, convinced that doing so would end the "insurrection." To free up troops to push north along the rail line, they first needed to dismantle networks of resistance around Manila, particularly in Aguinaldo's home province of Cavite. In October, Governor-General Elwell Otis issued directives to "attack and severely punish these Cavite insurgents."[28]

The Marines were to march down the peninsula and take the crossroads village of Noveleta. Smedley's "A" Company was placed at the head of the column. Just as they were about to go, the company captain was reassigned, leaving the teenage Butler in charge.

As the Marines marched south, the peninsula and road narrowed. At times the infantrymen had to walk single file, surrounded by swamp. Trigger fingers swelled in the heat. Butler led the column around a corner toward the causeway to the mainland. Suddenly, a group of Filipino soldiers who had been lying in wait opened fire from a trench.

"A" Company dove to the ground. A sergeant named Alex McKinnon—"a wild impulsive Irishman," Butler later recalled—leaped to his feet and started shooting back. As Butler grabbed him by the wrist to pull him down, a bullet shredded McKinnon's arm.[29]

The company to their rear started shooting, creating a deadly crossfire. Some Marines jumped into the swamp. Spattered with McKinnon's blood, his men waiting for his orders, Smedley felt his stomach shrink into a ball. In his very first battle, he'd just led the entire battalion into an ambush. His mind went wild with regret and fear. An image came to him of his mother, Maud, spanking him over her lap as a little boy.[30]

Butler later tried to describe the instinct that took over in moments like that one. "The feeling of a human being next to you," he would write, "with the knowledge that he is probably just as much frightened as you are seems to break the spell, and the natural desire to hide from each other any weaknesses gives courage to both."[31]

Rising unsteadily to his feet, he ordered the men to fire. What Butler didn't know, what no one had told him, was that just three years earlier

Filipino insurgents fighting under Aguinaldo and Gen. Santiago Álvarez had used that very choke point to wipe out at least four hundred Spanish soldiers.

But the Americans had an advantage. Thanks to an inspired piece of tactical preparation, the gunboat USS *Petrel* was sweeping down the coast to their right in support of the advance.[32] Its shells whipped by and exploded across the Filipino positions. The Marines roared and charged into the haze.

Flanking through rice paddies, the Americans chased the insurgents into Noveleta. Fresh waves of gunfire came from nipa-grass huts. Butler's men took refuge in a trench. A private named John McDonald peeked over the edge, then snapped backward, a crimson stream running down his face. The company surgeon rushed over and, pulling fingers through McDonald's blood-soaked hair, breathed a sigh: the bullet had only grazed the skull. But when the doctor sat McDonald up to get a better look, the private's forehead burst open. A second shot had hit its mark. Butler and the men returned fire and charged, leaving McDonald's limp body behind.[33]

In short order, Noveleta was in American hands. The rest of the province, and soon the island, would follow. The Marines sang "My Country 'Tis of Thee" under a mango tree, then went back to base, burning houses along the road.[34]

Later that day, an orderly sent to bury the dead noticed that McDonald was still breathing. The private woke from a coma two weeks later and was shipped home to a Philadelphia naval hospital. Thomas Butler regularly visited the twenty-four-year-old soldier who'd served under his son, and used his position in Congress to secure him a lifelong pension—a rarity in that war. But McDonald would never see again; the second bullet had shattered his optic nerve.

Butler often talked about his first battle. In his memoirs, he spoke honestly about the fear he'd felt—often as a comic foil to highlight the strenuous duty he'd endure in wars to come. But though those retellings often included the shattering of McKinnon's arm, Butler does not seem to have written or spoken publicly about what happened to Private McDonald. Perhaps that trauma was too much for him to process and bear. But for the rest of his life, Butler held on to the newspaper clippings his mother sent him about his father's visits to his blinded comrade in the hospital.


When I visited Noveleta over a century later, I met a man named Salvador Garcia. He was ninety years old. He wore a blue hat that said "NAVY," a Masonic ring, and a white polo shirt. Embroidered above his heart were a bald eagle and the words "Proud to be a USA American."

Garcia was hanging out in the mayor's office. Though he had traveled about as far around the world as a person could go, he'd always come back to his hometown. "All the people here I know and they know me," he said. "Also, I am the one who is running the cockpit here. You know what the cockpit is?"

I thought of airplanes and ships.

"A cockpit is where they hold the cockfighting."

"Oh, yes," I said. "An actual cockpit."

He laughed hard. "I'm a big small-time cockfighting aficionado."

Garcia was born in Noveleta in 1927, twenty-eight years after Butler, McDonald, and the Marines crushed the insurgency in his town. He grew up under the U.S. colonial regime and was forced to learn English in American-run schools.

His strongest memories began when he was fourteen, when the Japanese soldiers arrived. The invasion of the Philippines started on December 8, 1941, ten hours after the attack on Pearl Harbor. By the end of the month, the Americans were trapped on the nearby Bataan Peninsula, and the Japanese were in control of Noveleta. They gathered all the able-bodied men eighteen years and older and drove them away on trucks, never to be seen again.

For three years, young Salvador and the rest of the survivors lived as virtual slaves to the Japanese. They watched their food supplies dwindle until there was nothing but *kamote,* a type of sweet potato. The Americans returned in 1945 and with the help of Filipino guerrillas drove the Japanese out. A year later, President Truman granted the devastated islands their long-belated independence—minus a few carve-outs for preferential trade as well as space for U.S. military bases, much as the Platt Amendment had done with Guantánamo in Cuba.

Garcia had dreamed of going to college, but there was little chance of that in postwar Noveleta. So he signed up for a job as a steward's mate with the richest, most powerful institution he knew, the U.S. Navy.

The military was still legally segregated then. But it was not clear where Asians and Pacific Islanders, including the American-but-not-American Filipinos, were supposed to fit. Once, at a naval station in San Francisco, Garcia tried to board a military shuttle with another Filipino. After a few seconds of confusion, the driver told one of them—Salvador didn't remember which—to sit with the whites in the front, and the other to sit in the back.

"What did you say?" I asked.

"I said, 'Oh, gosh. What a life.'"

Eventually Garcia moved up the ranks. He was granted U.S. citizenship in 1952, the year he turned twenty-five—a benefit he'd never enjoyed despite having been born on U.S. soil. He served on an aircraft carrier in the Vietnam War. One of his daughters became a nurse in California. A son followed him into the Navy. When Salvador retired, he finally went to college.

Here was a man who represented the promise, or at least some promise, of America. Despite incredible odds and blatant discrimination, in a life roiled over and over again by the vicissitudes of U.S. (and Japanese) imperialism, he had grabbed onto the slimmest of opportunities, held on, and prospered.

I tried to ask what he studied in college, but he didn't seem to hear me. Instead he said, "At the time they were hiring some ex-Navy men to Iran. You know Iran?"

"Iran?" I assumed I had misheard.

"Bell Helicopter in Iran. I spent two years in Iran and I was captured there."

"Captured? By who?"

"I was a hostage. Khomeini's soldiers."

My jaw dropped. When I looked through old newspapers later, I read about the Bell Helicopter employees who'd been imprisoned inside the Royal Tehran Hilton at the outset of Iran's 1979 revolution.[35] A group of Iranian revolutionaries fighting in the name of the Grand Ayatollah Ruhollah Khomeini had overthrown the monarch Mohammad Reza

Shah, who had himself been restored to power in a CIA-sponsored coup*
two and a half decades earlier. U.S. citizens were immediate targets. Garcia tried hiding in a bathroom when fighters stormed the hotel, only to be
dragged into the lobby.

"Woo! I was so scared. I thought—I was saying, 'Uh-oh, this is the
end.'"

One of Khomeini's soldiers told him to pull out his blue U.S. pass-
port. He looked it over and asked, "Are you American?" Garcia looked at
me and started laughing so hard his voice nearly whistled.

"What did you say?" I asked him.

"What can I say? I cannot deny that. I said, 'Pil-Am.'"

"Pil-Am?"

"Pil-Am. Filipino American."

Garcia and the other Bell employees were freed after a week. Khomeini's student followers stormed the U.S. embassy in Tehran nine months
later. Those fifty-two Americans would remain hostages for over a year.

"That's amazing," I said.

He smiled a big wrinkled smile. I looked again at the patriotic embroi-
dery above his heart.

"Okay," he replied. "I'll see you in the States sometime, maybe."


In late 1899, while the Army was chasing Aguinaldo north on Luzon, the
Marines fell back into waiting at Cavite. Waiting, Butler was learning,
was most of war. The brass stressed readiness with competitive drills, but
most of the time was passed with cockfights and bouts of heavy drinking.
Butler adopted a pony. He was assigned a room with his old friend from
boot camp and Guantánamo, Pete Wynne, which did little to alleviate
the drinking.

The victories meant soldiers could roam more freely, allowing them
to introduce a new, more personal element of occupation to the women
of Luzon. This, too, did not come without casualties: at the new Cavite
Naval Hospital, sexually transmitted infections outpaced every other

---

* Completing the circle, the CIA's top operative in Iran who oversaw the coup was Kermit
Roosevelt—Teddy's grandson.

malady, including gunshot wounds and malaria.[36] In a story recounted by a future Corps commandant for its supposed comedic value, one Marine complained of his Tagalog girlfriend: "When I asked her to explain things, she smiles like a hyena and says, *'No Sabe, Sargento!'* What the hell can I do about it? I can't tame her and I'm afraid to kill her."[37]

If the young Quaker took part in such things, he doesn't seem to have written about it. Butler later said he spent most of his nights so homesick he cried himself to sleep, only to be embarrassed by the memory the next day.[38]

In December 1899, a new major arrived at Cavite. At five foot four, forty-three-year-old Littleton W. T. "Tony" Waller was even shorter than Butler. His ego made up for his size. Waller was Waller's biggest fan, and he didn't care who knew it. He walked with his chest barreled out and groomed his graying mustache into a flashy imperial. It quivered when he barked in his aristocratic Virginia Tidewater drawl. Waller had won a small amount of fame within the Corps during an 1882 port intervention in Egypt, and commanded ship-guard Marines in the naval battle of Santiago de Cuba. He could also put away an unrivaled amount of alcohol. With a more "swarthy complexion," another Marine wrote, Waller "might have tied a bandana around his head, set his teeth in a knife athwart his jaw, and made a good Comrade Blackbeard."[39]

Waller was the virile model of soldiering manhood Butler had been looking for. He kept as close to the Virginian as possible, following him even on routine beach patrols. When Waller implemented a few of his suggestions on improving guard duty, Butler beamed in a letter to his mother: "Major seems to have every confidence in me."[40]

One day, a traveling Japanese tattoo artist showed up at Cavite. Guys took turns at the needle. One picked a favorite animal. Another chose a portrait of his wife. Butler chose the design that now meant more to him than any other in the world. The artist traced the eagle across the front of his shoulders, talons perched on the globe across his chest, the anchor and fouled rope behind. The tattoo immediately got infected, and Butler spent a few days knocked down with fever as a result.[41] But wherever he was, from then on, he'd wear the emblem of the United States Marines.

As Butler fell deeper into the rhythms of life on a forward base, he stopped writing home. Letters piled up from his parents. Maud became particularly prolific in the spring of 1900. Often using her husband's congressional letterhead, she sent near-daily updates on the family, life in West Chester, and politics. She took particular interest in the state of the fights over Marine Corps appropriations in the House; far less in the ceremonial duties of a congressman's wife. ("My forte is not in the line of entertaining gentlemen," she noted.)[42]

At the end of May, Maud sent her son a clipping from the *Philadelphia Inquirer*—an illustration of the battle cruiser USS *Newark*. "I always had a motherly instinct in the *Newark*. If thee had gone on her thee would perhaps have experienced some active duty," she wrote. Her clipping omitted the short accompanying item: the ship was carrying Marines to China, where a popular uprising was targeting foreigners.[43]

By early June 1900, the insurgency on Luzon had been severely weakened. Though the rest of the archipelago was by no means in American hands, it was secure enough to start moving Marines elsewhere. Orders came down for Major Waller to transfer with 104 enlisted men and eight officers to reinforce Guam. George Reid, Pete Wynne, and Smedley Butler volunteered to join him. Though Butler had heard nothing but bad things about the freshly captured Pacific island ("a Hell Hole," he'd written, ruled by a "tyrant" of a Navy captain), he jumped at the chance to follow his new mentor.[44]

Then the orders changed. The situation in China was rapidly deteriorating. The U.S. envoy in Beijing had requested Marines to protect Americans—starting, as Maud Butler had noticed, with the ones aboard the *Newark*. Now a full invasion was in the works. The Navy ordered Butler and the rest of Waller's detachment to head to China instead.

While I was in Manila, I found myself invited to a party of the Filipino arts set. A few of the islands' better-known movie stars were there, hanging out in an upstairs lounge decorated with the shell of an old jet fuselage. A pop-punk band from Mindanao was playing on the stage below, singing in a language the Manileño Tagalog speakers I was sitting with couldn't identify.

"I hear you're doing research on the American War," a film critic sitting at my table shouted over the din. "Was the guy you're following at Tirad Pass?"

I shook my head. That was a battle fought during the northward pursuit of Aguinaldo, in 1899; it's often known as the "Philippine Thermopylae" because it featured a small Filipino rear guard sacrificing itself against a much larger U.S. force. Only the Army was involved on the American side; Butler and the Marines were at Cavite at the time.

"That's a shame!" the critic said. "They're shooting a movie about it right now up in Tarlac. We could probably get you onto the set."

"I mean—I could go anyway."

"OK! You better be careful, though. Once they see a real live American there, they'll probably cast you as a villain."

That's how, on my last full day on Luzon, I ended up on the set of *Goyo: The Boy General*. The film was the second in a planned trilogy about the U.S. conquest of the Philippines. This was something new. Like Filipino society as a whole, the country's movie industry had seldom dealt with the collective trauma of American colonization. Instead, generations of filmmakers had channeled their anxieties into allegory: science fiction and horror flicks that told "imperialism's history in scenes of bloodcurdling terror, mild eroticism, and immensely pleasurable schlock," as the Filipino American film scholar José B. Capino has written.[45]

Then, in 2010, a young director named Jerrold Tarog, fresh off a short film about a haunted funeral parlor, read a Wikipedia article about Gen. Antonio Luna—a Filipino commander who served as chief of staff in the early months of the Philippine-American War. Tarog was captivated by the story of a brilliant, headstrong general who fiercely resisted the Americans—only to be assassinated on the orders of Aguinaldo, who was jealous of his rising power and fame.

The result was the first film in the series, *Heneral Luna*. It was released in 2015 by a Manila art-house studio, and promptly flopped on its opening weekend. Multiplex owners tried to rush it off their screens to make room for the next installment of Marvel's Avengers series.

But before *Luna* could be shunted from theaters entirely, a small group of Filipino students was able to see it, and in it, they recognized its groundbreaking potential. Tarog's film depicted Americans as they are rarely portrayed in Hollywood: duplicitous, relentless killers. The movie's real villain, though, was the divisions in Filipino society. At a crucial moment, the title character turns nearly to the camera and says: "If we are to become one nation, we must go through a radical change. My brothers and sisters, we have an enemy bigger than the Americans—ourselves."

Supporters rallied to sell out the remaining showings. *Luna* memes took over social media. Superfans calling themselves Lunaticos Bravos cos-played as Filipino heroes of the war. Ticket sales tripled from the first week to the second, despite the film being on half as many screens. By the end of the year, *Luna* had become one of the highest-grossing Filipino movies ever made.[46]

The sequel, *Goyo*, was about another officer: the dashing "Boy General" Gregorio del Pilar, who was killed by the Americans at Tirad Pass at the age of twenty-four. It was announced Marvel Universe style, in a post-credit teaser trailer following *Luna*. To star, Tarog tapped Paulo Avelino, a heartthrob known for romantic comedies like *I'm Drunk, I Love You* and *Status: It's Complicated!*

I arrived on the set in a large public park early on a Tuesday morning. It was the Fourth of July; or as it's been known in the islands since their belated independence, "Philippine-American Friendship Day."

As the critic had predicted, the casting director sized me up and decided to cast me as a U.S. soldier. When she realized they didn't have soldier's boots big enough to fit me, she assigned me to the prisoners of war. The costume department took my shoes and glasses, dressed me in a ratty wool uniform with the buttons popped off, and sprayed fake dirt on my face and bare feet. A tech snatched my phone away ("not period appropriate," she noted). Then I was lined up with my fellow "prisoners"—a mix of foreigners and light-skinned Filipinos who'd answered a casting call on Facebook.

The scene was of a prisoner exchange at a rural train station, in which the Filipinos were handing over captured Americans in a deal to buy the fleeing Aguinaldo time. Maj. Gen. Arthur C. MacArthur (Douglas's father) and another American general were to enter and exchange a bit of dialogue with their Filipino counterpart, Gen. José Alejandrino, while we prisoners of war shuffled in glumly behind him. I tried to channel what Butler might have felt if he'd been caught in a similar situation.

At first my debut as a Filipino film extra went smoothly. Despite the fact that I was barefoot and couldn't see without my glasses, I walked in on command, hit my mark, and glowered. Then we did it again. Then again. And again. It slowly dawned on me that I had signed up for a military-style exercise in repetition. I did not notice the monsoon clouds rolling in.

"Thirteen of our men in exchange for a cease-fire? They can't be fucking serious," the fake-bearded actor playing Brig. Gen. Loyd Wheaton said for the millionth time.

"MacArthur" snorted in agreement. "This is all a grand waste of our time. Otis won't—"

Just then, the winds picked up, and a sudden hard rain fell. Water burst through plastic sheets that doubled as a station roof.

"Fuck!" Alvin Anson, the actor playing the Filipino general, shouted as a torrent of water crashed into his face. Someone from the costume department ran over and shielded him with a plastic poncho. The camera crew rushed to cover their equipment.

"Where do we go?" one of the other prisoners asked me. It seemed we had to fend for ourselves.

Before long the water was rising over my feet, real mud mixing with the fake dirt. One of the other Americans, a former missionary named Andy, pointed to a tangle of thick black wires beside us.

"I get electrocuted all the time in the Philippines," he warned. "Nothing is grounded, the wiring is terrible, and it's two hundred twenty volts."

I flagged down a tech. He told me he wasn't worried. "You have no shoes on," he said, deadpan. "You'll go first."

The water kept rising. The concrete platform started to sag. The loudspeaker occasionally crackled in Tagalog. I put my hand on the station's brick wall to get my bearings. It was Styrofoam.

"Prisoners, you can go into the train car!" a production assistant helpfully chirped in English, and we cozied in with some "market women" and extras dressed as Filipino soldiers in their pin-striped blues. But the "train" had a gap-filled plywood roof, and water poured in over the dangling wires there, too.

By the time the rain stopped, the sun had dropped low over the Zambales Mountains. Tarog called it a day. As cast and crew took turns wading through a moat that had risen around the fake train station, I asked an assistant director about the electricity. Why hadn't they turned off the lighting rig when the downpour started?

"When it's been on for that long, it gets too hot to turn off just like that in the rain," she patiently explained. "We could blow a transformer. Or start a fire."

Clouds of steam were evaporating off the lights. It was like the empire in which we'd trapped ourselves and millions of others in places like that a century before: Too dangerous to turn off. Too dangerous to keep on. I turned to look for my fellow Americans, making their way across the water.

# FOUR

## NORTHERN CHINA

The trouble in China, like so much in Smedley Butler's life, began back in that auspicious summer of 1898. After months of heavy rain, dikes built to contain the Yellow River along the fertile central plains failed.[1] Millions were left homeless. In what seemed like mockery from heaven, the floods were followed by an even more crippling drought. "We ate corn cobs to get by. Some people did not even have corn cobs—they ate cotton," a survivor remembered.[2]

The ruling Qing dynasty, ensconced hundreds of miles away in the Forbidden City of Beijing, seemed indifferent to the farmers' plight. Christian missionaries—mostly Americans, British, and Germans—opened their doors to starving families. But many of the plainspeople were suspicious of the foreigners. Some thought they might have even caused the flood and famine by offending the gods with their strange religion.

It was in this atmosphere of hunger and suspicion that a new kind of figure appeared on the plains. Some wore red turbans. Others went barechested, sporting flowing black scarves around their waists. They traveled from village to village, spreading the word about a way to end the cycles of disaster through a magical style of fighting.

A villager from Shandong Province named Wang Qingen remembered his first encounter as a teenager. The visitors took him and four friends to a clearing outside his village and told them each to think of a favorite deity. Wang chose Lord Guan, the warrior. Perhaps imitating the missionaries, he made a sign of the cross, then did a traditional Chinese kowtow—bowing his head to the ground three times. Then he felt the spirit take over. "It was like a dream. I rode a bench and it became a horse. I rode a rope and it was a dragon. I climbed a locust tree to challenge the gods."[3]

The young men trained for weeks, first with wheat stalks, then knives and swords. Finally, the visitors revealed their purpose: they were building a holy army. "We must practice hard," the fighters told Wang. "Then we can drive the foreign devils back into the ocean and protect our homes."

At first, the fighting bands took names based on their preferred fighting styles, such as "Big Sword Society" and "Plum Blossom Fists." As the movement spread, and attacks on Christians and their missions accelerated across the central plains, the fighters united under a single name: Yihequan, or "Righteous and Harmonious Fists." Unfamiliar with Chinese martial arts, English-speaking missionaries described them with the closest word they had: Boxers.

This all had come at an inopportune time for the Qing dynasty. For two and a half centuries, the ethnic Manchu house had ruled a diverse empire stretching from the Pacific to the Tibetan Plateau, and from Southeast Asia to Mongolia. But their power had weakened. The British had invaded twice during the nineteenth century—the second time in an alliance with the French—to force the Qing to tolerate the trafficking of opium, especially that grown in British India.

As a result of the Opium Wars, the Qing had granted land concessions and trading privileges in port cities such as Shanghai and Tianjin. The British annexed even more territories, including Hong Kong. France leased five hundred square miles of southern Guangdong Province, which it administered as part of its colony of French Indochina (now Vietnam, Laos, and Cambodia). Germany seized Qingdao, a port on Shandong's Pacific coast. Russia had taken part of Manchuria. Most disturbingly to the imperial family, Japan, which the Qing considered an inferior power, won a shocking victory in an 1895 war and took Taiwan.

Like the farmers, Beijing elites were disturbed by the foreign encroachment, but their response took a different form. On June 11, 1898—the day after Huntington's Marines landed eight thousand miles away at Guantánamo, while Butler was still in boot camp—a group of intellectuals had launched a democratic reform movement. They even convinced the twenty-six-year-old Guangxu Emperor to join them, with plans to create a constitutional monarchy.[4]

But the Hundred Days' Reform was thwarted by the real power in China: the ruthless and skillful Empress Dowager Cixi. She had not risen from a status as a low-ranking teenage concubine to the de facto ruler of the world's most populous empire without learning how to outmaneuver a relative. Cixi threw her nephew under house arrest, executed six of his most prominent advisers, and sent the rest of the would-be reformers fleeing for their lives.

That meant the Empress Dowager, not her reform-minded nephew, was the leader to whom foreign diplomats appealed to counter the Boxer threat in late 1899 and early 1900. Cixi didn't need foreigners to remind her of the threat a fanatical sect could pose: she'd first come to power during the Taiping Rebellion, an 1850 revolt that began when a Cantonese cult leader who studied with a Southern Baptist missionary from Tennessee declared that he was Jesus Christ's younger brother and tried to overthrow the Qing. More than twenty million people had been killed in that fourteen-year war.[5]

But the hard-line conservatives at court, led by the militant Prince Duan, suggested an alternate strategy: instead of trying to contain the troublemakers, the Qing should ally with them. Perhaps these "righteous fists" might accomplish what the government could not: stop the foreign encroachment entirely.

By the summer of 1900, the situation was ready to explode. Drought refugees flowed north into Tianjin and Beijing, carrying stories of massacres on the plains. Boxer bands looted foreign shops, burned churches, and destroyed train and telegraph lines.

"The country is full of the wildest rumors and threats. The people have nothing to do but talk and they talk of killing the foreigners and Christians," Susan Rowena Bird, a missionary from Ohio, wrote in her journal in rural Shanxi Province. "We feel that the end may not be far off for any of us."[6]

Many in Washington had been waiting for a moment like this one. Some of the United States' most powerful families had gotten rich in China, often in tandem with the Opium Wars. The first U.S. multimillionaire, John Jacob Astor, made part of his fortune smuggling opium into China. The Forbes, Delano, and Cabot families of Massachusetts used their narco-profits to found enduring political dynasties.* By 1900,

---

* Warren Delano Jr. wrote: "I do not pretend to justify the prosecution of the opium trade in a moral and philanthropic point of view, but as a merchant I insist that it has been a fair, honorable and legitimate trade; and to say the worst of it, liable to no further or weightier objections than is the importation of wines, Brandies & spirits in to the U. States, England, &c." Delano

it had become an article of faith that China's "limitless market" was the key to America's global future. Senator Henry Cabot Lodge, an ally of Theodore Roosevelt and scion of the opium-smuggling Cabots of Boston, wrote a month into the war with Spain: "All Europe is seizing on China, and if we do not establish ourselves in the east, that vast trade, from which we must draw our future prosperity, and that great region in which alone we can hope to find the new markets so essential to us, will be practically closed to us forever."[7]

In early 1900, Secretary of State John Hay got the Europeans to agree to an "Open Door" policy, in which any Western power (or Japan) could do business in China, but none would dominate. Such a proposal from the upstart United States would have been turned aside "with a shrug and a smile" a few years earlier, Lodge crowed, "but to the power which held Manila Bay, and whose fleet floated upon its waters, they were obliged to give a gracious answer."[8]

With the Boxer crisis, the opportunity for more assertive intervention was at hand. The European powers had spent the last decade carving up Africa along lines drawn at a conference in Berlin; it seemed clear that China's continent-sized empire was to be next. Alfred Thayer Mahan, President McKinley's naval adviser, wrote a series of articles arguing that China was a "carcass" soon to be devoured by "the eagles" of Europe and Japan— and that America should grab a spot on the perch. With McKinley's big-business backers in mind, he declared: "Every step forward in the march that has opened China to trade has been gained by pressure; the most important have been the result of actual war."[9]

On June 5, the U.S. diplomatic minister in Beijing called for U.S. warships to join the international force massing in Bohai Bay near Tianjin. Knowing Congress was unlikely to approve a third overseas war in two years, McKinley made a fateful decision: he became the first president in U.S. history to order the full-scale invasion of a sovereign country without seeking legislative approval.[10] Congress did not challenge him.

On June 17, Maj. Littleton Waller's most promising lieutenant wrote

---

was the maternal grandfather of Teddy Roosevelt's cousin and fellow president, Franklin Delano Roosevelt. John Forbes Kerry—the former senator, secretary of state, and Democratic presidential nominee—is a descendant of the Forbes family.

his mother as he sped north aboard the USS *Solace* through the South China Sea:

> There has been a revolution in China as nearly as we can make out and all the European Powers have landed their Marines and Blue Jackets and we are to represent the great "American Republic." . . . It is needless to say I am the happiest man alive.
>     Thy affectionate son,
>     *Smedley D. Butler*[11]

One hundred and seventeen years later, another warship was racing in the opposite direction through the South China Sea. After years of preparation, China's first aircraft carrier, the *Liaoning*, was finally combat ready.

On July 7, 2017, the sixty-thousand-ton ship arrived off Hong Kong for its official debut.

General Secretary Xi Jinping had timed the showing to take place on the heels of a state celebration: the twentieth anniversary of the end of British rule over Hong Kong. For the Chinese Communist Party, the 1997 handover was a signal reversal of what it calls the "Hundred Years of Humiliation"—a period that officially starts with the First Opium War in 1842 and ends with the establishment of the People's Republic of China in 1949.[12] The invasion of the allies to halt the Boxer Rebellion in 1900 plays a central role in that narrative.

Many Hong Kongers, probably rightly, saw the aircraft carrier's arrival as a show of force, meant to intimidate the territory's pro-democracy movement into submission. But the primary audience were the powers across the seas. Xi had spent his first five years in office asserting China's global might in a way not seen since the Qing dynasty's height. On the economic end, there was the "One Belt, One Road" initiative—a worldwide development project of pipelines, highways, railroads, "streamlined border crossings," and ports, with the ultimate goal of putting the Middle Kingdom back at the center of global trade.

On the military side, Xi's government was outstripping the defense spending of every other nation, with the glaring exception of the United

States.[13] The Chinese defense ministry had announced plans for at least two more aircraft carriers. Part of this new fleet's job, a ministry spokesman said, was "safeguarding sovereignty" over what China now claims as its "territorial seas"—a large swath of the Western Pacific that includes mostly uninhabited islands and resource-rich sea lanes also claimed by Vietnam, Brunei, Malaysia, Indonesia, the Philippines, and Japan, as well as Taiwan.[14]

Watching all of this carefully were officials in the United States, who consider most of those lanes neutral territory (in which it, as the world's largest naval power, enjoys de facto primacy). The U.S. Navy defends that claim through confrontational "Freedom of Navigation Operations"—entering contested spaces and conducting military exercises, in effect daring the Chinese military to respond.[15]

While visitors and the press gathered to gawk at the *Liaoning*, I was stuck nearby in the Hong Kong International Airport, stranded overnight by the sudden no-fly zone declared for the carrier's debut. When I finally arrived, bleary eyed, in Beijing, Chinese state television was filled with images of exuberant visitors lining up to ride the elevator to the *Liaoning*'s flight deck, gawk at rows of J-15 Flying Shark fighter jets, and strike poses waving the red flags of modern China and Chinese-ruled Hong Kong. Official press restrictions were relaxed, ensuring the images would be transmitted all over the country and the world.

In case any of that was too subtle, an anonymous man visiting the aircraft carrier from nearby Guangdong Province spelled out the message for a reporter from the *New York Times*: "This shows our country is growing up," he explained. "We can compete with the United States now, because you bully us."[16]

On June 18, 1900, the USS *Solace* arrived in Bohai Bay. Eight nations' warships jockeyed for position, more interested in spying on one another than coordinating an invasion or avoiding collisions. It took Major Waller two days to flag down a German freighter to ferry his Marines ashore. As with his arrival in Cuba two years earlier, Smedley Butler found himself once again standing alongside Pete and George, on a ship off a freshly bombarded foreign coastline, with no idea what lay in store.

The fleet's first step had been to seize control of the Hai River delta by shelling and raiding the installations that guarded it: the Dagu Forts. This was of great strategic importance, as controlling Dagu meant controlling both the rail line and the Hai River. Upstream at Tianjin, the river fanned into a system of canals and waterways that ultimately connected nearly all of China. One of these offshoots was the northern spur of China's Grand Canal, which led directly to Beijing.

Butler and the rest of Waller's detachment stumbled into camp beside one of the captured forts at around three in the morning, stepping around sleeping bodies and hot piles of manure. They awoke to a cacophony of empires. British officers sat beneath the Union Jack alongside turbaned Sikhs from British India and knife-wielding Gurkhas drafted from Nepal. North African *zouaves* and Indochinese *tirailleurs* downed their morning coffees under the French tricolor.[17]

Then there were the upstarts: Japan, whose European-style whites sparkled with global ambition, and Italy, whose black capercaillie headdresses masked their recent failure at colonizing Ethiopia. Most ostentatious were the Germans, in spiked leather helmets and mustaches styled after those of their emperor, Kaiser Wilhelm II. The impetuous forty-one-year-old German leader wanted the China campaign to announce his Reich's arrival as a world power; he had ordered his troops to fight in such a way "that no Chinese will ever again dare look cross-eyed at a German."[18]

The Marines were dressed in blue campaign coats. Their broad-brimmed felt hats, designed for fighting the Lakota, Cheyenne, and other native peoples on the Great Plains, made them look every bit the cowboys their allies expected them to be. After a late breakfast, Waller ushered the men aboard a commandeered flat-bottom coal train to head toward Tianjin.

The Marines had no maps. There was no briefing. They relied on what they called "Dame Rumor." Some heard that Boxers had mined the train tracks. Another Marine swore he'd read that white women were being crucified in Tianjin. Every so often the Marines had to jump off to repair the broken tracks in front of them. The grinding, halting ride did nothing to calm their nerves. Somewhere along the way, Butler heard a loud bang from one of the train's other cars. An eighteen-year-old Marine had become so overcome with terror that he'd shot himself in the heart.[19]

Ten miles down the line, the train caught up with a column of Russian infantry. Waller flagged down their commander, an officer named Savitsky, and offered to give them a lift to Tianjin. The shared ride didn't last long. Around 1 A.M. the train reached a bombed-out bridge. They would be continuing on foot from there. As he climbed the other side of the shallow ravine, Butler could see the glow of the fires burning in Tianjin.

"On either hand a flat, bleak country stretched away into nothingness," a lieutenant from New York named Frederic "Fritz" Wise recorded.[20] Within a few hours, bodies started appearing in the river, waterlogged and gray in the morning light. "Some drifted against the banks and stuck in the mud where wolfish dogs tore and gnawed at them." These were likely some of the Tianjinese who'd tried to flee the coming battle, only to be caught by Boxer sentries, robbed, and hacked to death.[21]

Tianjin in those days was divided into two sections. Closer in toward the coast were the foreign concessions: European-style banks, houses, and hotels where foreign citizens were permitted to live and work. Farther up the Hai River was the Chinese city of Tianjin, surrounded by ancient walls.

As the allied column neared the concessions, a volley of shells exploded in front of them. Any remaining delusions about China being an easily picked "carcass" were flayed in a hail of bullets. The whole company dropped to the ground. Butler found himself in the dirt next to Waller—who, with a salty smile, told the young Marines he was waiting to hear the sound of a shot going through someone's head. "A bullet that hits the skull sounds like a stone splashing into a pond," the major added. This did not help morale, Smedley later recalled.[22]

Butler reached blindly for rocks, built a little fort around his head, and peeked around the corner. The enemy was five telegraph poles ahead.

The Marines struggled to their feet. The ensuing fight was bloody—at least three Marines were killed—but it did not last long. Realizing the allies were badly outnumbered by the Chinese forces, the Russians beat a hasty retreat toward the safety of the rail line. Waller ordered the battalion to follow. But first, Butler asked the company sergeant for a report.

The sergeant did a quick head count. "Private Carter is missing, sir."

With a sigh and a grip on his rifle, Butler ordered four Marines to follow him. Another lieutenant came too. Near the Chinese lines, they found the private "groaning and writhing, in a mud puddle near the railroad track." White bone stuck out of his leg. As bullets whipped past, Butler and the other lieutenant made bandages out of their shirts, ignoring Carter's screams that they should leave him to die. They lifted the private as the other Marines got off as many shots as they could to keep the nearby Chinese forces at bay. It took another four hours to drag Carter back to camp.[23]

It was like Noveleta all over again: Waller and Savitsky had marched straight into an ambush, for want of a key piece of intelligence. Earlier that month, the Empress Dowager Cixi had officially put the hard-liner Prince Duan in charge of foreign affairs. With the invaders' seizure of the Dagu Forts, the last moderate voices in her court had been silenced, and the Qing committed themselves to supporting the Boxers. That meant the force the Russians and Americans had encountered was made up of both tens of thousands of fearless Boxers—now calling themselves Yihetuan, the *Militia* United in Righteousness—and Qing imperial regulars armed with powerful modern artillery, including guns produced by the world's leading arms producer, Germany's Friedrich Krupp.[24]

That evening, the promised allied reinforcements arrived. Among them were Col. Emerson H. Liscum's U.S. Army Ninth Infantry Regiment, fresh from the Philippines. Facing superior numbers, the combined Chinese forces fell back to the walled city, leaving the foreign concessions to the invaders.

Waller's Marines were placed at the head of the column. Butler braced for the horror. But as they reached the bombed-out churches and Tudor villas all they saw were relieved Europeans and Americans. There were no crucified white women in sight—just a man handing out beer bottles, one of which Butler gladly cracked open with his bayonet. The Marines paraded to cheers and the sound of the buglers playing the popular song that had become their unofficial anthem: "(There'll Be) A Hot Time in the Old Town Tonight."[25]

I knew from previous trips to China that I'd need to work with a translator or fixer, much as I'd done with Rica in the Philippines. But China's economic boom meant that all the journalists I contacted had full-time jobs. In Tianjin, though, I found a young teacher looking for cash to embark on a big step in the new Chinese life cycle: beating out millions of other young couples to rent an apartment with her fiancé. "Nelly," as she called herself in English, was polite and eager to show off her city's history. She met me at the bullet train in a checkered dress. Her hair was streaked with auburn—a foreign shade to match her adopted foreign name.

We decided to start by retracing the Marines' path from the coastline. At the gates of the Dagu Fort Ruins Museum, we ran across the sunbaked concrete into a blast of air-conditioned shade. When my eyes adjusted, I nearly jumped. Massive Qing soldiers and Boxers crawled out of the walls in bronze, pointing swords and a cannon in our direction. On the other wall, huge brass inscriptions in English and Chinese laid out the lesson the exhibit was designed to instill: "A weak nation will inevitably be bullied. Only a strong country can thrive in peace."

I asked Nelly if she'd been to the museum before.

"Yes, of course. In school," she said, folding her parasol. "On Tomb-Sweeping Day."

The exhibit traced the history of China's encounters with a rapacious outside world. It opened with portraits of Columbus, Bartolomeu Dias, and Vasco da Gama, whose explorations were in part aimed at finding a route to the fabled riches of Kublai Khan. An exhibit showed Qing officials confiscating British opium. Cannonballs and long Qing rifles from the British and French sieges of Dagu during the Opium Wars lined the hall.

At last we reached the climax. Under a title card reading "National Calamity," placards introduced the "Eight Power Allied Force" that attacked the forts on June 17, 1900. Nelly instantly recognized the photos of foreigners looting, pillaging, and executing captives. She had studied the Boxer War in school: under the centralized state curriculum, each of China's hundreds of millions of students goes through it once in eighth grade, then again in high school, in preparation for China's devilish national college entrance exam, the *gaokao*.

I asked if she still remembered the details. She laughed. But she remembered the basic thrust: China was weak. The foreigners were greedy. "The Qing were closed off from the—what do you call it, the worldwide development of technology."

"The Industrial Revolution?"

"Right. They did not believe in modern things, like electricity."

I later found an official teacher's guide. It recommends using Yihetuan poems and songs to "arouse students' interest" before detailing the horrors of the war. At the end of the unit, teachers are instructed to ask: "How can we wash away this historical shame?" Suggested answers include improving education, technology, and strengthening the Chinese armed forces. The teacher is told to impart: "Only when the country is rich and strong, standing in the forest of the world powers, can we wash away this history of humiliation."[26]

The taxi back to Tianjin took half an hour on the expressway. On the way we passed groves of identical apartment towers, some literally rising before our eyes. The Chinese government had decreed the land the Marines and their allies fought their way through a century before the "Binhai New Area"—a planned community for three million people, featuring two free trade zones, a spaceship-like library, and assembly plants for Boeing and Airbus passenger jets. A skyscraper was under construction; within a few months its top floor would be higher than the new One World Trade Center in New York.

"Bubble housing," Nelly explained with a sigh. "They build more, the prices go up more. But someday maybe no one will want to buy it."

We got out of the cab near the site of the former foreign concessions. The European architecture is, if anything, grander than it was in Butler's day: Renaissance archways, art deco balconies, and the gray colonnades of banks that look like they dropped through a time warp from Victorian London. The Notre Dame des Victoires church, torched by the Boxers, had been rebuilt to its neo-Gothic splendor.

We were not the only tourists. Visitors from all over China, wallets stuffed with the disposable renminbi of the new middle class, had also flocked to Tianjin, eager to get a glimpse of real Western architecture for a fraction of the cost of a trip overseas. A sign beckoned passersby to an "Authentic European Restaurant." Other visitors posed for selfies hugging the oversized matryoshka dolls that dotted the former Russian concession.

In "Marco Polo Square," built as the Piazza Regina Elena during the days of the former Italian concession, a family from Xi'an stopped to admire an Italianate fountain featuring a statue of Winged Victory. In the style of overcautious tourists everywhere, the father wore his backpack on the front.

As Nelly chatted with him, I noticed we were standing near the former location of the barracks where Butler's company had bivouacked in 1900. They'd been in bed one night when a pair of shells came through the roof, raining twenty square feet of concrete onto their heads. ("Luckily no one was severely hurt," Smedley wrote his mother.) The British soldiers across the street were not so lucky; the shell that landed in there killed one and wounded four as it tore the building to pieces.[27]

I asked Nelly what the father thought of the Western buildings.

"He says they are OK," she translated. "But he is disappointed so many are reconstructions."

The final assault on the Chinese city of Tianjin began on July 13, 1900. To guide Butler's company, Waller conscripted a twenty-five-year-old engineer from Iowa named Herbert Hoover, who'd moved to the foreign concessions to oversee a coal mining project. The doughy engineer told Waller he knew his way around the city walls from his regular horseback rides with his wife, Lou. Butler was surely pleased to learn that Hoover was a Quaker.

But when young Herbert followed the Marines over an earthen wall and slid onto the battlefield, he froze. The air was choked with smoke. Fat bullets rained down, spitting mud up as they hit the ground below. The Marines were supposed to link up with the Ninth Infantry, but they were nowhere to be seen. Hoover had led them to the wrong place—a cemetery, no less.[28]

Butler shouted down the line, asking Hoover where to go next. By his own admission, the future president was useless. ("I was completely scared, especially when some of the Marines around me were hit," Hoover wrote in his memoirs.)[29] The Marines tried to dig shallow trenches to take refuge, but they kept hitting water. Screams echoed down the line as man after man was struck. As Butler sloshed through a mud patch to rescue a wounded Marine, he felt a sharp, burning sensation in his right thigh. At first, he thought the wounded man had kicked him. Then he saw the hole, clean through the muscle. Collapsing in pain, he crawled to a nearby grave mound for shelter. His blood pooled in the watery ground.

Before going to war, Butler had dreamed of getting shot—"not too seriously, but sufficient to leave a scar."[30] He hadn't expected it to hurt this much.

A hand grabbed him. It belonged to Henry Leonard, a fellow lieutenant from Cavite. A sergeant, Clarence Sutton, took his other arm, and together they dragged Butler off the field. At some point, Leonard got shot in the arm as well, but continued dragging his friend to safety. Delirious and in shock, Butler leaned on Sutton for the long walk back to the concessions. Someone gave him a swig of brandy to ease the pain.

In the hospital, Butler learned the battle's toll. Leonard's left arm had to be amputated. The man Butler tried to rescue had died. The Ninth Infantry, stuck alone on the extreme right side of the allied line, had taken heavy losses; its commander, Colonel Liscum, was among the eighteen killed. One in seven of the 750 coalition soldiers who'd fought in the battle died.[31]

That night, a Japanese engineer saved the allies from disaster. Rushing forward under fire, he set off a guncotton grenade beside the city walls, blasting himself and the main gate to pieces. The allies burst into the city and slaughtered everyone they found. An American photographer who entered the next day saw "a holocaust of human life." Bodies, young and old, littered the stone streets. The stench of rotting flesh wafted through the ruined buildings. The allies estimated that as many as ten thousand Chinese combatants and civilians had died.[32]

Inside the city walls, the allies buried their dead and burned the Chinese. Then they got down to the real pastime of imperial warfare: looting. The British, French, and Germans were most practiced at the craft, but the Great Game's newest entrants proved quick studies. In a burned-out official's residence, the Marines found a lode of silver bullion. They estimated its value at $376,000—more than $11 million today. With the authorization of the secretary of the Navy, the bullion was packed on barges by the Marines and sold to a J. P. Morgan representative in Shanghai.[33]

The U.S. returned the money to China two years later as part of the postwar negotiations. But somehow, ninety-five pounds of Chinese silver ended up back in the hands of the Ninth Infantry. It was made into a silver punch bowl, which they named after their slain colonel. Officers of the

"Manchu" Ninth still drink from the Liscum Bowl in official ceremonies to this day.[34]

Nelly asked if I wanted to visit the Boxer shrine in Tianjin.

"There's a Boxer shrine in Tianjin?" I replied.

She took me to the neighborhood of Hongqiao, just west of where the old city walls had stood. Around the spot where Hoover froze and Butler bled, there was a Holiday Inn with a built-in shopping mall.

The shrine, it turned out, was an active, three-hundred-year-old Daoist temple to the scholar-god Lü Dongbin: master of internal alchemy, vanquisher of devils. It had served as headquarters for the Yihetuan commander Cao Futian during the war—an appropriately mystical space for a leader whose followers believed he could turn himself invisible and be in two places at once. (Cao's supposed connection to the divine did not dampen his brutality. According to one account, his men castrated and decapitated a man ahead of the Battle of Tianjin—possibly a deserter— and left his dismembered corpse as a warning outside the temple gate.)[35]

Around the brick-and-timber bungalow were faded Yihetuan flags and racks of rusting *guandao,* heavy bladed spears on six-foot poles. I lifted one; it must have weighed forty pounds. Nearby, in the center of the yard, stood a bronze statue of Cao flanked by his fellow Boxer commander Zhang Decheng and Lin Hei'er, known as the "Holy Mother of the Yellow Lotus" and leader of the local unit of the women's army, or Red Lanterns.

As I walked closer, I noticed there was something going on behind the statue. On the grass at the edge of the compound was a group of people holding swords tied with red and yellow handkerchiefs. They punched in unison, slicing the air with their blades. The metal flashed white in the sun.

My God, I thought. They're back.

I quickly realized the fighters looked more like my aging parents than guerrilla reserves. The women wore patterned exercise blouses, the men sweaty T-shirts. They mimicked the movements of their instructor: a short, older man with a stringy black comb-over. He wore a cream-colored silk uniform whose trousers hung loosely over a pair of red-striped tennis shoes.

When the class took a break, the teacher introduced himself. "Master Baoshun," he crooned, bowing slightly as he extended his hand. He asked Nelly where I was from.

"Ah," he replied when she told him. He nodded at one of his students. "Her son is a doctor in Los Angeles."

"Can you ask what they're doing?" I asked Nelly. She listened to his answer, then scrunched her nose. "I'm sorry, I don't know how to say it in English." She repeated his answer slowly in Mandarin. I recognized the last word: *quan*.

"Like Yihequan?" I asked, referring to the original name of the "Righteous and Harmonious Fists." The elderly students laughed.

Baoshun smiled. "Like the Boxers," he said.

He told Nelly the four goals of his martial arts method, waiting patiently as I wrote each down:

1. Defend against invaders
2. Self-protection
3. Keep fit
4. Create harmony

"The Yihetuan were simple farmers," he told me. "They answered the government's call to defend our land. With our martial arts and our military power, foreigners won't invade us again—China isn't weak like it used to be."

That last line had become familiar. But the rest didn't match the history I'd read. Far from answering a government's call, the Yihetuan had started as a rebellion against the Qing, and infighting ultimately plagued the effort.

But those were not the sort of details modern Chinese schools would teach. The idea of divisions in the face of a foreign invasion was as taboo as the fact that peasants rose up without government approval in the first place. A schoolteacher I met elsewhere in China was so nervous about his knowledge of Boxer-era infighting between the government and guerrillas that he spent most of our conversation reminding me not to repeat his name.

The story I heard most frequently in China about the Boxer War was the sacking and looting of the Old Summer Palace—the once-majestic complex of royal mansions and gardens on the outskirts of Beijing. The ruins are now a national tourist mecca, a kind of "Hundred Years of Humiliation" theme park. But any damage the palace suffered during the Boxer Uprising was incidental, because nearly all of it had been ransacked and burned by the British and French forty years earlier, during the Second Opium War. Perhaps it was more useful to imagine that China's future rival—the United States—had been involved in the destruction of a national treasure.

Such negotiations with the past are, of course, true everywhere. "Ordinary folks . . . are likely to be more emotionally drawn to a past that fits their preconceptions—a past they feel comfortable and identify with—than to a past that is 'true' in some more objective sense," Paul A. Cohen, an American historian of China, has written.[36]

Baoshun said something to Nelly. "He wants to know if you would like a lesson," she translated.

I realized he was serious. "Oh, OK."

The students cleared a circle by the outer wall. The master indicated I should raise my hands, palms up and together, like a butterfly. Then he punched me in the throat, stopping his hand just as his knuckle brushed my skin.

Defend ourselves against invaders, I thought.

The class applauded.

With the looting over in Tianjin, there was little for Butler to do but watch the hole in his leg heal and wait. In letters home, his attention hopped from the weather ("hotter than Cavite") to his friend ("poor Leonard") who'd developed gangrene on the stump of his amputated arm.[37] As a reward for his bravery and to fill the void left by the dead and wounded officers, Butler was breveted to captain. A few days later, he turned nineteen.

By late July 1900, the question on every soldier's mind was when they were going to Beijing. Weeks earlier, the Empress Dowager had issued an ultimatum for all legation staff to leave Beijing within twenty-four hours. The chief German diplomat in China had been killed on the way to the Qing foreign office the morning after. The surviving diplomats and their families had decided to dig in, defended by a thin line of embassy guards, including a small contingent of Marines. Surrounding them was the main force of the Chinese regular army along with a quarter of a million Boxers. Beyond them all, in the innermost palaces of the Forbidden City, was the Empress Dowager herself.

"Dame Rumor" again ran wild. On July 5, the *New York Times* had declared: ALL FOREIGNERS IN PEKING DEAD. The story was false, based on erroneous British reporting, but it had catalyzed international attention. Like the Cuban and Philippine wars that overlapped with it, the Boxer Uprising coincided with the rise of the daily newspaper. Editors had access to more stories from around the world than ever before, and they were learning how to use the uneven drumbeat of developments to hook readers. Tales of swarthy turbaned bandits attacking desperate Western women made for hot copy. A Chicago newspaperman compiled poorly sourced and secondhand accounts into the popular book *Massacres of Christians by the Heathen Chinese, and Horrors of the Boxers*. A British filmmaker was filming "Attack on a China Mission"—a four-minute short in which Boxers kill a missionary before British sailors rush in to rescue his family—at a cottage in East Sussex. (The English audience at its premiere demanded an immediate repeat viewing.)[38]

The fear and hope reflected in letters from home overcame any reluctance the Marines might have had about heading back into the fray. Butler just prayed his leg had healed enough to go. On August 4, he jotted a note to Maud, covering any dread he was feeling with Rooseveltian swagger:

> Nothing new, preparations all made, expect to run against 30,000 chinamen tomorrow morning. Don't be worried about me. If I am killed, I gave my life for women and children, just as dear to some poor devil as thee and Horace are to me. Lots of love to all, Good bye.[39]

Nineteen thousand men set off for the ninety-mile journey, including twenty-five hundred U.S. soldiers and Marines. The first resistance came at the hamlet of Beicang, where Qing general Dong Fuxiang's Chinese Muslim troops and their Boxer allies were waiting. Dong's goal, the allies realized too late, was not to defend Beicang so much as to kill as many of the invaders as possible before they reached the capital. His troops destroyed a dike on the left bank of the river, pinning the French and Russians behind floodwaters and a curtain of artillery fire. That left the Japanese to again take the heaviest losses, directly attacking and overwhelming the Chinese positions.*

As the column ground northwest, the veneer of order fell apart. It was early summer in China, when the dry, hot air blows in from the Gobi Desert, heating the North China Plain like a furnace. The rice boats the Americans' Chinese servants were tugging up the canal lagged behind them. Butler felt lucky to befriend a veteran Marine, an old Greek immigrant with big gold earrings, who was willing to share the moldy bread and cheese he'd filled his knapsack with before leaving Tianjin.

The Marines were told not to drink any water they found, but in the infernal heat that was impossible. "On one occasion we found a big earthen bowl of water in a hut that we stormed," Butler wrote. "We drank lustily and immediately became ill."[40]

The Japanese at the front of the column decided to avoid the heat by leaving every day before dawn. The French took the opposite tack and hung back until dark. The Americans were stuck in the middle, departing just before the sun reached its zenith. Clouds of dust blew into their eyes and peeling noses. Their horses died in the road. Sergeants yelled every insult they could think of, trying to push the Marines on by force of rage. (Pete Wynne took particular pleasure in joining in the harangues.) With his leg still not fully healed, Butler often only made it by grabbing the musty haunches of a mounted officer's horse and letting it drag him part of the way.

---

* According to a local historian, at some point, the British fired a "chlorine gas cannon." The poet and journalist Li Boyuan elaborated two years later: "People only had to inhale the gas to die where they stood; they had no need to be in the vicinity of those cruel shells when they landed." This would be revelatory if true: most Western historians state that the first chemical weapons were deployed by the Germans during World War I, fourteen years later. If such weapons were used in China, it was in violation of European law. The powers had banned the use of poison gas at the first international conference on arms control at the Hague a year before. Li wrote that the allies "had reserved them for attacks on savages." Indeed, when chlorine gas was used first on the battlefield by the Germans, they did so against Algerian troops fighting for the French at the Battle of Ypres. Thanks to Jeffrey Wasserstrom for pointing out the poem. See Wang Jingmo, 天津静海旧话 [Tianjin Jinghai History] (Tianjin Shi: Tianjin gu ji chu ban she, 2007), 38–39, via Google Translate, and Douglas Lancashire, *Li Po-Yuan* (Boston: Twayne Publishers, 1981), 175n32.

The good news was that the drought was starting to break, deplet-ing the Boxer forces as some men returned to their fields. The bad news was that meant nights of torrential rain. And Butler, like most of the Marines, hadn't been issued a tent.

On August 13, they finally reached Beijing. "I could not help being impressed with the dignity of the walls surrounding the ancient city. There were miles of massive battlements, with huge gate houses," Butler wrote.[41] The Marines darted between the low-slung houses of the capital's outer city to avoid sniper fire along the road.

Eventually they reached the gate called Dongbianmen, where an im-posing corner fortress rose to a peaked red-and-green roof. A bugler with the U.S. Army Fourteenth Infantry dropped his instrument and moun-taineered his way to the top. Others followed. They set fire to the five-hundred-year-old corner tower, watching until the flames blasted through its three-century-old ceiling, and opened the gate.

Waller called his favorite teenage captain over, and together he and Butler climbed the ramp to see what was waiting on the other side. It was another set of walls. ("Peking was all walls," Butler later recalled.)[42] Chi-nese troops were taking potshots at the entering infantry. Waller ordered Butler's company to take out the snipers. Butler hustled down to the road, shouting for the men to hurry through the gate. As he turned to follow them, a bullet zipped through the air. Pain exploded through his lungs, and the world went black.

The Chinese government restored the burned-out tower at Dongbianmen in the 1980s. When I visited, it housed a modern art gallery run by an Australian. A small sign outside the door pointed to graffiti left by Russian and American soldiers during the Boxer War. I made out a name in Cyril-lic letters, "Goshka Falaleev," and penknife carvings reading "Stickel" and "Paul F."

The world's best repository of Boxer memory lies a few hours south at Shandong University, in the capital of the province where the upris-ing began. Past the School of Marxism and a statue of the region's most revered native son, Confucius, I took an elevator to the Center for Boxer

Movement Studies. Professor Su Weizhi was waiting at a long table with two colleagues.

The meeting opened formally with a recitation of credentials. Then Su leaned forward and spoke. "Professor Su welcomes you," the junior colleague translated. "The Boxer issue is so big and so complicated. We are glad to hear you want to do research on the Boxer movement." We would chat for a while in the office, he explained, then continue the conversation over lunch.

For decades after Mao Zedong's Communists won control of China in 1949, there had been little collaboration between Chinese and Western scholars. The end of the Cold War and reforms under Mao's successor Deng Xiaoping in the 1970s had opened new possibilities, but obstacles remained. Much of the best historical material remained scattered in Western archives, and the steep language barrier meant many scholars couldn't understand each other's work.

Su told me that foreigners make the mistake of looking at the Boxer War through the eyes of their own countries' missionaries, diplomats, and businessmen, instead of the people whose country they invaded. The junior colleague dutifully translated. Then he paused, and added, carefully: "Their opinions on the Boxer Movement and the Chinese people are not—objective, maybe."

"Are not objective," I repeated, making sure I understood.

"Yes," the junior colleague said, pausing to see if I would respond. I didn't, and Su went on.

Unsurprisingly, the professor's understanding of the rebellion was more nuanced than that of the martial arts master at the Boxer shrine. He framed the events through a century of Chinese political thought. "Revolutionaries from the capitalist class" initially opposed the Boxers but later came to praise their "heroic spirit," he explained, channeling Marx and Mao. He added, with a nod to the power-and-wealth-seeking policies of Xi Jinping: "After all, that kind of spirit is necessary for a nation to move toward independence, toward prosperity."

I asked him if he thought the memory of the Boxer Rebellion influenced modern Chinese policy. Was China less likely to intervene in other countries because of its own relatively recent experiences with imperial invaders?

He bristled. "No, no impact to speak of. The Chinese government knows that if it wants to develop its economy, it has to open it up to the world, and open it permanently." The interpreter said something to him in Mandarin and laughed nervously.

I decided to push the issue. China's expansionist designs were hardly a secret. On my trip through Asia, I'd been surrounded by signs of it: Filipino newspapers were filled with reports of the new Chinese military airstrips, radar, and antiaircraft guns on artificial islands in the South China Sea. Philippine president Duterte's trolling about his country's American War was in part a means of pivoting away from the increasingly unreliable United States and toward China—which on the one hand was providing him with massive infrastructure investments, and on the other was rattling its saber over Filipino islands it claimed were inside its "territorial seas."[43]

When I'd landed in Beijing, I had been greeted at customs by a huge "One Belt, One Road" banner. At the same time the aircraft carrier *Liaoning* was leaving Hong Kong a few days later, China inaugurated its first overseas military base in Djibouti, across the Gulf of Aden from the Arabian Peninsula. A U.S. Navy base was positioned just a few miles away. "It's like having a rival football team using an adjacent practice field," a U.S. analyst said with alarm.[44]

Given all that, I felt I had to restate the question: "Do you think China can become an imperial power in the world again—in the sense that the members of the 'Eight Power Allied Force' were a hundred years ago?"

The interpreter's eyes widened. Su, apparently understanding enough English to get the gist, laughed. The two went back and forth in muted tones. It seemed the interpreter did not want him to answer.

But Su did anyway. "The 'China Threat' discourse is absolutely groundless. China will not invade another country. The Chinese government has made this commitment." You could look to history, he said: the Great Wall of China was built for defense.

I told him the United States usually says the same thing about itself. "When we invaded Iraq in 2003, the Bush administration said that they were doing it for defense."

Su's expression hardened. "These are really political issues that are beyond our research." Then he smiled broadly. "Besides, there are many examples in international history that invading countries don't come to a good end!"

The interpreter studied my face for a reaction. "Maybe except America," he added, politely.

As the three professors huddled, I realized I'd overstepped. I resolved to smooth things over at lunch.

Then the third colleague, who had not said anything until then, came over to my side of the table. "I am sorry that Professor Su has another engagement and cannot join for lunch," he said. Also the junior colleague couldn't make it. Neither could he.

I thanked them and went back to the campus hotel to eat alone.

When Smedley Butler awoke, he was inside Beijing's walls. It felt like someone had taken a sledgehammer to his chest. "Stand back and give him air!" a Marine shouted. Another ripped open his jacket and shirt and cussed: "He's shot through the heart."

Butler knew that wasn't true, but he couldn't catch his breath to reply. Then the unit's bugler looked closer. The second button on his jacket was flat as a toadstool. The bullet had cracked Butler's breastbone and flayed a chunk of Latin America off his chest tattoo before ricocheting away. "Needless to say, I have kept the button," Butler wrote his mother.[45]

Despite themselves, the allies' chaotic, rivalry-ridden assault had broken the last of the Chinese resistance. Racing to be first into the legations, the Japanese and Russians hit the same section of wall before dawn, drawing Qing units from across the city. This left the southern battlements, where the British and Americans arrived, more lightly defended. Two British Indian regiments, the Seventeenth Rajput and Twenty-Fourth Punjab Infantry, found their way into a sewer and emerged in the legation quarter.[46]

The Americans halted their advance beside Tiananmen, the monumental entrance to the Forbidden City. The U.S. commanding officer in China, Gen. Adna R. Chaffee, may have wanted to avoid the further bloodshed he would have provoked by violating the sacred space in the presence of the Empress Dowager. But she wasn't there. Once word came that the invaders had breached Beijing's innermost walls, Cixi gathered her nephew and closest relatives, a handful of staff, and a favorite concubine and fled west in a convoy of mule carts.

On August 16, confident the royals were gone, the allies marched into the imperial palace. Smedley Butler was chosen to represent the First Marines. He passed through a gate that for five centuries had been used only by emperors, expecting to find mountains of diamonds, rubies, and pearls. To his great disappointment, he only saw a bunch of paintings, uncomfortable furniture, and some gold-leafed columns that chipped when poked with a bayonet.[47]

With their supply lines exhausted, coalition forces were expected to "forage" for food in the capital. The Marines spent the rest of their time foraging, as Butler put it, for anything "that looked good to us."[48] They took coins, candlesticks, porcelain, and ponies. Officers arrived to find Marines patrolling in stolen silk boots and pajamas. General Chaffee noted the looting in his official report, as well as "indiscriminate and generally unprovoked shooting of Chinese." He estimated the rate of civilians to actual Boxers killed during mop-up operations at fifty to one.[49]

These stories did not stay in China. Foreign journalists, out of Boxer horrors to report, turned to their own countrymen for material. Tales of postwar abuses soon reached the United States, where misgivings some had started feeling about their country's imperial exploits were beginning to harden into an antiwar bloc.

The criticism boiled over in late 1900, when the *New York Sun* profiled the Rev. William Scott Ament, a Congregationalist missionary who expropriated money and houses from Chinese civilians after the war.[50] The story got the attention of the most famous writer in America, Mark Twain. Twain had initially supported the war with Spain, only to become enraged when the would-be liberators turned around and "benevolently assimilated" Puerto Rico, Guam, Hawai'i, and the Philippines. In an essay penned for a literary magazine, Twain used Ament's crimes in China to blast the hypocrisy and greed—and impending blowback—he now saw at the heart of the entire American imperial project:

> Extending the Blessings of Civilization to our Brother who Sits in Darkness has been a good trade and has paid well, on the whole; and there is money in it yet, if carefully worked. . . . But Christendom has been play-

ing it badly of late years, and must certainly suffer by it, in my opinion. She has been so eager to get every stake that appeared on the green cloth, that the People who Sit in Darkness have noticed it—they have noticed it, and have begun to show alarm.[51]

The American public was more interested in personalities than policy. The reaction to Twain's essay turned into a mud fight not over U.S. actions in Asia but over Ament's personal reputation and the specific amounts the missionary was alleged to have extracted. Stung by the controversy, the Anti-Imperialist League—of which Twain was a vice president—edited out the most incendiary parts of his essay for later publications.[52]

Years later, Butler would look back on his role in the looting of Beijing with equally belated shame. "I suppose we shouldn't have taken anything, but war is hell anyhow and none of us was in the frame of mind to make it any better," he would write.[53]

In the moment, though, he had to find other ways of dealing with his ambivalence and the stress of the campaign. One night, the Marines threw Major Waller a birthday party. Junior officers sat in a corner, smashing looted Buddhas in hopes of finding something valuable inside. Butler and his friends killed a mule and cut out its liver, which they served with bacon and rum. Soon there was only rum. Butler got so thuddingly drunk that he started belting out an old sea chanty—"Down along the coast of the High Bar-bar-ee!"—until he passed out on the table, nose first.[54]

The surviving Marines were sent to Japan soon after for some R&R. Butler never got off the ship. He developed a raging fever at Nagasaki and was left in the care of a "colored fire man named Padmore." The fetid water he'd been drinking in the Chinese countryside, it seems, had caught up with him. "The gunshot wounds had weakened me," he reflected. "The typhoid fever finished the job." He fell into delirium. In nightmares he relived the horrors of the battlefield. Years later, he told his family he'd experienced death on that ship.[55]

Maud and Thomas crossed the continent to see Smedley's ghostly pale, ninety-pound frame descend from the ship at San Francisco. It had been a year and a half since he had left for the Philippines. Thomas had written Littleton Waller expressing his worry about Smedley's condition in the meantime. Maud had been more sanguine. When a West Chester newspaper republished a short profile depicting her as a weeping mother, she wrote the editor to say she was "extremely annoyed" and that the "hysterical displays" attributed to her were "a lot of silly sentiment I never possessed." (The editor issued a retraction, saying: "The many readers of the News who know Mrs. Butler will fully believe the above and at the same time sympathize with her under such trying circumstances. Mrs. Butler is a heroic woman and to credit her with saying soft things is unfair and discourteous.")[56]

Despite the controversies over looting, the China campaign again made the Marines into national stars. The next year, Buffalo Bill would replace the "Battle of San Juan Hill" section of his Wild West Show with a reenactment of the Battle of Tianjin and the capture of Beijing. The posters featured a Marine stabbing a Boxer with a bayonet at the gate where Butler had been shot.[57]

Two thousand Main Liners turned out to the Assembly Building in West Chester on January 17, 1901, to see Smedley Butler receive a ceremonial sword. The recently promoted Capt. Henry Leonard received a gold medal for saving the town's new favorite son. He accepted it with his remaining hand.[58]

The war hastened the Qing dynasty's end. But the fall did not happen overnight. The allies contented themselves with the internal exile of Prince Duan and the execution of several officials and Boxer leaders including Cao Futian. The Empress Dowager (and her still-imprisoned nephew) were allowed to remain in power. In exchange, the foreigners got what they had really wanted all along: money.

In September 1901, the parties signed one of the "unequal treaties" Nelly and her classmates had to memorize in school. Known as the Boxer Protocol, it required the Qing to pay 450 million silver taels, worth roughly $10 billion today. The Russians demanded almost a third; the Germans nearly a quarter. The Americans took the smallest share among the major powers—about 7 percent. The Qing customs system became, in effect, a "debt collection agency" for foreign governments. The Qing also agreed to allow foreign troops in twelve cities, including Tianjin, and to dismantle the Dagu Forts.[59]

McKinley's successor, Theodore Roosevelt, would sign a broad new U.S.-China commercial treaty in 1903, renewing the long-held hopes for a marriage of U.S. industry and the world's most populous market. Satisfied, Roosevelt could stand at the Mechanics' Pavilion in San Francisco in 1903 and declare: "Before I came to the Pacific Slope I was an expansionist, and after having been here I fail to understand how any man . . . can be anything *but* an expansionist!"[60]

Ordinary people paid the biggest price. An estimated one hundred thousand Chinese were killed in the war; most who died had taken no part in the uprising. In defeat, the Yihetuan had left the people of the plains worse off than before as the Boxer Indemnity sapped the resources they needed to survive. "In the beginning, when it was the Big Sword Society, they used slogans like, 'Kill the rich and give to the poor!' 'Kill corrupt officials and work for the people!'" a survivor from Shandong Province remembered. "But they never put those slogans into practice."[61]

Even the missionaries, whose stories had given the allies the pretext they needed to invade, were abandoned. Susan Rowena Bird was executed by Boxers in late July, alongside five other Americans and several Chinese Christians in Shanxi Province. The Marines and soldiers were 275 miles away at the time. They never got closer.

For the elite intellectuals behind the failed Hundred Days' Reform—whom the Empress Dowager had sent into exile before the invasions started—the disaster helped clarify a reimagining of their country. They could no longer afford to be the borderless Da Qing Guo, the Great Qing Kingdom, expecting tribute and kowtow from countries that no longer showed them fear or respect. They would need a new national identity as a modern nation-state.

One of the reformers, the journalist Liang Qichao, had spent part of his exile in Hawai'i. From Honolulu, he kept tabs on the news back home, met refugees from the Boxer and Philippine Wars, and saw the young men boarding U.S. warships to head across the Pacific. He had no doubt the United States was "the preeminent rising power of the world," as a colleague wrote. "In the past, we were fearful of the savage ambition of absolute monarchs, but now the desires of the mighty capitalists are even more to be feared," an unsigned editorial in Liang's newspaper observed.[62]

Liang believed a reformed China could eventually assert itself among the new powers. But another member of Liang's circle, a philosopher and physician known to his Western contacts as Sun Yat-sen, believed reforms wouldn't go far enough. What China needed, Sun thought, was a revolution.[63]

# FIVE

**W**hile Butler was resting and healing at his parents' house in West Chester, the United States' first Asian quagmire was entering a dangerous new phase. Throughout the first months of the war, the U.S. had been nearly undefeated on battlefields across Luzon. Realizing the Filipinos could not win in direct confrontation, in late 1899 the fleeing president Emiliano Aguinaldo had ordered his troops to throw away their uniforms and melt into the countryside to mount a guerrilla insurgency.

Filipino generals had been urging such a shift for months, arguing that their knowledge of the terrain, connections to the local population, and experience with the climate were their best advantages to exploit. Aguinaldo had resisted, possibly out of a belief that a conventional victory would be held in higher esteem by other nations. But with President McKinley coming up for reelection against the antiwar Democratic populist William Jennings Bryan, the embattled Filipino leader now calculated that his best option was to raise the cost of the war in both money and lives and force American citizens to demand a withdrawal.

Guerrillas on Luzon inflicted heavy losses, using snipers and booby traps. Their most feared tactic was the "bolo rush": leaping out of the bush with guns and sharpened bolo knives—a farm tool similar to a machete—and overwhelming a hapless patrol.[1] American soldiers chasing these guerrillas were pulled ever deeper into the hinterlands. Along the way, they picked up local words. *Bundók*—Tagalog for "mountain"—was given an American twang and made into slang for any wild and remote place. It was only by going to the "boondocks," the soldiers learned, that you could get the measure of a country.[2]

To finance the insurgency, the soldiers on Luzon seized the supply of the islands' most valuable export: a strong, flexible fiber harvested from a cousin of the banana plant known as *abacá*. Americans called it "Manila hemp," and before synthetics came along, it drove the global economy. Shipbuilders used its fibers to weave ropes and sails. Electric companies ran abacá belts through their city-powering generators. The oil boom minting millionaires in Texas and California depended on miles of "Manila drilling cable" pulsing through the derricks. Even the people counting the money needed abacá to make their office supplies: they're called "manila envelopes" for a reason.

U.S. commanders wanted to destroy the hemp supply to starve the insurgents out, but they were overruled by Washington and Wall Street. There was simply too much money to be made from the export crop. Instead, the Americans looked south of the big island toward the Visayas—a group of six major islands and scores of smaller ones in the middle of the Philippine archipelago.

Most promising was the island of Samar—a lush, mountainous expanse, shaped like a butterfly's right wing, where abacá grew thick. Samareños had not taken part in the revolution against Spain; they spoke a different language than the peoples of Luzon and considered them nearly as foreign as the Iberians. They were equally indifferent to the fight against the Americans. In January 1900, U.S. forces were ordered to Samar to, as a commander put it, "render a sufficient quantity of hemp available for the American market as soon as possible."[3]

Aguinaldo also had designs on Samar. In 1899, he had sent one of his most trusted generals, Vicente Lukban, to bring Samar and its neighboring island, Leyte, into the Philippine Republic.[4] An accomplished Tagalog lawyer with a waxed mustache, Lukban was a committed bourgeois revolutionary: tortured by the Spanish, then exiled by them along with Aguinaldo to Hong Kong, he had commanded Filipino forces to a string of victories against Spain during the brief American alliance.

In his year on Samar, Lukban had learned that managing the islanders took more political than military skill. He learned to speak Samareño and married a local woman. In the island's mountainous interior, he forged a tentative alliance with an aggressive apocalyptic cult, the Dios-Dios, on promises of mutual protection. When Lukban learned the Americans were coming for Samar's abacá supply, he went on a propaganda offensive, spreading word that their true purpose was "raping, pillaging, and 'annihilating us later as they have the Indians of America.'"[5]

But the Samareños mostly ignored him. The people of the lowland farms and fishing villages were too busy trying to recover from the ravages of a recent typhoon. They just wanted to be left alone. Quietly, Lukban ordered his lieutenants to kill and burn the houses of any Samareño caught collaborating with the enemy.[6]

If the Americans had known that, they might have taken advantage of the tension between the Luzon-led revolutionaries and the locals to divide and conquer Samar. Instead, they bulldozed over everyone. When Lukban's small guerrilla bands started harassing the island's hemp ports, U.S. commanders moved to cut off the entire island's food supply. The Americans slashed fishing nets, burned crops, and shot livestock, including the beefy water buffalo, known as *carabao,* that were often a village's most valuable possessions. Along the way they would sing their marching song: "Underneath the starry flag / civilize 'em with a Krag."*

On Luzon, the Americans had experimented with a carrot-and-stick approach. Battlefield victories were followed by projects to build roads, rail lines, telegraph stations, and hospitals. Schools where children could be taught English and American propaganda were seen as "more beneficial than troops." These tactics had been adapted from the U.S. government's experience conquering and controlling American Indian populations on the North American frontier.[7]

But that was not to be the approach on Samar. Unfortunately for everyone, the Americans' arrival on the mountainous island coincided with a fight over strategy among the U.S. colonial command. With his reelection on the line, McKinley had divided the job of governor-general overseeing the Philippines in two: William Howard Taft, a federal judge from Ohio, was put in charge of civilian affairs, overseeing the promised "benevolent assimilation." Meanwhile, a new military governor-general— Gen. Adna R. Chaffee, the erstwhile commanding officer of U.S. forces in

---

* The full song was known as "Damn Damn Damn the Filipinos," a parody version of a Civil War march. The melody is best known today as the tune of "Jesus Loves the Little Children." The M1898 Krag–Jørgensen, a bolt-action, side-loading rifle, was a standard-issue firearm for Marines.

northern China—was entrusted with overseeing those areas still deemed to be in "rebellion."

The two governors did not get along. Chaffee deemed Taft hopelessly naïve after he called Filipinos, with equal parts racism and paternalism, "our little brown brothers"—who, the future president had said, in time and with proper tutelage, could develop the "Anglo-Saxon political principles and skills" for self-rule.[8]

Eager to prove Taft wrong by demonstrating the greater efficacy of the iron fist, Chaffee ordered the use of the tactics he'd learned in his thirty years of war against the Apache, Cheyenne, and other Native American tribes: concentration, devastation, and harassment.[9] Like the Boxers, Lukban's soldiers were branded "bandits," placing them and their fates outside the law. It was a tactic Americans have used against insurgents ever since, evolving into more modern variants such as "criminal," "subversive," and "terrorist."[10]

Some Samareños reluctantly turned to Lukban for protection. In 1901, with McKinley now elected to a second term, the U.S. soldiers in Samar felt free to push back harder. In August, the Ninth Infantry arrived aboard the U.S. Army transport Liscum, named after their late colonel killed at the Battle of Tianjin. Four companies of the "Manchu Ninth" were assigned to towns along Samar's southern coast.

The sleepy fishing village of Balangiga was assigned to Company C. Its commander, Capt. Thomas W. Connell, was a by-the-book West Point graduate who had fought in the Santiago campaign in Cuba, alongside Liscum in China, and on Luzon. In strict accordance with his mandate, Connell ordered the port closed and the village's rice and fish stocks destroyed, ignoring the villagers' protests.

In their downtime, the men of Company C nursed their physical and psychic wounds from the Boxer War with tuba, a local coconut wine. ("When fresh tastes like cider, and is hell on fire when fermented," a soldier noted in a letter home.) On September 21, 1901, two soldiers got into an argument with a local tuba vendor and drunkenly threatened to abduct a waitress. The woman's brothers ran over and beat the soldiers to a pulp.[11]

The next day, September 22, Connell ordered the people of Balangiga to gather in the town's plaza. Those who heeded the call found two medium-sized conical canvas tents—tepees, basically—pitched on the north side of the municipal hall. At Connell's signal, the soldiers arrested all of the men, at least 143 people. They were then divided into two groups and stuffed into the tepees, which had been designed to sleep only sixteen people each.[12]

For six days, the Balangiganons' only respite from those torturous conditions were periods of forced labor. This included chopping up the sweet potato and taro vines the villagers needed to survive the coming wet season—plants the men of Company C thought were merely underbrush. Each evening, the soldiers confiscated the sharpened bolo knives they'd distributed among the prisoners for the job.

But the Americans in Balangiga proved as adept at monitoring their situation as they were at recognizing crops. Some of the men imprisoned in the overcrowded tents, the Company C soldiers failed to realize, were Filipino guerrillas from elsewhere on Samar, who had come to secretly train the locals in the art of armed resistance at the invitation of the town's police chief, Valeriano Abanador. By failing to distinguish between insurgents and villagers, and abusing them both, the Americans had done what Lukban could not: unite disparate factions of islanders in a common, national cause.

On the morning of September 28, 1901, as the soldiers of Company C sat down in their mess tent for breakfast, they were assaulted from all sides by rebel fighters, including many of the prisoners escaped from the tents. Forty-eight U.S. soldiers were killed, along with twenty-eight Samareños, in what Americans called the "Balangiga Massacre." It was the worst U.S. military disaster since Gen. George Custer showed up unprepared at the Little Bighorn. *Collier's Weekly* likened it to the Alamo.[13]

To reach Balangiga, I flew with Rica Concepcion, the fixer I'd hired in Manila, to the city of Tacloban on neighboring Leyte. Then we set off across a long bridge that winds like a red dragon across the channel islands of the San Juanico Strait. At the entrance to Samar, rifle-toting Filipino soldiers manned a checkpoint. They were on guard, Rica explained, for both Maoist guerrillas who still patrol its mountains and ISIS fighters trying to use the sparsely populated island to slip out of Mindanao into Tacloban. No one seemed to care who was going into Samar.

For an hour we drove down the coastal highway, passing thick abacá groves, until we crossed a small river bridge and reached Balangiga. In the main square stood the San Lorenzo de Martir Parish Church, with its Romanesque arches and squat bell tower. Across the way was the municipal building, painted aquamarine.

Between them stood the most visceral monument I had ever seen: dozens of life-sized, gold-painted statues arrayed in a horrific tableau. In the middle were the men of Company C, forever frozen around their breakfast table, as if in a nightmare. Their faces twisted in horror as they faced a stylized doorway—representing the doors of the church—out from which burst furious Samareño men, beginning the bolo rush. More fighters in conical *sarok* hats crawled in from the sides. Police Captain Abanador directed the action with his bolo and baton from a pedestal. Above them all hung a representation of golden church bells in a stylized belfry, gleaming in the noonday sun.

I stood in front of the monument for a few moments, absorbing its ferocity. Then we headed over to the municipal building. Amid curious looks, Rica explained to a receptionist that I was an American interested in learning Balangiga's history. Minutes later we were ushered upstairs into the office of the mayor, Randy Duran Garza. We sat down at an intricately carved wooden table. The town's seal, featuring a silhouette of Abanador and two golden bells, hung on a beige wall.

Garza was slight, with black hair and a youthful face. He seemed eager to meet but reluctant to talk, perhaps embarrassed about speaking English with me or Tagalog with Rica, instead of his native dialect of Samareño. So I opened the conversation with what seemed like an obvious statement: "I assume from seeing the monument in the square, that the memory of this event is very important."

"Yes, yes, of course," the mayor replied, in an unexpectedly deep voice. "Every year, we are celebrating the Balangiga Encounter."

Rica and I exchanged a confused glance. Celebrating?

"September last year we had a reenactment," Garza continued. "But this year we are preparing so it will be an annual reenactment for the Balangiga Encounter."

"Can I see it?" I asked.

A short time later, the mayor's IT guy, a short young man with spiked hair named Pewie Cerilla, came in with a gray laptop and a CD-ROM.

The video opened with shots of a meticulously built set: a nearly scale replica of the church, full-sized nipa-grass houses complete with porches and windows, a courthouse, and a jail—a stand-in, in local memory, for the prison tepees. Even the replica Krags looked accurately rendered. Hundreds of spectators watched from folding chairs and standing along the sidelines—it was staged on the soccer field of the town's elementary school.

It seemed a hundred more people were in the pageant itself. The priest was played by a real priest. A member of the city council played Police Captain Abanador. The "Americans" were all young Balangiganon men, most of whom had to dye their hair blond for the part.

"That's me," Pewie said, pointing to a villager in a pink shirt, white pants, and flip-flops.

The pageant begins with scenes of tranquil village life, interrupted by the arrival of the soldiers of Company C on the USAT *Liscum*—a large prop boat built around a pickup truck. The soldiers in blue disembark and raise a U.S. flag. Everyone stands at attention for a full rendition of "The Star-Spangled Banner," played over the loudspeakers.

Then the abuses start. The soldiers point their guns, mock and shove the villagers, and overturn market baskets. One "American" throws a Balangiganon woman onto the grass. He pantomimes unzipping his pants as she screams in palpable horror. As the violence reaches its crescendo, the video's editors cut to a shot of the waving U.S. flag.

The music changes from somber to driven. A few dozen men and one woman converge at the center of the field, holding lighted torches and sheathed bolo knives. Abanador stands in front with his baton, barefoot and dressed in a simple cotton uniform. He gives directions in Samareño as the public-address announcer explains the plan over the loudspeaker in English: Filipino officers disguised as women would sneak in weapons from outside the town, hidden in hollowed-out bamboo containers and nipa coffins. Meanwhile the only woman among the plotters, Casiana Nacionales, would sneak up to the jail under the American soldiers' noses. At the moment the attack began, Nacionales would spring the prisoners—townspeople and trained guerrillas both.[14]

"The dawn of September 28, 1901, promised a perfect day," the announcer says. "The Americans, after a mess call, settled down for a hot breakfast in a relaxed atmosphere." Company C gathers at a bamboo table under a canvas tent. As they sit, the bleached-blond youths in blue uniforms give each other high fives—an instantly recognizable, if anachronistic, sign of their Americanness.

Abanador strolls past. As he passes the American sentry, Pvt. Adolph Gamlin, he swings his baton, grabs the replica Krag from the soldier's hands, and smashes the rifle butt toward his face. The announcer repeats his words in Samareño: "Atake, mga Balangiganon!" People of Balangiga, attack!

The air is filled with the ringing of church bells. Bolo men cut the ties on the mess tent, trapping screaming "Americans" underneath the canvas flaps. Some of the soldiers scramble for cover, running across the soccer field at full speed in every conceivable direction. Some are cut down by the prisoners. Others run straight into the waiting bolos of men bursting out of the church, led by Casiana Nacionales, defiantly waving her rosary.

As I watched the actors tumbling like acrobats, fighting and pretending to cut each other's throats, I thought of the testimony I'd read of one of the massacre's survivors:

> The scene in the blood-soaked shack was awful, with dead and dying all around. I particularly remember one man bleeding from a gaping wound in his forehead, sitting bolt upright on the ladder in front of our shack, dying. Another soldier, Private Armani, was slashed across the abdomen and was suffering intense agony. Private J. J. Driscoll was crawling on his hands and feet like a stabbed pig, his brains falling out through a wound he had received.[15]

"That's me!" Pewie repeated, as his on-screen self lunged at an American. "I had to be careful. I was carrying a real bolo."

Soon, there are blond Americans lying motionless across the field, a smaller number of Samareño fighters beside them. "On that September morning," the announcer says, "the pent-up emotions suppressed for centuries finally surfaced, when every Balangiganon risked his all for freedom and liberty."

The audience grows quiet. Everyone knows what's coming next.

News of the Balangiga Massacre rocketed out of the Philippines on the wires and straight onto front pages across the United States in the last days of September and first days of October 1901. Many accounts made sure to highlight the Filipinos' alleged posthumous mutilation of the Americans' bodies.[16]

It could scarcely have come at a more vulnerable moment for the Americans, politically. The night before the massacre, a group of soldiers returned from a supply trip to Leyte with staggering news: President McKinley was dead. He'd been assassinated at a world's fair* in Buffalo by an anarchist who'd lost his job as a steelworker in the 1893 depression. The assassin, Leon Czolgosz, had been troubled in part, a friend later said, by the "outrages committed by the American government in the Philippine Islands."[17]

Teddy Roosevelt was now president, the youngest in the history of the United States. The last thing the new leader needed was a public reminder that his "splendid little war" against Spain—the war that had made him an international star—had never really ended, that civilians who were supposed to greet Americans as liberators were furious enough to kill them instead. He raged at the War Department. It was "unpardonable" for an officer to be "surprised," Roosevelt said. If the commanding officer in Balangiga, Captain Connell, "escapes death, he will, I presume, be at once placed under arrest and tried by court-martial."[18]

The acting secretary assured Roosevelt that Chaffee, the military governor-general, had already ordered an investigation.[19] But as the official may have already known, Connell had not escaped. He had jumped

---

* The Buffalo "Pan-American Exposition" featured a special "Outlying Possessions Exhibit" organized by the Smithsonian. A few buildings away from the Temple of Music where McKinley would be shot, visitors could tour a model Filipino village, learn about the "clothes [Filipinos] wear, what they eat . . . [and] their games and amusements." Also on display, according to a syndicated newspaper article from 1901, were "curious native weapons captured by our troops" and "the famous Manila hemp in huge skeins."

out his window ahead of an onrush of bolo men, only to be stabbed to death in the street.

Chaffee believed the massacre proved he, not Taft, had been right all along. "We are dealing with a class of people whose character is deceitful, who are absolutely hostile to the white race and who regard life as of little value, and, finally, who will not submit to our control until absolutely defeated and whipped into such a condition."[20]

To accomplish this, Chaffee ordered a new crop of generals to subdue all remaining trouble spots. For Samar, he appointed Brig. Gen. Jacob H. Smith. It was a dangerous choice. "Hell Roarin' Jake" was legendarily corrupt and a drunk. Court-martialed three times for insubordination and dogged by creditors, Smith had only gotten his general's stars, the military historian Brian Linn has written, because of "his longevity, his physical bravery, and the mistaken belief that he planned to retire."[21]

But Smith had the one qualification Chaffee wanted: he'd spent twenty-seven years as a captain in the wars against American Indians in the west, and he was versed in the tactics of concentration, devastation, and harassment Chaffee believed were necessary.[22]

The revenge began before Smith even arrived. On September 29, the day after the massacre, cables flew from Chaffee to his subordinate, Brig. Gen. Robert P. Hughes, to investigate the affair. Hughes ordered the Eleventh Infantry on Leyte to cross the San Juanico Strait and "make a desert of Balangiga." That afternoon, they bombed the village into flames from five hundred yards offshore with the guns of the USS *Pittsburgh*. By October 8, an Army captain could report: "With the exception of the stone walls of the church and a few large upright poles of some of the houses, there is today not a vestage [*sic*] of the town of Balangiga left."[23]

To exact vengeance across the rest of the island, Smith turned to the group of men he knew would show the natives no quarter. He called for three hundred Marines from Cavite, under the command of Smedley Butler's mentor, Maj. Littleton Waller. On October 24, 1901—nearly a month after the massacre at Balangiga—Smith instructed Waller: "I want no prisoners. I wish you to kill and burn. The more you kill and burn, the better you will please me. I want all persons killed who are capable of bearing arms against the United States."[24]

"Capable of bearing arms," Smith clarified, meant any boys at least ten years of age.

Waller would later insist that he relayed Smith's orders without the instruction to commit genocide. But Smith also surely knew that the Virginian could be counted on to be as brutal as possible. He would be avenging the "Manchu Ninth"—the regiment who'd fought and died alongside his Marines at Tianjin and Beijing. "Place no confidence in the natives, and punish treachery immediately with death," Waller ordered. He added: "We have also to avenge our late comrades in North China, the murdered men of the Ninth United States Infantry."[25]

Among Waller's Marines were John H. Quick, freshly awarded his Medal of Honor for signaling under fire at Guantánamo and given the rank of gunnery sergeant. Other names on his roster would soon become similarly elevated luminaries of the Corps: David Dixon Porter, Alexander S. Williams, and Hiram Bearss.

Butler, then on duty at the Philadelphia Navy Yard, would surely have been among them had he not contracted his near-fatal case of typhoid in China and been sent home. Not only was his mentor leading the mission, but the officer at Cavite who selected the troops for Samar was his former captain at Guantánamo, the newly promoted Lt. Col. Mancil C. Goodrell.

Waller set up his headquarters at the village of Basey, about forty miles west of Balangiga. When he learned that some locals had been accused of smuggling rice to Filipino forces, he ordered their entire barrio destroyed. Then he set about burning nearby villages. For weeks, Waller's Marines destroyed rice, killed carabao, and burned homes. They also did what the military commanders had wanted to do all along: confiscate and burn supplies of "Manila hemp." If the Marines believed a village was giving information to Lukban, they burned it. If they found items they believed belonged to the Ninth Infantry, they killed the people who had them in their possession—and burned the village as well. Pvt. Harold Kinman wrote his sister that his company was "hiking all the time killing all we come across."[26]

That was still not enough for General Smith. In early December, one of Waller's lieutenants, John H. A. Day, handed the major a new order, written in Smith's distinctively calligraphic scrawl. It read: "The interior of Samar must be made a howling wilderness."[27]

Smith and Waller's fixation on total destruction of the insurgency led to one of the most confounding episodes of the Philippine-American War: the "March across Samar." Just before New Year's Day 1902, Waller led fifty-six Marines, two Filipino scouts, and thirty-three porters on an expedition to find a route bisecting the island, up the Lanang River and across the mountains. Despite warnings from Army personnel on the island's east coast, and the unavailability of the company surgeon, he pushed forward, driven by his "desire for some further knowledge of the people and the nature of this heretofore impenetrable country."[28]

It was the height of the monsoon. With the river too swollen to travel, the Marines tied up the boats and continued on foot, but the trails disappeared into mud. Soon, they realized they were going in circles, crossing the same part of the river again and again. They camped. But the ensuing days only got worse. Their maps fell apart. Lost, cutting their own trail, they sometimes found themselves trying to climb waterfalls. Boots disintegrated. Skin sloughed off the Marines' feet, leaving open sores. Leeches clung to their legs. They were running out of food, and it was too wet to light fires. Rations ran to a single piece of raw bacon per man.

Waller decided to take thirteen of the most able-bodied Marines and push forward as fast as he could, leaving Capt. David Porter in charge of the remainder. He kidnapped a Samareño family—"2 men, 2 women, and a boy of about 12"—and forced them to lead his fragmented unit back to Basey, where he summoned a mission to rescue the main column.[29] Eleven Marines died from exposure. Nearly all the rest ended up in the hospital.

Waller—mortified, delirious with fever, and, if his track record was any guide, probably drunk—blamed the Filipinos. He accused the scouts of intentionally leading his men to their deaths.

Lieutenant Day used a new torture technique the Americans had recently learned from the Spanish—the "water cure," an even-more-brutal precursor to waterboarding*—to force a porter into a vague, confused confession of

---

* A private with the Thirty-second Volunteer Infantry on Luzon described the process: "Lay them on their backs, a man standing on each hand and each foot, then put a round stick in

having attacked one of the Marines with a bolo. Day shot the porter dead on the spot. Waller then ordered the rest of the Filipinos in the party executed. Day threw together a firing squad and killed ten of them. The number was probably symbolic: eleven dead Filipinos for eleven dead Americans.[30]

The Marines would wrest a heroic narrative from the fiasco. As its veterans went on to become senior Marine Corps generals, Waller's blood-soaked disaster was revised into the "March across Samar"—a story of survival used to inspire the island-fighting campaigns of the South Pacific and jungle counterinsurgencies to come. For the rest of their lives, whenever one of the survivors entered a chow hall, all Marines present would rise and say: "Stand, gentlemen! He served on Samar."[31]


In the modern-day Balangiga pageant, Littleton Waller is one of the few Americans identified by name. The actor playing him wears a cowboy hat and carries a silver revolver instead of a Krag. He's also the only Marine who is not forced to bleach his hair.

Though Balangiga had been burned to the ground by the time Waller's Marines arrived on Samar, the pageant's designers used them to represent the entire American retaliation. Smith's "kill and burn" order is read verbatim over the loudspeaker. No music is played. For five agonizing minutes, the only sounds on the field are shooting and screaming. Marines in khaki uniforms murder a girl in a summer dress and bayonet villagers in front of the church. Fire is set to the nipa houses, which burn so ferociously it seems like the modern houses behind them might be consumed as well.

At the climax of the action, a few Marines climb the fake church belfry, carefully remove the gold-foil-wrapped bells, and haul them away.

The importance of those bells cannot be overstated. In the century since they were taken, they have become the embodiment not only of the memory of the 1901 massacres, but the entire trauma of colonization—for Balangiga, Samar, and in many ways the Filipino nation. Representations

---

the mouth, and pour a pail of water in the mouth and nose, and if they don't give up pour in another pail. They swell up like toads."

of them are everywhere in the town. Beyond the bells in the pageant, the monument, and the city seal, there was also a "Run for the Balangiga Bells" ultramarathon and a Balangiga Bells painting competition. Mayor Garza displayed a photo of two of the looted bells in his office.

The bells in turn became symbols of military sacrifice for the Americans. They were brought back to the United States: two displayed in a brick shrine at a military base in Wyoming; a third given to the Ninth Infantry and eventually housed at a U.S. Army museum in South Korea. The Wyoming plaque claims the bells were the signal to start the massacre of Company C. Though the historical evidence for this is thin, by asserting a connection between the bells and murdered soldiers, their theft was transformed into an act of vengeance—a narrative that also helpfully glosses over the Americans' wholesale devastation of Samar and its inhabitants.

Contests over objects imbued with the weight of history are fights over the meaning of the past. In the United States, similar fights have occurred with regularity over statues, or the singing of historically freighted songs. That was why the U.S. military and Filipino nationalists argued so bitterly and for so long over the bells' return. Was the story of Balangiga—of the whole history of U.S. expansionism, perhaps—a story of Americans trying to improve the world, only to be unfairly attacked and forced into justifiable revenge? Or was it a story of oppression, rape, and murder, culminating in the looting of three sacred objects from a church?

I realized this was likely the reason I'd been given a VIP welcome into the mayor's office in the first place. My status as an American journalist, Garza seemed to think, might put me in a position to relay to the U.S. government his plea that the bells be returned. Several of his aides asked if I'd ever seen the bells myself. A receptionist asked me if it was true that they were made of solid gold.

The Balangiganons were not alone in their fascination. Duterte, the Filipino president, also loved talking about the bells. For him they were a convenient distraction from his authoritarianism and abuses, and a handy refrain to needle the United States and signal his shift toward China—a way to affirm his country's position in a post-American world. Three weeks after my visit to Balangiga, during his annual State of the Nation address to the Philippine Congress, Duterte turned toward U.S. Ambassador

Sung Kim and demanded: "Give us back those Balangiga bells. They are ours."[32] He was met with deafening applause.

Then, unexpectedly, it happened. In 2018, Donald Trump's defense secretary, the retired Marine general James Mattis, authorized the bells' return. Shouts of congressional protest followed. Wyoming's Republican delegation blasted the giveaway of "a memorial to American soldiers killed in action." The bipartisan House of Representatives human rights commission called on Trump to withhold the bells as a bargaining chip to force Duterte to end his policy of mass killings under the cover of his "War on Drugs."[33]

But Mattis understood, perhaps in the face of the Philippines' pivot toward China, that a new narrative of U.S.-Filipino relations was needed. In a brief speech at their handover in Wyoming, the retired Marine general emphasized instances of Filipino and U.S. soldiers fighting side by side—in World War II, Korea, Vietnam, and most recently against ISIS in Marawi. Paradoxically, he reassured the audience—particularly the "Manchu command" of the Ninth Infantry—that their predecessors' actions would not be disavowed: "To those who fear that we lose something by returning the bells, please hear me when I say that bells mark time, but courage is timeless."[34]

On December 15, 2018, 117 years after they were stolen, Duterte stood in front of a crowd of dignitaries, Catholic clergy, Mayor Garza, and hundreds of cheering locals. He pulled a rope attached to the largest bell's clapper, and its ringing was heard in Balangiga once more.

Watching the ceremony from half a world away, I wondered: What happens now? Will the bells, now returned, lose their symbolic power? Could the memory of the massacre fade with them? Or will they become central to a new narrative of righted wrongs, inspiring future generations to ask new questions and seek more substantive justice—in both their relationship with their former colonizer and at home?

Before I left the mayor's office during my visit, I had asked Mayor Garza how Balangiganons felt about Americans today. He answered by talking about the Americans in his own family. One of his sisters married a U.S. diplomat and followed him to Saudi Arabia. A brother was a retired U.S. Marine. The reenactment and his demands for the bells' return, he assured me, were just about pride, and teaching young people about the past.

But he must feel conflicted, I said—going outside his office every day, seeing so many reminders of a brutal war.

"No," he answered. "It doesn't affect because it's already finished. We must embrace the reality now. Forget the past."

"But you said it was important to remember the past."

"Yeah," the mayor responded. "For the history."

"But this is what I'm confused about. It's like—you have to remember and forget at the same time."

The mayor didn't hesitate. "Yes," he said.

Chaffee's attempt to assuage President Roosevelt and the American public with a campaign of vengeance and terror backfired. News of the atrocities on Samar soon became as big a scandal as the massacre of the Ninth Infantry itself. Stories from elsewhere in the Philippines followed, thanks to soldiers' letters that began slipping past military censors and into newspapers.

Perhaps the most shocking revelation for Americans came from Brig. Gen. J. Franklin Bell, whom Chaffee had appointed to "pacify" the rebellious province of Batangas, on southern Luzon, at the same time he hired Smith. Citing General Order 100, a standing Civil War code that left wide latitude for dealing with guerrillas, Bell ordered civilians rounded up into what he called "zones of protection."

The soldiers, some of whom had been in Cuba, knew exactly what these were: "a *reconcentrado* pen," one soldier called it, using the Spanish general Weyler's original term for concentration camps, "with a deadline outside, beyond which everything living is shot . . . It seems way out of the world without a sight of the sea—in fact, more like some suburb of hell."[35] A Georgia Democrat read the letter into the *Congressional Record*.

Scrambling to undo the public relations damage, Chaffee ordered Waller, Day, and Smith arrested and court-martialed. Their trials in Manila became national spectacles across the mainland United States. (Butler kept tabs on the case from Charleston, South Carolina, where he was posted on regimental guard duty at a lackluster sequel to the Buffalo World's Fair. A week after Waller was arrested, Smedley wrote his father to say that he would apply to head back to the Philippines "if nothing else turns up.")[36]

The layers of abuse ran deep in the military court: Waller's lawyer, Maj. Edwin F. Glenn, the Army judge advocate responsible for counter-intelligence on Samar, was about to face his own court-martial for subjecting Filipinos to the "water cure." In his testimony, Day claimed he was just following orders. Waller passed the buck to Smith, revealing the dramatic "kill and burn" order on the stand. Of the three being tried for abuses on Samar, only Smith would be convicted: his sole punishment to face an oral rebuke by the court, and to take his long-overdue retirement.

Waller had no regrets. "I have lived up to the motto of my corps: 'Semper Fidelis: Semper Paratus.' I have carried my colors where no white foot has trod," he wrote Pete Wynne's father. To a reporter, Waller crowed: "I left Samar a howling wilderness. They tried to make it that for us, but we made it a howling wilderness for them."[37]

Roosevelt thumbed his nose at the critics, too. He lumped antiwar voices like Mark Twain with Jim Crow architects like Senator "Pitch-fork Ben" Tillman, whom he could dismiss more easily as a hypocrite for condemning torture and concentration camps in the Philippines while supporting lynching at home.

"Keep in mind that these cruelties in the Philippines have been wholly exceptional, and have been shamelessly exaggerated," the president told a crowd at Arlington National Cemetery on Memorial Day 1902.[38] This would become a familiar motif among apologists of U.S. empire: the insistence—all evidence to the contrary—that abuses are rare, sponta-neous, and limited; that they are not "who we are."

The day after Smith's conviction, Roosevelt declared combat operations in the northern Philippines over. Aguinaldo's war had failed. The Filipino founding father had sacrificed too many allies and waited too long to start his guerrilla campaign. U.S. soldiers under Brig. Gen. Frederick Funston—with the help of members of a rival ethnic group to the Tagalogs on Luzon, the Macabebes—had arrested Aguinaldo on March 23, 1901. Lukban was captured by the Army and local scouts in the mountains of Samar on February 18, 1902.

The worst of the fighting in the Philippines was still ahead, and would continue for more than a decade, as the United States "pacified" its first

Muslim insurgency in the southern provinces of Mindanao and the Sulu Archipelago. But most Americans just wanted to be reassured that they could stop paying attention to the war. Annexing their first major overseas colony had cost, by that point, forty-two hundred American lives and $600 million (over $18 billion today). It had resulted in the deaths of some twenty thousand Filipino combatants and as many as three quarters of a million Filipino civilians.[39] It was a staggering price for a group of islands few Americans had heard of before the war began. Even the expansionists started to wonder if there might be easier ways to build an empire.

# SIX

On a sweltering day in December 1902, Smedley Butler was standing waist-deep in a watery ditch. He dunked his shovel into the mud. Mosquitoes darted across the rust-colored ripples. Their bites itched like poison. He couldn't decide what he hated more: this marshy hell, the solid rock his unit had to chip through the day before, or the admiral whose idea it had been to build this stupid canal in the first place.

The ditch Butler was wading through was located on the Caribbean island of Culebra, part of the new U.S. colony of Puerto Rico. Butler was twenty-one years old now, a fully confirmed captain after his bravery in China two years earlier. That meant he was in charge of a full company of Marines: a company that had been ordered to dig a three-hundred-yard canal across a tiny isthmus on the sunny cay.

Butler was convinced the task was make-work—a punishment. A few days before, his Marines had beaten a Navy company in a race to install guns on a Culebra hill. They'd celebrated by firing a shell over the flagship USS *Mayflower,* where Admiral George Dewey himself was in command. A few hours later, the Hero of Manila Bay had tasked Butler's company with cutting a waterway through the little isthmus, so the admirals could cruise to their battleships in the island's inner harbor without having to go all the way around the peninsula.

"It is a damned outrage to make the Marines do all the work," Butler griped in a letter to his mother, "but we showed them what we could do."[1] In three and a half days, his Marines had dug halfway through the isthmus—good enough, the admirals decided, to hand the rest of the work to some conscripted Puerto Ricans, under Butler's supervision.

Deep in the muck, Butler couldn't see the larger purpose of the military exercises. Teddy Roosevelt's administration was engaged in a diplomatic fight to secure land to build a far more sophisticated canal across a

much bigger isthmus: the mainland of Central America. The exercises off
Puerto Rico were, in part, to make sure the Marines and sailors were fit
and ready in case muscle was needed on the mainland to see the administration's aims through.

All the territories the United States conquered between 1898 and 1902
had one thing in common: they were islands. In many ways that insular empire had been conceived by one man: McKinley and Roosevelt's
naval adviser, Alfred Thayer Mahan.

Mahan was literally an offspring of academia and the military. He
was born on the grounds of the U.S. Military Academy at West Point—
his father an engineering instructor whose students included Ulysses S.
Grant, William Tecumseh Sherman, and Thomas "Stonewall" Jackson;
his mother the daughter of the headmistress of a nearby girls' school. Defying his parents' wishes, young Alfred enrolled at the Naval Academy.
He quickly proved one of the worst sailors in Navy history—crashing or
running aground nearly every ship he commanded.[2]

Fortunately for his crews, Mahan took up writing instead, and became the most influential military theorist in the world. His big idea:
sea power, not huge land armies, was the key to empire. That simple
concept, drawn primarily from his reading of the history of Britain in
the Napoleonic Wars, won Mahan powerful fans in industry and politics. It also made his works required reading in every rising power with a
coastline, from the Kaiser's Germany to Meiji Japan. It was the seagoing
complement to Frederick Jackson Turner's "free land": a rationale for
conquering islands all over the world in the name of free movement and
free trade.

Mahan prophesized that the United States would become a worldwide commercial and military power, its merchant fleets dominating the
"great highway" of the seas, protected by what with work and money
could become the world's greatest navy. Because of the limited range
of the era's steamships, such a system required a network of bases and
coaling stations. It was Mahan who thus pushed McKinley to annex
Hawai'i in 1898; Mahan whose naval board had called for the colonization of Guam and American Samoa, the fortification of Puerto Rico, the

purchase of the Virgin Islands from Denmark, and the construction of a full-blown naval station at Guantánamo Bay.[3]

One final link was needed to close the vast chain of commercial and military control. At the time, to get from New York to San Francisco—or from Guantánamo Bay to China—a ship had to sail thousands of miles around the tip of South America. Mahan's solution was to cut the route in half by building a canal across the isthmus of Central America.

Like many of his ideas, this one wasn't new: Europeans had dreamed of punching a hole through Central America since the conquistador Vasco Núñez de Balboa first spotted the Pacific from a Panamanian hilltop in 1513. The Spanish had considered all the thinnest spots to cross. There's a pinch in southern Mexico, 120 miles wide, known as the Isthmus of Tehuantepec. Nicaragua is 140 miles wide, with a large lake and navigable river taking up much of the expanse. The narrowest point of all—an isthmus of an isthmus—was Panama, where a mere 30 miles separated the Atlantic from the Pacific.

Americans had first started fantasizing about routes through Central America during the California gold rush of 1848 to 1855. Seeing an opportunity, Nicaragua's government granted rights to the railroad magnate Cornelius Vanderbilt to patch together a lucrative ferry system of riverboats and stagecoaches. It was so profitable that a "filibustering" mercenary from Tennessee named William Walker tried to take over all of Nicaragua, only to be driven out by a force Vanderbilt had sponsored from Costa Rica.

At the same time, the New York shipping firm of Howland & Aspinwall got permission from the Colombian government, which governed Panama, to build a railway across the narrow isthmus. The Panama Railroad opened in 1855, quickly becoming the most valuable holding on the New York Stock Exchange.[4]

Mahan and those who would become his most committed fans watched closely as France moved closer to the final step of digging a canal across Panama in the 1880s. The French investors tapped the famed architect of Egypt's Suez Canal, Ferdinand de Lesseps, to oversee the project. His attempt ended a decade later with twenty thousand workers dead, eight hundred thousand investors ruined, and the oceans no closer together than they had been for three million years.[5]

Teddy Roosevelt, naturally, was an early and avid Mahan fan. A year before he went to war in Cuba, he wrote Mahan a letter affirming his desire to build an isthmian canal "at once."[6] De Lesseps's disaster merely convinced him the U.S. should dig through Nicaragua instead. But there was one last set of players waiting to show their cards.

The surviving French investors of de Lesseps's fiasco had hired the Wall Street law firm of Sullivan & Cromwell to dispose of their remaining assets—mostly excavation machines left rusting in the Panamanian jungle. But Sullivan & Cromwell's founding partner, William Nelson Cromwell—an ambitious Brooklynite with flashy white hair, bright blue eyes, and a silver tongue—saw no reason to settle for scrap fees. In conjunction with the investors' representative, the cagey ex-mercenary Philippe Bunau-Varilla, Cromwell embarked on a campaign to lobby the McKinley and then the Roosevelt administrations to abandon the Nicaragua route, and held up de Lesseps's half-dug ditch as a shovel-ready alternative.

Cromwell's ace in the hole was Senator Mark Hanna of Ohio, a multimillionaire industrialist and the chairman of the Republican National Committee. Cromwell had spent years cultivating Hanna as an "intimate friend," often through large donations to the RNC.[7]

In mid-1902, Cromwell and Bunau-Varilla helped Hanna write a rousing floor speech extolling the advantages of the route through the Colombian isthmus. Sympathetic engineers bent Roosevelt's ear about Panama's shorter width, superior harbors, and the advantages of the existing American railroad. In an inspired example of early guerrilla marketing, they also sent every senator a Nicaraguan postage stamp showing one of that country's many active volcanoes. At the eleventh hour, Bunau-Varilla agreed to slash the investors' asking price for the Panamanian route from over $100 million to $40 million.[8] Even at a discount, the steep price tag attested to the incredible importance of this fifty-mile-long strip of land: it was double what McKinley had paid Spain four years earlier for the entire Philippine archipelago.

The U.S. government agreed. On June 28, 1902, Congress voted to finance a canal across Panama.* Bunau-Varilla's French investors would

---

* In truth, either way, some U.S. business interests would have made out handsomely. The Louisiana senator who championed the Nicaraguan route had his own secret investment at stake. See Espino, *How Wall Street Created a Nation*, Kindle loc. 353.

recoup some of their losses. Sullivan & Cromwell's founding partner would get an $800,000 check for his services.[9] But no one would get paid unless the Colombian government signed off on the deal.

While the negotiations with Colombia dragged on into the spring of 1903, other pieces could be put into place. Mahan, who knew that a future canal would have to be defended from rival powers, had called for the creation of more military bases across the Caribbean and Central America. It was also critical for the Americans to keep the isthmian republics situated along the route to the canal from falling under the influence of rival powers.

Honduras was one such vulnerable point. The country, one of the northernmost in Central America, stuck out like a dorsal fin into the sea lanes leading to the proposed canal. The country was in default to British banks, raising the specter of an invasion from one of Britain's nearby colonies. As Thomas Butler had written in a confidential memo to Smedley, during the Culebra maneuvers a few months earlier: "I believe the time is close at hand when the American people will conclude that it will be cheaper and wiser to assume control over these South American republics."[10]

There were also Americans getting rich in Honduras, thanks to a new hit product on the U.S. market: the banana. Sweet and soft, with an exotic flair, a dozen bananas could be bought for the price of two apples from American greengrocers. That was because importers had discovered that they could buy the yellow marvel so cheaply off poor Honduran farmers that, even with the cost of shipping, they could sell it at bargain prices and still rack up massive profits.[11]

An Italian American family from New Orleans, the Vaccaro brothers, had received generous concessions of prime banana-growing land along Honduras's north coast in exchange for agreeing to build a railroad. The Vaccaros turned to their larger competitor, the United Fruit Company, to help finance the project.[12]

In February 1903, the Honduran general Manuel Bonilla launched a coup against the government. His forces took the port city of La Ceiba, near the Vaccaros' property. Alarmed, the Vaccaros wired the customs collector in New Orleans. Word from him reached United Fruit's general manager in Louisiana, who sent a message to his headquarters in Boston to notify the Navy and the State Department of the need for military protection.[13]

Just over two weeks later, on March 20, 1903, a Marine battalion from Culebra dropped anchor off the Honduran port of Puerto Cortés. "We arrived here this morning at two o'clock, prepared to land and shoot everybody and anything that was anything that was breaking the peace," Smedley Butler wrote his mother from aboard the USS *Panther*. "We leave tomorrow morning for [La] Ceba [*sic*], a small place up the coast where we may find some American interests that need protecting."[14]

The all-white Marines seethed with contempt for the Hondurans, many of whom in the coastal areas were Black. In his letter to Maud, Smedley mocked the size of the rebels' "spicecake" warship. A welcome salute given by the rebels' marine infantry was greeted with roars of laughter from the Americans—which, Butler noted, "did not add to the dignity of the occasion."

For the next few weeks, the Marines waited off the Honduran coast, itching for an opportunity to come ashore and kill. "The rebels here are becoming rather restless," Smedley wrote his mother on March 26. "Our company is to go ashore if anything happens so I am anxiously waiting for a nigger to throw a stone."[15] (Butler, as often happened during his campaigns, does not seem to have saved his mother's response, so we don't know how she replied. Maud may have objected to the coarseness of the racial epithet, though likely not the militaristic sentiment.)

Ultimately little shooting was necessary. The Marines' show of force was enough to forestall a British intervention and convince both sides of the Honduran conflict to leave the American banana companies and their assets alone. Bonilla's troops marched unimpeded to the seat of government, Tegucigalpa, and forced the army to surrender. "The capital has fallen and the revolution is all over but the shouting and there is plenty of that left, it seems," Butler wrote Maud on April 14, no doubt disappointed, as the Marines prepared to leave.[16]

The Roosevelt administration immediately recognized the conservative general as the legitimate president of Honduras.[17] In gratitude, Bonilla extended the duration of the Vaccaros' land concession to seventy-five years, and gave them a century-long lease over the port of La Ceiba. (The brothers would rename their company Standard Fruit, which eventually formed part of the Dole Food Company.) United Fruit, sensing new opportunity, bought up huge Honduran tracts of its own.

A few months after Butler and the Marines left, the short story writer William Sydney Porter, better known as O. Henry, published a novel about a lightly fictionalized version of Honduras. To capture the Central American country's blend of destabilized democracy, an economy dominated by a single export crop, and the ever-present shadow of U.S. military and market control, he used a new term. He called it a "banana republic."[18]

Over the ensuing decades, the Marines would invade Honduras at least six more times to protect the interests of the banana companies and prevent other empires' interference, until a client military could be formed to ensure U.S. profits and the passage to and from the Panama Canal.[19]

Sometimes the fruit companies handled the invasions themselves. In 1910, the Russian American merchant Samuel Zemurray and a semiretired General Bonilla boarded a decommissioned Navy gunboat near New Orleans with a platoon of mercenaries and sailed for Honduras. Once Bonilla was installed for a second nonconsecutive term, he rewarded Zemurray with massive concessions for his new banana company, Cuyamel.[20]

In 1930, Cuyamel merged with United Fruit. Zemurray eventually became the president of the combined firm. (United Fruit rebranded in 1990; it is now known as Chiquita Brands International.)

Thanks to its wealth, size, and connections at the highest levels of the U.S. government, United Fruit would dominate Central America for decades to come. In 1954, the Central Intelligence Agency orchestrated the overthrow of Guatemala's president, Jacobo Árbenz. The Americans accused Árbenz of Communist sympathies, but his real crime was trying to expropriate uncultivated farmlands and redistribute them to the poor. (He offered to compensate United Fruit, but at the grossly deflated rates the company had spent years claiming its land was worth for tax purposes.) The CIA director, Allen Dulles, as well as his brother, Secretary of State John Foster Dulles, had a long-standing association with United Fruit: they had both represented it as attorneys with the firm of Sullivan & Cromwell.[21]

Decades of civil war and U.S. corporate and military interference have made the "Northern Triangle" of Guatemala, Honduras, and El Salvador one of the most dangerous parts of the world to live in. Honduras has become known as a narco-state. Its president, Juan Orlando Hernández, was accused by U.S. federal prosecutors in 2021 of providing paid protection for cocaine traffickers and collaborating with a cocaine laboratory outside Puerto Cortés.[22] (An official Honduran government spokesperson denied the allegations.)

Hundreds of thousands of impoverished people have been forced to flee north, seeking refuge in the country that took generations of their peoples' wealth. Some have tried to find safety by traveling in "caravans" that attract the attention of international media, with hopes that having more eyes on them will lend protection on a dangerous road and engender sympathy at their destination. Conservative politicians and commentators in the United States use the images of the caravans for their own ends, in attempts to stir up nationalist sentiment. With no apparent sense of irony, they routinely refer to the fleeing refugees as "an invasion."[23]


In August 1903, the Colombian Senate rejected Roosevelt's proposed treaty for the creation of a canal zone through its Departamento de Panamá. The Americans had proposed a six-mile-wide concession stretching from the Pacific port of Panama City to the Atlantic port of Colón.

The sticking point was sovereignty. Decades earlier, in exchange for the right to build the Panama Railroad, the firm of Howland & Aspinwall and its protectors in the U.S. government had accepted Colombian law and oversight and allowed the Colombian military full use of the line. The government in Bogotá expected to have the same privileges over any future canal.

Roosevelt scoffed. In a letter to Rudyard Kipling, the imperialist poet who had written "The White Man's Burden," he mocked those who thought a "corrupt pithecoid community" like Colombia was "entitled to just the treatment that I would give to, say, Denmark or Switzerland."[24] Secretary of State John Hay insisted the Americans would set up their own courts and enforce their own regulations throughout the zone and its ports. The Americans also wanted the right to send in their own troops or police whenever they declared an emergency.

When the news arrived that Colombia refused to ratify the treaty, reporters raced to Roosevelt's mansion on Long Island. They found the chairman of the Senate Foreign Relations Committee, Shelby Cullom of Illinois, fresh from lunch with the president. "I do not think we are ready to abandon Panama yet," he told them.

"But . . . how can the canal be built without the treaty?" a reporter asked.

"Well, we might make another treaty," the senator replied cryptically. "Not with Colombia, but with Panama."[25]

Cullom had presumably learned what was happening behind the scenes. William Nelson Cromwell, despite his obvious conflicts of interest as the lawyer for the canal's investors, was personally advising Roosevelt's secretary of state. Months before, Cromwell had sent his craftiest agent, the former journalist and wildcat banker Roger Leslie Farnham, to coordinate with a secessionist clique of Panama City bankers, merchants, and other elites intent on making sure the canal did not pass them by.

When Farnham returned to the States, he had gone to his old employer, Joseph Pulitzer's New York *World,* and planted a story that made Panamanian secession sound inevitable if the Colombian government did not go along with the canal. "This plan is said to be easy of execution, as not more than 100 Colombian soldiers are stationed in the State of Panama," the unbylined article said. Farnham had told the editors to expect action on November 3, Election Day in the United States, when the public would be distracted.[26]

On November 2, 1903, right on schedule, people living near Panama's Manzanillo Bay sighted a warship steaming down the isthmus toward the city of Colón.

Today, Colón, Panama, is a crowded metropolis of nearly three hundred thousand souls, pressed along the Atlantic shore. First built by the Americans as a terminus for the Panama Railroad, it looks and feels like a Caribbean port town: tiered concrete buildings in fading pastels; market stalls filled with fresh green chayotes, red mangoes, and cassava root. Cuban salsa music pulses out of stereo speakers on the street, briefly mingling with a grinding Colombian *cumbia* from a passing car.

It is also one of the poorest cities in a country already riven by extreme inequality. Clean drinking water, electricity, and paying work are in short supply. Colón's poor are predominantly Afro-Panamanians. That community in turn divides itself into two groups: the West Indian children and grandchildren of the Caribbean laborers who came to build the American canal, and the *afrocoloniales,* descendants of the enslaved Africans originally brought by the Spanish conquistadors to haul goods over the older overland route between the oceans. Those two populations do not always see eye to eye.

I met an afrocolonial named Marcia Rodriguez for lunch on a spring day. Around her neck she wore a gold-painted conch shell dangling off a chunky wooden necklace.

"Our people were not interested in the canal," she told me over a bowl of rice and chicken stew. "Maybe they understood it, but they did not know why they had to give up their property to make a canal. I think it felt like the worst injustice—apart from slavery, the second worst injustice that ever happened to them. [The Americans] took away their lands, their houses, everything."

Rodriguez recounted stories about her grandmother, Zoila Jaramillo Requena, who had been a teenager in 1903. Her family lived on a jut of land outside Colón that people used to call Punta de Toro—the point of the bull. Back then the family was not rich, she said, but they were comfortable. They owned their land and some cattle.

"My abuelita came from a time when she could not read nor write. It was forbidden: one, for a woman, and two, because her ancestors had come with the history of slavery, in which you did not have the right to learn to read," she said. "If they caught a Black man writing, they killed him."

Instead of texts, many afrocolonials passed their history down through rituals of song and dance. The most important memorial comes in the annual pre-Lenten carnival, when they hold their "Festival of Devils and Congos." In some variations of the dance, a man dressed as the Devil plans to kidnap—enslave—the women of the community. But the *reina,* or queen of the carnival, has a premonition in a dream that "a man with gold teeth" is coming to take her away. While a chorus of Congos distract the Devil—"el diablo tun tun," the Devil is knocking, they sing—the reina emerges from her palace armed with a large wooden cross and grabs him from behind. They wrestle until they both fall on top of the resounding drums.[27]

Zoila was a reina. Rodriguez is, too.

"What does it mean to be a queen?" I asked.

"The queen is the one who always has the last word," she said. "They passed down a great deal of information to me, because one day I would be a reina. Now it is my turn, and it is my responsibility to keep fighting to keep what little my people left behind."

She told me her grandmother had taught her a song about what happened in 1903.

"Could you sing it?"

"Yes, I can. But I don't have any drums, so you will just have to imagine them."

I promised I would.

She closed her eyes and began:

*Dicen que Garrote un cuarto feliz*
*lo hizo Ferrari cuando llegó ahí.*
*Llorenlele, llorenlela.*
*Ahí viene la flota que nos va a matar*
*Ay, corran, señores*
*Corran de verdad*
*porque a todos los negros los van a matar*

It means:

*They say that Garrote is a happy quarter*
*Ferrari made it so when he got there*
*Cry, oh cry, oh cry*
*Here come the warships to kill us*
*Ay, run, people*
*Run like you mean it*
*Because all the Black people they are going to kill*

Marcia did not know who Ferrari was. Perhaps he was someone who was relieved to have escaped all the way to Garrote, a village about forty

miles up the coast from Colón. "All I know is that there were white men
with guns, and they made the people run in terror, thinking, 'Okay. Supposedly we were freed [from slavery], and now what is happening?'"

She sang me the final lines:

> *"Auxilio y auxilio," gritaba Simeón.*
> *"Son americanos. Llegaron a Colón."*

> *"Help us! Help us!" cried Simeón.*
> *"They're Americans. They're coming to Colón."*

On the evening of November 2, 1903, the USS *Nashville* reached Colón
just ahead of the Colombian warship *Cartagena*. Buoyed by the American show of force, the Panama City conspirators swung into action on
the other side of the isthmus, bribing the isolated Colombian regiment
in the provincial capital and convincing them to defect. The conspirators
raised the flag of the new Republic of Panama—which was promptly sent
to William Nelson Cromwell to present as a gift to President Roosevelt.
A Colombian gunboat fired shells uselessly into the city, killing a Chinese
immigrant shopkeeper in his home. He would be the only direct casualty of the revolution. The new republic was born on November 3, just as
Cromwell's bagman, Roger Farnham, had predicted.[28]

But the new republic was not yet assured. Four hundred U.S. Marines were rushed to Colón to ensure the rest of the Colombian army did
not interfere with the secession—arriving, appropriately, aboard a cruiser
named the USS *Dixie.* They landed in the rain and dark on the night of
November 5, under the command of Maj. John A. Lejeune, the round-
faced, thirty-five-year-old son of a Confederate captain from Pointe
Coupee Parish, Louisiana. The U.S. government formally recognized
Panama the next afternoon. It took longer than that for most on the isthmus to learn they were living in a new country.

The new nominally independent Panamanian government named
Philippe Bunau-Varilla, the French investors' representative, its ambas-
sador to Washington. He immediately crafted a new treaty granting the
United States "all the rights, power and authority" over the planned Canal
Zone, as if it were the "sovereign of the territory."[29]

J. P. Morgan was made the new republic's chief financial representative, charged with handling the $40 million payment from the U.S. government to the French investors and a $10 million payment nominally meant for the new government in Panama City. After setting aside some money for immediate expenses, Panama "was left with $6 million, which Morgan invested, very profitably, in New York City mortgages."[30]

As it slowly dawned on Americans what had happened, many were floored. A *New York Times* editorial declared the isthmus "Stolen Property." When Mississippi senator Hernando Money learned the details of Bunau-Varilla's treaty, he exclaimed, more accurately than he may have realized: "It sounds very much as though we wrote it ourselves!"[31]

Even the Panamanian businessmen who had orchestrated the break with Colombia were furious when they learned the extent of what Bunau-Varilla had given away. Popular tradition in Panama has it that one of the conspirators spat in the Frenchman's face.

Once again, Roosevelt and his fellow expansionists justified their actions by citing destiny, racial superiority, and their supposedly innate capacity for "good administration." Elihu Root, the secretary of war, found precedent in China: just as the Empress Dowager's court had shown an "incapacity to protect the rights of others" during the Boxer Uprising, Colombian leaders had proven they "could not maintain order upon the Isthmus." Roosevelt lied to Congress in his next State of the Union address, claiming that "the people of Panama," supposedly enraged over Colombia's rejection of the treaty, "rose literally as one man." (Senator Edward Carmack of Tennessee cracked: "That man was Roosevelt.")[32]

The new U.S. Canal Zone was ten miles wide. It split the new country in two and included tens of thousands of people living on farms and in towns from Colón to Panama City—including the family of Marcia Rodriguez's grandmother, Zoila Jaramillo. In the weeks following secession, a cavalcade of U.S. warships arrived on the isthmus to ensure it stayed taken.

On December 10, 1903, Smedley Butler's battalion left Puerto Rico aboard the USS *Prairie*. After a brief stop at Guantánamo Bay—to participate in the official handover ceremony of the base to U.S. control—they arrived in Colón. Rumors were rampant about what awaited them in the brand-new republic. Some said Colombia might try to reinvade.

Others said the Germans were trying to establish a beachhead near the future canal. "The young hopefuls among the Lieutenants are clawing the air and clamoring for war, bloody war, ten thousand Columbians [*sic*] killed before breakfast and all that sort of rot, but thy gentle little son is not thirsting for any more gore, especially his own," Butler wrote his mother, perhaps sarcastically.[33]

Butler was assigned to the regiment of his mentor, Littleton Waller—fully rehabilitated after his court-martial, now a lieutenant colonel. Waller had called for his most trusted subordinates: survivors of his murderous March across Samar—including Hiram Bearss and Alexander S. Williams—and his best men from the China campaign—Butler, George Reid, and the one-armed Harry Leonard as his adjutant. Pete Wynne came, too, still drinking heavily and unable to shake off the tubercular cough he'd picked up on the road to Beijing.

Waller's regiment was posted halfway down the Canal Zone, at a location the old French engineers had called Bas Obispo. This was perhaps the most critical point in the project: the continental divide whose rocky layers had thwarted the French engineer de Lesseps's naïve plan for a sea-level canal. American engineers decided to reduce the amount of digging required by installing a system of locks, which could raise ships on one side and lower them on the other, like a series of aquatic elevators. But major excavation would still be needed. The spot was known, Butler was tickled to learn, as Culebra—just like the barrier island in Puerto Rico where he and the Marines had to dig their own little canal a year earlier.

The Marines named their outpost Camp Elliott, after George Elliott, the pipe-smoking Alabaman from the Battle of Cuzco Well who was now the Marine Corps commandant. For the next few months, they set up living quarters, customs houses, and post offices. They went on reconnaissance missions through the rocky hills and made topographical maps for the engineers, standing by as the American administrators decided what to do with the roughly forty thousand Panamanians who now found themselves the residents of a colonized zone.[34]

Once, the Marines went down to Panama City and challenged the locals to a baseball game. Butler played catcher. Hiram Bearss, a former college athlete in Indiana, took the mound. Pete Wynne, perhaps owing to his chronic illnesses, was the umpire. "We won 19 to 4," Butler boasted in a letter home. "We had our eyes on the ball and knocked it all over the Isthmus."[35]

As it became clear that Colombia was not going to start a war to get back its lost territory, the Marines drew down to a skeleton force. Smedley watched Leonard, Reid, and Pete Wynne all leave. Waller gave Butler every job imaginable—shifts as quartermaster, commissary and ordnance officer, and utility man.[36] Butler's first stint in Panama ended on March 7, 1904.

Two months later, on May 4, a whistle blast sounded outside Bas Obispo. The first group of West Indian contractors in derby hats and denim overalls stepped forward with their machetes and began cutting through the jungle.[37]

# SEVEN

In the fall of 1904, Butler was a nervous wreck. After leaving Panama, he had reported home to the Philadelphia Navy Yard, where he was posted as captain of the Marine guard on the permanently docked USS *Lancaster*. One night, a high school football buddy invited him for dinner at his family's opulent home, where he met his friend's older sister, Ethel Conway Peters.

Ethel was twenty-four—about a year older than Smedley. Maud and Thomas would find her family's WASP credentials impeccable: one of her great-great-grandfathers was a delegate to the Continental Congress. Her paternal grandfather was a railroad baron who helped found Atlanta.[1]

More important for Smedley, Ethel had an easy laugh, an upturned nose, and a penchant for adventure. A few years earlier, she had saved a newspaper clipping about the exciting lives of wealthy Philadelphia women who followed their husbands to exotic postings around America's growing empire.[2] The Marine captain intrigued her, perhaps because he seemed to represent an escape from the confines of her upper-class upbringing to a daring life abroad.

Smedley launched a lightning courtship. In late September, he dashed off a note on Marine stationery urging Ethel to join him in a "flank movement"—meeting him secretly during a layover at the Pennsylvania Railroad's Broad Street Station while the rest of her family traveled on. "I don't like this sort of thing but if we are to avoid suspicion heroic measures must be adopted," he wrote. "I am determined to see you [even] if my head is lost in doing it."

He pleaded for Ethel to let him know whether she was serious about him "in a hurry." "There is a Regiment going to the Philippines next month," he warned. If she did not plan to return his affections, he would volunteer to "go back to the rough soldiering, with nothing to look forward to."[3]

Butler's mood calmed when Ethel kept the date at the train station, and those that followed. They adopted secret love codes in letters to one another: private abbreviations accompanied by the numbers "1 2 3 4." He started calling her "Bunny," because she could wiggle the end of her nose. She eventually started using the pet name herself.[4]

They wed on the last day of June 1905, in a Jersey Shore ceremony of white lace and Marine brass. Smedley's middle brother, Sam Butler, was his best man. Ethel's sisters Edith and Hope were maids of honor. Littleton Waller was an usher.[5]

The marriage of a congressman's soldier son and a daughter of one of America's most elite families drew a storm of national press coverage. Headlines like IDEAL AMERICAN SOLDIER SURRENDERS TO CUPID cemented the incipient fame Butler had gained in war. One article described President Roosevelt as "one of Captain Butler's most ardent admirers."[6]

Having Bunny on his arm gave him confidence about his future career moves as well, especially when she made it clear she was eager to head abroad. As soon as the engagement was secured, Butler put in for a transfer to the Philippines, for both of them. He and his new bride would be assigned to the new U.S. naval outpost on the west side of Luzon at Subic Bay. A few days after the wedding, the newlyweds boarded a steamer for the fourteen-thousand-mile journey to their first home. With the Panama Canal still under construction, they crossed the Atlantic and went through the Suez Canal in Egypt. As they stopped for honeymoon calls along the way in Italy, Yemen, India, and Singapore, Ethel was surely dreaming of her new life as half of a young power couple in a tropical colony.[7]

Then they got to Subic. Onshore was where she would be living: dilapidated old Spanish barracks surrounded by a jumble of grass huts, mosquitoes, and mud. The Mount Pinatubo volcano loomed in the distance. The adjacent village of Olongapo was little better, as far as Ethel was concerned. Filipinos had set up bars, *tiendas,* and dance halls to cater to the servicemen. The Marines put on their favorite forms of entertainment, including boxing matches and blackface minstrel shows. A Polish-born Marine named John J. Gordon set up a tavern in a bamboo pavilion. The

Marines nicknamed it "Gordon's Chicken Farm," for the eager Filipinas said to hang around the dirt dance floor.[8]

Though three years had passed since Roosevelt declared an end to combat operations in the Philippines, the archipelago was not yet fully under U.S. control. U.S. forces were busy tangling with fierce Muslim resistance in the south. But those areas were, literally, the Army's province. The Marines were tasked with implementing Alfred Thayer Mahan's vision and establishing American sea power on Luzon.

Manila Bay, where Smedley had been posted five years earlier, was too shallow for the Navy's new class of battleships. So Mahan's advisory board had looked west, across the mountainous Bataan Peninsula to neighboring Subic Bay. Subic was smaller but deeper, and also emptied directly into the South China Sea. There was a wide, flat shore to build on. It was the Pacific's answer to Guantánamo.[9]

Every month, Smedley disappeared to lead training exercises in the Bataan hills, leaving Ethel alone to manage the house and make small talk with Mary Fay Pendleton, the half-deaf wife of the commanding officer. Smedley would return ten days later, ragged, sunburned, and distant. Then he'd head to Olongapo.

After a few months, Ethel got pregnant. Bunny now spent her time "making little dresses and laughing at the indications of a prize fight taking place within," Smedley wrote his father. In November 1906, with the aid of the post surgeon, she gave birth to a healthy girl.[10] They named her Ethel. Butler nicknamed the baby "Snooks."* He threw a party for the men where they all got roaring drunk.

Despite his joy at becoming a father, Butler's behavior around this time started becoming more erratic. He wrote Maud and Thomas in a careless scrawl in late December 1906 that he couldn't "find the time to bath [*sic*] or shave on many days let alone write long letters."[11] Once, on a training march through Bataan, he tied a recalcitrant Marine to a tree by his wrists. (Butler later claimed the man had tried to attack a corporal with a shovel.)[12]

At one point, he even submitted a furtive request to resign his com-

---

* It started as a joke—"Snooks" was the nickname of the tallest man in the regiment, and the baby was immediately "adopted" as the smallest. But the nickname stuck.

mission and go home.[13] Ethel would have none of it. She had tried to be sanguine about life at the rugged base. She dismissed a bout with disease as a "slight tropical complaint."[14] She trudged through monsoon floods to attend her only real form of entertainment—her regular bridge games. She put up with Smedley's moods, and had even accepted the lack of a suitable Episcopal priest to baptize her baby. What she couldn't accept was the possibility that her husband might throw away his career—and with it her hopes for an exciting, worldly life—after just a few months together.

"I have opposed it from the beginning and would never give my consent to it, so consequently it had just sort of evaporated," Ethel told her grandmother and father. "It was simply a wild idea, principally due to his extreme nervous condition."[15]

At the time, the political situation around the Pacific was becoming equally unsettled. The former allies in the Boxer Rebellion had begun turning on one another. Japan had struck first, destroying much of Russia's Pacific fleet to take control of Korea and a key Manchurian port in 1905. The United States helped settle that conflict by hosting peace talks, an effort that netted Roosevelt one of the first Nobel Peace Prizes.

But Roosevelt had not intervened primarily in the interest of peace. Mahan had warned for years that Japan might go to war with the United States over its island colonies in the Pacific.[16] (Officials in Tokyo knew the importance of sea power and island bases to their imperial designs—they were reading Mahan, too.) By helping negotiate the treaty that ended the Russo-Japanese War, Roosevelt was helping to ensure that America's emerging rival did not emerge from its victory too strong.

In late 1906, the United States and Japan began tumbling toward war. The immediate crisis was triggered by, of all things, a school board vote in San Francisco. The city was the hub of transpacific immigration in the United States; for decades, its white majority had forced the children of Chinese and Korean immigrants into their own segregated school. On October 11, 1906, the board of education declared that students of Japanese descent had to attend the "Oriental Public School" as well.[17] As empowered white mobs attacked Japanese businesses and stoned Asian immigrants in

California, the Imperial Japanese government accused the United States of violating a treaty protecting immigration and trade.[18] That raised the specter of retaliatory attacks on U.S. merchant fleets in the Pacific, to which the Roosevelt administration would feel compelled to respond.

U.S. planners determined that if war broke out with Japan, American forces would concentrate for the counterattack at Subic Bay.[19] That required fortifications to protect the entrance to the harbor. In the spring of 1907, Butler was ordered to take fifty Marines to the edge of the stubby peninsula at the mouth of the bay, at a spot the Americans called Macmany Point, and install a defensive gun battery.

The mission was arduous from the start: some of the guns were twenty-six feet long, weighed nine and a half tons, and had to be moved uphill through dense jungle vegetation.[20] But it was only after Butler's team reached Macmany Point that they understood exactly how difficult their task was going to be. First, they realized an advance team had installed the wrong gun mounts. Then the rain started. The work dragged on for days, then weeks. Uniforms mildewed, and flies mauled their faces. Meager rations of hardtack, canned beef, and coffee ran out.

As the Marines' hunger and exhaustion reached their breaking point, they tried to wave down a Navy supply tug that made regular runs to a tiny island in the middle of the bay. It never responded. "It didn't even know we were alive," Butler would later recall.[21]

Realizing his men had for all intents and purposes been abandoned, Butler decided: to hell with his orders. He commandeered a local fisherman's outrigger, known as a *banca*. With two enlisted men—a Corporal Lytle and a Private Thompson—he embarked on a five-mile voyage across Subic Bay, to grab the needed provisions himself.[22]

As the little boat cruised out into the bay, the skies darkened. Suddenly a fierce thunderstorm erupted. The banca rocked violently in the wind and rain, then began taking on water. Their paddles floated away. The little flour-sack sail was blown into oblivion. Because Butler had not informed anyone at base of his journey, he knew there would be no rescue; the tiny boat would be essentially invisible from shore. The three Marines paddled the banca with their hands through the deadly waves, trying desperately to reach the flickering lighthouse beacon ahead.

Five hours later, Butler appeared at the naval yard, half-drowned and covered in mangrove mud. The yard commandant, apparently drunk, found this very funny, and told Butler to take whatever he needed in a tugboat. But as soon as they left, they got caught in another squall. The trio somehow wrestled the tug across the bay to Macmany Point, only to find the storm had washed away their makeshift dock. So they started tearing off pieces of the hull and lashing them as ballast to the supplies. The other Marines darted into the waves to bring them ashore.

Butler's commanders were not as amused as the yard commandant had been. In their eyes, he had bucked discipline, risked the lives of two enlisted men, and damaged a perfectly good Navy tug. Moreover, he showed no remorse, blaming the command for leaving him and his men to starve. In light of his erratic behavior, and his evident stress, he was ordered to submit to a physical and psychiatric evaluation.

On June 19, 1907, Butler was transferred for observation to the Cavite naval hospital. "Patient seems constantly depressed, complains of constant dull pain in epigastrium and sensation of a ball rising in throat at times, emotional and according to his statements 'has crying spells without any apparent reason,'" the base surgeon recorded. "Suffers from insomnia. Bowels slightly irregular."[23]

The doctors diagnosed Butler's condition as "Dyspepsia nervosa . . . incident to prolonged service in the tropics." After he was released from the hospital, Smedley, Bunny, and Snooks were put on a ship back to America.

Butler's banishment from Subic would become a signal event in his life. The question is what, exactly, it signaled. Butler biographer Hans Schmidt saw the defiant, risky crossing as an example of the "style and flair" that would win Smedley a shelf of medals in the years to come. To military critics of his later antiwar and anti-imperialist activism, it may have seemed like early evidence of a man losing his mind.

To try to figure out what was going on inside his head, I decided to cross Subic Bay myself. I headed there one morning with Rica, the fixer. A few hours up the highway from Manila, we arrived at a checkpoint marked "Subic Bay Freeport Zone." A digital sign flashed in deference to President Duterte's vicious "war": "This is a drug free workplace. Let's keep it that way."

Subic had continued to be the major U.S. naval outpost in the Asian Pacific for nearly a century. It was particularly important during the Cold War, when it served as a threat to the Soviet Union and China and a staging post for troops heading to and from Vietnam. Then, in 1991, a few months before the Soviet Union collapsed, Mount Pinatubo erupted catastrophically, killing hundreds of people and leaving the base and bay drenched in toxic sludge. When negotiations with the Philippine government over paying for repairs and the increased cost of upkeep broke down, George H. W. Bush's administration decided to abandon the bay.[24]

A powerful Filipino senator, Richard J. Gordon—the son of a former mayor, and grandson of the Marine founder of the seedy "Chicken Farm" in Olongapo—got permission to turn the former base into a free trade and tourism zone. It still had a base-town feel—rectilinear streets, traffic signs that drivers actually obey, checkpoints on the way in and out to maintain an atmosphere of security. (That illusion was maintained at the pleasure of Duterte's government: a forty-three-year-old Filipino man had been shot in the stomach and left to die in front of a former Navy Air Station chapel in the zone a few months before, in a graphic reminder of the reach of the War on Drugs.)[25]

"Filipinos were always wondering what was in here when Americans held the base," Rica told me as we drove in. She'd seen the inside for the first time when she'd come to cover Pinatubo's eruption. She could still picture the buildings and the bay covered in ash.

Wanting to get as close to Butler's experience as possible (without the near drowning, I hoped), I asked Rica where we might be able to hire a proper banca. For that, she said, we'd need to pass through the base and into Olongapo. We passed bars with names like "Cheap Charlie's," "Coco Lips," and "The Wet Spot," whose sign invited visitors to *"come and make it happen."* I scrolled through the Olongapo Facebook page as we drove down the strip. It was full of messages from Filipinos looking for absent servicemen fathers.

Rica told me we were looking for "Johan's dive bar." I kept an eye out for a place even dodgier than the rest. It wasn't until we pulled up that I realized that was the bar's actual name: Johan's Beach & Dive Resort. Iggy Pop's "Lust for Life" jammed on the speakers. A poster of two Filipinas in bikinis waving from a Jet Ski advertised the bar's sports-tourism offerings, including diving, banana boat rides, and something called "jungle survival." (Butler, I thought, got to do that one for free.) On the tawny beach, shirtless white retirees shared pizza with their decades-younger Filipina wives and girlfriends.

The banca Rica found belonged to a local fisherman, a skinny Olongapeño named John. He called himself and his boat "Popoy." Sitting cross-legged on the stern, he steered us beneath the colossal black and orange cargo ships that now dominate the bay. The detritus of the global economy floated around us: Downy fabric softener packages and Nestlé candy wrappers bobbed in the foam. Popoy's fellow fishermen used Gatorade bottles as markers for their traps. The air near the docks was heavy with diesel.

As we hugged the coast, Popoy told us about the hole the Americans' departure from the bay had left in Olongapo. His father had been a ship welder employed by the Navy who worked a night shift for double pay. Popoy still remembered the night rate: 560 pesos, worth about $43 today. But the money dried up after the base closed. Opportunities for locals in the "Freeport Zone" were scarce. The women of Olongapo turned to what they called the *"reh-tay-rees"*—the shirtless American, Australian, and English men on the beach—for financial support, Popoy told us with a mix of jealousy and resentment.

After an hour and a half, Popoy steered us onto a little pebble beach on a sparkling emerald cove. This was Macmany, or close to it.

Inside a lean-to onshore, in the shade of a talisay tree, a young Tagalog woman named Perlyn was teaching colors to her three-year-old daughter, Jeyln. They spoke in a language shaded by the empires that had conquered and passed through the bay: Malay, Khmer, Chinese, Spanish, and American.

"Verde," Perlyn said, handing her daughter a green crayon.

The little girl ignored it and picked up another.

"Or-ange," Perlyn said, slowly. She picked up a blue crayon, colored in a circle on the page, and pointed to it. "Blue*berry*."

Jeyln scrunched her nose. "Blue mangga?" (It means mango in Tagalog.)

Perlyn's father-in-law, Sixto, sat across a big wooden table. The nutmeg skin on his bald head and chest testified to decades in the sun. "Kano?" Sixto asked Rica, gesturing to me and using the shorthand for *Americano.* "He says they used to love the Americans," Rica translated. "Even during 'target practice.'"

"Target practice" was the regular bombing runs the Army, Navy, and Marines had staged on beaches all around the bay from the 1950s through the 1980s. Sixto told us that he and his friends would rush into the water right after to dive for scrap metal. They sold it to junk dealers for a few centavos a kilo.

Once, in the 1980s, Sixto's friend picked up something and dropped it in their banca. It exploded, killing the friend instantly and maiming the others. Sixto pointed to a series of jagged scars on his left side. "Grenade. From a M203. I know because it was shaped like an egg." He took a Marlboro out of a clear plastic jar and lit it, blowing smoke out his nose.

"You didn't get angry at the Americans after that?" I asked.

He shrugged. "After that I just went diving again."

"He didn't feel anything," his wife, Josephine, interjected. "He just started drinking more."

Another husband with another tangle of physical and mental scars courtesy of U.S. Naval Base Subic Bay, I thought. Another wife left to pick up the pieces.

With Rica translating, I told Sixto and Josephine the story of Butler's voyage across the bay. I asked if the details sounded plausible. The couple was mostly just surprised the Marines had gone hungry in the first place. Mangoes, cashews, soursop, and different kinds of bananas all flourished on the stubby peninsula, and there were lots of fish in the sea.

The storms, though, that sounded right. Sixto guessed Butler had gotten caught in the *habagat,* the season when the monsoon blows from the southwest and clouds swell with rain.

"Can you make it to the other side in a banca without a motor?" I asked.

"Of course," Josephine replied, patiently. "Not everyone can afford a motor."

I thanked the family for their hospitality, and Popoy and I pushed the outrigger into the water. Gray clouds stirred over distant Bataan as we reached the open bay. I climbed up on the prow. A wave swelled to the level of my eyes. Popoy sailed expertly over it.

I tried to imagine if Butler had sat like this, facing the wind, maybe trying to spot Bunny and the baby onshore. I tried to picture what it must have been like for him there, on the waves, after eight years of near-constant deployment, of killing and nearly being killed, risking it all for a hungry company in the face of a command that was proving indifferent to their lives. He was facing deep instability at that moment: daunting personal transformations as a husband and a father, an urgent threat of war against the rising power across the Pacific. Was he desperate? Careless? Suicidal? Was this his first protest—his first act of defiance against the institution that controlled his life? Or perhaps he had just been happy to breathe a moment's peace, on his own little boat in the blue sea, before the storms came raging back in.

Perhaps I should go back and try it again without the motor, or maybe wait for a thunderstorm, I thought. But no boat could transport me into Butler's mind. No letters of his from that year made it into the archives, if he wrote any. The Navy doctors' diagnosis—a "nervous breakdown," as Butler later summed it up—was written to serve the goals of a bureaucracy in which individuality is pathologized and trauma's clarifying nature ignored. All I could see were the traces of those traumas around the bay: the bodily scars and abandoned children, the English words taught by a Filipina mother to her daughter, the town built into dependence and now made to struggle on its own.

But merely trying to cross Subic Bay was not, in itself, an act of insanity. We made it to the other side just fine.

In the end, Butler's mission at Macmany Point was for nothing. The war scare of 1906 and 1907 died down. Roosevelt and the Japanese emperor entered into a "gentleman's agreement" in which Tokyo agreed to informally limit immigration to the United States, while Washington pledged to respect the rights of Japanese immigrants already living there.

Moreover, as Butler's chaotic attempt to install the guns had shown,

Subic could not be fortified quickly, and the Marines were not yet up to the job. Army officials, jealous of the increasing importance and funding of the Marines, used the opportunity to argue that U.S. Naval Base Subic Bay had proven too vulnerable and too far from the mainland to be used as a launchpad in a war against Japan.[26]

Looking back, it seems like that might have been a moment for officials on both sides of the Pacific to pull back from the brink. Butler would argue, decades later, that the Philippines should be given "their independence at once." "Every military and naval man in Washington who knows the situation in the Far East will tell you that they can't be defended against a real attack," he would tell a reporter. "Sooner or later, if we hold onto them, America will be jerked into a damn war before we know what it's all about."[27]

But bureaucracies are where real madness always lies. Unwilling to draw down, Roosevelt and his advisers simply decided to shift their future war plans from the Philippines to the closer-in territory of Hawai'i, and start the long, slow buildup of forces at Pearl Harbor instead.[28]

# EIGHT

## NICARAGUA

The decision to build the transoceanic canal in Panama set off a chain reaction four hundred miles up the Central American isthmus in Nicaragua. The president there, José Santos Zelaya, had been eager to host the United States' canal in hopes of turning his republic of cattle ranchers and coffee farmers into a global transit hub. When Roosevelt and Congress sided with the Panama conspirators instead, Zelaya rolled back concessions for U.S. companies, raised taxes on foreign investors, and began looking for partners who might be interested in building a rival canal, including the Germans and Japanese.[1]

By that point, Teddy Roosevelt had codified his interventionist instincts into a formal policy for the Western Hemisphere. "In flagrant cases" of "wrongdoing or impotence," he had announced in an address to a joint session of Congress, the United States would act—"reluctantly," of course—as "an international police power."[2] Roosevelt pitched this as a "corollary" to the old Monroe Doctrine. But it was, as the historians Serge Ricard and Walter LaFeber would argue, mostly a new idea.[3] Whereas Monroe—and his secretary of state, John Quincy Adams—had been trying to ward off interference from Europe, Roosevelt declared the United States had the power to commit imperial interference of its own in Latin America and the Caribbean—regions Americans would soon start referring to as "our own backyard."

Roosevelt's presidency ended in March 1909. While he set off on an international retirement tour—a hunting safari in the Belgian Congo and British East Africa, hobnobbing with the Kaiser outside Berlin—Roosevelt's former secretary of war William Howard Taft took over the White House. Roosevelt had handpicked the portly bureaucrat for the Republican nomination, in large part owing to Taft's experience administering to America's growing empire: as civilian governor of the Philippines, overseeing the secession of Panama, and as provisional governor of Cuba.

Taft was more conservative than Roosevelt on economic issues. While T.R. pursued a domestic agenda of regulatory reforms and antitrust prosecutions, Taft shared the late President McKinley's affection for corporate power. To run his State Department, Taft tapped Philander C. Knox, a corporate lawyer from Pittsburgh who had played a key role in the formation of J. P. Morgan's U.S. Steel Corporation. The senior attorney in that deal was the Panama Canal's Wall Street mastermind, William Nelson Cromwell. Knox had then teamed up with Cromwell again on the canal, as Roosevelt's attorney general. (When Roosevelt asked Knox to provide a justification for the U.S. intervention, he allegedly told the president: "I think it would be better to keep your action free from any taint of legality.")[4]

Knox's friends from Pittsburgh were heavily invested in Nicaragua. When Zelaya threatened to revoke the concession at the Pittsburghers' La Luz y Los Angeles gold mine, in Nicaragua's Mosquitia Province on the Atlantic coast, the investors wrote the new secretary of state to ask for "protection in the premises." Unsubtly, they reminded him that La Luz and other nearby mines were owned by "Pittsburgh capitalists, some no doubt known by you."[5]

In late 1909, sensing an opportunity, the governor of Mosquitia Province, Gen. Juan José Estrada, launched a coup against Zelaya. Estrada shrewdly chose as his top aide Adolfo Díaz, an otherwise unremarkable conservative colonel who happened to be the chief accountant at La Luz.

Knox sent an operative to make contact with Estrada and Díaz in the provincial capital, Bluefields. U.S. businessmen poured in money and supplies to support the putschists. Pittsburgh industrialist William Rees, the treasurer of La Luz, reassured his employee, Díaz: "Our good friend Knox will help us all he can."[6]

When Zelaya executed two American mercenaries who'd come to assist Estrada and Díaz, the State Department swung into action. In a blistering public letter dated December 1, 1909, Secretary Knox denounced Zelaya as "a blot upon the history of Nicaragua," and announced official U.S. support for Estrada and Díaz's business-friendly revolt. "The Government of the United States is convinced that the revolution represents the ideals and the will of a majority of the Nicaraguan people more faithfully."[7]

But as Knox knew, it would not be the Nicaraguan people that Zelaya would have to answer to.

Smedley Butler's road to Nicaragua began with a few detours. After his ejection from Subic Bay, he was put on a recruiting desk in Philadelphia. His health didn't improve. Chalking his "nervousness," headaches, weight loss, and lethargy to chronic malaria contracted while digging the canal off Puerto Rico, a Navy medical board ordered him to take sick leave "in a dry mountainous region" for at least eight months.[8] Maud and Thomas had a wealthy friend from their Quaker meeting who owned a coal mine in West Virginia, so Thomas made a call.[9] Bunny and Snooks made a home on the mountain while Smedley tried his hand at being a coal boss.

Life at war had done little to prepare Butler for his first civilian job. The strategies he'd learned for motivating Marines—alternating bromides with public humiliation—boosted production but enraged the mostly Eastern European immigrant miners.

Once, a drunk superintendent came after him with a gun. Butler summarily disarmed him and kicked him into the snow.[10] Another time, Smedley hopped into a coal car, only to realize too late that someone had removed the brake stick. He hurtled down the mountain and crashed into a train of parked cars, smashing several ribs and bruising himself from head to toe. When the mandatory nine-month leave ended, Bunny suggested he go back to active duty.[11] It seemed safer for him there.

Upon his return to the Marine Corps, Butler passed an examination board to be promoted to major—his first rank as a field officer, qualifying him to lead an entire battalion of as many as one thousand Marines. ("Everybody rather expected me to retire but I fooled them," Smedley wrote to his mother and brother Sam after getting the top score on the exam.)[12] Whatever doubts the commanders had after Butler's episode at Subic Bay were overshadowed by those results and his previous record—and no doubt by his father's status as a key member of the House Committee on Naval Affairs, which handled funding for the Marine Corps.[13]

Smedley spent a year back at the Philadelphia Navy Yard—enough time to see the birth of his second child, Smedley Junior. In November 1909, he was given command of the Third Battalion of the First Marine Regiment. It would be based in the new Canal Zone, but it wasn't expected to stay there. Four days after Knox sent his note denouncing Zelaya, Major Butler and his "Panama Battalion" boarded the auxiliary cruiser USS *Buffalo*, bound for the Nicaraguan Pacific port of Corinto.

As soon as he heard the Marines were coming, Zelaya resigned and fled to Mexico.

"Everything is quiet and peaceful as a Quaker Meeting on a hot Sunday," Smedley complained to Bunny after arriving. "This is a d—d fool expedition anyhow," he added soon after. "I would really like to know what Father's friend Philander Knox is trying to do."[14]

For the first weeks of 1910, Butler stayed on the ship off the dusty Corinto pier. In the mornings he sent out two parties to trawl for fish. At night, he tossed and turned in the inexorable cabin heat.

As a newly minted major, he eventually realized he could give himself permission to leave the ship. In February, Butler led a small reconnaissance party south down Nicaragua's main railroad: through the liberal college town of León; the capital, Managua; the indigenous city of Masaya; and Granada, the wealthy conservative stronghold at the edge of Lake Nicaragua.

The reconnaissance would prove its military value on Butler's missions in Nicaragua to come. For the moment, it felt like sightseeing. The beautiful volcanoes and deep blue crater lakes Butler stopped at along the way served mostly to remind him of how alone he was. In an epic twenty-seven-page letter to his "Precious Ones" (he had begun calling himself, with fulsome sentimentality, their "Daddie Piddie"), Smedley rambled mournfully about how much he missed his family. He included in the envelope an interestingly shaped leaf he had presumably plucked from the jungle.[15]

In the cities, Butler got the chance to do something else he'd rarely done as a junior officer: meet people outside the chain of command. He drank with American newspaper correspondents and met the crush of U.S. businessmen flocking to strike it rich in the Central American republic. All of them had opinions about his mission. In conservative Granada ("by far the most desirable City of the Republic"), he was ushered in to an audience with an "old Spanish don"—the head of the Lacayo family, one of the richest in Nicaragua, who lectured him on who he thought the ideal leader of Nicaragua would be.[16] Butler escaped the harangue only to arrive at his quarters at the Hotel Alhambra, where he was "forced to listen to the ideas of several [more] men on what the United States should do."[17]

These encounters triggered something new in Butler, or perhaps combined his older frustrations into something different and more potent. When he got back to Corinto, worn out and running on four hours' sleep, he unloaded about his mission in a letter to Maud and Thomas.[18]

First, he laid into the Nicaraguans—"Spigs," he called them, "the most worthless, useless lot of vermine [sic] I have struck yet, even worse than our 'little brown brothers' the Filipinos." (At least those "F— will fight and these dogs won't," he spat.)

But then he spun toward a new target: his fellow Americans. "What makes me mad is that the whole revolution is inspired and financed by Americans who have wild cat investments down here and want to make them good by putting in a Government which will declare a monopoly in their favor," Butler told his parents. "The whole business is rotten to the core, and I am ashamed to think a Republican Administration is, if anything, assisting the revolution."

There was no "patriotic movement" in the conflict or the mission, he concluded. "The whole game of these degenerate Americans down here is to force the United States to intervene and by doing so make their investments good."

Other senior officers shared Butler's concerns. Rear Admiral William Kimball, the commandant of the U.S. expeditionary squadron off Corinto, grumbled in an official report to Taft's secretary of the Navy: "I have never been able to understand how the comparatively small American commercial interests backing the revolution could control practically the whole American press and give such generally false views."[19]

For Butler, this was more personal. If a shooting war started, he and his Marines would be some of the ones risking their lives. Those who survived would bear the shame for what they had done. As he wrote his parents from Corinto: "The poor common people are the only sufferers, as is always the case, and their blood will be on our heads."[20]

The words ring hollow today, given the invective he had just hurled. Patronizing sympathy and racial animus can be close cousins, living side by side in one trained to view the people around them solely as objects for pity, utility, or scorn. But even so, the moment represented a quiet turning point in Butler's thinking. For the first time, he was beginning to question the ulterior motives behind his mission—even if he wasn't ready to give up his role in that mission just yet.

Like Butler, I arrived in Nicaragua by way of Panama. The route afforded a spectacular view of the country's eponymous great lake from the air, and the twin volcanoes jutting from its center. A white cloud of super-heated gases hovered over the peaks.

Nicaraguan politics were no less volatile in 2019. For a year, protesters had been in the streets demanding the removal of President Daniel Ortega and his ruling party, the Sandinista National Liberation Front, or FSLN. Hundreds of dissidents had been killed, hundreds more jailed, tortured, or disappeared.[21] Journalists were routinely beaten and harassed; a Nicaraguan investigative reporter was shot to death on live television.[22] Four days before I landed in Managua, the national police had charged and beaten hundreds of students, activists, and a small number of Ortega's former Sandinista allies demanding the release of political prisoners. At least 164 people were detained.[23]

One of the dissident Sandinistas arrested at the protest was Mónica Baltodano. She had been one of the most senior guerrilla commanders in the revolution that overthrew the Somozas—the murderous family dictatorship that ruled Nicaragua in the decades following the U.S. occupation.

Baltodano's signature moment as a guerrilla had come in the city of Granada in 1979. In documentary footage, she is seen wearing a beret over her frizzy brown hair, big round glasses, and a red-and-black Sandinista bandanna. "Specify your commander! Say your name—your full name!" she shouts at the government troops through a window, holding her machine gun just out of sight. The defeated colonel of the Somozas' feared militia—the U.S.-trained Guardia Nacional de Nicaragua—appears, wrapped in the Nicaraguan flag, unable to conceal his humiliation at being forced to surrender to a woman. Mónica greets him with a beaming smile.[24]

I went to meet the *comandante* one morning at a safe house in a quiet neighborhood. Though she had long ago broken with her former comrade, Ortega—calling his presidency a dictatorship and a return to Somoza-style rule[25]—she still had friends in the regime. One, it seemed, had intervened to have her freed.

In addition to having played her own crucial role in Nicaraguan history, Baltodano had become a leading chronicler of her people's long war against dictatorship and empire. Her major work, *Memorias de la lucha sandinista*—Memories of the Sandinista Struggle—comprised four volumes of oral history with key figures from the revolutions of the twentieth century. In talking to her, I hoped to find the connections between the conflicts and invasions of Butler's day and the crises facing Nicaraguans now.

When she opened the door of the house, two tiny yipping dogs bolted down the driveway to meet me. Baltodano had naturally aged since the scenes filmed of her in the 1970s, her old chunky glasses replaced by frameless lenses. But the smile looked the same.

We sat down at a round table that filled most of a tiny office. The rest of the room was taken up with boxes. She apologized for the mess. She had to keep moving to stay ahead of Ortega's security forces, and had not had time to unpack.

"Latin American history has been a history with a high level of gringo presence, of course," Baltodano told me in cheerful but pointed Spanish. "But in Central America, and in particular Nicaragua, the United States has been *extremely* present. And that is why Sandinismo developed as an anti-imperialist force."

The philosophy can be traced back to the movement's namesake: Augusto César Sandino. Sandino grew up in Niquinohomo, a small town outside Masaya. In 1927, at the age of thirty-two, Sandino launched a revolution against a puppet president and the still-present U.S. Marines—or, as Sandino called them, "the claws of the enormous eagle with its curved beak bloody with the blood of Nicaraguans."[26]

For six years Sandino and his original Sandinistas battled the Americans in the jungles of northern Nicaragua. (Many of the Marines who fought against Sandino in the renewed campaign had trained and served under Butler; others, especially Lewis "Chesty" Puller, would become Marine legends in their own right.) When the Marines withdrew from the country in 1933—part of the same era of renegotiation with Latin America that saw the Platt Amendment in Cuba repealed—Sandino turned his attention on the client army the Americans had trained and left behind: the Guardia Nacional.

It was a fatal move. The chief of the Guardia, Anastasio Somoza García, ordered Sandino killed in 1934. Two years later, Somoza staged a coup d'état and launched what would prove to be a multigenerational dictatorship.

Throughout their reign, Baltodano emphasized, the Somozas—Anastasio, the father, and his sons Luis and Anastasio Somoza Debayle—used the Guardia as an instrument of absolute control: starving, beating, electrocuting, and killing thousands of Nicaragua's poor, the family's enemies, and anyone who might inconvenience their rule. Eight U.S. presidents knew all about it. All of them continued funding their regime.[27]

"I will tell you that, yes, the United States was present, they were present back then supporting the Somozas during all their forty-three years of dictatorship," Baltodano told me, her eyebrows raised knowingly. "The Somozas faithfully represented the interests of the United States, they favored [U.S.] businesses, their investments, their explorations for control of the mines, all the important business sectors. Trade was above all with the United States. It really was, as they say [Franklin] Roosevelt once said of Somoza: 'He is a son of a bitch, but he is our son of a bitch.'"[28]

This partnership grew especially strong during the Cold War. Anastasio Somoza García supported United Fruit and the 1954 CIA coup against Guatemala's Jacobo Árbenz.[29] The U.S.-trained anti-Castro Cuban exiles launched their failed 1961 invasion at the Bay of Pigs from the Nicaraguan beach of Puerto Cabezas.

In the 1950s, a group of Nicaraguan students and activists struck back against Somoza's repression. They called themselves Sandinistas, in honor of their anti-imperialist hero. The name was itself an act of rebellion, Baltodano told me, because the dictator had tried not only to bury Sandino's body but "to make his story disappear as well." The story of Sandino's resistance had been rediscovered by Carlos Fonseca, a radical librarian who became a leader of the anti-Somoza uprising.

The connections Fonseca and his activist colleagues forged with their predecessors went even further than that, as Baltodano has documented through her oral histories. One of their first steps was to make contact with Sandino's former lieutenants in exile.[30]

Still, the new Sandinistas were different from their namesakes in significant ways. Many of the youngsters were Marxists. Sandino was not: he lived and died a proud member of Nicaragua's Liberal Party—"a petty-bourgeois caudillo, a social bandit," one commentator described.[31] But Fonseca and the other founders of the FSLN recognized the power of Sandino's example to inspire the masses; under his banner, they launched what would prove to be the decisive Sandinista uprising in 1978.

All the women in Baltodano's family joined that fight. One sister blew off her hands trying to build a bomb. Another was tortured with electrocution by the Guardia Nacional and later killed. Mónica herself was imprisoned for nine months in the squalid Central Jail of Managua, where she was beaten and tied to a wall, before resuming her guerrilla activity and helping to bring down the dictatorship.[32]

The last of the Somozas, Anastasio Somoza Debayle, fled into exile in 1979. He was assassinated by Sandinista agents in Paraguay a year later.

Although he would come to dominate Nicaraguan politics afterward, Daniel Ortega had been a secondary figure throughout the Sandinista revolution. His pragmatic "Third Way" branch had clashed with the more orthodox Marxist-Leninist streams of the Sandinista Front. ("Ideologically, he was always one of the weakest because he was always very lazy," Baltodano told me with a wry smile.) But Ortega quickly maneuvered his way to the top of the new ruling junta, becoming Nicaragua's first post-Somoza leader in 1981.

So how did a revolutionary movement come to be led by someone she called a dictator? I asked Baltodano.

"I do believe that it will be necessary to do much deeper research to answer that," the comandante replied.

If anything, back in 1909, Butler had underestimated the influence the American "wild cat" investors had on U.S. policy in Nicaragua. A new way of making money was emerging in North America. Built on the system of railroad financing—the one that had made his and Ethel's families wealthy—a new breed of bankers was finding ways to turn money into more money: refinancing debts and providing capital for expansion. They used their securities—stocks and bonds—to take over companies they invested in. To ensure their profits were prioritized, they often moved to choose the client companies' managers themselves.

While the Marines were learning to land on foreign beaches, the bankers were learning to expand beyond the U.S. borders too, starting with a loan to Mexico by J. P. Morgan in 1899. They also experimented with financing foreign wars: U.S. bankers had supported the British seizure of Boer South Africa from 1899 to 1902 and Japan's war against Russia in 1904 and 1905.[33] It was only a matter of time before the investors wanted to select the leaders of the countries they were investing in as well.

During his presidency, Theodore Roosevelt had realized the potential of private finance to participate in systems of control. Between 1904 and 1907, he had "solved" a debt crisis in the Dominican Republic by transferring the Caribbean country's debt from European bondholders to Wall Street (ultimately the Morgan-linked Guaranty Trust Company), while taking over its customs system.[34] It was a privatized spin on what the powers had done to China under the Boxer Protocol, borrowing from the way the British Empire had used private corporations to colonize places like North America, India, and Egypt.[35] To Americans skeptical of imperialism, it could be sold as what the banks called "receivership"—seizing assets to ensure repayment of a debt. It was just that, instead of a bank taking over a railroad, in this case the banks were taking over a country, supported by the full force of the U.S. government and military.

Even with that arrangement, Washington had not always gotten its way. U.S. officials' abiding belief in "the white man's civilizing mission" had led them to see the darker-skinned Dominicans as "people who were naturally followers"—only to find themselves manipulated by Dominican leaders with their own agendas, as the financial historian Emily Rosenberg has written.[36] But the system worked well enough. U.S. sugar and railroad companies had profited, and the banks increased their business.

Officials in Washington saw a possible future: one that carried the moneymaking potential of their recent imperial adventures without the horrors—and public backlash—of the Philippine War, the dependence on foreign allies in China, or the mounting costs of keeping Cuba and Puerto Rico as "protectorates." Hiding in a supporting role, the U.S. government would indirectly expand its influence over domestic affairs without having to take on the responsibilities associated with the formal colonialism of its European rivals. President Taft called it "substituting dollars for bullets." Other commentators scrubbed the violence out completely, dubbing it "dollar diplomacy."[37]

The recipe was simple: In order to accept lucrative U.S. bank loans, targeted countries would have to also accept U.S. financial advisers. Those advisers would then "reform" the countries' customs collection agencies, putting the country in receivership. They would also force the country to replace its existing monetary system with one based on the gold standard—the basis of the U.S. dollar at the time. The reserves guaranteeing that currency would be "safely deposited in New York."[38]

Taft likened "dollar diplomacy" to a parent helping "weaker," "backwards" children. "Our aim has been to do good for good's sake," he pledged.[39] Through financial control, the United States could ensure peace through fiscal and "moral accountability," eliminating the need to send troops overseas. "True stability," Knox added, "is best established not by military but by economic and social forces."[40] But as Butler would learn firsthand, bullets were still very much needed to ultimately guarantee control.

In May 1910, Butler's Panama Battalion was rushed to Bluefields to protect Estrada and Adolfo Díaz's rebels, who had not yet unseated Zelaya's appointed Liberal successor, José Madriz. Butler informed the government troops' commander that he would retaliate against any attack on the rebel-held city, but that he had no objection to the Conservative rebels "shooting outwards."[41]

State Department operative Thomas Moffat, the architect of the 1907 Dominican receivership plan, swooped in to put the final pieces in place: Madriz would resign, leaving Estrada to become Nicaragua's president. Adolfo Díaz would become vice president, to the glee of his former employers in Pittsburgh. The new Nicaraguan government would also hire a professional financial "expert" arranged by the Wall Street banks of Brown Brothers and J. & W. Seligman and Co.

The problem the experts faced was that there was no pretense under which Nicaragua's assets could justifiably be seized. Unlike the Dominican Republic, Nicaragua under Zelaya had enjoyed a good credit rating, a treasury surplus, and a stable currency.[42] So the bankers had to get creative. They invented a new debt: they would repay Adolfo Díaz and his fellow generals for the costs incurred during their coup.[43]

This did not go over well with middle-class and poorer Nicaraguans. In 1911, Estrada banded with disgruntled tradesmen in an effort to prevent his rivals from moving against him. He failed and was forced to step down, making Adolfo Díaz president of the republic.

Díaz's political ascent was matched by an economic coup from Washington. On January 4, 1912, Brown Brothers and J. & W. Seligman formed the new National Bank of Nicaragua. It was incorporated in Connecticut and run out of Brown Brothers' offices in lower Manhattan.[44]

It didn't take long for the immediate effects of "dollar diplomacy" to be felt. The Nicaraguan economy quickly deteriorated. Diáz drained the budget surplus to pay his supporters, then risked inflation by secretly printing more paper money.[45] When Philander Knox made a "goodwill visit" to Nicaragua in March 1912, he was greeted with violent demonstrations against Díaz and his American backers.

The leader of the national legislature, Dr. Ignacio Suárez, welcomed Knox with a warning. The secretary's visit, he said, had "awakened fears and misgivings in timid minds, who see in it a peril to our autonomy." Suárez quoted George Washington's farewell address, in which the first U.S. president warned that "an attachment of a small or weak towards a great and powerful nation dooms the former to be the satellite of the latter."[46] The legislator's implication was clear: Nicaraguans would defend their sovereignty and independence from imperial control as fiercely as the American revolutionaries had, over a century before.

I was driving up the highway between Managua and Corinto when I spotted a large faded billboard rising over a bank of *capulín* trees. Two figures stood triumphantly against a faded pink background, each with one arm around the other, their free hands signaling to an unseen crowd.

The figure on the left was Daniel Ortega. Beside and slightly beneath him was Rosario Murillo Zambrana, his vice president, who is also his wife. Above them was the couple's slogan: *Cristiana, Socialista, Solidaria*—Christian, socialist, and in solidarity. Beneath them was another slogan partially in Murillo's looping handwriting: "A time of victory! By the grace of God!"

The overt religiosity of Ortega's new slogans was a sharp contrast to the tone the Sandinistas, especially the more Marxist elements, struck during and after their 1978–79 revolution against the Somoza dictatorship. (Augusto Sandino himself had said, when asked if he had religious beliefs shortly before his assassination in 1934: "No, religions are things of the past. We are guided by reason."[47]) But it was emblematic of the more "ecumenical" style of Ortega and Murillo's current rule, in which they forged alliances with conservative elements of Nicaraguan society—bankers, businessmen, police, and the Catholic Church. To maintain a degree of popular support, they papered over these new ties, along with their creation of a quasi-police state, with copious symbols of leftist international solidarity.[48]

Things had not started out that way. When Ortega had emerged the first time, taking the leadership of the Sandinista junta in 1981, his government tried to implement a program of social improvements including agrarian reforms and a massive literacy campaign. As soon as they got started, however, a coalition of former members of the Somozas' Guardia Nacional and allied business interests launched a counterrevolution. The "Contras," as they were known, were armed and financed by the CIA.

As Contra death squads massacred and raped their way through the Nicaraguan countryside throughout the early 1980s, President Ronald Reagan called them "the moral equal of our Founding Fathers."* CIA-trained commandos shot rockets at oil storage tanks in Corinto. The Contras blew up bridges, factories, fishing boats, hospitals, childcare centers, food warehouses, and schools. In response, Ortega turned to the Soviet Union and Cuba for support.[49]

---

* Most Americans remember this because of a uniquely American scandal. When the Democratic Congress banned funding for the Contras, the Reagan administration hatched a scheme to illegally funnel money and weapons to them anyway, in part by using their profits from weapons sales to Iran. It became known as the Iran-Contra Affair and resulted in a string of nationally televised hearings. About a dozen Reagan administration officials were indicted. Several were convicted. Most were pardoned by George H. W. Bush, on the recommendation of his (and later Trump's) attorney general, William H. Barr. (Bush had likely been tied up in the scandal as vice president as well.) Appropriately for a story involving Nicaragua, the face of the scandal was a Marine: Lt. Col. Oliver North, who oversaw the scheme as a member of the National Security Council. North's conviction was overturned after an

The war and Ortega's first term as president ended at the same time, with his loss in a 1990 election. The first Sandinista government had made crippling and destructive errors of its own—especially its early attempts at seizing indigenous peoples' lands, which provoked a separate, shorter-lived counter-revolt. But, as the anthropologists Jennifer Goett and Courtney Desiree Morris have written, such wounds were "overshadowed by the tremendous resources and energy the U.S. dedicated to sabotaging the revolution."[50]

Ortega immediately began plotting his return. He sidelined dissenters in the FSLN. When Murillo's daughter from a previous marriage accused Ortega of having sexually abused her since she was eleven years old, Murillo disowned her.[51] Ortega reconciled with the Catholic Church, pledging to revoke Nicaraguan women's century-old right to therapeutic abortions. He lastly cut a deal with the corrupt center-right president to rewrite election laws in his favor.[52] In 2006, Ortega won back the presidency with just 38 percent of the vote and a former Contra leader as his running mate. (He subbed in his wife as his second-in-command in 2017.)

During his first years back in power, Ortega depended on the largess of his Venezuelan ally, Hugo Chávez, who promoted his country's oil wealth as an alternative to U.S. economic hegemony. Ortega and Murillo used Venezuelan money to buy up media outlets and hand out tax breaks and other perks to loyal businessmen.[53] In 2013, Ortega's imitation of "dollar diplomacy" reached absurd heights when he began confiscating private and indigenous lands on behalf of a Chinese company that promised, at long last, to build a transoceanic canal through Nicaragua. (That plan was, at the time I visited, apparently on hold.)

When oil prices fell and Venezuela's economy collapsed, Ortega's government revenues went with it. In the spring of 2018, after the Nicaraguan government announced cuts to social security, protests erupted in several cities. On April 18, a gang of Sandinista Youth members savagely

---

appeals court ruled witnesses might have been affected by testimony he had given against other Reagan administration officials in exchange for congressional immunity. On Bush's involvement, see Arun Gupta, "Let's Talk About George H. W. Bush's Role in the Iran-Contra Scandal," *Intercept*, Dec. 7, 2018.

beat demonstrators in Managua. The crackdown only made the protests grow.

Across Nicaragua, protesters began chanting "¡Daniel y Somoza! ¡Son la misma cosa!" (Meaning: Daniel and Somoza are the same thing.) Loyal paramilitaries dismantled barricades and murdered marchers. Elder guerrillas taught a new generation to fight back against the pro-government troops with homemade mortars and slingshots. On the way out of Managua, I had passed convoys of riot police on guard for anti-government demonstrations.

Ortega and Murillo had survived the protests by shielding themselves under the mantle of anti-imperialism. They accused the protesters of being, essentially, latter-day Adolfo Díazes: puppets carrying out a coup d'état financed and organized by the United States. In a speech addressing loyal Nicaraguans as "children of the homeland of Diriangén, Sandino, and Rubén Darió," Ortega called dissidents "terrorists" and *"golpistas"* (coup plotters), and denounced as murderers "those that finance, encourage, and justify these crimes" for the purpose of, as he claimed, "putting the [Nicaraguan] people in chains again."[54]

It was effective enough. Ortega did not even have to present evidence of an attempt at U.S. control of the protests. All he had to do was invoke the national heroes—above all Sandino—and let history and memory do the rest. As much as former allies like Mónica Baltodano would contest the point, Ortega and Murillo were still, as far as most of the world was concerned, the faces of the Sandinista movement. Just not on the *particular* billboard I was driving past: some brave soul had smacked Daniel and Rosario in the mouths with balloons of red paint, blotting out their faces almost entirely.

In the summer of 1912, "dollar diplomacy" collapsed in Nicaragua. A punishing drought had pushed rural refugees into cities. When the U.S. official now in charge of Nicaraguan customs—fresh from a similar job in the Philippines—opposed loans to import grain on the grounds that it would swell public debt, protests erupted. Poor and indigenous Nicaraguans began ransacking wealthy haciendas in search of food. Some of the wealthiest elites were beaten, raped, and tortured.[55]

On July 29, seeing the tidal wave of popular resentment against President Adolfo Díaz and his American backers, the Nicaraguan war minister, Gen. Luis Mena, tried to stage a coup. Mena fled to Masaya with six hundred troops, where he joined up with the forces of a popular young Liberal general, Benjamín Zeledón. The allies declared their intent to overthrow the American-puppet president, hold new elections, and take control of "symbols of national sovereignty" including the railroads and banks.[56]

One of the rebels' most likely targets was the new U.S.-run National Bank of Nicaragua, whose first manager, W. Bundy Cole, had arrived weeks earlier with his wife and five-year-old son aboard a United Fruit ship.[57] As word came that rebels were closing in on the capital, Cole rushed a personal telegram to the Park Avenue residence of James Brown, one of the partners at Brown Brothers, requesting to know, urgently, "if anything was being done in behalf of our interests."

Cole got back comforting news. "I had a reply stating that everything possible was being done," the banker later recalled, "and that Major Butler would arrive there shortly from Panama."[58]

"Well here we are again on our way to Corinto," Smedley Butler wrote Bunny and the children from aboard the USS *Justin*. "I had hoped, when I left that 'hole' . . . never to see it again, but you never can tell from where you sit how your picture is going to look."[59]

While the Marines unloaded their supplies at the Pacific-side port, Butler took a phone call from the U.S. consul in Managua. Mena and Zeledón's rebels were already bombarding the city. As he had as a younger man in China, Butler would have to make his way to a besieged capital on a road laden with hostile forces. But this time, he knew the route: it was the same rail line he'd gone "sightseeing" down two years before.

Butler's Panama Battalion began the ninety-mile journey under cover of darkness. They arrived in Managua around 10:30 A.M. By luck they timed it perfectly, arriving after Mena had retreated into the countryside but before his rebels could cut off the railroad from the port. In a nod to the true purpose of the mission, Butler stationed half his Marines in Brown Brothers and Seligman's National Bank.[60]

The rebels were gaining strength. Tradesmen and indigenous people were flocking to Zeledón and Mena's army, drawn by promises of school, food, and a restoration of dignity. "Citizens, let us take back our rights!" Zeledón implored in a widely circulated leaflet. "Without liberty there is no life, without equality there is no light, without national autonomy an empire of chaos reigns."[61]

Calls for reinforcements to back up Butler's battalion rang out across the United States. "No Latin-American country more severely tries the patience of the big Anglo-Saxon guardian," the *Cleveland Plain Dealer* editorialized. "No one of the baby republics so richly merits a spanking on general principles."[62]

On September 4, a full expeditionary force of 1,150 Marines arrived under Col. Joseph H. Pendleton—Butler's former commanding officer at Subic Bay. Butler was ordered to head to Granada, where Mena had established his headquarters. To preserve a patina of neutrality, Butler was ordered to load his train with Red Cross supplies and food, and to hang a U.S. flag on the front. He ordered the locomotive moved to the center of the train, behind several flat cars, for its protection.

On the way, they had to pass a fortress on a hill above Masaya called Coyotepe, where Mena's ally, Zeledón, was now positioned. When they reached it, the rebels fired three shells at them. The train clambered to a halt. Butler sent a message to Zeledón, who agreed to a conference inside his lines.[63]

Zeledón was just two years older than Butler—his thirty-third birthday was weeks away. After a decade of war and service in Zelaya's diplomatic corps, he found himself in charge of hundreds of men on the battlefield. But—also like Butler—he was still answering to a senior commander, in his case Luis Mena. Butler quickly learned another similarity between himself and his Nicaraguan counterpart: Zeledón would not be easily bullied.

The rebel's men blindfolded Butler and two other officers and led them to a location beyond the far side of Coyotepe. When Butler's blindfold was removed, he saw a "short plump man with a dark mustache," smartly dressed in a Panama hat and civilian clothes.[64]

Butler, on the other hand, looked like hell. He was suffering a relapse of malaria, waking up in the middle of the night with a 104-degree fever—"so stiff," he'd written Bunny, "I could hardly roll over in bed." His eyes were sunken and bloodshot. He had lost at least ten pounds after a week of eating "nothing but quinine and limeade."[65]

Apparently not thinking much of the Marine, Zeledón addressed him belligerently. Butler told him, with some bluster, that his orders were to "go through to Granada, and that I was going to carry them out."[66] When Butler slipped and mentioned that Colonel Pendleton had come to see the situation himself, Zeledón demanded to speak with the more senior officer. Butler threw up his hands and agreed, glad to have more time to recover from his illness.

Negotiations dragged on for two more days. When Pendleton threatened to drive the rebels off Coyotepe by force, Zeledón demanded to speak with an even-higher ranking officer, Admiral William H. H. Southerland. The next day, Zeledón wrote a letter formalizing his protest. The handwriting was elegant and careful, a mark of class the American elite had prized until they'd adopted the typewriter not long before.[67] The wording also reflected Zeledón's education as a lawyer: "I will not bother going into the axiom of international law that says that countries, however small, are to be accorded the same respect and the same considerations as stronger countries; nor will I bother reminding you of the longing expressed by the Father of American Independence, George Washington, that the grandeur of your country be based in respect for its laws and in its nobility with the other countries of the world."[68]

Zeledón did, however, remind Admiral Southerland that the "illegal" President Díaz had an agreement with "the bankers from New York" not to operate trains on Nicaraguan soil during wartime. The rebel army wished to pursue "friendly relations with your powerful Government and wonderful people," he assured the admiral. "But I do not want it as a conquistador in my country, which I love with all of the capacity of a citizen who was born free, who has lived free, and will die free."

Butler dismissed the missives as "hot air" from "the Spigs." "The Colonel is moving up five hundred more Marines, and we will attack them tomorrow morning unless they give in in the meantime," he wrote Bunny.[69]

Before dawn on September 19, Butler led his battalion to the edge of Coyotepe Hill and waited for the 6:00 A.M. deadline for Zeledón to surrender. At "ten seconds of six," a white flag appeared. Warily, Butler ordered the Marines back onto the train to continue on toward Granada. Butler rode at the front of the lead car.

Night had fallen by the time the train reached the center of Masaya. Butler looked out ahead, the tracks illuminated by a single lantern positioned beside him. Out of the darkness, a figure appeared on horseback, riding in their direction. When the rider was ten yards away, he pulled out a revolver and fired directly at Butler. The shot missed, hitting the corporal sitting just behind him.

"My heart!" the corporal yelled. (In fact, he had been shot in the hand, which had been on his chest at the time.) Butler shouted for the train to stop and took off running after the man on horseback. Too late, he realized the lone gunman's approach was only the rebels' opening move. Dozens of fighters appeared and opened fire on the stopped train. Marines scrambled to their sixteen mounted machine guns and lit into the attackers. The whole train became "a mass of shooting tongues of flame," Butler would later write.[70]

The Marines' Nicaraguan engineer got the locomotives roaring again. The train lurched out of the ambush and began speeding toward Granada. In twenty minutes, four Marines had been wounded. Sixty-eight Nicaraguans were dead.[71]

Butler was livid. Zeledón, he was convinced, had set him up. It was about that time when Butler's men started noticing a look in him: a menacing, piercing stare, made more pronounced by eyes still bloodshot and sunken from fever. They started calling him "Old Gimlet Eye," after an old Anglo-Saxon hand tool used to drill holes through wood. Butler swore that, when he returned to Masaya, he would see those responsible for the ambush hanged.[72]

Granada, a city of wide plazas and picturesque churches on the shores of Lake Nicaragua, is one of the oldest Spanish cities in the Americas. Named in honor of the conquest of the last Muslim stronghold in Spain, it owes its wealth to its position as a stopover for trade between the inland waterway and the Pacific Ocean.

That combination of money and cosmopolitanism led to an early openness to "Americanization." In 1856, when the Tennessee filibusterer William Walker tried to take over Nicaragua, he made Granada his capital, winning the support of the city's conservative cattle-ranching elites with his U.S.-style entrepreneurism and the promise of an interoceanic canal. By the time the ranchers learned that Walker planned to seize their haciendas and replace them with U.S.-style slave labor camps run by his American lieutenants, it was too late to save their city. Fleeing the capital ahead of the arrival of troops sponsored by Cornelius Vanderbilt, Walker ordered the city burned to the ground. His men left behind a sign: "Here was Granada."[73]

Almost exactly fifty-six years later, in September 1912, Smedley Butler was threatening to do the same thing if the rebel general-in-chief, Luis Mena, did not surrender. "The firing of even a single shot at us will mean an attack by this entire force, big guns and automatics," Butler warned. On the other hand, Butler promised Mena he would strictly obey his orders of "absolute neutrality" if the rebel leader guaranteed the Americans the use of the railroad.[74]

To Butler's shock, General Mena sent a message back saying he was willing to make the deal. But no sooner was Butler's mission completed than word arrived that U.S. policy had changed: The State Department had grown tired of waiting for "dollar diplomacy" to work. They wanted the "neutrality" pretense to end, the Marines and Navy to side with Adolfo Díaz's government troops, and the Nicaraguan rebels destroyed.[75]

"This goes back on all the things I have told the rebels and I am, therefore, to be made scapegoat after I have done all the hard work," Butler complained to Bunny.[76]

On the moonlit night of September 24, Butler walked through the deserted streets of Granada to explain the situation to Mena in person. Passing the cathedral and the main plaza, he arrived at the smaller Convento San Francisco. The general was lying on his back in the shadows, surrounded by weapons stockpiles lit by a pair of hanging lanterns. Mena, Butler realized, was gravely ill, apparently in an advanced stage of kidney failure.[77]

"I told him the whole sad story," Butler wrote Bunny soon after. If Mena agreed to "unconditionally surrender himself, and all his men in Granada," the Fighting Quaker promised the "Admiral would take care of him and remove him from the country," sending him to the new U.S. hospital in the Panama Canal Zone. "Mena pondered for a while, but finally consented."[78]*

Destroying the remaining rebels meant defeating Benjamín Zeledón's forces atop Coyotepe. On October 2, with nearly a thousand Marines and sailors surrounding the five-hundred-foot hill, Pendleton sent up terms of surrender. Zeledón replied at 5:00 A.M. the next morning: "I will mount with my forces the resistance the case calls for, and that the dignity of Nicaragua demands."[79]

This time, Zeledón also wrote a letter to his wife—his "beautiful Estercita"—and his children. "Destiny appears to have made its pact with . . . the traitors to drag me to a certain and cruel end with the brave men who remain with me," the rebel commander wrote. "Do not cry, do not grieve, because in spirit I will accompany you always."[80]

Butler's battalion began climbing the hill before dawn on October 4, in two single-file lines, holding hands to keep together in the dark. At 5:15 A.M., they linked up with Pendleton's Marines, who approached from the other side. Zeledón's men had dug trenches into the hillside, which they had surrounded with barbed wire. The Marines cut their way through with bayonets and leaped into the trenches. Amid the cacophony of gunfire, screams, and bugle calls, a Marine captain noticed "about one hundred and fifty of the enemy" running down the slope.[81] The Americans fired after them, but the small band of rebels disappeared around a bend. Benjamín Zeledón, it seems, was among them.

From the top of the hill, the Stars and Stripes waving behind him, Butler could not help but admire the vista: the great lake, the rolling fields, and the smoke wafting lazily out of the Masaya volcano to the west. There was not a cloud in the sky. He looked down into the city of Masaya, where Díaz's puppet government troops had massed under the command of the Conservative general Emiliano Chamorro. From half a mile away, the Marines could hear the gunfire as the *federales* raided the last holdouts of Zeledón's revolutionary army. Butler later swore he could hear their screams.[82]

---

* Despite Butler's concerns over his legacy, it was Mena who ended up bearing Nicaraguans' derision for his betrayal of the 1912 revolution. To this day, when a boastful person is suspected of lying or breaking a promise, Nicaraguans will say, "¡Esta dijo Mena!" ("That's what Mena said!") and make an obscene gesture with their index finger and thumb.

climbed Coyotepe while I was in Nicaragua. Ortega's government had tried to turn the hill into a tourist site. But due to the unrest, there were only a handful of kids from the nearby indigenous settlement of Monimbó at the top, along with a bored tour guide, his little brother, and their curly-haired dog. The grass was trampled and brown. The sun beat down overhead.

The hilltop itself wasn't the only thing I'd come to see. After the patriarch of the Somoza clan, Anastasio Somoza García, took power in 1936, he modernized the old fortress. Beneath the surface of the hill where Butler had battled Zeledón's forces a few decades earlier, the new dictator installed a concrete prison. Over the ensuing decades, the Guardia Nacional used the prison to torture and murder countless enemies of the Somoza regime. It is said that survivors were driven mad by the darkness. After I paid the guide an entrance fee, he unlocked the iron gate and led me down the concrete stairs.

It was black as night in the prison. The air was musty and cold. If I hadn't known it was midafternoon, on one of the hottest days of the year in Nicaragua, I couldn't have guessed the time, season, or hemisphere. I tried to keep pace with the guide's flashlight without tripping over his brother or the dog.

We passed multiple small cells. With the cool detachment of someone who had been through there many times, the guide flatly rattled off their former capacities: eighty prisoners in this one, eighty-five in that, and so on. "Here is one of the torture chambers," he said, blandly, as he swung open a rusted door. It screeched, startling the bats that had been sleeping on the ceiling behind us. "The prisoners in here lost all sense of time because they didn't know whether it was morning, afternoon, or night. I'll shut off the light so you can see."

It was an ironic choice of words but apropos. Lost in the darkness, I became entirely disoriented; transported, if only for a few seconds, into a vision of what it might have been like for the Guardia's victims unlucky enough to enter that room. I saw beyond the chamber into thousands of others like it. I imagined the detainees still hidden at Guantánamo, those subjected to similar horrors in the CIA's "black sites," and immigrants driven to madness or suicide under stress and solitude in prison camps within the United States itself. There was something painfully unifying about their experiences. The dehumanization and atomization of enemies, real and perceived, was a great commonality across the empire, bridging the vast gulfs of time and space such methods were meant to create.

My thoughts were interrupted when the guide flicked the light back on. I shivered. We continued down the hall. His beam traced the concrete walls, illuminating dark stains that I realized were blood.

The strategic hill above Masaya was an important theater of the Sandinista Revolution of 1978–79, just as it had been in 1912. The last of Somoza's Guardias bombed the Sandinistas from Coyotepe; some of the revolution's final casualties occurred at the base of the hill, in the spot known as La Barranca.[83]

When the Sandinistas won, my guide explained, they took over the underground dungeon at Coyotepe. He showed me a cramped room where they had imprisoned Guardias who had tortured them.[84]

With Coyotepe fallen and the railroad under American control, the Marines turned their attention to other major cities of Nicaragua. This next stage of conquest did not always go smoothly: at León, two hundred revolutionary fighters fired on the entering Marines and sailors, killing three. "It is terrible that we should be losing so many men fighting the battles of these d—d spigs—all because Brown Bros. have some money down here," Butler wrote Bunny, in a racialized flash of the instincts that would infuse his future antiwar polemics.[85] But the Marines overcame the last bastions of resistance, and before long all Nicaragua was under U.S. occupation.

Butler's final mission in Nicaragua was to supervise a presidential election—a "fine free" one, he called it sarcastically—in order to legalize the position of "our American protégé," Adolfo Díaz.[86] After a few years under the control of the former Pittsburgh mining accountant, the historian Peter James Hudson would write, "Nicaragua had become a mere item in the accounting ledgers of Wall Street."[87]

Butler put aside whatever misgivings he was nursing and spent his last weeks in Nicaragua enjoying the spoils of victory. The U.S. ambassador and Colonel Pendleton both penned glowing reports singling out his bravery, conduct, and initiative.[88] President Díaz presented him with two cannons from the Convento San Francisco. Butler also visited a reopened gold mine in the countryside managed by his fellow Quaker veteran of the Battle of Tianjin, Herbert Hoover.*

The mission was capped with a banquet hosted by the representative of Brown Brothers and Seligman, W. Bundy Cole. A British guest stood and toasted Butler as the "Kitchener of Nicaragua."[89] He may have felt pride at the comparison to the famed British conqueror of Sudan, who had in effect trained the Scottish sergeant who trained him all those years before. Or perhaps the setting at the banker's banquet amplified his misgivings.

Worrying that the dwindling contingent of Marines would not be sufficient to keep control, Butler argued for the creation of a new force of U.S.-sponsored colonial troops to police the country in the Americans' stead.

"Tuesday," Butler wrote Ethel in late 1912, "I spent talking 'Mounted Constabulary' to the Bankers and other controlling interests in Managua. . . . This proposition all the decent people—to say nothing of the representatives of our investors—heartily endorse and approve of."[90]

Butler would personally implement his idea for a "native militia" a few years later in Haiti. It would take another decade for Butler's suggestion to come to fruition in Nicaragua. But in 1925, training began of a mounted constabulary under American command. Two years later, Butler's brainchild was designated the sole official armed force of the country. It was renamed the Guardia Nacional.

There is one more story worth telling about Butler's time in Nicaragua. The rebel leader Benjamín Zeledón had indeed escaped the Battle of Coyotepe. At 5:00 P.M., on October 4, 1912, Butler had cabled Admiral

---

* Hoover was hugely capitalized in Nicaragua. By 1912, he owned shares in more than thirteen Nicaraguan mines. But he was also an example of the fact that there are no guarantees in business, even when you have the Marines on your side. Hoover's company had trouble finding workers thanks to the unrest. The mine Butler visited, Oroya Leonesa, went out of business in 1920 "without ever paying a dividend," according to Hoover's biographer George H. Nash.

Southerland in Managua: "Government forces have captured Zeledon and have asked me if we want him. Am sending force to Masaya at once to preserve order so if you direct me I can have Zeledon sent back here under guard. . . . Personally would suggest that through some inaction on our part someone might hang him. Please direct me at once."[91]

No American action was taken. Somewhere between Coyotepe and Masaya—probably near La Barranca—the lawyer-general was killed.

While Butler and his battalion got ready to head back to Managua, the *federales* threw Zeledón's corpse on the back of a horse and paraded it through the towns at the base of the Masaya volcano. They meant it both as a victory party and a warning to any who dared stand against them and their American allies.

In the small village of Niquinohomo, the grisly procession passed a white one-story house with blue shutters. Hearing the noise, the seventeen-year-old son of a wealthy local coffee farmer and a poor native coffee picker went outside to watch. The teenager's eyes grew wide with horror as he recognized the mutilated corpse of his hero—"killed," as he would later remember, "by bullets of Yankee soldiers serving the interests of Wall Street."[92]

It was at that moment, Augusto Sandino would later say, that he swore to carry on Zeledón's fight against the United States and its proxies for the rest of his life.[93]

# NINE

## THE CANAL ZONE

E thel Conway Peters Butler was thirty when she moved with her three-year-old daughter and infant son to the Panama Canal Zone. It was April 1910, and the isthmus was the fourth home in five years of marriage to which her husband's career had taken her. By contrast, Ethel's favorite sister, Edith, never married nor had children. She made a name for herself as a painter and seemed to travel where she liked—to Europe, to visit their relatives in Atlanta. She even visited the Butlers at Subic Bay, staying only until she got bored.

Mrs. Butler on the other hand was becoming just that: Mrs. Butler, the Marine officer's wife, "Bunny." Though she found herself in her dream life of globetrotting adventure, she realized that the price was to have her movements dictated by, and her identity eclipsed by, her ever-more-famous husband.

There were only four other women on the SS *Ancon*, the ship Ethel took to Colón: two other wives whose husbands were in the Zone, the Butlers' nanny, and a stewardess. Every night at dinner, Ethel was forced to sit on the captain's right-hand side. He "is very hard to talk to and thinks us rather empty-headed, I guess," she wrote her grandmother. Most of the space on board was taken up by canal workers and cement.[1]

While the women weren't given respect as individuals, sending white women as a group to the Canal Zone had become a national priority. After rashes of disease and accidents provoked an early exodus of skilled workers, it had occurred "to officials that women might indeed be the key to success," as the historian Julie Greene has written.[2] Married men were given more spacious houses, and the U.S. government paid wives' travel expenses from the States. Ethel and the other wives were expected to do their part through domestic management, keeping their husbands

comfortable and productive, and defending their households against in-
festations of aggressive jungle insects and tropical diseases.

The dynamics could be alienating: women's clubs were set up to stop
"social discontent" and alleviate housewives' "isolation, monotony, and
boredom."[3] During his visit to the gold mine owned by Herbert Hoover's
company in Nicaragua, Smedley would write a letter to Ethel in which he
described the American ladies who'd hosted him for tea. "The usual type
of wives doomed to life in the bushes," he'd call them, "but very polite,
well behaved, [and] quite well dressed."[4] As Ethel may have noted, he did
not elaborate on what "type of wife" that was.

But living in the jungle was the price she had to pay to reunite their
growing family. Smedley greeted his wife and children on the dock at
Colón, then they set off together for the hour-and-a-half train ride to
their new home at Camp Elliott. "We had many views of the bed of
the canal—it is really inconceivable, the vastness of it," Ethel wrote her
grandmother of the trip. "I should think people would be discouraged
but I never saw such a busy wideawake place. Engines and trains pounding by and long lines of cars filled with dirt or stone or rubbish. Just
perpetual motion."[5]

Camp Elliott was perched on a hill overlooking the construction. The
Butlers were in a two-story house, raised off the ground on stilts for ven-
tilation and to prevent rats from nesting. Ethel adored the view from the
screened-in porch. "Very pretty at night with all the barracks and bunga-
lows lighted up," she wrote her grandmother, "quite like the view by night
from the Miyako Hotel in Kyoto." Smedley's office was across the street.

The house also came with a cook named Josephine. She, like many of
the men digging the canal, came from Barbados. Ethel told her grandmother the family was also looking for "a boy to wait on table, run er-
rands, keep shoes (and house) cleaned etc.," but that young male servants
"were very hard to find. Not like [in] the Philippines where they're as
plentiful as cocoanuts—or bananas."

Indeed, as much as the Canal Zone was a place of sweeping gender
disparities, it was even more rigidly stratified by race. Instead of formally
designating spaces as "white" and "colored," as was being done in the
Southern United States, officials divided the payroll: U.S. citizens—nearly

all of whom were white—were listed on the "gold roll." Everyone else, especially the workers doing the most dangerous jobs of actually constructing the canal—the vast majority of whom were Black—were relegated to the "silver roll."[6]

Silver rollers were forced to use separate building entrances, ate worse commissary food, and were housed in poorly built shacks in so-called native towns. Nonwhite women were doubly discriminated against: paid even less and consigned to jobs as waitresses or house servants. Only white American civilians were granted paid vacation—six weeks in the States— and a month of sick leave every year.[7]

Apartheid was billed as a mark of American modernity in the Zone, as much of an advance as its hospitals and movie theaters. The project's chief sanitary officer, Col. William Gorgas, argued that separating whites from everyone else would protect them from disease.[8] (This was not a fringe idea: Gorgas was the president of the American Medical Association at the time.)

To differentiate themselves from the "natives," white residents started calling themselves "Zonians." The colonial culture they built would define life in the Canal Zone and politics in Panama for generations to come.

Smedley's long missions to Nicaragua in 1910 and 1912 overlapped with Ethel and the children's stay in Panama. Although she had moved to Panama to be with him, she was left alone in the house on stilts with Josephine and the kids for months at a time. Once, she returned from a shopping trip to Panama City to find that Smedley had deployed to Nicaragua without saying goodbye. Many of her letters to him throughout that time were filled with longing: "Precious one I am so proud of thy wonderful power and brain and abilities," she gushed in one, "my ittie Piddie!—good night for the present—am writing in thy own boudoir!"[9]

Absent as he often was, Butler's exploits in Nicaragua increased his fame and cemented the couple's status in the Corps. Smedley was given command of Camp Elliott, the same position his mentor, Littleton Waller, had held seven years earlier. As many of Smedley's old friends were being drummed out or dying (Pete Wynne, his body wrecked by alcoholism, died of tuberculosis in March 1912), Smedley's star was rising. The base was a must-see for visiting dignitaries because it was positioned near the most critical part of the project, the Culebra Cut—the channel through the continental divide that had doomed Ferdinand de Lesseps's earlier French attempt. Smedley was at the railroad to personally receive President Taft on his visit in 1910. After Taft reviewed the battalion, Ethel hosted the prodigious head of state, and his famously relentless appetite, for a buffet luncheon in the Camp Elliott bandstand.[10]

Each day, the Butlers' house would shake with the noise of nearby dynamite blasts, steam shovels, and rockslides. At quitting time, the train whistles would moan as they carted out the dead.

Today, Panama City has several museums dedicated to the history of the canal. Many tourists flock to the Museo del Canal, housed in a French Second Empire hotel that was the headquarters of de Lesseps's company. Sightseeing buses seem to prefer the Miraflores Visitor Center, where the tour begins with an IMAX movie and ends on a veranda where guests can watch ships passing through one of the canal's famous locks and dams.

I, on the other hand, was the only visitor on a sunny Saturday afternoon at a small gallery in the working-class neighborhood of El Marañón. Set up in a former Protestant chapel built by workers from Barbados in 1910, the Afro-Antillean Museum of Panama features family heirlooms and black-and-white photos captioned in English and Spanish. Its small collection is almost all the physical memory that remains of the thirty thousand West Indian workers who did almost all the work of actually digging the canal.[11]

Teddy Roosevelt had wanted the canal completed with white labor, but the managers weren't willing to pay the salaries white Americans were accustomed to. An early attempt to import workers from China was stymied by U.S. anti-Chinese exclusion laws. Recruiting African Americans would have angered employers in the U.S. South.[12]

There were not nearly enough people in Panama to do the job, had they even been willing: the number ultimately needed for construction was equivalent to more than one-eighth the new republic's entire population. That left the U.S. government to rely, as the French had, on workers from the Caribbean. Their stories are mostly absent from the better-funded museums, which focus on celebrating the technological feats and leaders involved. But in the humid basement of the Afro-Antillean Museum, at a table covered with a vinyl cloth, the librarian handed me a bound blue volume. The faded gold embossing on the cover read: *Letters from Isthmian Canal Construction Workers.*

The letters had been solicited in 1963 for a competition held in anticipation of the canal's fiftieth anniversary. One hundred and twelve entries were verified for inclusion. First prize was $50.

The entrants knew who they were trying to impress. Many included compliments about American officials ("Lots of fevers . . . but Doctor Gorgas try his best"). A few concluded with an exuberant "God Bless America!" The letters also manifested a genuine pride in their accomplishments. A West Indian immigrant named Reginald Beckford, a jeweler by trade, recounted his fellow workers keeping and awarding each other fossilized sharks' teeth they had found deep in the rock—hopeful proof that millions of years earlier the two oceans had indeed been connected. "Some must suffer for the good and welfare of the others for where [there] is no Cross there may be no Crown," a worker named Harrigan Austin wrote.[13]

Suffer they had. The ways to be injured or killed in the digging seemed endless. Workers were electrocuted, ripped apart by explosions, crushed by falling rocks and equipment, and run over by trains. Far fewer died of yellow fever under the Americans than under the French, thanks to Carlos Finlay and Walter Reed's work in Cuba showing that mosquitoes transmitted the disease. But the control methods were crude. A Bajan (as people from Barbados are known) named Joseph Brewster recalled having to buy himself a "small bottle containing kerosene and coconut oil, which was rubbed on the exposed parts" of his body to keep biting insects away.[14]

It was not an infallible solution. "I saw mosquitoes, I say this without fear of exaggeration, by the thousands attack one man," wrote a worker named Alfred E. Dottin. "There were days that we could only work a few hours because of the high fever racking our bodies—it was a living hell."[15]

I kept flipping through the letters. Horror resonated on page after page:

I recollect on one occasion shovel 210 fell over covering 6 men. The crane had to be brought to raise this shovel. All the men died . . . [16]

The flesh of men flew in the air like birds. Many days johncrows feed on the bowels of men around the jongles [*sic*] . . . [17]

As the lightning flashed it caught a galvanized sheet iron afire it ripped it off the small shanty and struck the foreman of a [European] Spaniard right above his chin . . . the shock went through his body . . . he was killed [instantly] . . . [18]

The Engineer applied his brakes suddenly, and the tiles from both cars ran together, caught the brakesman between the two sets of tiles and squeezed him to sudden death . . . [19]

I shall never forget the train loads of dead men being carted away daily, as if they were just so much lumber . . . [20]

As I was lost in reading, the door creaked open. A pair of older women walked in. It turned out the weekly meeting of the museum's Society of Friends was scheduled for that day. The coordinator asked if I wanted to stay.

While I helped the ladies set up the metal folding seats, other members filtered in. Though nearly all were born in Panama, they greeted each other in the Caribbean English they learned from their parents and grandparents. That language itself, I learned, was a symbol of the West Indians' difficult position on the isthmus: caught between the English-speaking empire that exploited them and the Spanish-speaking Panamanian majority that has never fully accepted them.

"They refuse to speak English and they discriminated against us because we spoke English," said a woman in an orange-and-green-printed summer dress with close-cropped salt-and-pepper hair. "But if you didn't speak English, you couldn't be employed by the Americans."

Her name was Ines Sealy. It was her eightieth birthday. (The meeting would conclude with the singing of "Happy Birthday" to her in English and Spanish, over servings of bread pudding with vanilla ice cream.) Sealy was born in Panama City to a Bajan father who'd worked in the construction of the canal and a mother who'd come as a girl from Saint Lucia. After retiring from the canal commissary in 1992, she got the last laugh on the monolingual Panamanians: selling them her skills as a translator and English teacher so they could find work in the Canal Zone.

"What brings you to Panama?" Ines asked me.

I told her about Smedley Butler, and my travels to learn about the legacy of America's empire.

"Ah," she said, with a little laugh. "You're studying how they had a spoon in everybody's soup."

West Indian workers were at the bottom of the hierarchy in the canal construction. Above them were Southern Europeans, mainly from Spain and Spain's former colonies. Those "semi-white" workers, as U.S. government officials sometimes referred to them, were, in turn, paid worse and ranked far behind the white American managers, many of whom had transferred to Panama straight from the ongoing occupations of the Philippines, Puerto Rico, and Cuba.[21]

Atop the pyramid was the chief engineer, Lt. Col. George Washington Goethals. Goethals had previously run Army logistics for the U.S. conquest of Puerto Rico. He saw digging the canal as a kind of war, too: against the land, the elements, and foreign rivals. The American press could not praise him enough for his work ethic and brutal efficiency. President Taft and Goethals posed together for souvenir postcards in matching white suits.[22]

"In all my years . . . I have known of only one benevolent dictator," Butler would later say: "General George W. Goethals."[23]

The workers saw him as an oppressor. "Going to work on the labor train was like mingling with cattle on a drive," Alfred Dottin, one of the West Indian canal builders, noted in his 1963 letter. "If you were ever seen getting off the trains before they stopped, you would be arrested and sentenced to 10 days in jail."

Thanks to the treaty Philippe Bunau-Varilla negotiated with the United States back in 1903, the U.S. enjoyed "all the rights, power and authority within the zone . . . which the United States would possess and exercise if it were the sovereign of the territory." The residents who were not born U.S. citizens were afforded few rights. In a 1907 case arising from the murder of a Bajan woman by her laborer husband, the U.S. Supreme Court affirmed that—as in the Philippines, Puerto Rico, and other recently annexed islands—the Canal Zone was "foreign in a domestic sense," and that the U.S. Constitution thus did not apply to its residents.[24]

Zone police were recruited mostly from the ranks of veterans of the imperial wars, and wore a uniform copied from Teddy Roosevelt's Rough Riders in Cuba. Caribbean immigrants were hired to police their side of the color line. Some infiltrated labor organizing attempts and reported activists to U.S. officials, who were in turn given "sweeping powers of deportation."[25] The police also swept the Zone to root out gambling, prostitution, and murder.

Standing behind them all was the most powerful armed force on the isthmus. The Marines stood ready to act as a police auxiliary—to "quell riots, strikes, and popular uprisings, to provide support for endangered presidential administrations, and to oversee elections," as Greene, the historian, has written. The Marines were, as one of Butler's predecessors at Camp Elliott (and a future Corps commandant), John H. Russell, told Goethals, "as essential for the completion of the Canal as the steam shovel."[26]

But at times, the troops' combination of entitlement and aggressiveness threatened to upend the whole project.

On July 4, 1912, Butler attended an Independence Day sports competition in Balboa, on the outskirts of Panama City. It was billed as a friendly competition between the Marines, a team of civilians, and the Army's Tenth Infantry. But Butler had deeper hopes. The Tenth had arrived in Panama a year earlier and seemed poised to supplant the Marines. A Marine win, Smedley imagined, might show the War Department which branch was fittest to oversee the security of the Zone.[27]

There appears to have been some dispute over who won. The argument devolved into a fight, and the fight became a riot. It spilled across a wide boulevard—named, appropriately, Fourth of July Avenue—into Panamanian-controlled territory, and the red-light district of Cocoa Grove. At some point, the troops, "a bunch of whom were plenty drunk," a Panamanian newspaper reported, turned their energy on the local establishments, "throwing chairs, tables, liquor bottles, etc." Some tore down street signs and threw lighted firecrackers into buildings and carriages. Others began manhandling and beating sex workers.[28]

Panama City was an international place. There were Spanish anarchists and Bengali peddlers. Chinese merchants wore lapel pins with the picture of Sun Yat-sen, the revolutionary physician who had just declared a new Republic of China. West Indians played dominoes and discussed the latest stories in *La Prensa,* a newspaper that had been edited by the Jamaican-born Black nationalist Marcus Garvey in Colón until a few months before.

That is to say, the spectacle of foreigners in Cocoa Grove—even drunk, noisy foreigners—was not unusual. So the fact that the bars started shuttering their doors is an indication of how dangerous locals perceived the riot to have been. Some Panamanians heard the Americans' aggressive, inebriated chants—possibly about their interservice rivalry, if not about the Fourth of July in general—and interpreted them as political taunts at their expense. An Afro-Panamanian saloon owner pushed several Marines out of her club. Women threw bottles at the troops. Boys hurled rocks. A crowd ran to grab a nearby Panamanian policeman, shouting: "¡Los americanos se habían vuelto locos!" (Meaning: The Americans have gone insane.)[29]

The Panamanian National Police were eager for an opportunity to reassert their authority over Panama City. Three days earlier, they had been pushed aside as Zone Police took over the capital to manage a preliminary presidential election. With that vote now over, and the U.S.-preferred candidate now on his way to certain victory, the officers charged into Cocoa Grove with rifles, revolvers, and clubs. When the Americans started punching, kicking, and choking the Panamanian police, the officers fired into the crowd, then charged. A bartender from California was bayoneted to death. At least two Marines, three Panamanian police, and several civilians were seriously injured.[30]

Butler, meanwhile, had stayed back in the Canal Zone, no doubt savoring the victory he was certain his Marines had won, when he overheard someone talking about the riot. He raced to the red-light district and found bedlam. "I tried to hurl thunder at the men, but they were beyond the rational stage," he later wrote. He ordered his military police to round up all the Marines and soldiers they could, but Panamanian police had gotten to some of them first. One Marine private later recalled being marched through the street in his underwear, then thrown into a filthy cell with "9 or 10 negroes."[31]

Butler called Goethals, infuriated. ("God-Damned Black Cowards," Smedley wrote his father of the incident; his men, he said, were "just children playing and were bitten by mad dogs.") Goethals called the outgoing puppet president, Pablo Arosemena, and in short order the arrested servicemen were released back into U.S. custody. Butler's final task was to make restitution to the injured Panamanian police—"ten dollars a jaw to settle for the facial damages," Butler later groused.[32]

Panamanians were equally enraged. "A large majority of the Americans feel themselves superior to any Panamanian. This is inherent in their race, in any race of conquerors," the newspaper *Los Hechos* wrote.[33]

Instead of offering restitution to the shopkeepers and working-class residents of Cocoa Grove, U.S. officials demanded that the Panamanians pay a substantial indemnity to *them*. A nineteen-year-old Panamanian police officer was convicted of the murder of the American bartender. He died in jail before he could be sentenced.[34]

As negotiations over the indemnity dragged on, further violence between off-duty American troops and Panamanians erupted in Panama City and Colón, killing several on both sides. The U.S. ordered the national police to hand over all their rifles. This step was so egregious, even the president the Americans had helped install could not stay silent. "This attitude toward a sovereign state which has given to the U.S. evident proofs of friendship and loyalty is incomprehensible," he wrote. U.S. officials simply demanded his compliance, referring back to the 1903 canal treaty that gave the Americans the right to intervene in the port cities at any time.[35]

For Panamanians, the Cocoa Grove riot and its fallout would become an enduring symbol of U.S. domination over their lives—proof that, nearly a decade after the U.S. had engineered their separation from Colombia, they were not independent at all.

For Chief Engineer Goethals, the tumult hardened his conviction that the Canal Zone should be completely cut off from the rest of Panama. In 1912, he had told a Senate committee that no one should inhabit the

Canal Zone "excepting the necessary operating force and the military." The tens of thousands of Panamanians still living in the "native towns" of the Zone were a security hazard, he explained—and, citing Dr. Gorgas's racist theories, a sanitation risk. Once construction was completed, an uninhabited jungle would provide the optimal buffer for canal defense.[36]

"What would you do with the people you have got there now?" a senator asked the chief engineer.

"I would drive them all out of there," Goethals replied.[37]

Today, the former Fourth of July Avenue is a busy highway called Avenida de los Martires—the Avenue of the Martyrs. The leafy parklands of Ancón Hill in the former American Zone lie on one side. On the other, where Cocoa Grove used to be, are crowded pink and green apartment buildings topped with billboards for Pepsi and presidential candidates.

A mile or so farther stands a series of monuments depicting young people climbing fences and a streetlight. Several are carrying the Panamanian flag. The statues represent the martyrs the avenue is named for—killed not in the riot that occurred under Butler's watch but one that occurred decades later, in many ways as a result.

Following Goethals's recommendation, on December 5, 1912, President Taft signed an executive order authorizing the depopulation of the Canal Zone. Zone police posted notices reading: "You are hereby notified to remove or destroy your building."[38]

Over forty thousand Panamanians were displaced.[39] Cities older than Jamestown or Plymouth Colony were forcibly vacated, land that had been farmed for centuries abandoned. Like the Cubans and the Filipinos before them, the Panamanians were used and betrayed. Because their own government was complicit in the U.S. colonial project, they had even less recourse. In 1914, an anonymous group of victims penned a protest letter to Goethals. Though the writers knew they would be "smothered by the indifference" of "the powerful and rich Government of the United States," they kept faith that "the All Powerful, the only impartial judge without a salary, the giver of truth and justice, will know how in good time to crucify those guilty of what we are suffering at the hands of the imperial Yankee represented by you."[40]

Over the decades that followed, Panamanians were occasionally allowed across Fourth of July Avenue to gawk at the luxurious homes and grassy lawns of the Canal Zone. "As a child living in Panama, I saw the Zone as a place of desire and denial," the Panamanian historian Marixa Lasso has written. "There was something magical about the contrast between the jungle and the towns with their impeccable lawns, swimming pools, and air-conditioned houses. . . . At the same time, the chain-link fences with 'Do Not Trespass' signs and checkpoints at the gates of the twelve military bases were a constant reminder of the Zone's many restrictions."[41]

By the early 1960s, some Panamanians were inspired by the Cuban Revolution to demand a degree of sovereignty over the Canal Zone. Some even demanded the U.S. hand over control of the canal itself. Panamanian nationalists won a symbolic victory in 1963, when President John F. Kennedy ordered that the Panamanian national flag—a quartered red, white, and blue banner—be raised beside the Stars and Stripes in civilian areas of the Zone.

"Zonians"—the majority white U.S. citizens living inside the fence—were livid. They tried to pressure the Canal Zone's governor, Maj. Gen. Robert J. Fleming, U.S. Army, into rescinding the order. But Fleming had neither the power nor inclination to do so. He had come to resent the chauvinism of the Americans he oversaw. "They've been isolated so long they've developed a reactionary mentality," Fleming told the *Saturday Evening Post*. "It's the perfect place for the guy who's 150 percent American and 50 percent whiskey."[42]

Fleming blunted the flag order in cut-the-baby-in-half fashion: he would stop flying the U.S. flag in front of Canal Zone schools, police stations, and post offices, so that a Panamanian flag wouldn't be required. This only infuriated Zonians more. "We want just the American flag flying—it proves our sovereignty. The next step, if they have their way, will be just to fly the Panamanian flag," an outraged seventeen-year-old girl in Cristóbal, the Zone town outside Colón, told *Life* magazine.[43]

In early January 1964, Zonians staged protests, raising the U.S. flag everywhere they could. The students at the American-run Balboa High School (mascot: the Bulldogs) walked out of class and raised Old Glory on the school flagpole overlooking the canal, then started a round-the-clock vigil to prevent it from being taken down. The local Elks Club and Veterans of Foreign Wars lodges provided the students with blankets and meals.

Word that the Zonians had raised their flag crossed Fourth of July Avenue. On January 9, a group of students from the premier high school in Panama City, the Instituto Nacional, marched to Balboa High carrying a silk Panamanian flag. A Zone police captain informed them that they could not proceed, "since there was only one pole and a U.S. flag already flew on it," as one historian described. The Panamanian students began singing their national anthem—the "Himno Istmeño," or Isthmian Hymn—only to be drowned out by Balboa Bulldogs and their parents belting out "The Star-Spangled Banner." A scuffle broke out, and the Panamanian flag was torn. Zonians shouted: "Panamanians, go home!"[44]

The students went back across the fence line, kicking over trash cans and throwing rocks at streetlights. Then a larger group of Panamanians appeared along the fence line carrying flags, rocks, and Molotov cocktails. A few tried to tear down what they called the Valla de la Vergüenza—the fence of shame—to plant their flags on the American side. Zone Police fired tear gas. Panamanians threw rocks. The Americans opened fire.

Nineteen-year-old Ascanio Arosemena* was shot through the lung and aorta, likely while trying to help wounded protesters escape. He would be the first "martyr" to die. Panamanian protesters smashed traffic lights and burned cars with Canal Zone license plates. As the riot escalated, the U.S. embassy was stoned and a U.S. government library burned down. Rioters broke into businesses symbolic of American imperialism. Sears was looted. The new Pan American Airlines building, Chase Manhattan Bank, and the Goodyear and Firestone tire outlets were sacked.

Unrest spread across Panama. Army barracks were set on fire at the U.S. base at Río Hato. American employees were evacuated from the banana plantations of the Chiriqui Land Company, a Panamanian subsidi-

---

* No known relation to the puppet president Arosemena from fifty years earlier.

ary of United Fruit. By the morning of January 13, 1964, at least twenty Panamanians and four U.S. soldiers had been killed.[45]

The flag riots made the cover of *Life* and were featured in *Newsweek*. The *New York Times* blamed both sides: the Zonians' "colonial mentality" on the one hand; the Panamanians' "unjust, unfair and ungrateful" nature on the other.[46] American conservatives insisted the riots were a Communist plot.

Panama recalled its ambassador and broke off relations with the power that had midwifed the country into existence six decades before. Those ties were reestablished a year later, after President Lyndon Johnson opened negotiations on a new treaty aimed ultimately at handing control of the canal to Panama. The terms were finalized more than a decade later by President Jimmy Carter and Panama's de facto leader, the U.S.-trained commandant of the Panamanian Guardia Nacional, Gen. Omar Torrijos.

The treaty was bitterly opposed by U.S. conservatives. The Canal Zone "is sovereign United States Territory every bit the same as Alaska and all the states that were carved from the Louisiana Purchase," Ronald Reagan said in a 1976 campaign speech. The future president lied profligately about the history of the canal, claiming falsely that "our Navy did not intervene to bring about the secession of Panama," that the Panamanians "knew what they were doing" when they let Bunau-Varilla give away their rights in the Zone, and implied that Americans—as opposed to Caribbean conscripts—had done the actual digging.[47] (Conservative Republican Senate candidate S. I. Hayakawa said, more cheekily: "I think we should keep it. We stole it fair and square."[48])

Though the nationalist anger stoked by the canal fight would help Reagan win the White House a few years later, in the moment, the U.S. hard-liners lost. Proponents of the treaty argued that in an age of nuclear missiles and aircraft carriers too big to fit through the locks, the canal had outlived its military usefulness. So long as the treaty ensured the canal would remain an "open and neutral" artery of global capitalism— and that, ignoring the contradiction, U.S. warships could "go to the head of the line" whenever they needed to go through—Panama could do as good a job as Egypt had done since it took control of the Suez Canal in 1956.[49]

Two-thirds of Panamanians ratified the Torrijos-Carter treaties in a national plebiscite in 1977. The U.S. Senate followed suit months later. On October 1, 1979, with Panamanians parading with salsa bands and terrified Zonians hiding inside their homes, the Canal Zone was dissolved as a formal entity.[50] Its American institutions were handed over one by one: U.S. Army forts became residential areas and export processing zones. Balboa High School became a training center for canal employees, renamed for the first protester killed in the 1964 riots, Ascanio Arosemena.

The Zone would remain depopulated. Most of it today is Parque Nacional Soberanía—Sovereignty National Park. The abandoned Panamanian towns within, as well as the former Camp Elliott, are covered by jungle.

And on December 31, 1999—ninety-six years after the Marines helped sever the Republic of Panama from Colombia for the purpose of building it—Panama at last took sovereignty over the Panama Canal.

B utler had been on hand to see the first water flow through the canal. On Friday, October 10, 1913, in Washington, D.C., at exactly 2:01 P.M., the new president, Woodrow Wilson, tapped a telegraph key. It sent an electric current to Galveston, Texas, which traveled via submarine cable to Panama, then continued down a local circuit on the isthmus. One minute later, forty tons of dynamite blew up the Gamboa Dike, and millions of gallons of water flooded the Culebra Cut.[51]

Alfred Thayer Mahan, the military theorist who had pushed for Americans to dig the canal in the first place—nearing the end of his life at seventy-three—read about the triumph at his home in the Hamptons. Philippe Bunau-Varilla went to Panama to witness the blast in person. Arnold Alexander, a West Indian immigrant, wrote in his letter that he was at work putting the finishing touches on the new Empire Bridge when he heard the explosion. He stood and watched as the water rushed below.[52]

One of Butler's Marines was the first man "to pass in a boat through the hole in the Gamboa Dike," Smedley boasted in a letter to Maud. "One of the canal superintendents remarked . . . as he saw his little canoe shunt over the rapids that, 'By God if there ever is anything dangerous going on anywhere you will always find one of Butler's men right in the middle and always first.'"[53]

Smedley doesn't mention whether Ethel was there to witness it, too. It is likely she was resting nearby. A month earlier, she had stood at the bottom of the Cut, marveling at the man-made canyon and the stopped machinery. She was nearly eight months pregnant at the time. Eleven and a half days after the water began flowing through the canal, she gave birth to the couple's third and final child, Thomas Richard Butler, at Camp Elliott.

O n my last day in Panama City, I signed up for a walking tour with Víctor Peretz, a member of the indigenous Guna people, who runs a local nongovernmental organization for kids. We met late in the afternoon at the edge of the Spanish colonial Casco Viejo neighborhood, in front of the American Trade Hotel.

The white stucco manse was built in 1917 as an office building and luxury apartment by one of the conspirators in the 1903 secession plot, the Panamanian merchant banker Ramón Arias Feraud.[54] After Butler and the Marines sealed the secession with their show of force, Arias's American Trade Developing Company was given one of four banking contracts to handle U.S. government disbursements in the Canal Zone. His accountants thus helped handle the financial end of the "gold and silver" system of segregation.[55]

In the century that followed, the inequality and privation fostered under that system mired many of Panama City's oldest neighborhoods in poverty. Some, such as Casco Viejo, were transformed by a wave of gentrification that followed the Panamanian takeover of the canal. (When a consortium that included Arias's great-grandson bought back the abandoned office building to turn it into a boutique hotel in 2007, it was a graffiti-covered shell. Rooms when I was in town started at $359 a night.)

Other neighborhoods were unchanged. Víctor had promised to show me the "other side" of Panama City. So we turned our backs on American Trade and walked down into the barrio of El Chorrillo. It had been an overcast day, but the sun was finally starting to peek out as we walked down the cracked street. The buildings were mostly concrete, a few with tin roofs, with laundry hanging out to dry on clotheslines. Some boys were playing soccer. I picked up a strong whiff of chili dogs, before realizing Víctor had stopped to buy one fresh off a griddle at the back of a little white van.

Founded by West Indian canal construction workers in 1915, the barrio is best known for a few former residents: the boxer Roberto Durán, the poet Héctor Miguel Collado, and—most notoriously—the Panamanian dictator Manuel Noriega.

Noriega rose through the ranks of the National Guard of Panama, a force created during the Cold War along the lines of the Somozas' militia in Nicaragua. While being paid by the U.S. government to spy on leftist movements in Panama in the early 1960s, he enrolled at the U.S. Army's School of the Americas training center, then based in the Canal Zone. (Noriega's fellow alumni included the future heads of death squads and secret police across Latin America.) In 1970, Noriega was made Panama's chief of military intelligence. A year after, he was formally put on the payroll of the CIA.[56]

The Americans knew Noriega was running cocaine through Panama—in drugs, as in all things, the land bridge was an ideal nexus for trade. But he was too valuable an intelligence asset to give up. Among other things, Noriega let the Americans use the Canal Zone as a listening station to help run the CIA-managed coup in Chile in 1973 and helped carry out sabotage and spying against the Sandinistas in Nicaragua.[57]

After the 1981 death in a plane crash of Omar Torrijos, the de facto leader who had negotiated the canal handover, Noriega restructured the police and Guardia Nacional into a new army—the Panamanian Defense Forces (PDF)—and made himself its leader. At the same time, he reduced his personal involvement in narcotrafficking and concentrated on laundering drug money, using the almost entirely unregulated banking system set up in the early days of American rule over the Canal Zone to enrich himself.[58] By seizing all the levers of U.S. imperial control, Noriega became so powerful he did not even have to become president. He would choose Panama's leaders, and they would work for him.

In January 1989, a former director of the CIA, George Herbert Walker Bush, became president of the United States. Noriega, who had started working with Bush in 1976, must have thought he had won the lottery.[59] But with the Cold War coming to an end, Bush was pivoting to a War on

Drugs as a new frontier for defense contracts, surveillance, and a pretext for military control.

Once in office, Bush turned on his erstwhile employee, calling for Noriega to step down and imposing crippling sanctions on Panama. On December 15, 1989, the Panamanian national assembly named Noriega the country's "maximum leader of national liberation" and symbolically declared war on the United States.

The next day, a group of U.S. troops got into an argument with PDF soldiers at a roadblock in El Chorrillo. A Marine lieutenant named Robert Paz was shot. He died soon after at Gorgas Hospital in the former Canal Zone.[60]

On December 20, citing the Colombian-born U.S. Marine's death as a justification, the United States invaded Panama for the second time. The invasion was code-named "Operation Just Cause." Just before 1:00 A.M., two stealth fighters dropped a pair of two-ton bombs near the PDF's barracks at Río Hato. Paratroopers dropped across the countryside in what at the time was the largest U.S. airborne operation since World War II. An Army battalion fought its way down the Panama Canal from Colón.[61]

The brunt of the attack fell on El Chorrillo, where Noriega had built his personal headquarters, the Comandancia. Apache helicopters and armored vehicles fired volleys of missiles past the balconies of tenements as PDF forces returned mortar fire and rocket-propelled grenades. The barrio's residents fled or prayed under their beds. By 6:00 P.M., the Comandancia was in American hands. But Noriega was not there. He would resurface days later inside the Vatican embassy. It would take ten more days—including a siege during which U.S. troops blared a psych-ops playlist including Black Sabbath, Lee Greenwood's "God Bless the USA," and Twisted Sister's "We're Not Gonna Take It (Anymore)"—for the longtime U.S. operative to surrender.[62]

Víctor, who was twenty-eight when I met him, was not yet born in 1989. But having spent so much time in El Chorrillo, it seemed some of the trauma of what the locals call La Navidad Negra—Black Christmas—had worn off on him. He made sure to stop every time we passed graffiti marking the event, which was often: "Dec. 20, National Mourning" on a peeling corner; faded spray paint asking "How many died? 20–12–1989," across from a construction site promising new luxury condominiums. Artists were planning a mural that would feature a helicopter gunship over the words *Ni Olvido, Ni Perdón*. Neither forget nor forgive. An advertisement for a USAID project stood uneasily nearby.

We passed through a street market called "Salsipuedes." That means "get out if you can"—a reference to the street gangs that had dominated the neighborhood since the invasion. One gang had decorated a home-goods store with fresh graffiti—"20–12–89 *Fuera de Latinoámerica Yankee Asesino*"—out of Latin America, Yankee murderer.

I asked Víctor some of the gangs' names.

"Let's see. There's Los B.B.'s. Vietnam. Iraq. Pentágono . . ."

Funny names for people angry about Yankee imperialism, I observed.

He laughed. "Yes, I guess so. But look over there." He pointed down a block of decaying tenements that ended at the bay. On the other side of the water stood the skyscrapers of the Panama City financial district.

The banking system housed in those towers—the system first set up in Panama by financiers such as Ramón Arias and their American friends—ultimately eclipsed the value of the canal itself. The bankers who occupy those buildings have outdone Noriega, not to mention the gangs of El Chorrillo, in brazenness: much of an estimated $7.6 trillion in worldwide hidden offshore holdings—8 percent of the world's wealth—flows across the isthmus under the cover of generous bank secrecy laws.[63]

The money is often hidden in so-called shell corporations—companies that only exist on paper, to shield assets from lawmakers, regulators, and competitors. It stands to reason that such arrangements would be rife in Panama: it was, after all, a country godfathered into existence by Sullivan & Cromwell, the Wall Street law firm that pioneered the earlier concept of the "holding company," which allows trusts to hide their assets and evade regulation designed to limit their size.[64]

In 2016, millions of documents were leaked from the Panamanian law firm Mossack Fonseca. Nicknamed the Panama Papers, they revealed a global network of shell corporations used to commit fraud and evade taxes and international sanctions. The money of drug traffickers, the most powerful families in the Chinese Communist Party, Russian mafia, and American billionaires mixes, flows, and comes out untraceably clean along the banks of the Panama Canal. Some of the illicit funds were converted into real estate, in the form of the white-hued glass-and-steel towers shimmering before us.[65]

A former financial-crimes prosecutor in Panama singled out the tallest of the skyscrapers, a soaring white hotel and condominium complex, as a particularly egregious "vehicle for money laundering." The building's first sales manager was an admitted Brazilian money launderer with ties to Russian organized crime.[66] Its investors and buyers included a confessed cocaine smuggler from Chicago and Russians charged in multiple countries with human trafficking.[67] A few months before my visit, that building had been the scene of an armed standoff between the Panamanian government and security staff, caught in a fight between the building's ownership group and the American family that had licensed their name to it.[68]

"Do you recognize it?" Víctor asked me, pointing to the infamous high-rise across the bay. "The big one, taller than all the others. Looks like a sail."

I squinted. "Is that—"

"Yes!" he said. "The famous Trump Tower. Trump Tower Panama."

# TEN

## VERACRUZ

On a sweltering morning back in March 1900, three Americans and their indigenous guide climbed down from a Pullman railway car a few dozen miles from Tampico, a port town on the Gulf of Mexico. They hiked for miles in the subtropical heat, through dense vegetation, until they reached an area where a thick cloud of steam floated above a bubbling pool of black tar. The vapors burned their nostrils. The indigenous people living nearby called such pits *chapopote* or *nut*. Some had set up makeshift fences to keep straying livestock from getting pulled under.[1]

The party's leader, Edward L. Doheny, was a prospector. Forty-three years old, born in Fond du Lac, Wisconsin, he sported a thick, prematurely white broom mustache. Doheny had gotten his start surveying the seized Kiowa and Comanche territories in Kansas and Oklahoma with a federal team. He then spent years on his own traveling across the former Mexican lands of the western United States—the modern-day states of California, Nevada, Utah, Arizona, New Mexico, Texas, and parts of Colorado and Wyoming, all seized in the 1846–48 Mexican-American War—in search of silver and gold.[2]

Doheny's fortune came when he had noticed a horse-drawn wagon hauling *brea*, or pitch, in the formerly Mexican city of Los Angeles. The driver told him the stuff flowed freely in a nearby park and was sold as cheap fuel to factories nearby. Doheny bought a parcel of tarry land and, with the help of his partners and thirteen-year-old son, dug a well. They struck oil, setting off the Southern California oil boom.

Oil was a young industry at the time, geared mainly toward kerosene for lamps. It was dominated by John D. Rockefeller's Standard Oil, which, through its network of subsidiaries, refined three-quarters of the petroleum drilled in the United States. The only other known oil fields in the world were in the closed-off Russian Empire and the Dutch East Indies.[3] So when one of Doheny's fellow Wisconsinites, the president of the Mexican Central Railway, invited him to take his private railcar two thousand miles southeast to inspect the tar pits outside Tampico, the driller jumped at the chance.[4]

Facing his first chapopote, Doheny kicked over the makeshift fence and squatted beside the bubbling ooze. Carefully, he traced a finger across its surface. He held it briefly next to his white mustache, studying the vapors. Then he put the tar-soaked finger in his mouth, touched it to his tongue, and smiled.[5]

In January 1914, Butler and his Panama battalion were given transfer orders to the Gulf of Mexico. Smedley and Bunny sadly packed up their lives at Camp Elliott, a place they had learned to call home for four years. In anticipation of the danger waiting in Mexico, Ethel and their children were booked home to Philadelphia.

Butler was told nothing about the mission. All he knew was that, despite his efforts to convince the War Department otherwise, the U.S. Army Tenth Infantry was being given sole command over the Canal Zone. He was furious at this, furious at being ripped from his family, and had a throbbing toothache to boot. "To have the Marines, who took this place, withdrawn *entirely* before the ships go through is terribly hard," he wrote his mother. He promised he would apply for a transfer back to Philadelphia, "as soon as I find there is nothing doing in Mexico."[6]

There was, in fact, a lot going on in Mexico. While Butler had been busy in Central America, the United States' immediate neighbor to the south had fallen into a complicated civil war. For over three decades, the dictator Porfirio Díaz had ruled Mexico with a philosophy of terror and technocracy. He imprisoned enemies, fixed or canceled elections, ordered critics killed, and prosecuted wars of enslavement and ethnic cleansing against native peoples. The period was known as the Porfiriato, and its net effect was to make Mexico's ruling class and a small middle class wealthier, while keeping the vast majority of Mexicans very poor.

American elites profited as well. Díaz had come to power with the support of New York financiers and Texas landowners. By the end of the Porfiriato, U.S. citizens owned an astounding 130 million acres of Mexican territory—nearly 27 percent of what was left after the 1846–48 Mexican-American War. Foreigners controlled more than half of Mexico's coasts and borderlands and most of its railroads. Some Americans oversaw haciendas where workers toiled in conditions a State Department investigator reported were tantamount to slavery. Along the Gulf coast, where Edward L. Doheny had struck oil in 1900, U.S. oil companies (and one key British competitor) were making millions drilling between the port cities of Tampico and Veracruz—a stretch they called the Faja de Oro, or Golden Lane. As was the custom wherever Americans ran things, segregation was observed: white U.S. citizens on the platforms, Mexicans on the oil-soaked ground.[7]

Sensing the naked inequality was brewing unrest, Porfirio Díaz had allowed a liberal landowner, Francisco Madero, to run against him for Mexico's presidency in 1910. When it seemed Madero might win, Díaz had him arrested. Madero called for a general uprising. Facing an explosion of dissent and violence, Díaz resigned. He rushed to his most profitable Atlantic port—Veracruz—where he boarded a German-flagged steamer and fled for France.

In an attempt to build a stable coalition, the victorious Madero appointed some of Díaz's technocrats to be his advisers and ordered his revolutionary army to lay down its arms. The commanders who had helped Madero oust Díaz in the name of land reform and redistribution felt betrayed. The most radical—Francisco "Pancho" Villa in the north and Emiliano Zapata in the south—declared the revolution would continue against him. But just as the rebels were preparing to move against Madero in February 1913, he was overthrown by someone else—the belligerent conservative Gen. Victoriano Huerta.

Huerta was a military man and a longtime Díaz loyalist. He had joined Madero's revolution because he sensed which way the winds were blowing, but his heart was never in it. He had made a simple calculation: he and his Mexican Federal Army units were in the capital; Pancho Villa and Zapata's rebels were farther away. For his opportunistic overthrow of the originator of the Mexican Revolution, the bald and bullying Huerta would be known to future generations of Mexicans as "The Jackal."

Huerta's coup was carried out with U.S. support. President William Howard Taft liked the conservative general, who, he imagined, might restore the "firm hand in Mexico" Taft had admired in Porfirio Díaz.[8] After Madero and his vice president had been arrested by Huerta's agents, Taft's ambassador, Henry Lane Wilson, hosted Huerta at the U.S. embassy in Mexico City. As the general plunged into one of his legendary drinking sessions, the U.S. ambassador promised him that the United States would recognize him as president if he pledged to protect American property.[9] Madero and his vice president were assassinated four days later in a clumsily staged "attack" en route to a federal penitentiary.

But, as Huerta would not be the last to learn, the trouble with doing business with the United States was that, while Americans subverted democracy abroad, they still practiced a limited form of it at home. Huerta's coup took place in February 1913. But Taft had lost the election a few months before. (Teddy Roosevelt, bored in retirement, had launched a surprise third-party bid, splitting the Republican vote.) With just a few weeks left in his term, Taft decided to withhold recognition, and punted the Huerta problem to his successor.

That successor, Woodrow Wilson, was very different from his predecessors. Wilson was the first Democrat to occupy the White House in two decades, the first Southerner elected since the Civil War, and an academic. Over the course of his career as a political scientist—which included the presidency of Princeton University—Wilson had adapted Teddy Roosevelt's Progressivism into a new liberal idealism. His goal was not to ensure U.S. global supremacy, as Roosevelt wanted, nor unfettered American capitalism, as Taft had sought, but peace, justice, and democracy by promoting the ideal social order. It just so happened that, to Wilson, that ideal social order looked a lot like the racially stratified antebellum South in which he was born.

Wilson's foreign policy was less well formed.[10] He ran on the old neo-Confederate Democratic platform, which condemned America's "experiment in imperialism" as "an inexcusable blunder."[11] On Election Day, twenty thousand Filipinos gathered in Manila to hear the ousted president Emilio Aguinaldo and a new generation of Filipino leaders cheer Wilson's victory and its implicit promise of Philippine independence.[12] The peoples colonized under McKinley, Roosevelt, and Taft were further encouraged when Wilson chose the anti-imperialist stalwart William Jennings Bryan as his secretary of state.

But foreign policy had barely come up in the election. If it had, Wilson might have been forced to admit he had supported annexing the Philippines, Hawai'i, and Guam in 1898; and that while he believed the Philippines and Puerto Rico might *eventually* have self-rule, he had warned against giving "the generous gifts of complete individual liberty or the full-fangled institutions of American self-government" to "undeveloped peoples, still in the childhood of their political growth." Nor was he philosophically opposed to Frederick Jackson Turner's brand of expansionism. To the contrary, Wilson had been an early, influential collaborator of Turner's, who helped shape his Frontier Thesis when he taught Turner as a graduate student at Johns Hopkins.[13]

Still, Wilson had heard enough about Mexico to know that General Huerta was everything he hated in a leader: a belligerent, authoritarian drunk who'd taken power in a bloody coup. Over the course of 1913, Wilson dispatched "a mix of diplomatic agents, consular officers, intelligence officers and wealthy businessmen with White House connections" to collect intelligence in Mexico.[14] He was horrified to learn of his ambassador's role in Huerta's coup and fired him. Wilson sent his own envoy, John Lind, to demand that Huerta hold free elections and relinquish power. Huerta refused.

Much of the information Wilson was getting about Huerta and Mexico came from the clique that had carried him to Washington. As a relative political newcomer, Wilson had only been able to finagle the Democratic nomination through the help of the Southern Democrats—especially the powerful boss of the Texas Democratic Party, Edward M. House. House, who went by the unearned nickname "Colonel," became Wilson's top unofficial adviser, bringing with him his close ties to banking, real estate, and the oil industry on both sides of the Rio Grande. House had persuaded Wilson to appoint several of his Texas cadres to cabinet posts.[15]

Colonel House's Texas clique was particularly interested in a specific part of Mexico: the Golden Lane. In 1908, Henry Ford had unveiled the first mass-produced automobile—the gasoline-powered Model T— sending demand for petroleum soaring. Among the firms that flocked to the Golden Lane to capitalize on the boom was the Texas Company, a relative newcomer in the petroleum game that would soon shorten its name to Texaco.

The Texas Company's directors had supported Madero's revolution against Díaz in exchange for his support for their drilling operations. With Madero dead, they shifted their allegiance to Venustiano Carranza, the governor of Coahuila—the Mexican border state white Texas settlers had split off from three-quarters of a century before. The oilmen knew that Huerta favored European partners, such as the British oil magnate Weetman Pearson, whose Mexican Eagle Petroleum Company was based in Veracruz. They also knew and trusted Carranza, with whom they had been doing business for years. When Carranza declared his state in rebellion against Huerta—enlisting Pancho Villa as a general in his "Constitutionalist" army—the future Texaco began pushing for the Wilson administration to support the rebels' bid.[16]

In November 1913, the oilmen's lawyer in Mexico City, William F. Buckley Sr., wrote his old friend from Austin, Colonel House. In addition to Texaco, Gulf, and Standard Oil, Buckley was connected to an even wealthier Texan: James Stillman, the chairman of the powerful National City Bank of New York, where many of the oil profits were deposited. Stillman was the Democratic Party's wealthiest donor, and at that very moment engaged in delicate negotiations with Wilson over what the president hoped would be his signature domestic reform: the Federal Reserve Act. So when Buckley spoke, House—and thus Wilson—was sure to listen.

What Buckley had to say was this: The war between Huerta's *federales* and Carranza's Constitutionalists was getting out of control. Attacks were mounting against American property. Revolutionaries had blown up U.S. mines and disrupted the coffee harvest in Veracruz. Fighters had even attacked and looted the estate of Colonel House's cousin Henry, who ran Texaco's operations in Tampico. If something was not done soon, he warned, the U.S. oil companies might be forced to cease production. Or, worse, a European power might invade and take over the Golden Lane for itself.

The value of the oil riches under the Golden Lane was not news to anyone in Washington. U.S. Navy spies had spent years gathering intelligence on the oil resources available between Tampico and Veracruz. As the war between Huerta and Carranza's forces had worsened, the Navy Department cabled its office of intelligence to "immediately estimate minimum force required . . . for the protection of oil wells, pipelines, pumping stations, and oil in storage."[17]

But now the oil companies were ready to ask directly for help. Buckley told his old friend, Wilson's chief adviser: "We all believe here that there is but one solution of this difficulty, and that is American intervention."[18]

In late February 1914, Smedley Butler was summoned to the flagship USS *Florida,* in the Gulf waters off Veracruz. Rear Admiral Frank Friday Fletcher met him at the gangway. The "Big Admiral" asked Butler, as Smedley recounted soon after to Bunny, "if I wanted a good job."[19]

Waiting aboard to meet them both was Wilson's new personal envoy to Mexico, John Lind. Lind had gotten the appointment not because of any particular knowledge of Mexican politics (he had none), but because he was a reliable Democratic Party operative: a former progressive governor of Minnesota who was friends with Secretary of State Bryan.[20] All Lind knew was that General Huerta was a dictator and a thug—"a Frankenstein devoid of all moral judgment," as he called him.[21]

The Texas clique had persuaded Lind that their neighbor, Carranza, would be an improvement. Lind had also read the glorious reports of Pancho Villa's victories against Huerta's forces, filed for *Metropolitan Magazine* by the socialist activist John Reed. The charismatic Villa—whose battlefield skill was exceeded only by his talent for self-promotion—would soon be featured in a hit movie, combining real battle footage with staged dramatic scenes, produced by the rising Hollywood filmmaker D. W. Griffith. The media blitz convinced Lind that the Constitutionalists could unseat Huerta if given the right push.

Lind was anxious to get started. If the Americans waited to act, he feared, they would find themselves in a repeat of the Boxer War: racing to Mexico City against European rivals, left to squabble over the spoils. Boxer echoes were everywhere he looked—news that the British were stockpiling machine guns at their Mexico City embassy brought to mind the siege of the legations in Beijing. The move "in effect places the Huerta

Government, so far as the Powers are concerned, in the same class with China and the semi-civilized countries of the East," Lind wrote.[22]

Fortunately, Lind had an expert on hand: a battle-scarred Marine, a veteran of the race to Beijing, who had recently put his legation-storming experience into action in Nicaragua. It was too dangerous to let Butler in on the details of the plan in earshot of the sailors on the ship. So on the first day of March, Admiral Fletcher took Smedley ashore and invited him onto a private railcar. Fifty miles out of town, near Xalapa, Butler was given his instructions: he was to pose as a civilian and make his way by train to Mexico City, collecting intelligence for an all-out invasion.

"In plain language," Butler later reflected, "I was to be a spy."[23]

Butler's cover story wasn't deep. He was introduced in Puebla state as the nephew of Samuel Morse Felton Jr.—Bunny's real-life uncle who had been president of the Mexican Central Railway a few years before. Posing as an investor, Butler was given access to the electric power plant, the city water system—"all the sights boring to a tourist," he wrote, "but vitally important to an invading army."

Back aboard the train, Butler climbed into the soaring mountains and descended into the Valley of Mexico. As he looked out on the mountains of Popocatépetl, the "smoking mountain," and Iztaccíhuatl, "the white woman"—said in Nahuatl lore to be the resting places of legendary Aztec lovers—it occurred to Butler that he was following the route that Cortés and the conquistadors had taken before him.

Butler was also retracing the steps of his predecessor Marines. In 1847, in the decisive campaign of the Mexican-American War, U.S. troops had seized Veracruz, then advanced two hundred miles inland along much the same route to capture Mexico City. The seaborn force had included 314 Marines, who marched under U.S. Army Gen. Winfield Scott in one of their rare inland invasions of the nineteenth century. Marines would immortalize their role in the capture of the Mexican military academy, Chapultepec Castle. They dubbed it "the Halls of Montezuma,"* and eventually featured it in the Corps hymn.

---

* The name was an anachronism: Chapultepec was built by a Spanish viceroy in 1785, more than two and a half centuries after the Aztec emperor Moctezuma Xocoyotzin was killed during the invasion of Hernán Cortés's conquistadors.

When he arrived in Mexico City, Butler changed his cover story. Now posing as a Secret Service agent looking for a criminal who'd supposedly enlisted in the Mexican army, he took detailed notes on military installations and eavesdropped on foreign diplomats' conversations. On his last day as a spy, Butler got enough of a sight of the Marines' beloved Halls of Montezuma to determine that "with artillery the top of the hill could be smashed to kingdom come." Then he hightailed it back to Veracruz, taking care to hide his maps while on the train.

After he rejoined the fleet, Butler sat down with Lind to draft the war plan. Butler would lead a thousand Marines inland by train, their speed and security guaranteed by the American employees of his uncle-in-law's former railway. In the capital, the Marines would fan out, disabling military strong points and seizing the radio station.[24]

Lind added the coup de grâce: the Marines would arrest Huerta and put the capital under U.S. military occupation until Carranza's forces arrived, or President Wilson decided what to do next. If Butler had any objection to his role in this planned regime change, he did not make a note of it.

In late March, Secretary Bryan cabled to say that the president was taking Lind and Butler's recommendations under consideration.[25] Powerful Democratic supporters, including the media mogul William Randolph Hearst—who was one of the biggest landowners in Mexico—were agitating to finish the job of 1848 with an all-out annexation. ("Our Flag should wave over Mexico as the symbol of the rehabilitation of that unhappy country and its redemption to humanity and civilization," Hearst would write in a full-page signed editorial two years later.[26])

As they waited for word, Butler noted that his spy run had solidified his reputation with the command. "My position in this Fleet is now assured and I spend my time running around in admiral's barges and being patted on the back by the whole crowd," he wrote Bunny from offshore at Veracruz.[27] It would eventually burnish his legend with the public as well: A decade later, with the help of a younger Marine turned pulp fiction writer, Butler would spin the experience into a sensationalized boys' novel called *Walter Garvin in Mexico*. In it, the lightly fictionalized hero narrowly escapes the clutches of Huerta's soldiers at Veracruz—though not before they rip off his shirt, revealing a familiar Marine Corps emblem tattooed on his chest.

But as the weeks went by in March 1914, Wilson cooled on the idea of a Butler-led march to Mexico City. Though his hatred of Huerta had only grown, like future presidents considering involvement from the Balkans to Syria, he had to weigh his preferred outcomes against the risk of getting swamped in a civil war. Mexico, owing to its massive size and relative wealth, could not be subdued as easily as the smaller Central American republics. So instead, Wilson hedged his bets: He lifted an arms embargo, facilitating the legal sale of arms to Carranza and Pancho Villa's northern rebels.

Meanwhile, he would keep the Marines, including Butler, and several warships off the Golden Lane, waiting for the moment to launch a more strategic strike.

Veracruz today remains Mexico's most important Gulf port, the maritime gateway to the east coasts of the Americas, as well as to Europe and Africa. Its busy shipyard, where forklifts load multicolored containers onto ships long into the night, is in turn a terminus on a rail network that connects as far north as Illinois, and a node on a highway system that can reach essentially anywhere on mainland North America. Because of that geography and infrastructure, Veracruz remains a supremely valuable prize for anyone trying to transport anything—whether oil, cars, or narcotics.

Mexico's illegal drug trade also traces its origins to 1914. In December of that year, Woodrow Wilson signed the first federal law limiting the sale of manufactured drugs. Until then, opium and cocaine had been legal and widely available across the United States. Cocaine was famously one of the titular ingredients in Coca-Cola; home shoppers could order morphine and hypodermic needles from the Sears Roebuck & Co. catalog. (Marijuana would not begin to be criminalized in the United States until 1937.)[28]

But concern had risen over the high numbers of opium addicts among the U.S. soldiers occupying the Philippines. Lawmakers were also looking for ways to criminalize new behaviors to feed an increasingly profitable system of underpaid prison labor, which had arisen in part to replace the free labor provided by enslaved African Americans. In that atmosphere, rumors spread freely that drugs such as cocaine would lead some, especially Black people in the South, to "disregard the barriers that society had established between different races," as the Mexican historian Gabriela Recio has written.[29]

In 1919, the states ratified the Eighteenth Amendment, prohibiting the manufacture, sale, and transportation of alcohol. The feds soon began targeting narcotics as well. As Americans became familiar with black markets during Prohibition, an international division of labor emerged: Canada specialized in supplying Americans with illegal liquor, and Mexicans took the lead on opium.

The era set a pattern that would endure: Mexicans transported the drugs across the border; Americans provided the customers and the cash. If rival officials or smugglers caused trouble, Americans would use the weapon-smuggling channels they established during the Porfiriato and revolution to provide the traffickers with guns to defend their turf. Rampant corruption in both the U.S. and Mexican federal narcotics enforcement systems ensured minimal interruption.

In the late 1970s, a Cuban exile named Alberto Sicilia Falcón made a breakthrough in Tijuana. Sicilia had apparently been trained by the CIA as a weapons smuggler in the effort to overthrow Fidel Castro. He made a deal, through a Honduran intermediary, to transport Colombian cocaine to the lucrative U.S. market. When the U.S. Drug Enforcement Agency tried to crack down on him, they ran into "strange pressures from Washington," as the researchers Peter Dale Scott and Jonathan Marshall have written.[30]

Sicilia was eventually double-crossed by his Mexican associates. His replacement as kingpin, Miguel Ángel Félix Gallardo, an ex-cop from the northwestern state of Sinaloa, organized competing trafficking operations into the first Mexican drug cartel.[31]

The Mexican gangsters were the beneficiaries of an American double game. It was the 1980s, and the Reagan administration was trying to link Communist Cuba and Sandinista Nicaragua to the narcotics trade in an effort to boost public support for U.S. involvement in Central America's civil wars. Ordered to crack down on "narcoterrorism," the DEA shut down Colombian distribution routes through the Caribbean, forcing more cocaine through Mexico. The result was that Félix Gallardo's Mexican cartel ended up handling 90 percent of the cocaine supply for the U.S. market.[32]*

After Félix Gallardo was betrayed and arrested by Mexican Federal Police in 1989, his syndicate splintered into competing factions. One of Félix's top lieutenants, Joaquin "El Chapo" Guzmán, founded the powerful Sinaloa Cartel. The hired muscle of the influential Gulf Cartel, based in the border town of Matamoros, broke off and formed one of the drug world's most feared gangs, Los Zetas. In the early twenty-first century, the competition over the billions to be made, fueled by American guns and money, exploded into a vicious nationwide war that would kill as many as 250,000 people.[33]

In 2011, I was sent to Mexico to cover the drug war for the Associated Press. My job was mostly to edit dispatches from Mexican correspondents on the carnage consuming their hometowns. Each day, I would field a barrage of nightmarish reports of severed heads discovered in plastic bags and armed men slaughtering bar patrons. More than once I had to politely decline a dispatch about the bodies of suspected informants being found hanging from a highway bridge. "Sorry," I told one, "we've already had two stories like that this week."

In September 2011, thirty-five corpses were found dumped beneath an overpass outside the Port of Veracruz. All showed signs of torture. Most had been strangled, one shot in the head, the rest bludgeoned to death. A message scrawled on a sheet warned: "This is what will happen to all the Zeta shits that don't leave Veracruz. This *plaza* has a new owner."[34]

---

* At the same time, the CIA was contracting the Mexicans' Honduran middleman, Juan Ramón Matta Ballesteros, to run weapons and supplies south to the Nicaraguan Contras. Scott and Marshall cite evidence that Félix Gallardo's associates hosted a training camp—run by the CIA under the cover of the Mexican federal police—where Contras trained as well. Lawyers for men accused of the 1985 murder of a DEA agent in Guadalajara alleged in U.S. federal court that "various agencies of the federal government, including the CIA," were allowing Félix Gallardo to smuggle cocaine into the United States in exchange for his support in the fight against the Sandinistas. The U.S. attorney on the case did not dispute the claim. See Kim Murphy, "Cover-Up Alleged in Drug Agent's Death," *Los Angeles Times*, Aug. 19, 1988, and Ryan Grim, Matt Sledge, and Matt Ferner, "Key Figures in CIA-Crack Cocaine Scandal Begin to Come Forward," *Huffpost*, Oct. 10, 2014.

It was the announcement of a new phase in the drug war. Over the next seven years, Veracruz would become an epicenter of the violence—rocked by waves of murders and reprisals by the cartels, and deadly interventions by the Mexican military with the support of the U.S. government. By 2018, there were more unmarked graves than municipalities in Veracruz state.[35]

In reality, "cartel" is a misnomer when it comes to Mexican organized crime. The word refers to a group of political actors or businesses that collude to control prices and production. The most powerful cartels of the twentieth century involved the oil industry: Standard Oil and its successors were part of several, many of which were later recombined into ExxonMobil. For many years, the most notorious cartel among Americans was the Organization of the Petroleum Exporting Countries, or OPEC, whose 1973 oil embargo caused great economic pain around the world.

The DEA had applied the term to Félix Gallardo's operation in the 1980s half-mockingly, because he had brought together competing racketeering syndicates.[36] Even after the syndicates went back to fighting one another, the name stuck. "Cartel" carried the sense of the kind of wealth and influence produced by collusions of corporate and political power that the Mexican gangsters wanted to emulate. But in the end, they could only approximate the violent destructive power of the real thing.

On April 9, 1914, one month after Butler's spy run, a U.S. Navy crew in Tampico was in desperate need of gasoline. Their go-to sources—gas stations run by a Standard Oil subsidiary and Weetman Pearson's Mexican Eagle—had been severely damaged in battles over control of the city between Carranza's Constitutionalists and Huerta's *federales*.[37]

The ship was the USS *Dolphin*—the same gunboat that had saved, after nearly wiping out, the Marines at Guantánamo Bay sixteen years before. Its captain learned about fuel cans stored in a German warehouse and sent nine sailors up a canal in a rowboat to collect them. Either the owner neglected to mention, or the officer ashore did not care, that the warehouse was in restricted territory. The sailors were loading the gas cans when they were confronted by Huerta's troops. The Mexicans shouted in Spanish. The Americans shouted in English. Before anyone knew what was going on, the Mexicans were pointing their rifles at the Americans, who immediately surrendered.

When word of the sailors' arrest (and prompt release) reached the commander of the U.S. squadron off Tampico, Rear Admiral Henry Mayo, he was incensed. Mayo was one of the last of an old school of U.S. Navy commanders, who, having come up at a time when long-distance communications were in their infancy, were entrusted to make decisions independent of the chain of command. He seized on the fact that two of the sailors had been detained aboard a U.S.-flagged vessel—the dinghy—and declared it "an assault on sovereign American territory." Mayo demanded a public apology: the Mexican federal army was to "hoist the American flag in a prominent position on shore and salute it with twenty-one guns."[38]

It was the pretext Wilson had been waiting for. "Really, it was a psychological moment, if that phrase is not too trite to be used," the scholar-president confided to a journalist. "There was no great disaster like the sinking of the *Maine*." Instead, the case for war would hinge entirely on whether Americans could be made to see the incident as a "series of insults to our country and our flag."[39]

As with the *Maine* sixteen years earlier, the newspapers made everything they could out of the "Tampico Affair." On April 16, 1914, William Randolph Hearst devoted the first four pages of his flagship *San Francisco Examiner* to the deployment of the U.S. fleet, with headlines such as GUNS OF TWO GREAT U.S. FLEETS MENACE MEXICAN COASTS and WHY HUERTA MUST APOLOGIZE. To sell readers on how easily this battle would be won, the editors juxtaposed a four-column picture of shipboard Marines at attention beneath the guns of the battleship *Arkansas* with a photo illustration of Mexicans selling bananas on Tampico's main canal.

As that day's paper was being put together, Ethel, in Philadelphia, was sending a worried letter to Smedley in Veracruz. A contact in Washington had called to tell her that, if Huerta had not fired the salute by six o'clock, the invasion would begin. "I wish thee were with thy own old battalion. I'd feel so much more comfortable," she wrote.[40]

Smedley had just written his own note to her. "Something might be doing," he acknowledged. Admiral Fletcher had ordered him to head for Tampico. He rushed the letter off, with his $50 paycheck enclosed, on a collier ship headed for the States.[41]

Five days later, on April 20, Wilson asked Congress for approval to use armed force against Mexico. His speech was an early example of the Wilsonian rhetorical formula of war: a promise of limited involvement wrapped in a grandiose moral appeal. He called Huerta a usurper and asserted that Mexico constitutionally had "no government." "We seek to maintain the dignity and authority of the United States," Wilson claimed, "only because we wish always to keep our great influence unimpaired for the uses of liberty."[42]

On the morning of April 21, 1914, while Congress was still debating the proposed resolution, the invasion began.

Commodore Manuel Azueta, chief officer of the Mexican Navy's Gulf fleet, had just eaten a late breakfast at his house on Calle Benito Juárez when he heard people running and shouting through downtown Veracruz. He threw on his uniform and hurried to the military headquarters to report for duty to Gen. Gustavo Maass, who was in charge of the city's defense. When he got there, he was informed that the Americans were invading Veracruz—and that Maass had already fled with his troops.[43]

A native-born Veracruzano of Huasteco descent, Azueta had seen the capabilities of the U.S. military firsthand. He had traveled the world as a young sailor, including a stint in the Spanish-ruled Philippines. In 1909, Azueta had captained the Mexican ship that whisked José Santos Zelaya, the nationalist president of Nicaragua, out of Corinto—skillfully avoiding detection by the U.S. sentries as Butler's Marines steamed up from Panama. In 1902, he had taken his seven-year-old son, José, to a New Jersey shipyard to see Mexico's newest gunboats being built.

The "Tampico Incident" had convinced commanders on both sides that the invasion, if it happened, would come there. But two days before, on April 19, Secretary Bryan learned from a U.S. consul that a German freighter was carrying a shipment of arms for Huerta, bound for Veracruz.[44] Wilson's cabinet had determined that Veracruz was a better strategic point for an invasion anyway: As Butler's spy mission had shown, it would be a key entry point for any invading army trying to move on the capital by rail. It was also home to Texaco and Standard's main foreign rival—the British Pearson's Mexican Eagle.

Azueta rushed back home and told his wife, Manuela, that he was going to the nearby national naval academy, the Escuela Naval Militar, to organize the cadets into a defense. The commodore knew the school well. He had been its director for ten years. It was strategically positioned near the port, with an accessible flat roof and iron balconies ringing the upper floor on all sides that would be perfect for picking off invaders. Manuela suggested her husband change into civilian clothes to avoid detection.

When Azueta arrived at the Escuela Naval, he walked into the court-yard, took off his hat, and shouted: "To arms, boys! Our homeland is in danger! ¡Viva México!"[45]

As the nervous cadets rushed to get their weapons, Azueta changed into his white naval uniform and climbed to the roof. He could see the American battleships *Utah, Florida,* and *Montana* moving freely in the bay, along with the auxiliary cruiser *Prairie.* Waves of launches filled with Marine reinforcements and blue-jacketed sailors from the Navy were headed for shore.

From the roof, Azueta also saw the first stirrings of resistance in the streets. The eldest Veracruzanos had been children during the American siege of 1847; it was burned into the city's memory that Gen. Winfield Scott had refused a cease-fire to save the women and children. This time, some of the citizens had organized themselves into an ad hoc Society of Defenders of the Port of Veracruz. Before abandoning the city on Huerta's orders, Maass had directed his lieutenants to distribute rifles to this resistance.[46]

The decision quickly paid off. About half an hour past noon, a sniper hit Cpl. Daniel Haggerty, a U.S. Marine atop a hotel rooftop, killing him instantly. More shots rang out from across the city. The *Prairie*'s guns let loose in reply.

Seeing the bluejackets and Marines pressing into the city, Azueta ordered his 128 cadets to take their places on the roof and behind the partially shuttered windows, and open fire.

For a moment, picking off enemy soldiers at will, the young cadets must have felt they might repel the invasion themselves. But the tide quickly turned. A bullet from an American gun found the head of seventeen-year-old Virgilio Uribe, who was standing right next to Azueta. His blood splattered on Azueta's white uniform. Three small American launches in the harbor had taken notice of the gunfire and were racing toward the academy.

Realizing the academy's ammunition supplies were limited, the commodore shouted for the cadets to shield the windows and doors with furniture and crates, then waited for the Americans to close in further.

Then suddenly, the *gringos* stopped. Some in the front of their lines howled in pain. A hail of bullets roared at the approaching Americans from the corner outside the naval academy.

They were being fired by Azueta's son, José. Now a teenager, Pepe, as his friends called him, knew he had disappointed his father by enrolling in, then flunking out of the naval academy, and enlisting in the army instead. When General Maass had ordered the army's retreat hours earlier, José had stayed behind. He had snuck into the armory, a block away at the colonial Baluarte de Santiago, and hauled the French-made Hotchkiss machine gun into the street.

At first, José hid behind a lamppost, but it gave him little space to maneuver. That's when he pulled the gun into the open street. The gun fired hard and fast, but its weight kept pulling the boy's slight teenage frame down, which meant most of the shots went into the *yanquis'* ankles and knees.

A cadet called for Manuel Azueta, who rushed to a balcony on the side of the academy. He shouted to his son to be careful. But it was far too late for that. The commodore watched helplessly as José took a bullet in the right knee, then rose again and kept on firing. An unseen sniper took another shot, this time striking the teenager in the left leg.

A cadet rushed into the street to pull his injured former classmate, now screaming with pain, toward safety. As he dragged the teenager toward the academy building, a final shot rang out, hitting José from three hundred meters away.

The death knell for the naval academy's defense came, fittingly, from the sea. The *Prairie* unloaded its .50-caliber guns, punching holes through the school's façade and tearing its interior to shreds.[47]

Most of the cadets, and the commodore, managed to escape—thanks, largely, to the covering fire laid out by José Azueta. "Pepe" himself survived for several days at home. Mexicans remember him for a last patriotic act: refusing to accept the aid of an American surgeon sent by Admiral Fletcher. Before he died of sepsis from his wounds, Huerta promoted him to captain. He was nineteen. It was the same age Smedley Butler had been when he was made captain after being shot through the leg in China—trying to prove to himself, and his distinguished father, that he too was an honorable man.

The Azuetas were alone in neither their suffering nor their personal loss. "Almost every Veracruzan family treasures the memory of at least one heroic act: the young Judith Oropeza who threw bricks from her rooftop at the Americans; the prostitute nicknamed 'America' who set her ammunition belt on a flat roof and fired down at the *gringos*," the Mexican historian Enrique Krauze has written.[48]

Wilson was floored by the resistance. Everyone—his advisers, the military, the newspapers—had assured him the Mexicans would not put up a fight. When asked for comment on the first deaths of U.S. servicemen—just four in the first report—he stood "preternaturally pale, almost parchmenty," a magazine editor who witnessed the moment recalled. "The death of American sailors and marines owing to an order of his seemed to affect him like an ailment. He was positively shaken."[49]

The response to Mexican resistance on the ground was far more brutal. On April 22, the Americans launched a comprehensive takeover of Veracruz city. Marines went house to house, kicking in doors. Butler, who at the last minute had been sent back from Tampico to Veracruz, led one of the units. He and his Marines broke into one apparently empty house, only to be shot at through the floorboards. "We poured a volley through the floor and then ripped up the boards. There they were, two dead Mexicans dangling between the cross beams. Our fire had caught them."[50]

It was the first experience the Marines had with the kind of close-in urban combat that would become a staple of future battles from Hué to Fallujah. At every moment, they had to be on guard for an enemy jumping from a rooftop or a blind corner. The intimate encounters with the humanity of the people they were killing and the constant sight of the dead left even seasoned fighters scarred. (The U.S. estimated as few as 160 Mexicans were killed in the battle; the city historian of Veracruz places the number at 10,000. For U.S. troops, the official death toll was 22, with

70 wounded. "The casualty estimates vary so widely . . . that neither side can be taken seriously," the historian John Mason Hart observed.[51]

The trauma fed Butler's misgivings about the immorality and pointlessness of war. After learning that his father had joined a minority in the House that voted, belatedly, against the invasion, he wrote: "I was glad thee voted against approving the president's move and proud of thee for so doing." The sailors' arrests in Tampico that had supposedly prompted the invasion, he said, were a "joke."[52]

His family reinforced his view. "There was *no reason*" for the invasion, Ethel had written her husband, in a rare example of her political commentary, while the invasion was underway. "The president has gone ahead on his own authority and ordered you to land and some have gone to their deaths. If it is all a horrible mistake, will the country impeach him?"[53]

But Wilson was not impeached, and the occupation of Veracruz continued unabated. In May 1914, a U.S. military government was proclaimed over the port city. It was led by U.S Army Brig. Gen. Frederick Funston, the commander who had made his name in the Philippines overseeing the final betrayal and capture of Emilio Aguinaldo. (Mark Twain had snarked at the time: "It would be in the last degree unfair to hold Funston to blame for the outcome of his infirmity; as clearly unfair as it would be to blame him because his conscience leaked out through one of his pores when he was little.")[54]

Funston's staff included his fellow Philippine War veteran Douglas MacArthur, then a thirty-four-year-old Army captain.

Nearly half the active Marine Corps was sent to the Mexican city during the seven-month U.S. occupation as well. That coterie included John Lejeune (now a colonel), Fritz Wise (one of Butler's compatriots from the march to Beijing), and Littleton Waller (now a full colonel as well). On April 27, the honor of raising the first U.S. flag over occupied Veracruz was given to Sgt. Maj. John H. Quick. At last, Butler had a chance to spend time with the "Wig-Wag" hero of Guantánamo and the Battle of Cuzco Well.

Funston and the Marine commanders kept pushing for a chance to employ the war plan Butler and Lind had drawn up for invading Mexico City. But there was no longer any need, as Wilson saw it. The invasion had humiliated Huerta in the eyes of many Mexicans. After a final string of defeats at the hands of Pancho Villa and his fellow Constitutionalist general Álvaro Obregón in the north, Huerta resigned and joined his former mentor, Porfirio Díaz, in exile.

The Texas oilmen's favorite, Venustiano Carranza, became president. New plans were drawn up for oil wells and pipelines across the Golden Lane and elsewhere in Mexico. When Villa and Zapata turned against Carranza in December, in part because of his toleration of the U.S. occupation of Veracruz, the U.S. military made sure Carranza's troops were well supplied with guns, artillery, and field radios as fighting again raged across the country.[55]

Immiserated by the invasion, Veracruzanos were reduced to lining up to receive food aid from the Americans who had conquered them. In an effort to tamp down on any renewed insurgencies, U.S. troops oversaw the paving of streets and repair of buildings damaged in the fighting. Band concerts and movies were put on to entertain the residents and occupying troops.

Jack London, sent as a war correspondent for *Collier's* magazine, summed up the invaders' perspective: "In short, American occupation gave Vera Cruz a bull market in health, order, and business. . . . Verily, the Vera Cruzans will long remember this being conquered by the Americans, and yearn for the blissful day when the Americans will conquer them again."[56]

A French correspondent offered a subtler view. "The Mexicans are silent, but we can clearly see in their eyes their thought: at the first opportunity, they will show their hatred to the invaders," he wrote. On May 12, 1914, five thousand Veracruzanos had filled the streets for the funeral of José Azueta. The writer called it "the silent protest of the vanquished."[57]

José Azueta's name is read, with full military honors, by the Mexican president every year on September 13—the anniversary of the 1847 Battle of Chapultepec. Facing the imposing marble columns of the memorial known as the Monument to the Boy Heroes, the head of state recites the names of six cadets killed at the military academy by the Marines and U.S. Army during the Mexican-American War, as well as those of Azueta and his comrade Virgilio Uribe from Veracruz in 1914. After each name, an honor guard of armed cadets responds: "¡Murío por la patria!" (He died for the homeland.) The event is broadcast nationwide.

In 2020, the ceremony was scaled down, in keeping with the social-distancing requirements of the coronavirus pandemic. The honor guard wore black surgical masks. As Mexico's white-haired sixty-fifth president, Andrés Manuel López Obrador, prepared to read the martyrs' names, an announcer drew on the memory of their resistance against U.S. imperialism to rally the nation against the novel threat. ("In the present day, the battles are different. Today, we face a health crisis due to COVID-19 . . .")

Kept at home by the quarantine, López Obrador's supporters traded slogans, jokes, and emoji-laden patriotic bromides in a YouTube chat window. Off-screen, Mexicans were more divided about their president. "AMLO," as he is known, burst into national consciousness as an activist in the 1990s, when he was beaten and bloodied by police during a protest on behalf of poor and indigenous communities polluted by the state-run oil monopoly, Petróleos Mexicanos, or Pemex. But after his election in 2018, AMLO broke with the left. He embraced both his belligerent cross-border neighbor, Donald Trump, and his old foes at Pemex—vowing to spend billions shoring up the oil giant's finances, including $8 billion on a new refinery in a mangrove wetland in his home state of Tabasco.[58]

That contradiction was rooted in the oil monopoly's origins in the aftermath of the Mexican Revolution. The decade-long civil war ended in the 1920s with nationalism and pro-poor reforms ascendant, but the foreign oil companies more powerful than ever. In 1938, in an effort to put Mexico's oil wealth to work for its people, President Lázaro Cárdenas—a Constitutionalist army veteran who had served under Carranza and Pancho Villa—signed an order expropriating the U.S. and British-owned oil fields and refineries and putting them under the state-owned firm's control. Pemex thus emerged as a symbol of Mexico's reclaimed sovereignty, and a thumb in the eyes of the American oilmen who had inspired the invasion of Veracruz.

Cárdenas's political faction grew into the Institutional Revolutionary Party, or PRI, which by the 1950s had turned Mexico back into a one-party state. Empowered by its control over Mexico's oil wealth and, eventually, collusion with the drug cartels, the PRI's dictatorship-without-dictators seemed like it might last forever. But in the 1980s, oil prices fell, and Mexico was unable to repay the enormous debts it owed to U.S. and European banks.* The World Bank and the International Monetary Fund led a total restructuring of the Mexican economy, largely according to the dictates of U.S. corporations.

In 1994, the North American Free Trade Agreement, or NAFTA, opened the door for U.S. financiers including the former National City Bank of New York (now Citibank) and Chase Manhattan (now JPMorgan Chase) to restructure Mexican capital, labor, and resources. U.S. manufacturers proliferated in the borderlands. Organized crime flourished. In 2014, exactly one hundred years after the U.S. invasion of Veracruz, the PRI-led congress voted to once again allow foreign companies to drill for oil and gas in Mexican lands.

John Mason Hart has dubbed these arrangements "the Neo-Porfirian economy." Social scientists use another term. They call the augmented nineteenth-century ideology of individualism for those who can afford it—in which all of society is rebuilt as a marketplace, all citizens reduced to producers or consumers, in a world made possible by the seizure of power and resources by private enterprise—"neoliberalism."

Like the original Porfiriato, neoliberalism proved disastrous for most Mexicans. The left-leaning Center for Economic and Policy Research found that between 1994 and 2014, Mexico's poverty increased and wages barely went up. Many family farms were destroyed, with far too few manufacturing or service jobs to compensate for their absence. Millions had little choice but to move to overwhelmed cities or take their chances trying to cross the border into the United States. In turn, Americans kept flooding Mexico with cash and weaponry to continue the drug wars, including billions in U.S. military assistance to the Mexican government under the 2007 Mérida Initiative, also known as "Plan Mexico."[59]

López Obrador rode the resulting frustration to the presidency. In December 2018, a crowd of 160,000 packed the Zócalo, the storied Aztec square at the center of Mexico City, to hear him declare in his inaugural

---

* Ironically, many of those loans were financed by so-called petrodollars, excess profits from the members of the OPEC oil cartel that had been deposited in U.S. and European banks. Those banks, desperate to move some of the money elsewhere, had found Mexico—an oil-exporting country that was not part of OPEC—an attractive place to park the cash, so long as Mexico seemed able to pay the loans back with interest.

address: "The neoliberal political economy has been a disaster, a calamity for the public life of this country."[60]

But it quickly became clear that the former activist was more interested in demagogy than policy. Critics saw AMLO's obsession with reviving the fossil fuel industry as indicative of a dangerous, nationalist nostalgia for a misunderstood past. "In Mexico, development was always oil-driven. It was a historic error. The fact that oil brings in income doesn't mean it creates optimal development, and this government is falling into the same trap," an analyst observed.[61]

A backlash had emerged against neoliberalism north of the Rio Grande as well. Though the United States on the whole had once again come out on top in its relationship with Mexico, in terms of corporate profits, consumer prices, and overall economic growth, the benefits were so widely, if unevenly, distributed that most Americans did not notice them. What they did notice were the invisible ideology's effects closer to home: the slashing of the U.S. social safety net, the evisceration of labor protections, costly foreign interventions, and especially the 2007–09 financial crisis—in which banks who had gambled with their savings were bailed out but regular people were left to suffer on their own.

Just as the rejection of neoliberalism led many Mexican voters to López Obrador, the backlash in the United States drew a significant minority of Americans to Donald Trump, a failed real estate mogul who rejected neoliberalism rhetorically while furthering its most pernicious qualities.[62] Despite their many differences, the two leaders recognized each other as fellow travelers in a global wave of populism, as disaffected people all over the world turned toward alternative ideas of social organization: running the gamut from socialism to authoritarianism to fascism. Trump's brand of populism was, like AMLO's, steeped in nostalgia for an idealized past. Trump's faction also similarly fetishized the extraction and burning of domestic oil, gas, and coal. But more importantly, it sought to reclaim a mythical sense of past "greatness" by restoring the power of those it saw as "real Americans"—who were usually understood to be white and native-born.

That understanding required a demonized other. And all along, Trump had singled out Mexicans as a prime target. He launched his campaign with a speech in which he called Mexicans drug dealers, criminals, and rapists, and made his signature campaign promise to build a wall to keep them out. (A wall, he falsely pledged, that Mexico would pay for.) To see Mexico as a place of alien violence—which one could simply seal off with a physical barrier—required ignoring the ways in which Americans had participated in and instigated that violence all along, and the ways in which we had profited from doing so.

The historical throughlines—from early twentieth-century imperialism to that of the early twenty-first, from the chaos spurred by Porfirianism to the crises marking the end of the neoliberal turn—were perhaps easier to see from south of the border. For the Mexican historian Enrique Krauze, the invasion of 1914 was a clear precursor to the forever wars that may be hastening neoliberalism's doom. On the hundredth anniversary of the U.S. occupation of Veracruz, he wrote of its similarities with the 2003 invasion of Iraq: "To help remove a dictator who had seized power in a coup d'état, to channel and direct the radical groups that opposed him, to safeguard the interests of the oil companies active in the area, to forestall interference from other national powers, and to teach the citizens of an unfortunate country about the virtues of democracy."[63]

Smedley Butler, as he turned sharply against war later in his life, would home in on one of those causes above the others. "A French phrase, 'cherchez la femme,' advises you to search for a woman whenever there is a shady deal put across," Butler would tell a radio audience around 1935. "But I feel it more to the point, in these times, to look for the oil deposits when you are trying to get at the bottom of deep international intrigue."[64]

# ELEVEN

## HAITI

On December 16, 1914, a pair of U.S. Navy gunships slipped into Port-au-Prince Bay, the gateway to Haiti's capital. They sat idling for a day, provoking nervous speculation among the city's residents. The next afternoon, at approximately one o'clock, eight Americans were seen hustling toward the republic's central bank, the Banque National de la Republique d'Haïti. They were Marines, disguised in civilian clothes. They chose the hour knowing that most people in the business district would be indoors on their lunch breaks, resting from the heat.[1]

The undercover Marines burst into the bank, brandishing revolvers and canes. The Haitians inside were alarmed. For all appearances, the Caribbean republic's most important bank was being robbed. And in fact, it was: some of the bank's French and American clerks, apparently in on the plan, handed over seventeen heavy wooden boxes, prepacked with gold bars, valued at roughly $30,000 each.

The Marines hoisted the boxes into a wooden wagon waiting outside. Then they rushed back toward the wharf, passing still more undercover Marines posted along the route. The boxes were loaded onto a motorboat and stacked under a weighted cargo net, surrounded by twenty-five more Marines armed with rifles. In short order, half a million dollars' worth of Haitian gold—more than half of Haiti's total government reserves—was aboard the U.S. gunboat *Machias,* headed for a vault on Wall Street.[2]

Haitians were outraged. "How much was taken? By what rights?" the newspaper *Le Matin* demanded to know.[3] The robbery was just the most recent example of a century of abuse by foreign powers since Haiti—the world's first Black-run republic—won its freedom in one of history's most spectacular events a century earlier: the 1791–1803 Haitian Revolution.

For overthrowing their oppressors and freeing themselves, Haitians had been rewarded by Europe and the United States with exclusion and economic isolation. In 1825, in exchange for belated diplomatic recognition (and under the threat of French naval bombardment), Haiti's leaders agreed to pay their former enslavers in France a crippling indemnity of 150 million gold francs. To pay it off—which Haiti eventually did, in full—the country's leaders accumulated even more foreign debt.* In 1880, Haiti gave France's Crédit Industriel et Commercial a charter for a central bank, hoping it might lead to relieving the burden. In 1910, President Taft's secretary of state, Philander Knox, had negotiated a new agreement with Haiti in which French, Germans, and Americans would split the bank's ownership shares.[4]

The Haitian central bank's new U.S. offices were located at 55 Wall Street, inside the headquarters of James Stillman's National City Bank of New York (known today simply as Citibank). Supervising the operation was new City Bank vice president Roger Leslie Farnham—the journalist-turned-operative last seen as Sullivan & Cromwell's point man in the Panama conspiracy. Within a few years, Farnham began advising Wilson's secretary of state, William Jennings Bryan, on Haitian matters.

Bryan was eager for the advice. By the summer of 1914, Haiti's cash-strapped government was in turmoil. The foreign-run Banque Nationale added to the burden by speculating with government revenues, destabilizing the Haitian *gourde,* and withholding funds from the Haitian state by prioritizing reimbursements to foreign bankers when the government coffers were bare. As unrest spread, a series of unfortunate accidents befell Haiti's presidents: One was killed when an ammunition depot exploded and destroyed his National Palace. The next died soon after, purportedly of poisoning. A succession of military coups followed.

The opening for more direct U.S. involvement in Haiti came thanks to a shocking turn of events in Europe. In July 1914, the heir to the throne of the Austro-Hungarian Empire was assassinated while visiting his colony of Bosnia and Herzegovina. The political killing set off a showdown

---

* The amount of the indemnity was renegotiated a few years later to 90 million francs—five times France's annual budget at the time. The French economist Thomas Piketty estimated the amount France owes Haiti at upward of $28 billion. Haiti did not finish paying off the interest on the loans taken to pay off the predatory debt until 1947. See Marlene Daut, "When Haiti Paid France for Freedom: The Greatest Heist in History," *Africa Report*, Jul. 2, 2020.

between competing European alliances that resulted in what would become known as the First World War. With France and Germany now busy killing each other across the Atlantic, Farnham saw a chance to take over Haiti's central bank entirely. It was he who convinced Bryan to approve the heist.[5] Once Haiti's gold reserves were stashed away safely on Wall Street, Farnham got hungry for more.

Farnham knew that Bryan distrusted banks. (In 1896, the agrarian populist had famously accused East Coast bankers of intending to "crucify mankind upon a cross of gold.") So he appealed to Bryan's overarching fear of getting sucked into the new European war. The banker showered the State Department with a stream of implausible rumors about German designs on Haiti, which, had they in the least been true, would have augured a Kaiserreich colony six hundred miles off Florida.[6]

That was the stick. The carrot was a promise that, if a U.S.-friendly puppet president were to be installed in Haiti, politically connected corporations including United Fruit would set up shop there. Most important, Farnham suggested to Bryan, a client government in Port-au-Prince could ensure U.S. control over the Môle Saint-Nicolas—the harbor facing Guantánamo across the Windward Passage, which was now a key sea lane for traveling to and from the recently opened Panama Canal.

Throughout late 1914, the Navy Department drew up detailed plans for an invasion and occupation of Haiti, down to where to build the baseball fields that off-duty Marines would use and where to buy rum. Taking over foreign cities had become so old hat for the U.S. military that it was developing an actual template: some of the plans were simply repurposed from the recent invasion of Mexico, with instructions reading: "REWRITE LETTER INSERTING PORT AU PRINCE FOR VERA CRUZ, MEXICO WHEREVER IT APPEARS."[7]

The looting of the Banque Nationale proved a crucial step. The newspaper Le Matin observed, apparently fulsomely, that an "appalled public" was left to rely "on the wisdom of the [Haitian] government, which, firmly in its rights, will know how to defend the interests of the Republic." Bryan's dismissive reply to that government—in which he called the heist "merely a withdrawal of funds by the authorities of a private bank"—did not quiet the simmering rage.[8]

Disgraced by the incident, yet another Haitian president was forced to resign. Farnham and Bryan were pleased with his replacement, a fifty-six-year-old general named Vilbrun Guillaume Sam, who signaled openness to an arrangement with the United States—possibly a Dominican-style "receivership" in which a U.S. bank would take over the Haitian customs system.

But Sam would not get a chance to cut a deal. Accusing the new president of being a "thief" and "traitor" who "wants to give up our custom-house to the Americans," a nationalist physician named Rosalvo Bobo channeled public outrage into an uprising in the north of Haiti. In response, Sam ordered the arrest and execution without trial of suspected sympathizers in the capital. Relatives of the slain prisoners, bereaved and furious, stormed the partially reconstructed National Palace. They chased Sam to the nearby French legation and killed him. Then they threw his corpse into the street, where it was dismembered by the mob.[9]

Having destabilized Haiti's government through an armed robbery, Woodrow Wilson then used the murder that came in its wake as a pretext to invade. The following day, July 28, 1915, Wilson ordered Rear Admiral William Caperton aboard the USS *Washington*—which had been waiting off the coast of Haiti for months—to seize control of Port-au-Prince. By 5:45 P.M., 330 Marines and sailors were ashore just outside the capital. They marched in double columns into the center of the city, shooting and killing a handful of Haitian resisters. Port-au-Prince fell without a single American casualty.[10]

Though Bobo fled the onslaught to nearby Cuba, his rebels in the north—known as "Cacos"—would not be defeated so easily. Caperton radioed for more Marines. Col. John Lejeune, acting in the absence of the commandant, ordered an advance base brigade of two regiments to deploy to Haiti.

Littleton Waller, the "Butcher of Samar," would command all U.S. ground forces in the Black Republic. To lead the First Battalion of his First Regiment, Waller chose his favorite Quaker Marine.

I n the fall of 1915, Smedley Butler set out with Waller and a Marine battalion across northern Haiti to dismantle the Caco resistance. They traveled on a fortified train through the fertile plains surrounding Cap-Haïtien, the republic's main northern port and second-largest city. In the near distance rose the jungle-covered peaks of the Massif du Nord.

In letters to his "Dear Old Dad," Thomas Butler, Smedley explained the purpose of the mission. Word was spreading across Haiti that the Americans had installed a new puppet president: a milquetoast former senator named Philippe Sudré Dartiguenave. Wilson's new secretary of state, Robert Lansing, had dictated the terms of a new treaty to put Haiti's entire economy under the control of a U.S.-appointed financial adviser.[11] Anti-American sentiment was surging. Demonstrations broke out across the country. Caco insurgent attacks against the Marines increased in frequency and severity.

Some of the Navy brass had proposed bribing the Cacos into submission. Waller wanted a more violent response. The colonel, Butler told his father, "is of the old-fashioned school that believes the way to end a row with a savage monkey is to first go into the region or territory occupied by that monkey and find out how savage he is."[12]

The roots of Littleton Waller's racism ran deep. Both sides of his tangled family tree had played instrumental roles in turning his home state of Virginia into a powerhouse of enslavement. His eighteenth-century ancestor Col. John Waller was a pioneer of the trade; among the people he claimed as property was "Toby" Waller, the African man identified in Alex Haley's 1976 novel, *Roots,* as Kunta Kinte.[13] Waller's maternal grandfather was Virginia governor Littleton Waller Tazewell, who, after a bloody 1831 insurrection led by the enslaved rebel preacher Nat Turner, spent the rest of his life campaigning for the expulsion of Black people from the United States. Among those killed in Turner's rebellion were the wife and children of a slaver named Levi Waller, likely a distant relative.[14]

Waller, the Marine, was fiercely proud of that family history. (His full name, which he was not shy about using, was Littleton Waller Tazewell Waller.) As a teenager in the 1870s, he served in the Norfolk Light Artillery Blues, an ex-Confederate militia likely charged with enforcing "anti-vagrancy" laws meant to intimidate freed Black citizens. Waller saw his experience enforcing racial apartheid at home as the highest qualification for his work in the Caribbean. "I know the nigger and how to handle him. The same quality is going to be needed in

San Domingo*," he told Lejeune as the Haiti operation began.[15] One can imagine Waller smiling under his imperial mustache as he used the slave name of the country he was invading, as his ancestors and their French counterparts had done before him.

Haiti and the idea of Black freedom it represented had played foundational roles in U.S. history. The loss of Saint-Domingue had ended Napoleon's dream of a vast French American empire, forcing him to sell his planned breadbasket—the 530 million–acre Louisiana Territory—to Thomas Jefferson at fire-sale prices. That new territory, and the fight over whether and how to extend slavery into it, helped foment the Civil War. Jefferson in turn lived in fear of "another Saint Domingo" consuming him, perhaps in his plantation bed outside Charlottesville.[16] And he was not alone: The future Commandant Lejeune grew up in Pointe Coupee, Louisiana, a town that carried the memory of a failed 1795 uprising in which enslaved African Americans had tried to win their freedom by torching planters' homes, only to be captured and executed before they could act. A leader of that uprising, an enslaved man named Jean Baptiste, had recruited others by promising: "We could do the same here as at Le Cap"—meaning the city later called Cap-Haïtien, which the Haitian revolutionaries had burned to the ground two years before.[17]

Terrified of Haiti's capacity to inspire, white U.S. elites did everything they could to demonize the country and suppress the memory of its revolution. But the model of self-emancipation through armed revolution and the reality of Black people in positions of national power continued to inspire uprisings throughout the American South, including Nat Turner's. At the Virginia Secession Convention of 1861, soon-to-be Confederate Gen. Henry L. Benning warned that, once slavery was abolished, America would have "black governors, black legislatures, black juries, black everything. . . . We will be completely exterminated, and the land will be left in the possession of the blacks, and then it will go back to a wilderness and become another Africa or Saint Domingo."[18] (Fort Benning, home of the reconstituted School of the Americas, is named after him.)

---

* The slave colony that became Haiti had been known as Saint-Domingue. It was simply a French translation of "Santo Domingo"—a term the Spanish had used at times for the entire island otherwise known as Hispaniola. It should not be confused with the identically named capital of the modern-day Dominican Republic.

The Marine Corps was shaped by those histories as well. One of the most celebrated moments in Corps history was the 1859 arrest of the radical white abolitionist John Brown at Harper's Ferry, Virginia, by Marines under U.S. Army Col. Robert E. Lee. (A painting of Brown's arrest hung in the Library of the Marine Corps when I was last there.) The failed raid, which has been called a dress rehearsal for the Civil War, was meant to inspire an uprising against slavery along the lines of the Haitian Revolution. One of Brown's jailers reported that in the days before his hanging, the devout abolitionist consoled himself by reading a biography of the Haitian Revolution's most famous leader, Toussaint Louverture.[19]

When the Confederacy and U.S. slavery were destroyed by an interracial (though segregated) Union army, Woodrow Wilson had been an impressionable eight-year-old in Augusta, Georgia. Decades later, as a young scholar, he denigrated attempts at fostering racial equality during the post–Civil War Reconstruction era as having "held the South back from her natural destiny of regeneration." As president, Wilson allowed his cabinet secretaries to resegregate the federal workforce. On February 18, 1915, as the plans for the invasion of Haiti were being finalized, Wilson had hosted a private screening of one of the first movies ever shown at the White House: D. W. Griffith's *Birth of a Nation.* Essentially a three-hour-long advertisement for the Ku Klux Klan, the film presented Black characters (portrayed mostly by white actors) as sex-crazed killers. Griffith quoted Wilson's academic opus, *A History of the American People,* in the film.[20]

Also at the White House screening was Josephus Daniels, who, as Wilson's secretary of the Navy, was the senior civilian overseeing the Haiti invasion. Before entering politics, Daniels had edited the *News & Observer* in Raleigh, North Carolina. In 1898, Daniels used his newspaper to promote the overthrow of a multiracial governing coalition in the nearby city of Wilmington; the white conservative insurrection that followed is considered the only successful domestic coup d'état in U.S. history.[21] In another issue, Daniels published a piece by the Ku Klux Klansman "General" Julian Carr, who declared that "Haiti and Liberia are object lessons for mankind" of the dangers of allowing the "negro balance of power over white civilization."[22]

In other words, the most senior military and civilian officials who led the invasion of Haiti saw themselves as defenders of a racial order that was challenged by Haiti's very existence. Left to his own instincts, an unreconstructed racist like Waller—with Lejeune, Daniels, and Wilson above him in the chain of command—might have pursued a policy of extermination in Haiti beyond even what he had attempted on Samar during the Philippine War.

But Waller was increasingly putting his trust in Butler, a Northerner who had grown up in a very different tradition. Butler's Quaker family abhorred slavery; both Thomas and Maud's fathers fought for the Union to end it. (Ethel's grandfather Richard Peters had personally enslaved at least twenty-one people around Atlanta and used slave labor to build his Georgia Railroad, but Smedley was not close with his in-laws.[23]) Nonetheless, Black Philadelphians rarely lived alongside whites, especially in the cloistered suburbs of the Main Line.

Back in 1899, the University of Pennsylvania had invited a promising young sociologist named W. E. B. Du Bois to study this situation. He quickly identified the root of informal segregation as "color prejudice," known today as racism. The typical Black Philadelphian had no difficulty understanding he faced a "widespread feeling of dislike for his blood," Du Bois wrote. But whites in the Quaker City were "quite unconscious of any such powerful and vindictive feeling. They regard color prejudice as the easily explicable feeling that intimate social intercourse with a lower race is not only undesirable but impracticable if our present standards of culture are to be maintained."[24] This quiet confidence in a white-supremacist ordering of the world meant that in "respectable" white homes like the Butlers', race was seldom discussed at all.

Butler thus moved through Haiti unencumbered by ghost stories of the Black Republic or ancestral fears of Black revenge, and could think more strategically than his superiors. Instead of directing his Marines to "place no confidence in the natives," as Waller had on Samar, Butler made efforts to develop good relations with Haitian porters and guides. Rather than seeking to turn the northern plains into a "howling wilderness," he directed his men to scrupulously follow the rules of engagement—not firing unless they were fired upon. And instead of dismissing their "animal-like babble," as Stephen Crane had the Afro-Cubans at Guantánamo, he took the time to notice that they were speaking an unfamiliar language, Kreyòl (not "very pure French, much like the Filipino Spanish," Butler wrote Bunny, analogizing Haiti's native tongue to Tagalog)—and that it was a disadvantage that none of his Marines spoke it.[25]

Butler turned such insights into a strategy for more effective domination. He was able to perceive and then exploit the fault lines between the Caco insurgents and civilians. In the central Artibonite Valley, he noticed villagers' frustrations with a Caco commander, Pierre Benoît Rameau, whose men kept stealing their food and water. Butler appealed to the villagers by pledging to protect them, then humiliated Rameau personally by pulling him off his horse. When a Marine sergeant was killed by Cacos a few days later, village women sang a funeral hymn, signaling their shift in loyalty. Rameau was captured soon after.[26] Duly impressed, Waller praised Butler's "usual energy and judgment" in his report to the commandant.[27]

Butler's insights became the key to securing America's imperial foothold in Haiti. Though Butler did not realize it at the time, he was helping invent a new approach to warfare. It would eventually be dubbed counterinsurgency: the combination of military, political, and psychological methods employed by an occupying power with the goal of holistically defeating an armed resistance.[28]

In doing so, he was not rejecting white supremacy but channeling it. A few years later, Butler would explain to a Senate committee: "We were all imbued with the fact that we were trustees of a huge estate that belonged to minors. That was my viewpoint, that was the viewpoint I personally took, that the Haitians were our wards and that we were endeavoring to make for them a rich and productive property, to be turned over to them at such time as our government saw fit."[29]

That paternalism, as the historian Mary Renda has written, "masked as benevolent by its reference to parental care, but structured equally by norms of parental authority and discipline," became "the cultural flagship of the United States in Haiti."[30] Because Butler hailed from a place where, as Du Bois had written, white people were "unconscious of" their racism, he was the ideal vehicle for the rebranded form of violence it implied.

A century later, a Marine Corps Civil Affairs instructor was standing in his desert combat utility uniform in Quantico, Virginia, preparing to give a lecture on counterinsurgency to a class of fifty Marines. He pushed a plug of chewing tobacco to the side of his lower lip and held up a green paperback. "All right," he began. "*The Small Wars Manual*. If you have not read it, read it. It was written back in the 1900s and it still has relevance today. Trust me."[31]

The manual, codified in 1940, was based on the field notes of early-twentieth-century Marines. That group included Harold Hickox Utley, who served in Haiti under Butler, then deployed to Nicaragua to fight the original Sandinistas. Along with its more recent successor, the *U.S. Army and Marine Corps Counterinsurgency Field Manual* of 2006, the little green book provided the basis for what is now known as counterinsurgency doctrine, or COIN.

As the Civil Affairs instructor indicated, the original *Small Wars Manual* is still prized by Marines; the future Marine major general and defense secretary James Mattis recommended all of his officers reread it before deploying to U.S.-occupied Iraq.[32] As its introduction states: "The history of the United States shows that in spite of the varying trend of the foreign policy of succeeding administrations, this Government has interposed or intervened in the affairs of other states with remarkable regularity, and it may be anticipated that the same general procedure will be followed in the future."[33]

Because COIN doctrine prioritizes reducing civilian casualties over protecting one's own troops—part of its goal of winning "hearts and minds"—the doctrine remains controversial among some in the military. As another Marine Civil Affairs instructor remembered his first reaction to hearing about COIN (according to Jennifer Greenburg, the anthropologist who observed the Quantico class described above): "First you want me to kill them . . . now you want me to fucking take care of them? Make up your fucking mind!"[34]

To drive home the importance of COIN and Civil Affairs, the instructor pulled up a history slide. Under black-and-white photos of Marines, most likely in Nicaragua, a caption read:

> The Corps protected American citizens and business interests by intervening in the Dominican Republic (1916–1924), Haiti (1915–1934), and Nicaragua (1912–1933). In addition to providing stability and security

during these "Small Wars," Marines developed CA [Civil Affairs] doctrine "on the fly" as they built roads and schools, taught local citizens how to become civil servants, and raised the overall standard of living of these countries.

The instructor highlighted one old Marine in particular as an example to follow. Smedley Butler, he explained, had been successful in Haiti because he had relied less on his gun and more on language, culture, bearing, and restraint. "He was able to defuse the situation, make enemies back down, give the impression he had more men than he had," the major told the class. In summary, "he bluffed."

But as Butler and the instructor both knew, there is no such thing as a bloodless counterinsurgency. "We are Marines sent here to put an end to a condition that has become, through years of experience, second nature with these people, and no amount of carefully formed sentences will do the job," Butler had written his father from northern Haiti in October 1915. "Nothing will but a little shooting."[35]

By mid-October 1915, enough villages had been burned, bribes distributed, and Cacos arrested or killed that the Americans were in control of Haiti's northern coast. The Marines pushed farther into the mountains of the Massif du Nord. The summits are among the highest in a country whose name comes from the Taino for "mountainous place." Their nigh-impenetrable terrain had made those highlands the strongholds of Haitian independence fighters for over a century.

On the way, Butler wrote a letter to his youngest son, Tom Dick. The boy's second birthday was a few weeks away, but Smedley knew he likely would not have time to write then. "Thy father has been and will be quite busy for some time attending to his duties, the vast majority of which are causing him much discomfort, but he is doing all in his best style, so that when thee and thy Precious Sister and Big Brother grow up you will have no reason ever to be ashamed of him," he wrote. Waller, Smedley noted for Bunny's benefit, had authorized him to "go wherever and do whatever I please" in his mission to crush the Cacos.[36]

On October 24, Butler led thirty-eight Marines on horseback out of the city of Fort-Liberté in search of a Caco stronghold. At dusk, while the Marines were fording a river near the village of Bahon, the hills echoed with the trumpeting of conch shells. The Cacos opened fire. Only the inaccuracy of the Cacos' antiquated rifles, and the Marines' tactical use of their horses as shields, kept Butler and the rest of the platoon from being killed in the water. The Marines fought their way to a protected position, at the cost of a dozen horses and the mule carrying the platoon's lone machine gun. Butler's gunnery sergeant, Dan Daly—the short, wiry son of an Irish immigrant factory worker on Long Island—made his way back to the river, knifing several Cacos on the way. Daly cut the machine gun and ammunition off the dead mule, and brought the two-hundred-pound load back to the platoon. At dawn, the Marines "hunted the Cacos down like pigs," Butler later wrote.[37]

Over the following weeks, the Marines continued driving the Cacos back through the mountains. As of November 1, Smedley wrote Bunny, "I have marched 270 miles and ridden horseback 50 miles—total 320 miles in 43 days." He expected to double that by the middle of the month by "patrolling and reconnoitering the surrounding country trying to sweep it clear of Cacos"—"but," he cautioned, "they are as hard to catch as fleas."[38]

That was by design. The Cacos were heirs to a tradition of resistance that dated back to guerrilla fighters in the Haitian Revolution. They took their name from a native cuckoo bird that hides in the bush before striking at its prey. In the nineteenth century, farmers fighting under the Caco name rebelled against Haitian elites who, unable to imagine another way to generate wealth, tried to force them back onto plantations under the cover of the so-called corvée—a medieval French term for forced labor. Recognizing the corvée as slavery by another name, these earlier generations of Cacos had overthrown every attempt at implementing it at scale. In that sense, it had been the guerrilla Cacos, not the Haitian state, who had been the guarantors of the Haitian promise of freedom.

Using their knowledge of the terrain and skills of attacking and retreating, the Cacos drove Butler and the Marines to their wits' end. On one raid, the Americans stormed Fort Capois, the supposed stronghold of Josaphat Jean-Joseph—a Haitian army veteran turned Caco commander of the region of Grande-Rivière-du-Nord. But when they fought their way into the main fort, they found no one inside. "There was evidence of blood in many places, but no dead or wounded," Capt. Chandler Campbell reported.[39] Jean-Joseph's garrison had escaped up the mountain, using secret trails the Marines hadn't known about, apparently carrying their casualties with them.

Reconnaissance patrols eventually located their hiding spot: thirty-six hundred feet up a mountain above Bahon, in an old star-shaped redoubt called Fort Rivière. In a series of limited assaults, the Marines closed off all obvious escape routes. After midnight on November 17, 1915, three Marine companies and two Navy bluejacket detachments assembled on the three sides of the mountain and began climbing toward Fort Rivière.

Butler led Fifth Company from the west. They climbed through the night over the steep trails. As they gained altitude, the heavy tropical air grew cold and thin. The Marines took extra care to ensure the mules carrying their Benét-Mercié M1909 machine guns did not slip and fall off the side.

Near the top, the last of the vegetation disappeared, giving way to scattered boulders. There would be nowhere to hide when the fighting began.

As the sun rose over what the locals called Montay Nwa—black mountain—the brown brick parapets of Fort Rivière were still just out of view. From the western slope, Butler and his men could look straight down into the Citadelle Laferrière. That monumental fortress, perched on a lower peak, had been the jewel of a nationwide system of mountaintop forts meant for a desperate last-ditch defensive strategy: if the French or another slaving power reinvaded, Haitians would burn their cities and take refuge on the mountaintops, where they would make good on their motto: *libète ou lanmò*—liberty or death.

At 7:50 A.M., Campbell blew a whistle, and the Marines let loose a storm of automatic fire. Butler's column scrambled over the last ridge and rushed forward under heavy fire from the Cacos, only to find that the main entrance to the fort had been sealed. Then Butler spotted a small breach: "a drain four feet high and three feet wide extending back for fifteen feet into the interior."[40]

Sgt. Ross Iams forced himself into the opening first, followed by Butler's orderly, Pvt. Samuel Gross. Butler entered third. ("I had never experienced a keener desire to be someplace else," he later said.) He squeezed his way through the narrow space, deafened by echoes of gunfire pinging off the walls, and emerged in the middle of an open brawl. Cacos were shouting: "Touye yo!" (Kill them!) Butler fired his pistol at a Caco charging toward him and missed. He was saved, a heartbeat later, by a better shot from Gross. The three Marines got off as many rounds as they could as more Americans climbed out of the drain, one by one.[41]

For ten minutes, Marines and Cacos fought to the death inside the mountaintop fort, until the dirt floor was muddied with blood. Some of the Cacos, their antiquated rifles useless at close range, resorted to rocks and sticks. Realizing they were outgunned, the surviving resistance fighters tried to escape. Butler watched with both horror and relief as they climbed and leaped off the parapets, only to be mowed down as they fell by Campbell's machine gunners, who had been lying in wait.

Two days later, a small group of Marines climbed back up the mountain and dynamited the interior of the fort, Haitian bodies and all.

In the century since the slaughter, Fort Rivière was largely forgotten by Haitians and Americans alike. In 1931, a Haitian ambassador—perhaps embarrassed by the stories of such a catastrophic defeat—went so far as to deny that the remote mountain stronghold had ever existed, resulting in a public argument with Marine veterans of the battle in the press.[42]

One person who could not forget the battle was Butler. A few weeks after the massacre, Smedley had confided to Bunny: "The past several weeks seem like a horrible nightmare, such terrible work and such terrific excitement." He went on: "Of course at the time I thought it fine, but looking back at it the sight is not a desirable one—particularly those awfully shattered bodies at Fort Riviere."[43] Over the coming months and years, the gravity of what he had done would only weigh more heavily on him.

I hoped finding the site of the dynamited fort might give me some insight into a place that loomed so large in Butler's mind. So, in the spring of

2018, I flew to Cap-Haïtien, where I met up with my old friend Evens Sanon, whom I'd worked with closely during my years as a journalist in Haiti. About an hour after leaving the city (and a stop for Evens to pick up cigarettes), we turned onto an unpaved highway. We drove through a riverbed, passing billboards for a USAID project and market stalls selling American rice in bags stamped with the U.S. flag.

For a while, no one we stopped to ask had heard of a Fort Rivière. But as we neared Bahon, a few ears perked up, and soon we were pointed in the right direction. We turned onto an unmarked road into the forest and started to climb the foothills of Black Mountain, until we couldn't drive any further.

Walking past a group of *ti-kay,* a style of small wooden houses, I passed children playing with sticks, while the old folks chatted on the big roots of a shade tree. Smoke hung in the air, likely risen from a nearby fire pit where someone was burning wood into charcoal. I spotted a group of people gathered at the entrance to a *lakou,* a traditional arrangement of ti-kay around a central courtyard. A few were wearing white prayer caps. They looked at me with suspicion.

"Bonswa," I said.

"Good afternoon," someone replied in English. "Where are you from?"

The voice belonged to a man who was slightly older than the rest. He was dressed in a silver polo shirt and corduroy shorts, held up by a thick black leather belt. He spoke slowly and deliberately, with a rasp that suggested years of dedication to rum and cigars. "An entrepreneur from the boondocks," Evens muttered knowingly, so only I could hear.

The man said his name was Ramsey Sanon. (No relation to Evens, as far as we could tell.) He had lived for years in Miami but gave it up to come back to his mountain home. "I'm looking for a natural life," he explained. Then, as if one thought led inextricably to the other, he added: "There's not much time left."

"Until what?" I asked.

"The whole world is going to collapse. But only Haiti will survive. Ogou Fèray said."

I knew Ogou Fèray. He is said to be one the most powerful of the Haitian mystic spirits, or *lwa,* in his case associated with fire, iron, and war. Like many lwa, Ogou's origins lie with the Yoruba religion of West Africa. That faith was brought in chains to the New World, and combined with Christianity, other African pantheons, and a local brand of ancestor worship into the Haitian religion now known as Vodou.

"Are you an oungan?" I asked Ramsey. A Vodou priest.

He smiled knowingly. "We have a little shrine here in the lakou."

Smedley would not have been pleased to hear that. After Fort Rivière, Butler had been tapped to be the head of a new constabulary force, the Gendarmerie d'Haïti. As commander, Butler tried to put the final nail in the resistance's coffin by wiping out the practice of Vodou. This was not a new idea: in 1912, three years before the U.S. invasion, the Haitian Catholic Church had launched an "anti-superstition campaign" to suppress the rival peasant religion. As the Haitian scholar Lewis Ampidu Clorméus has written, the Americans found ready allies in a clergy eager "to take advantage of this new situation to further consolidate their hegemony."[44]

Butler saw "voodoo"—as the Marines spelled it, with baby-talk vowels and a lowercase "v"—as a source of the insurgency itself. "Ninety-nine percent of the people of Haiti are the most kindly, generous, hospitable, pleasure-loving people I have ever known," he told a Senate committee in 1921. "When the other one percent that wears Vici Kid shoes [a luxury brand from Philadelphia] with long pointed toes and celluloid collars stirs them up and incites them with liquor and voodoo stuff, they are capable of the most horrible atrocities; they are cannibals."[45] Here was paternalism again—the idea that Haitians only act under the influence of others. At that same hearing, Gen. Eli K. Cole cited "rampant" Vodouism as one of the justifications for the invasion.[46]

Officially, the Corps still takes that view. At the National Museum of the Marine Corps, a large *tambou* drum, looted during the occupation, is shown with the description "Haitian rebels used voodoo drums during ritual ceremonies to incite public insurrection." Butler's personal Gendarmerie flagpole topper is displayed alongside it.

Butler's Gendarmes raided shrines and arrested priests. They burned piles of sacred instruments and images of Catholic saints used in worship. As Ramsey told me on the forest mountain road, that loss of identity and historical memory was the cause of the coming apocalypse. "Ogou says that the world will end because people have lost their culture. They forget how they got their independence," he told me.

"Why will Haiti survive?"

"Because Haitians still have spirit possession. The world, they want to take it away from us."

Indeed, the crackdown backfired in rural places like Black Mountain, where people turned more deeply to Vodou as a form of resistance. Stories spread of the lwa themselves resisting. In one tale, Marines confiscated a massive *asòtò* drum only to have it start thundering on its own at Gendarmerie headquarters. Others among the faithful believed a Marine called "Captain Daybas" was so awed by the religion that he died and became a lwa himself. Vodouisant believe that the spirits can take over their bodies during ceremonies. When Daybas descended into a worshiper, it was said, the possessed person could only speak English until the spirit left.[47]

Ramsey motioned for me to follow him into the lakou. He showed me a stall made of blue tarps—the kind international aid groups handed out for people to use as tents after the 2010 earthquake in Port-au-Prince. Inside was a handmade wooden chair with a shiny red scarf draped over it. The air smelled unmistakably of the finest Haitian rum, Barbancourt, said to be the favorite of the gods. Then he led me to a thatch house with a roof of rusted corrugated tin, built over a dirt pit circled by a ring of bricks. This was the *peristyle,* the main sacred space of the court, where the spirits are called.

I asked him about the battle that took place up the mountain. I wondered what he thought about what Butler and the Marines did at Fort Rivière—if they bore some responsibility for what he said was going to happen to the world. He turned it over in his mind for a moment. "The way I look at it, it's not really them. It's their government. . . . They been ordered to come here. If they don't go, I mean, they would have put them in jail. I say do what you got to do."

I was unsure what to think about that. The Marines had all volunteered, if not fully realizing what they were going to be asked to do. Officers like Butler were the ones who gave the orders on the ground; grunts like Gross eagerly threw themselves into the maw. Perhaps Ramsey understood it structurally. Or maybe he was just telling me what he thought I wanted to hear.

I thanked him. Evens and I continued up the mountain. As we climbed past the forest, to where the trees thinned out, the path grew even steeper. Evens had to stop every few minutes to catch his breath and rest his six-foot-five, three-hundred-pound frame. It seemed his pack-a-day cigarette habit was catching up with him. Then, around a bend, I spotted them: the stone walls of Fort Rivière. They were damaged and jagged, showing clear signs of the dynamiting in 1915 and a century of erosion since.

The fort was still extremely far away. I asked a farmer how long it might take to get to it. "O, sa se yon bon mache," he replied. Evens and I looked at each other. When a Haitian from the mountains tells you that some-thing is a "good walk" away, that's far.

"I'll wait for you here," Evens said with a laugh.

I continued on, the farmer gamely offering to show me the way for a small fee. As I struggled up a precipice between the peak and the valley, it became clear why those particular Cacos had chosen this mountain as the place to make their last stand. I also realized how deeply committed Smedley Butler, and every Marine who climbed to the summit with him, had to have been to wiping out every last vestige of Haitian resistance.

One of the most painful ironies of the U.S. occupation was that while the Americans were crushing Vodou in Haiti, they were repackaging it as entertainment back home.

Many popular works came out of the nineteen-year occupation. For-mer Marine Lt. Arthur J. Burks—the pulp fiction writer who collabo-rated with Butler on *Walter Garvin in Mexico*—published a series of short stories about Haiti in the magazine *Weird Tales* in the 1920s.[48] One, titled "Voodoo," features the mutilation of a young American officer and sacri-fice of a naked teenage girl. Orson Welles sold out theaters with his 1936 "Voodoo *Macbeth*," a staging of the Scottish Play set on a fictionalized Caribbean island. The literary-minded turned to Zora Neale Hurston, whose ethnography *Tell My Horse* promised, according to her publisher, "VOODOO as no WHITE PERSON ever saw it!"[49]

But no occupation-era work had a bigger impact than a short chap-ter in William B. Seabrook's 1929 travelogue, *The Magic Island*. In it,

Seabrook, a journalist and World War I veteran from Baltimore, describes chatting with a Haitian tax collector about local legends of vampires and werewolves. Then Seabrook asks about "one creature I had been hearing about in Haiti, which sounded exclusively local—the *zombie*."[50]

The tax collector puts a hand on his knee. "Alas these things—and other evil practices connected to the dead—exist." They are, Seabrook paraphrases, a "soulless human corpse, still dead, but taken from the grave and endowed by sorcery with a mechanical semblance of life."

And with that, the zombie was introduced to America.

Some Haitians do believe that *zonbi,* the spirits of the recently dead, linger on Earth. The author had wandered into the murky underworld of the *zonbi kò kadav*—corpse-trapped spirits, or walking dead. Zonbi in this state are used as labor: "occasionally for the commission of some crime," as Seabrook wrote, but "more often simply as a drudge around the habitation or the farm, setting it dull heavy tasks, and beating it like a dumb beast if it slackens." The zonbi kò kadav, in other words, is a spiritual remembrance of Haitians' most scarring historical trauma: slavery.

Seabrook may have intended the story as a dark metaphor for the U.S. occupation itself. The chapter concerns a platoon of zombies sold as plantation labor to the Haitian American Sugar Company, or Hasco—one of the main businesses supported by the occupation. Seabrook contrasts the exoticism of Haitian magic with the firm's name: "American-commercial-synthetic, like Nabisco, Delco, Socony."* Yet, he writes, its U.S. owners were happy to profit from the dark arts. Where the field workers came from "was no concern of Hasco, so long as the work went forward."[51]

The chapter was adapted into the 1932 movie *White Zombie*. Hollywood's first zombie feature starred Bela Lugosi—fresh off his star-making turn as Dracula—as "Murder Legendre," a voodoo master who zombifies a blond ingénue who has come to Haiti to marry an American banker.

For a few decades, the zombie would remain racialized—often distinctly Haitian—lumbering into white anxieties over immigration and Black people migrating north.[52] But like Hasco, Americans did not ultimately care where our zombies came from.

In 1954, the sci-fi writer Richard Matheson wrote the postapocalyp-

---

* Standard Oil Company of New York, now the Mobil in ExxonMobil.

tic fantasy *I Am Legend,* in which a global pandemic has turned most of humanity into flesh-eating monsters. Matheson took a critical step: combining the shuffling posthumans with the parasitism of the vampire. One of Matheson's fans, the filmmaker George Romero, was inspired by the book to create his *Night of the Living Dead.*

Romero did not use the z-word in his first film. "We never thought of the creatures in our film as 'zombies' because, like everyone else at the time, we believed zombies to be those bug-eyed soulless beings that wandered the fields in Haiti," Romero later wrote.[53] But in the sequels he nodded toward his source material. In 1978's *Dawn of the Dead,* he put a telling piece of dialogue in the mouth of a Black protagonist named Peter, as the heroes watch a horde of zombies overrun a deserted shopping mall:

FRANCINE: What the hell are they?
PETER: They're us, that's all. There's no more room in Hell.
STEPHEN: What?
PETER: Something my granddaddy used to tell us. You know
Macumba? Voodoo. Granddad was a priest in Trinidad. Used to
tell us, "When there's no more room in Hell, the dead will walk the
earth."

Two tendencies have flowed through zombie literature since. For colonizers, zombie stories are powered by fears of revenge or contagion by the people they conquered. For a decade before COVID-19, the CDC, as the U.S. Centers for Disease Control and Prevention is known, used a program called "Zombie Preparedness for Educators" to teach middle schoolers about preparing for disasters.[54]

For the colonized, the zombie retains its older connotations: fear of abduction, assimilation, and losing one's soul. In 1977's global hit "Zombie," the Nigerian bandleader Fela Kuti mocks his country's postcolonial military: "Zombie no gon' go, unless you tell 'em to go . . . Zombie no gon' think, unless you tell 'em to think."

Smedley Butler would claim as much in the last years of his life. "Like all members of the military profession, I never had an original thought until I left the service," he would write in 1935. "My mental faculties remained in suspended animation while I obeyed the orders of the higher-ups."[55] This might have been a self-serving rationalization. Butler certainly exhibited plenty of ingenuity, along with motivated cruelty, in his decades as a Marine.

But then again, zombie literature, as it has evolved over the decades, is replete with examples of "intelligent zombies"—the undead still capable of creativity and individuality, even as they unquestioningly obey their drive to kill and consume. Maybe Matheson had it right: It was contagious. In stealing the zombie from Haiti, we became the zombies ourselves.

Two weeks after the massacre at Fort Rivière, in late November 1915, Butler started work on the Gendarmerie d'Haïti, eager to put the plans for the "mounted constabulary" he'd envisioned for Nicaragua into action. Unlike the Central American Guardias Nacionales, where locals like Anastasio Somoza would take leadership roles, deeper racism against Black people ensured the Gendarmerie would consist of white Marine officers overseeing Haitian enlistees. This was a compromise between the paternalists like Butler and the apartheid diehards. Butler assured his congressman father that his "little chocolate soldiers" would "do very well, in time, and as long as white men lead them." Littleton Waller summed up his contrary view in a letter to Lejeune: "You can never trust a nigger with a gun."[56]

Marines who volunteered for the Gendarmerie were given new Haitian ranks; as commandant, Butler became a Haitian *général de division,* with a pay rate of $8,814 a year. Haitian enlistees, on the other hand, earned just $120 a year as privates, up to $300 for sergeants. Members were issued surplus Marine uniforms with the Eagle, Globe, and Anchors removed. The Haitian coat of arms—palm trees and cannons under a "liberty cap" representing democracy—was pinned on their hats.[57]

Because the massacre at Fort Rivière had effectively broken the back of the Caco resistance for the time being, it felt safe for Smedley to start encouraging his wife to come down.

"I am so tired of campaigning and just want thee, *thee, thee,*" he wrote Bunny during a stopover in Guantánamo Bay, en route from Cap-Haïtien to Port-au-Prince. "We will be very happy and comfortable in Port au Prince, can make it just like Our Dear Old Camp Elliott and then I will be my own boss again with a command four times as large," he promised.[58]

Without her, Butler found it impossible to sleep through the night. His quarters in Port-au-Prince were in an old Haitian army barracks next to the destroyed National Palace. The old French colonial downtown around it was cramped, noisy, and oppressively hot. The mosquitoes drove him insane. Smedley tried to distract himself by working ten hours a day, often into the night.

Ethel was hesitant to come. Some nights, Butler may have regretted slipping the admission that he felt like he was living a nightmare—and the "awfully shattered bodies at Fort Riviere"—into his letter to her. What mother would want to bring her three children to a place like that?

But he probably could not help it. In addition to the traumatic stress he had suffered throughout his career, Butler was almost certainly reeling from what psychologists now call "moral injury": having done, seen, or allowed something that violated his deepest ethics. "War is an alternate moral universe where many of the rules and values we grew up with are revoked," the war journalist David Wood would write a century later of veterans of Iraq and Afghanistan. It is common, Wood wrote, for those with moral wounds to "react with cynicism or bitterness, to distrust authority; to be more prone to anxiety, depression; perhaps to seek comfort in isolation or the self-medication of drugs, alcohol, or overwork. Most common, to never talk about the war."[59]

The conflict inside Butler grew even more serious when, in February 1916, he got word that he had been awarded his first Medal of Honor, for his role in the invasion of Veracruz. Just three months removed from the slaughter at Fort Rivière, the house-to-house killing he had carried out in Mexico likely took on an even deeper level of obscenity. "I, even in my most puffed up moments, can not remember a single action, or in fact any collection of actions of mine that in the slightest degree warranted such a decoration," Butler wrote his mother. "I did my duty as best I could in Vera Cruz but there was absolutely nothing *heroic* in it."[60]

Not four months after he promised his two-year-old, Tom Dick, that he was doing everything he could in Haiti to keep his children from being ashamed, Smedley was now petrified by the vision that his sons, when they were grown, might "proudly display this wretched medal, or rather wretchedly awarded." Butler wrote Secretary Daniels to demand the medal be rescinded. Daniels ordered him to keep it.[61]

Indeed, more Medals of Honor were awarded for the Veracruz invasion than for any action before or since: fifty-six. It was a gilding so wildly out of proportion with a battle in which the U.S. troops were primarily fighting civilians—many of them untrained women and boys—that some smelled a cover-up. Exaggerating the heroism was a way of glossing over the realities of that invasion, and the terrible costs of the tide of Yankee imperialism in general. These were unpleasant truths best kept hidden as Wilson's 1916 reelection campaign began and the debate heated up over whether to intervene in the European war.

Perhaps hoping to drown out his demons with more fighting, Butler began hoping for a transfer to Mexico in support of Gen. John J. Pershing's "Punitive Expedition" against Pancho Villa.* But those orders never came. Smedley was stuck in Haiti, rearranging the pieces of the latest country he had helped rip apart. He took to signing letters to his wife and children: "Your loving, adoring, tired, lonely Dadda Piddie."[62]

---

* Villa had broken with Mexican president Venustiano Carranza. On March 9, 1916, Villa's División del Norte launched a cross-border raid into the tiny U.S. border town of Columbus, New Mexico, likely hoping to provoke an invasion and unite the warring Mexican factions against both his former ally Carranza and the United States. Wilson took the bait and sent ten thousand U.S. soldiers, led by Pershing, to capture the rebel leader. The invasion failed to produce Villa's hoped-for united front. But the "Punitive Expedition" also failed to capture him.

Smedley Darlington Butler in China, 1900. *Public Domain, Marine Corps History Department*

Massacre of Filipinos at Bud Dajo, Jolo Island, Philippines, 1906. One of the images Philippine president Rodrigo Duterte was referring to when he promised to "produce—from your archives—the photographs that you took of the people you murdered here in the Philippines." *Public Domain, National Archives and Records Administration*

Smedley and Ethel Butler's wedding, 1905. Maud Butler is in the feather hat; Thomas Butler to her side (far left). *Public Domain, Marine Corps History Department*

U.S. occupation of Veracruz, Mexico, 1914. From left to right: Capt. F. H. DeLario, Sgt. Maj. John H. Quick (standing), Lt. Col. Wendell C. Neville, Col. John A. Lejeune, and Maj. Smedley D. Butler. *Public Domain, Marine Corps History Department*

Littleton Waller in Haiti, 1915. *Public Domain, National Archives and Records Administration*

The "crucifixion" of Haitian insurgent leader Charlemagne Péralte, assassinated by Marines in 1919, in a photograph taken before his burial at the future Caracol Industrial Park. This image inspired generations of anti-imperialist resistance in Haiti. *Public Domain, National Archives and Records Administration*

Franklin D. Roosevelt (left) and unidentified colleague in Haiti, 1917, wearing the uniforms of Butler's Gendarmerie. *Courtesy of the Franklin D. Roosevelt Library*

Ethel ("Bunny"), Smedley Jr. ("Brother"), Thomas Richard ("Tom Dick"), Ethel ("Snooks"), and Smedley D. Butler in Haiti, 1916. *Public Domain, Marine Corps History Department*

The set of *Goyo: The Boy General*, a drama about the Philippine-American War, as a monsoon rain begins to fall. The author is the bearded prisoner of war, second from the left, 2017. *Courtesy of the Author*

A company of the Guardia Nacional Dominicana, one of the client police forces the Americans set up across Latin America, in San Pedro de Macoris, Dominican Republic, 1920. *Public Domain, American National Red Cross photograph collection, Library of Congress*

Butler's famous duckboards at Camp Pontanézen, Brest, France, 1919. *Public Domain, Marine Corps History Department*

Butler being sworn in as Philadelphia's Director of Public Safety by Mayor W. Freeland Kendrick, 1926. *Public Domain, Marine Corps History Department*

Smedley in Hollywood with (left to right) director John Francis Dillon, actress Pauline Starke, and screenwriter Elinor Glyn, 1926. Six years later, Starke, who got her start in a blackface role in D. W. Griffith's *Birth of a Nation*, would star in a Broadway adaptation of the zombie chapter of W. B. Seabrook's *The Magic Island*— the stage production that inspired *White Zombie*, Hollywood's first zombie feature, starring Bela Lugosi. *Public Domain, Marine Corps History Department*

Supporters of the Sandinista National Liberation Front (FSLN) protest on behalf of President Daniel Ortega in Managua, Nicaragua, September 1, 2018. *Rodrigo Sura/ EPA-EFE/Shutterstock.com*

Butler and the Marines in Shanghai, 1927. *Public Domain, Marine Corps History Department*

Butler addressing the Bonus Marchers on the Anacostia Flats, Washington, D.C., July 19, 1932. *Still from Fox Movietone News outtake, Moving Image Research Collections, University of South Carolina*

Gen. Douglas MacArthur's handiwork: the Bonus Marchers' encampment in flames in front of the U.S. Capitol, July 28, 1932. *Public Domain, National Archives and Records Administration*

Unidentified Marine at the January 6, 2021, pro-Trump insurrection at the U.S. Capitol. This photo was taken by another Marine, Christopher Jones, who came to document the riot as a journalist. Seconds after the photo was taken, the Marine putschist told his comrade he was "fake news" and should be shot. *Courtesy of Christopher Jones for 100 Days in Appalachia*

# TWELVE

## DOMINICAN REPUBLIC

I n 1916—while Butler was organizing the Gendarmerie and begging Bunny to leave Philadelphia for Port-au-Prince—the United States invaded the only uncolonized and unoccupied country left in the Caribbean. It happened to be right next door.

The circumstances in the Dominican Republic were specific, but the pattern had by now become familiar: local unrest and a presidential assassination, a cash-strapped government forced to take out a controlling U.S. loan (from City Bank, negotiated by Roger Farnham), and unfounded fears of creeping German influence. American commanders in Haiti, including Littleton Waller, were also getting fed up with mixed bands of Haitians and Dominicans attacking their bases in the north, then escaping—likely with the help of local Dominican officials—across the unpatrolled, undemarcated border.[1]

U.S. banks already controlled the Dominican customs system under the terms of the earlier "receivership," managed by J. P. Morgan through its subsidiary, Guaranty Trust. In the years leading up to the invasion, the Wilson administration had presented the Dominican government with a new list of demands: a U.S.-supervised presidential election, the installation of American financial supervisors, and the replacement of the Dominican military with a U.S.-organized National Guard.[2]

The invasion came when an anti-imperialist war minister, Gen. Desiderio Arias, tried to wrest power from the more pliant President Juan Jiménez. Two companies of Marines landed in the capital, Santo Domingo, under the command of now-Capt. Fritz Wise, on May 5, 1916. Refusing to countenance a full U.S. invasion on his behalf, Jiménez resigned without naming a successor.

Rear Admiral Caperton sailed from Port-au-Prince to Santo Domingo aboard the well-traveled USS *Dolphin* to demand Arias "disband his army and surrender his weapons by 0600 hours on 15 May or face a full-scale American attack."[3] Arias refused but retreated from Santo Domingo to the city of Santiago de los Caballeros, in the interior Cibao Valley. That left the oldest European-founded capital in the Americas in the hands of five companies of U.S. Marines.

Over the next few weeks, thousands of Marine reinforcements landed in the Dominican Republic. On June 26, the full Fourth Marine Regiment under Col. Joseph Pendleton—Butler's old commander in Nicaragua and at Subic Bay—started racing toward Arias in Santiago. The regiment moved as a "flying column"—a formation in which soldiers are equipped lightly enough to move quickly but well-stocked enough not to need resupplying from a rear base. It was a tactic derived in colonial warfare, having been employed in the past by the French in Algeria, the British in South Africa, and in modified form by the U.S. Army during the ethnic cleansing of the Great Plains.

Pendleton took advantage of the latest technology, including a complement of motorized trucks and eleven Ford touring cars to go with his usual mule carts and horses. This was new: the first experiments in motorized warfare were happening at that moment on the battlefields of France and Belgium. The U.S. Army had deployed its first motorized convoys just a few weeks earlier in Mexico in pursuit of Pancho Villa.

When the column neared Santiago, Arias surrendered, ending the Dominicans' best hope of stopping a full-scale occupation. Playing for time, the Dominican Congress appointed a nationalist diplomat, Francisco Henríquez y Carvajal, as interim president for six months. Henríquez agreed to accept a U.S. financial adviser but rejected the rest of Wilson's demands. While the parties bickered, Marines set out across the countryside to root out the last vestiges of armed resistance.

M y Dear Precious Darlings . . . We left Port-au-Prince at 11:00 A.M., September 1," Butler wrote Bunny and the kids in Philadelphia from the Dominican town of Comendador. After four days marching in heat and rain, a short train ride, and a marathon climb across the Sierra de Neiba mountains, Butler and his flying column of two hundred Marines and Haitian Gendarmes had found themselves just across "the 'border,'" as he wrote it, using scare quotes. "We just had lunch so must hurry back to Belladere"—a Haitian village about nine miles away—"to make my preparations for this raid tonight."[4] Where along that mountain road one country ended and the other began was anyone's guess.

The borderlands of the island of Hispaniola had changed hands, in whole or in part—first between France and Spain, then the governments in Port-au-Prince and Santo Domingo—no fewer than eighteen times over the preceding centuries.[5] For stretches the island had been governed as a single entity, under the Spanish crown in the fifteenth century, the French Republic in the late eighteenth, and under Haitian control from 1822 to 1844. A map adopted by the Dominican government in 1905 showed no single official dividing line at all.[6] In practice, the whole border region was a semi-autonomous zone where Haitians and Dominicans mingled freely—identifiable, if they were identifiable at all, by which language they spoke most: Spanish or Kreyòl.

The first real attempts at establishing border controls had come at the behest of the American customs officials in the years immediately prior to the invasion, born out of their eagerness to "rationalize" trade under the receivership and ensure that every possible international transaction was taxed. Those officials would be key sources of information for the Marines.

In the months preceding the raid, Butler had become personally frustrated with attacks on his new Gendarme posts in northeastern Haiti, emanating from the border zone. In July, fighters—likely a combination of Cacos and Dominican insurgents, known as *gavilleros*—had attacked a Gendarme position at Ferrier and overrun a station at Capotille. Citing the "constant uneasiness" in the area, he had taken his new Gendarmes on their first "drive"—a mission to, as he told Bunny, "clean up that district."[7]

Now, in the southern portion of the borderlands, he would lead an assault onto recognizable Dominican territory. His orders were to capture a Dominican insurgent named Celidiano Pantilion (or maybe "Pantillione"—the Marines were unsure of the spelling), as well as the nationalist Haitian lawyer Antoine Pierre-Paul, who had participated in a coup attempt against the Haitian puppet president, Philippe Dartiguenave, and was believed to be hiding in the mountains. But the Marines found nothing in the towns of Las Matas, San Juan de la Maguana, nor in the village known as either Bucá Creol or El Cercado.[8]

On September 11, 1916, the Marines arrived in the provincial capital of Azua in the middle of the annual saint's day fiestas, where they linked up with a column from Santo Domingo led by Butler's old friend from Panama (and Samar veteran) Maj. Hiram Bearss. "Our appearance caused the greatest confusion," Butler wrote his wife. "We took all the government buildings available for the men and horses and rented a little house for us officers."[9]

Most of the carnival-goers were understandably not happy to see the invaders. Someone offered them food; another warned, too late, that the bread had been poisoned. Over the next few days, as Marines fell ill, the flying column temporarily decamped to the nearby plantation of the American-owned Central Ansonia Sugar Company. All recovered. But for the rest of the trip, Butler wrote, "my stomach was absolutely no use to me."[10]

So went the rest of the mission: four weeks hard marching, sometimes covering more than thirty miles in a day, with no sign of "Pantilion" or Pierre-Paul. In the end, all Butler had to show for his borderland raid was a pair of seized rifles.

It was more successful as an exercise in intimidation. "We tried our level best to provoke hostile assault on the part of the natives living in the country through which we passed but to no avail," Butler wrote his father afterward, perhaps with a bit of self-aware sarcasm. "The people were most hostile in their attitude, but not enough so to give us an excuse for violence."[11]

With the Dominican insurgents temporarily cowed, the Wilson administration made it official. On November 29, 1916, Capt. Harry Knapp of the U.S. Navy formally proclaimed a military occupation of the entire Dominican Republic. The order justified this on the basis of alleged violations of the 1907 bank "receivership" treaty—specifically the Dominicans having since taken on more public debt (much of it courtesy of Roger Farnham and the National City boys) to finance crackdowns against internal insurrections.[12] The United States now effectively controlled the entire upper chain of the Caribbean: Cuba, Haiti, the Dominican Republic, and

Puerto Rico, as well as the archipelago soon to be known as the U.S. Virgin Islands. It would formally occupy all of Hispaniola until 1924.

U.S. commanders took Butler and his fellow officers' complaints about the "border" seriously. "The matter of fixing absolutely the boundary between these two countries, now unsettled and somewhat in controversy, is one of my hopes during my sojourn here," Rear Admiral Thomas Snowden, U.S. military governor of Santo Domingo, wrote the commander of the First Marine Brigade in Haiti in 1919. "Under the direction of the U.S. Geological Survey, a topographical and geological survey is about to be commenced and during its progress I hope to have the boundary line between the two Republics definitely settled and fixed for all time."[13]

Defining a nation's borders is necessary for controlling it. In order to tax, police, or bomb a place, it is useful to know exactly where one regime's rule ends and another's begins. That meant that the farther the United States extended its power beyond its own borders, the more it had to ensure the borders of the territories it was involving itself in were clearly defined. The closing of the Dominican frontier promised to signal "both the integration of the region into the national economy and polity, as well as the global economy, and into the arena of domination by the United States," the historian Lauren Derby has written.[14]

As one might suspect, many in the borderlands did not want that closing to happen. In 1920, the Dominican governor of the province of Monte Cristi, which is situated close to Haiti, complained to U.S. occupation authorities about Marines deporting his Haitian residents. "Most [of these] people are Haitians [who are] naturalized Dominicans, and some retain their nationality but have lived here for many years and are land owners," he wrote. He blamed the "unjust abuses" on Americans' unwillingness to follow Dominican law: specifically, the constitution of 1865, which guaranteed *jus soli,* or "right of the soil," birthright citizenship for anyone born on Dominican territory.[15] As the historian Anne Eller has written, the drafters of that constitution specifically had the children of Haitians in mind; it was drafted in a moment of heightened cross-island cooperation, as Haitian revolutionaries helped their Dominican counterparts win the country's final independence from Spain.[16]

Snowden ignored the provincial governor's objection. A true believer in "the white man's burden; the duty of the big brother," as the admiral once wrote Josephus Daniels, his focus was on controlling people he deemed inferior by restricting their movements.[17] His administration banned Dominican laborers from emigrating while regulating the immigration of nonwhite sugarcane-cutters, or *braceros,* from Haiti and the rest of the Caribbean.[18]

Soon after, the Americans passed responsibility for enforcing the frontier to their new local franchise of Latin American client police: the Guardia Nacional Dominicana. The composition of the force would be somewhere between the model used in Haiti and the model the Americans would employ in Nicaragua: at first the Guardia would be headed by white Marine officers, with Dominicans given leadership roles soon after. The blended approach was indicative of the confusion white Americans had over how to categorize Dominicans, who, while predominantly of African descent, on average had more European ancestry than their Haitian neighbors.

But filling the Guardia's native ranks was a challenge. Collaborating with the occupiers was anathema to most Dominicans (a star pitcher for the Escogido Lions of Santo Domingo, "Fellito" Guerra, became a national hero during the U.S. occupation when he refused a contract to play in the Major Leagues[19]). That left the Guardia to be filled by outsiders, social climbers, and those with a thirst for violence, such as a cattle thief and sugar mill guard named Rafael Leonidas Trujillo. Trujillo had direct Haitian ancestry, on his mother's side. But to ensure he would be accepted by the Americans as a junior officer, he elided that on his application, declaring he was a "white married man who did not drink or smoke."[20]

An early record of abuses, including credible allegations by a seventeen-year-old girl that Trujillo raped her multiple times, did nothing to slow his meteoric rise. Trujillo's American mentor, the future Marine Corps Gen. Thomas "Terrible Tommy" Watson, noted in a typical efficiency report that the snub-nosed lieutenant had "initiative, intelligence and good judgment," and was "one of the best in the service."[21]

For a few years, Marines and Guardias worked together to crush renewed gavillero insurgencies. As with Butler's Gendarmerie in Haiti, they made a particular point of attacking religious ceremonies based in African traditions. In 1922, a unit led by Marine Capt. George H. Morse Jr. slaughtered twenty-two followers of a professed Afro-Dominican prophet in the borderlands.[22]

In 1924, with U.S. financial control firmly established through the banks, the Marines withdrew from the Dominican Republic. The new president, Horacio Vásquez, named Trujillo head of the Guardia, which Trujillo redubbed the Ejercito Nacional, or national army. In 1930, elements of the army revolted against the president. Instead of trying to control them, Trujillo declared himself a candidate in a new election and won.

The Americans had not put him up to it, but they didn't mind having a friend in charge. Despite the fact that Trujillo's soldiers had assaulted would-be opposition voters, burned houses, and ultimately rigged him a 99 percent victory, President Herbert Hoover extended Trujillo his "cordial congratulations" and offered him "best wishes for a most successful term of office and the happiness of the people of the Republic under your wise administration."[23]

Trujillo became known as El Generalissimo, or simply El Jefe, the boss, establishing one of the longest-lasting and most repressive dictatorships in Latin America. In addition to overseeing a regime of murder and surveillance, Trujillo was a pathological narcissist (he renamed the island's highest mountain after himself and changed the name of the capital to Ciudad Trujillo) and an outrageous kleptocrat. He also had a reputedly insatiable appetite for sexual violence.[24]

El Jefe's power was built at the border. In 1929, Trujillo's predecessor, Vásquez, had negotiated a framework border agreement with the government of still-occupied Haiti. Trujillo's first priority as dictator was to work out the details. It took a while, but in 1936, two years after the last Marines finally withdrew from Haiti, Haitian president Sténio Vincent toasted Trujillo as his guest in Port-au-Prince to celebrate the finalized border treaty.

A year later, in the fall of 1937, rumors began spreading of people being killed, en masse, on the newly consolidated Dominican side of the border. By November 24, the whispers had grown pervasive enough for a brief report to appear in the U.S. magazine *The New Republic*. According to the correspondent, Harold Courlander—an anthropologist inspired to come to Hispaniola after reading William B. Seabrook's *Magic Island*—Haitians had been rounded up and "slaughtered without respect to sex or age" by Dominican Guardias acting with the assistance of local volunteers.

"Fires could be seen for a week, probable funeral pyres for hundreds of hapless victims who did not move westward fast enough," Courlander wrote. Busloads of wounded Haitians were seen moving across the border. One eyewitness told him "of seeing 400 Haitian dead" buried in a single grave. "Until more complete accounts arrive," Courlander concluded, "it will be impossible to estimate the real extent of this violence."[25]

Unbeknownst to the correspondent, the extent of the violence was already broadly known to U.S. officials, who kept it secret. A month earlier, the U.S. ambassador in Ciudad Trujillo had written Secretary of State Cordell Hull to report that "a systematic campaign of extermination" had been "directed against all Haitian residents."[26]

The slaughter is remembered in the Dominican Republic as El Corte—the cutting. An estimated twenty thousand people were killed for the shade of their skin, their accent, or just because.[27] But killing was only the first step. By "Dominicanizing" the borderlands and enlisting the population in genocide, Trujillo was embarking on a plan to solidify a racialized national identity that would provide the justification for his continued rule. His officials emphasized Haiti's "Africanness" against Dominicans' supposedly more European and thus "superior" culture and traits. Dominican schools taught pseudoscientific theories about the supposed inferiority and barbarity of Black—that is, Haitian—people (a trend that continued in Dominican textbooks into the twenty-first century).[28]

Trujillo had two audiences in mind. One was the United States. Many in the Dominican intelligentsia believed, with reason, that their relatively whiter, more Hispanic roots had convinced the Americans to end the occupation there ten years earlier than in Haiti. Dominican officials hoped that "'another' white country like the United States" would "understand their racial dilemma" and take their side in any regional disputes, as the Dominican American historian Edward Paulino has written.[29]

More important, they needed to convince the Dominican people that only Trujillo could stop the looming Haitian "silent invasion." His interim foreign minister at the time of the ethnic cleansing, Joaquín Balaguer, repurposed the native anger that had surged against Smedley Butler and the other Marines during the U.S. occupation into a new Dominican ethnonationalism, warning tendentiously that "the proximity of Haitian imperialism is more dangerous" than "Anglo-American imperialism."[30]

Demonizing the invented "other" was a political strategy being employed to great effect by the fascists in Spain, Italy, and Germany at the time. But Trujillo's version would survive all those regimes. Because the border remained strategically porous in spots—allowing the Dominican and foreign sugar-growing elites to continue relying on illegally immigrated and thus perpetually precarious Haitian cane-cutters—the specter of the Black invaders would never diminish.

Trujillo's personal luck ran out in 1961, when after thirty-one years in power he was assassinated with guns believed to have been provided by the CIA. (According to a later U.S. Senate investigation, the State Department feared Trujillo's violent excesses could pave the way for another Fidel Castro–type revolution.)[31] For the first time since the occupation, Dominicans had a chance to choose their own leader; they picked the leftist Juan Bosch. But Bosch was overthrown in a 1963 coup, supported and solidified by yet another U.S. invasion ordered by President Lyndon Johnson in support of anti-Bosch forces two years later. With the U.S. Marines and 82nd Airborne Division standing by across the country, voters went back to the polls and elected Trujillo's protégé, Joaquin Balaguer, instead.

During Balaguer's decades in power—which stretched, with interruptions, until 1996—Haitians in the Dominican Republic were restricted to sugar plantation colonies called *bateyes*. As that system slowly ended, and people of Haitian descent once again started moving into Dominican cities, Dominican nationalists began fighting to limit Haitian immigration and, if possible, expel those they considered *haitianos*.[32]

In 2010, a national assembly drafted a new constitution that excluded the children of people residing "illegally in the Dominican territory" from citizenship—effectively repealing *jus soli* birthright citizenship. Three years later, a newly created constitutional court went even further: It ruled that anyone who could not prove their parents, grandparents, or even great-grandparents had been legal residents when they were born were no longer citizens. The retroactive ancestry requirement went all the way back to 1929—the year Trujillo's predecessor, Vásquez, had worked out the border framework agreement under U.S. supervision. A deadline was set for June 2015, by which time all those affected were to register themselves and their families or face expulsion.

Though the law did not specify any particular race or ethnicity for deportation, everyone knew who was being targeted: Haitians and people of Haitian descent are the only major immigrant group in the Dominican Republic. As the deadline neared, millions braced themselves for another ethnic cleansing.

In November 2015, I went to the border. I approached from the Dominican side, crossing into Haiti over a dry creek bed near the mouth of the Pedernales River. Once I'd passed through exit customs, the only sign of the border itself was a squat orange concrete marker stamped with the year the border was made official: 1929.

In this limbo, about a mile up from the crossing, was a makeshift camp home to thousands of fleeing Haitians and Dominicans of Haitian descent. Most had been living on the barren patch for months, in shacks fashioned out of whatever they could carry or find: used cardboard, bed-sheets, old clothes, bits of tin.

A shack close to the road, with driftwood walls and a couple of ratty comforters for a roof, belonged to Peres Yves Jean and Mirlene Lamour.[33] Both Peres and Mirlene were born on the Haitian side of the border. They met as teenagers working on the far eastern tip of the island, near the all-inclusive Dominican resorts of Punta Cana. As adults they became sharecroppers on a Dominican farm outside the little town of Los Patos, on the southern Barahona peninsula. They and their seven children spoke mostly Spanish with Kreyòl mixed in. Peres and Mirlene loved dancing to Dominican music and telling Haitian jokes. Their kids, like most Dominican kids, loved baseball.

Because their parents had brought them illegally as children, Peres and Mirlene were not Dominican citizens. Each of their children—three boys and four girls—had a different legal status, based on whatever the arbitrary laws had been at the moment each was born. But almost all the kids should have been Dominican citizens, because they were all born on Dominican soil before the constitution was changed. (Their youngest, two-year-old Milana, was the exception.)

As I sat on an upturned plastic wash bucket, Peres told me what had happened to them that year. In March, three months before the registration deadline, he had been coming home from a day job when he was picked up by men in khaki uniforms and thrown into the back of a truck. Because he did not have identification, the men drove him fifty miles west to the nearest border crossing and left him on the other side. Peres waited until the truck disappeared, then headed back across the shallow river to the Dominican side. For two days, he walked through cattle ranches and banana groves, under the turbines of a wind farm, until he reached his family in Los Patos. Then they gathered their things and left.

For a few weeks, the couple thought they could stick it out in another town right next to the border, on the Dominican side. But as the deadline approached, the drumbeat of threats and violence got louder. Before Peres's express deportation, a Haitian man had been found hanging from a tree in a park in Santiago de los Caballeros, his hands and feet bound with black cord. On the night of the lynching a nearby crowd of Dominicans burned a Haitian flag and chanted: "Haitians out! If it's war they want, it's war they'll get."[34] Now Dominican neighbors began threatening their family. Someone flashed a hatchet blade. When they would turn on their favorite station, Radio Independencia, to dance to some bachata or reggaeton, they'd hear the disc jockeys bantering about how the coming expulsions would go.

"All the Dominicans who lived around us knew that our children were all born in the Dominican Republic," Mirlene told me, with an air of resignation. "But the hospitals and the big bosses, they didn't know that." The couple's seven-year-old daughter, Yahira, sat beside her, studying me with her deep brown eyes.

So they crossed the border. Conditions were dire. In the five months since they set up a home in the refugee camp, Mirlene had traded all their dishware and one of their two mattresses for food. Like most of the families now living on the dirt patch, they moved their cookfire inside the shack to protect it from the constant wind and dust storms. On each of the four days I spent at the camp, at least one shack caught fire. The only source of drinking water was the river. Cholera had just claimed the life of a neighboring family's son.

Despite the threats, and the televised images of school buses and soldiers preparing for a mass deportation, no ethnic cleaning materialized—at least not on the scale of Trujillo's 1937 massacre. A wave of international attention and threatened boycotts against the Dominican tourism industry saw to that. More quietly, in piecemeal fashion, Dominican authorities deported an estimated 80,000 people of Haitian descent over the next two years. Sporadic lynchings, including the hacking to death of a man of Haitian descent in the town of Hatillo Palma in August 2015, convinced as many as 130,000 more to flee on their own.[35] As many as three quarters of a million more people of Haitian descent remain in the Dominican Republic, at risk for violence or eventual deportation from a place that has built its identity, and sense of national self-worth, on an invisible line.

Though some may not realize it, Dominicans are trapped behind that line as well. The border on Hispaniola is proof of the political philosopher Frantz Fanon's dictum that "the colonial world is a compartmentalized world."[36] It was drawn at the behest of an imperial power, formalized in the interests of foreigners, and consecrated in blood by a dictator empowered and trained by the Marines.

Those officials knew, as do their successors today, that for capital and elites to flow freely, subject peoples cannot. Fears of uncontrolled movement are why, a century after Butler complained about the lack of a clear border on Hispaniola, the U.S. government still helps fund, train, and equip border patrols across the world, from Jordan to Kenya to Peru.[37] That list includes the Dominican Specialized Frontier Security Corps, or CESFRONT—likely the force whose soldiers, dressed in U.S.-style desert camouflage, picked up and deported Peres Jean. Each day, these heirs to the Guardia fan out across the borderlands Butler and the Marines once patrolled, keeping everyone, and themselves, in line.

# THIRTEEN

## PORT-AU-PRINCE

By the late fall of 1916, Butler had had enough. "Stop spending money like a drunken sailor on cablegrams and come down here," he wrote Bunny.[1] She did so a few weeks later with the kids. They all moved into a big house in the hills above Port-au-Prince, with a shaded garden and a retinue of Haitian servants. Smedley imported a used Stutz touring car the family nicknamed "the blue bird." Snooks and Smedley Junior, now nine and seven, attended a French-language school. Tom Dick, just past his third birthday, was learning Kreyòl and English at the same time—to the extent that, as Ethel noted in a letter home, "his impulse is to speak the Haitian tongue rather than his own."[2]

The Butlers quickly established themselves as the power couple of the occupation, hosting liquor-fueled parties that brought together Marine officials and the Haitian elite. Butler was promoted to lieutenant colonel, making him one of the highest-ranking officers in the occupation. Ethel was often called on to escort the unmarried puppet president, Dartiguenave, on trips throughout Haiti and at official functions. The position as surrogate first lady offered her more influence and personal freedom than at any previous posting. "If my two fathers could see me now!" she wrote in a letter to Smedley's parents and her own, recalling her thoughts at an official dinner. "The black president of the 'Black Republic' on my right, the ditto minister of finance on my left, and all the other members of the party tinted the same dusty hue."[3]

In January 1917, the Butlers threw a party for their most prominent guest yet, when the naval secretary, Josephus Daniels, sent his deputy on an inspection tour of the Caribbean. Franklin Delano Roosevelt was the scion of three of the United States' richest families. At thirty-five, he was already a fast-rising star in Democratic politics, thanks in large part to his famous last name.[4] (Franklin was Teddy's fifth cousin, once removed.

His wife, Eleanor Roosevelt, was Teddy's niece.) The official purpose of Franklin's trip was to inspect America's de facto colonies guarding the route to the Panama Canal on the eve of an increasingly likely U.S. entry into the World War. The subtext was to remind both the client governments and the Marines overseeing them who was really in charge.

FDR steamed into Port-au-Prince Bay aboard the flagship of the North Atlantic Fleet. The colonial city with the mountains above it reminded him of descriptions he'd read of Vesuvius over Naples.[5] When President Dartiguenave sailed through the bay to greet him, every U.S. warship fired a twenty-one-gun national salute—shaking the harbor, illuminating the sky, and covering the waves in white powder smoke. It was an unmistakable show of dominance.

Bunny hosted a welcome dinner at the Butler family home for Roosevelt and his entourage, which included the Marine Corps commandant, George Barnett, the Haitian president, and his cabinet. Then they headed down the hill for an officers' ball.

Smedley had "rented" the new National Palace, still partially under construction, for the occasion. The Marine officers of the Gendarmerie put in a wooden dance floor and thousands of electric lights. They decorated the space with palm trees, rifles, and cannons, likely in a pastiche of the Haitian coat of arms.[6]

Roosevelt was particularly bemused by the light-skinned Haitian women of the U.S.-supported elite in their Parisian finery; he noted that they wore "yellow-colored powder instead of flesh-colored powder on their countenances" in his summary of the trip. Like Bunny, he was fascinated and discomfited at the sight of Black people in positions of power. Ethel, as usual, accompanied Dartiguenave in the reception line.[7]

Roosevelt spent a few days of his trip hiking in the dense forests around Port-au-Prince. (The paralytic illness that would take away the use of his legs was still several years in the future.) Butler and Col. Eli K. Cole, who had relieved Littleton Waller as commander of U.S. ground forces in Haiti a few months earlier, accompanied the assistant secretary across the bay to tour the island of La Gonâve.[8]

FDR also lunched at the mountainside villa of longtime German residents of Haiti, the Tippenhauer family. "Because under the Haitian law only a citizen can hold real estate, and because citizenship is confined to people of color, Herr Tippenhauer married the daughter of one of the members of the Cabinet," Roosevelt recorded in an account of his trip.[9] The German government, he noted, had used those connections to acquire a sugar mill, railroads, ports, and several plantations.

This was not an idle observation. Roosevelt knew that Wilson's State Department was in the process of drafting a new Haitian constitution. Its most important change, from an American standpoint, would be an article allowing foreigners to directly own land in Haiti, without any residency or marriage requirement.[10]

In fact, one of FDR's personal goals for his trip was to prepare a private investment scheme in Haitian agriculture. His efforts to personally benefit from an imperialist project followed a long family tradition. Not only was his "Uncle Ted" the godfather and prime beneficiary of the first wave of U.S. global imperialism, both of his parents' families—the Delanos, and his paternal grandmother's family, the Aspinwalls—traced their fortunes to the China opium trade. The Aspinwalls in turn had reinvested their narco-profits into the Panama Railroad; Franklin's great-uncle, William Henry Aspinwall, was one of the founders of the city of Colón.[11]

Franklin was intellectually prepared for a life in imperialism as well: in his last year at Harvard, he had taken History 10-B: Development of the American West, taught by Prof. Frederick Jackson Turner. He later had a brief but enthusiastic correspondence about sea power with Alfred Thayer Mahan.[12]

The desire to survey as much real estate as possible may have been why, at the last minute, Roosevelt asked Butler to arrange a horseback trip for him to Cap-Haïtien. Butler gamely complied, outfitting Roosevelt in a Gendarmerie uniform and seeing his party off north. ("I was terribly disappointed not to be able to accompany them but I have not been able to mount a horse since the 15th of November," Butler wrote his parents, citing an apparently short-lived injury.[13]) On the trip, FDR climbed at least part of the way up Black Mountain to visit what he called "the famous Fort Rivière," where he learned about Butler's role in the massacre of the Cacos.

When he got back to Washington, FDR recommended Butler for his second Medal of Honor for the Battle of Fort Rivière.[14] Maybe Butler had been chastened by the refusal to rescind his first Medal of Honor. Perhaps he was loath to turn down a gesture from a rising star in U.S. politics. But whatever torment he still felt about that battle, this time, Butler accepted the award without complaint.

On June 19, 1917, an emergency meeting was held at the U.S. legation in Port-au-Prince. The topic was the impending Haitian government rejection of the State Department–written constitution, particularly the controversial new clause permitting foreign ownership of land.

Throughout the tropical morning, a stream of U.S. military and diplomatic officials had visited the National Palace to impress on Dartiguenave the importance of the provision. A State Department official later summarized their argument, swaddling the interests of American banks and corporations in a blanket of paternalism:

> It was obvious that if our occupation was to be beneficial to Haiti and further her progress it was necessary that foreign capital should come to Haiti, in order to establish new industries and stimulate agricultural production in the country. Americans could hardly be expected to put their money into plantations and big agricultural enterprises in Haiti if they could not themselves own the land on which their money was to be spent.[15]

For Haitians, land was synonymous with independence. After their ancestors overthrew French colonialism and slavery in 1803, ordinary Haitians were "less concerned with how foreign governments saw their country than with defending their access to land," the historian Laurent Dubois has written. At the height of the French plantation system in the eighteenth century, Haiti's soil had been one of the most stupendous engines of wealth in human history—the world's leading producer of both sugar and coffee at the time, by several orders of magnitude.[16] Control over the valuable land on which their forebears had toiled became the most important social issue in Haitian society. Land was "the only thing, they knew, that would provide them with real autonomy, dignity, and freedom."[17]

There were some in the Haitian elite who did not object to selling their nation's hard-won birthright to American banks and corporations, including President Dartiguenave. But as the client-president explained to Colonel Cole, the Marine commander, the decision wasn't his to make. The power to promulgate a constitution resided with the delegates of the Haitian parliament, who were at that moment meeting to decide the question. The leaders of both the Senate and Chamber of Deputies had made it clear that they intended to approve only a constitution constructed on their own terms, which included leaving the prohibition on foreign landownership in place.

If installing a fake president was not enough to ensure their goals were achieved, the occupation authorities would just dispense with the pretense of democracy entirely. "There was nothing else to be done but dissolve the National Assembly," Cole told a U.S. Senate committee a few years later.[18] To do it, he sent Smedley Butler.

Butler went to Dartiguenave to get an executive order. This was, the occupation authorities knew, the way Woodrow Wilson would prefer to have the last surviving democratic institution destroyed in Haiti: with a patina of administrative procedure—not to mention plausible deniability.

But the Haitian leader refused to see Butler. An aide whispered that the president was "very sick."[19] Butler explained that the president had no choice. Cole had told him that if "the president did not sign the decree," the Marine commander "would suppress the National Assembly myself and would recommend the establishment of a military government."[20]

The president, who was apparently indeed suffering from some kind of head cold, relented and issued the order, which was cosigned by four of his five cabinet members. But Dartiguenave insisted that Butler deliver the decree himself, in his role as commandant of the Gendarmerie. Butler said he was willing to do so. But, he warned the president, "there may be bloodshed."[21]

When Butler burst onto the parliament floor, the senators and deputies were in the middle of voting on ratifying their own version of the constitution. They began to jeer and hiss at the strongmen. Smedley ordered his Gendarmes, who had been detailed as security throughout the joint session, to seal the doors.[22] With the members now alarmed, the Marine strolled to the speaker's desk and calmly informed the presiding Senate leader, Sténio Vincent, that he was carrying a message from the president.

Vincent, a forty-three-year-old conservative from Port-au-Prince who had vocally opposed the occupation, asked Butler to hand him the order. He read it through his pince-nez glasses, then asked if he could read it aloud to the session. "I said, 'That is the reason I brought it down here,'" Butler later testified. But instead of reading the decree, the stentorian leader "entered into a vicious assault upon me and all other Americans, and referring to us as foreign dogs and devils dissolving the assembly."[23]

The Gendarmes loaded their rifles, prepared to fire in defense of their commander. Realizing the entire legislative body was now in the sights of its supposed security detail, and not wishing to have a repeat of the massacre of Fort Rivière on the parliament floor, Vincent gave in. Haiti's legislature was dissolved. It would not meet again for another twelve years.

Power, Butler knew, depended not only on violence but also on the control of information. If word got out of the Marines' role in the shuttering of parliament, Haitians would be scandalized. So he summoned the editors of all the national newspapers to Gendarmerie headquarters, where they were ordered not to publish any details. Later that day, according to a commission headed by Vincent, Butler had the records of the assembly's last votes removed from the parliamentary archives.[24] In a letter to John A. McIlhenny, a member of Franklin Roosevelt's inner circle, Butler added that he would later give him a "mouth to ear account" of what he had done. "Am afraid to write it," he explained, "for fear the Department of State might get a hold of this letter by means of the censors."[25]

Americans' ignorance of our imperial history can be traced in part to such cover-ups. "The presences and absences embodied in sources . . . or archives," the Haitian scholar Michel-Rolph Trouillot wrote decades later, "are neither neutral or natural. They are created . . . one 'silences' a fact or an individual as a silencer silences a gun."[26] By covering his tracks, Butler ensured there would be no accountability for the occupation's actions from either the Haitian or American publics, and that the story would be pushed to the margin of both countries' histories for generations to come.

With the legislature now abolished, the U.S.-written constitution was placed before a popular plebiscite in the summer of 1918. Polling places were overseen by Butler's rifle-toting Gendarmes, who were encouraged to actively campaign for the constitution's passage.[27] Less than 5 percent of Haiti's population voted. It passed overwhelmingly. In addition to the key clause permitting foreigners to own land, the final draft vested the legislative powers of the dissolved parliament in a "Council of State" appointed by the puppet president. It also contained a special article declaring: "All the acts of the Government of the United States during its military occupation of Haiti are ratified and legal."[28]

At the end of his life, Butler would look back at his actions at the Haitian parliament as one of his signature acts of gangsterism; the crime that above all others would make Haiti, as he would write in his *War Is a Racket* years, "a decent place for the National City Bank boys to collect revenues in."[29] Nearly two decades had passed since Butler first enlisted, hoping to free Cubans from tyranny. Now, one island over, he had personally helped destroy a democracy.

During my years living in Haiti in the late 2000s and early 2010s, I spent countless hours in the front seat of a car—most often in a patched-up SUV with the windows rolled down and my buddy Evens Sanon behind the wheel. As in America's former colony in Manila, traffic was so severe and the roads in such terrible condition that even going a few miles could take hours. It made the country feel much bigger than it was.

I learned a lot about Haiti's dismantled institutions in that traffic. Sometimes I'd be sitting behind an unregulated bus, overloaded with passengers sitting on the roof, clutching their belongings for a dangerous journey over the mountains. We might find ourselves breathing the exhaust of an eighteen-wheeler hauling cheap imported food, thanks to neoliberal trade policies that destroyed the country's farm sector. Other times we'd trail a bright-white armored personnel carrier of the United Nations' peacekeeping mission—a foreign blue-helmeted soldier, one of the thousands sent to enact the will of the United States and other foreign powers, glaring at me from behind an M2 Browning machine gun. If we were particularly unlucky, the highway would be blocked entirely by a barricade or burning tires. With Haiti's democratic institutions still in shambles a century after Butler dissolved parliament, grinding traffic to a halt was often the only way for angry citizens to make themselves heard.

This dysfunctional infrastructure was another of Smedley Butler's gifts to Haiti. In his counterinsurgency patrols and setting up of the Gendarmerie, he had run into constant headaches trying to move troops and equipment. U.S. investors—led by City Bank—had started funding a national railway just before the invasion. But it was so haphazardly built that its only real value was as an excuse for City Bank to collect on the debt the Haitian government had taken on to build it. (The railroad company's president was, naturally, Roger Farnham.)[30] The advent of the mass-produced automobile convinced Butler and his superiors in the military that turning horse trails and cow paths into a nationwide system of highways was the way to go.

But who would build them? Butler had learned that, under an old set of laws called the Code Rural, all of Haiti's roads were managed by the rural police, whose authority Butler's Gendarmerie had usurped.[31] The trouble was that the Gendarmerie could barely afford to pay any salaries on a meager $8,000-a-month road-construction budget, siphoned out of Haitian customs revenues by the American receiver general. Without better pay, farmers would not be eager to work for the Americans—especially a certain Main Line Quaker who, he was informed, had become "known throughout Haiti as 'The Devil.'" ("A fine reputation that," Butler commented, mildly annoyed, in a letter to his father.)[32]

Butler thumbed through his Marine translation of the old 1864 Code Rural. He noticed Article 54, which said that roads were to be "kept up and repaired by the inhabitants from each section . . . through which they pass."[33] It sounded innocuous, but as a Haitian legal commenter noted in 1872, the law as worded "gives rise to abuse," especially since it stipulated that workers would not be paid.[34] Nineteenth-century Haitian governments had used that law to justify the corvée—the return to slavery that earlier generations of Caco insurgents had risen up to defeat.

Smedley Butler thought the corvée sounded perfect. "We had little cards printed, notification cards, and lists of the names of citizens who should work on the roads," he told a U.S. Senate committee in 1921—convened to investigate abuses in the ongoing Haiti occupation after Wilson had left office and his rival Republicans had retaken power. "The Gendarmes then delivered these little cards notifying them that on a certain date they would report at a certain place and do their work or pay a certain tax."

"They had the option?" the committee chairman asked.

"They had the option," Butler replied. "Nobody had any money, so they reported for work." He compared it to a barn raising.[35]

Haitians saw easily through this veneer. "First, the work isn't paid," a corvée survivor told the Haitian historian Roger Gaillard years later. "Second, you worked with your back to the sun wearing nothing but pants. Third, they only sent you home when you were sick. Fourth, you didn't eat enough, just corn and congo beans. Fifth, you slept in a prison or at the construction site. Sixth, when you tried to run away, they killed you. Now then, is that not slavery?"[36]

A Baptist missionary from Pennsylvania told the Senate in 1921 that he had seen corvée workers "struck with such force by the Gendarme officer, and for the merest trifle, until they would fall like logs"; on at least one occasion he had "seen dead bodies covered with vermin, exposed and naked for days" near a corvée work site.[37] A Marine major admitted during that hearing that some corvée workers were killed trying to escape.[38] The Gendarmes, the Baptist missionary told the committee, were always Haitian—as with Trujillo and Somoza elsewhere, the white Marines elevated the most brutal of them to do the dirty work.

The road to the north opened under budget and ahead of schedule. Butler made the first drive from Port-au-Prince to Cap-Haïtien in his Stutz "blue bird"—though at one point he needed a corvée team to pull the car with ropes around a tricky bend. When Franklin Roosevelt cabled Butler to congratulate him on the project, Butler responded coyly: "It would not do to ask many questions as to how we accomplished this work."[39]

Smedley Butler defended his management of the corvée by claiming he only had the best interests of Haitians in mind. He would tell the Senate committee that he had gone so far as to execute Haitian Gendarmes who abused civilians. "The executions, of course, required the sanction and approval of the president of Haiti. He signed the death warrants. On one occasion we shot a Gendarme for shooting a prisoner. We never tolerated abuse of prisoners or the public."[40]

In addition to highway construction, Butler used thousands more prisoners to staff a factory that made uniforms for the Gendarmerie, as well as a bakery, a straw-hat factory, and carpentry and auto repair shops. But a few months after Butler left Haiti in 1918, the new brigade commander,

John H. Russell, decided that the practice had sparked too much of a backlash. He announced it would be officially abolished—as soon as "certain roads, needed for military purposes, had been opened up."[41]

The authoritarian mentality that characterized the roads' construction was reflected in the design of the highway system. So that the Marines and Gendarmes could control every part of the country from the capital, the highways connected regional centers to Port-au-Prince but not each other. When I lived in Haiti, in order to get from the south end of the Dominican border to the north end, a driver had to go fifty miles and several hours out of their way to Port-au-Prince, forcing them to pass through the stalled and smoking traffic of the capital on the way. Because it would be easier to control a single international port than the dozen former regional centers, most of the imports that have become the country's lifeblood now arrive in, and have to be trucked out of, Port-au-Prince as well. "Centralization did not simply leap out of the head of the American occupier," the Haitian geographer Georges Anglade wrote. "It was a centrality materially produced by the very demands of a dependent country to a center: the U.S.A."[42]

The result is that in Haiti today it is often impossible to do business, find work, or access education anywhere but the capital. As millions of people moved to a city whose road infrastructure was built to serve fewer than five hundred thousand, the streets of Port-au-Prince became largely impassable. Each day, its arteries clog with the cars and foot traffic of people trying to eke out a living, embittered by a broken system designed with imperial control, not their lives, in mind. In 1921, Roger Farnham boasted that the "beautifully done" Port-au-Prince-to-Cap-Haïtien highway made the transit possible "easily in twelve hours."[43] I often had to budget that long for the same trip a century later.

Military censors and cover-ups were some of the reasons Americans were unaware of what was happening in Haiti in 1917. Another was that they were distracted by the U.S. entry into a conflict that affected far more people directly, as nearly five million Americans were mobilized for the World War.

Though the children were happy in Port-au-Prince, and Smedley and

Bunny were in many ways at the apex of power and influence in their lives, Butler became obsessed with being transferred across the Atlantic. There was little fighting for him left to do in Haiti, and the work of managing a Black republic felt, to him and his government, inherently less important. The prospect of not proving himself in Europe, joining his comrades in battle against the world's most powerful armies, tormented him. "Had I remained in civil life, I could have gone to France at least as a Lieutenant, and saved my face," Butler groused to his parents in October 1917. "As long as the present gang stays at Headquarters, I will never be allowed to get into the show and will have to remain a Black Cop."[44]

In an effort to woo the Navy Department into approving his transfer, Butler tried to make himself indispensable to Roosevelt. FDR's plans for his personal investment scheme depended on a small circle of friends in the occupation. This group included John McIlhenny (the Louisiana-born civil service commissioner and soon-to-be chief U.S. financial adviser to Haiti had been one of "Uncle Ted's" Rough Riders in Cuba and was the heir to the Tabasco hot sauce fortune); another of FDR's cousins, Marine Maj. H. L. "Harry" Roosevelt; and McIlhenny's old friend at City Bank, Roger Farnham.[45]

Butler put the corvée to work for the FDR clique directly, using his prison laborers to offload freight Farnham was importing into the port of Saint Marc. He also offered to handle "any other 'roughstuff'" that might be needed, possibly meaning using the Gendarmerie to break strikes or intimidate competitors. When Roosevelt and McIlhenny informed Butler of their concerns that continuing German influence over Haiti's wholesale trade posed a threat to American interests, including their own, Butler said he'd take care of it. He suggested Roosevelt persuade the Haitians to symbolically declare war on Germany—which they did in July 1918.[46]

Plans for a formally incorporated Haitian trading company headed by FDR and McIlhenny—with Roger Farnham as a consultant—only fell apart in 1922 when McIlhenny, suffering a pang of ethics, decided he couldn't start work until he'd resigned as adviser to the Haitian government, and other investors lost interest.[47]

There's no evidence, at least none I found, that Butler held a financial stake in the scheme. Nor did his participation achieve his intended ends. Maud Darlington Butler, sympathizing as always with her son's desire to be at the center of the action, wrote him in the fall of 1917: "Sec. Roosevelt told thy father when he was in Washington last Monday they all fully realized thee should be in France, but they fear trouble when thee is taken away from Haiti and they can ill afford to send soldiers to Haiti at this time."

Given all the "splendid work thee is doing in Haiti," Maud said, as only a mother can, "I don't wonder they are having difficulty in finding someone to take thy place." But, she counseled, "I can wait patiently dear Smedley, and I wish thee will. I fear we are not near the end of the trouble and I don't suppose any of us realize what may be before us."[48]

The U.S. Occupation of Haiti, as it was officially known in Washington, lasted for nineteen years. Like the war in Afghanistan a century later, it seemed to get less popular with the American public with every passing season; yet four consecutive U.S. presidents—Democrat and Republican—left office without lifting a finger to end it. It took the fifth to bring the Marines home: Franklin D. Roosevelt.

Though FDR played key roles in both the invasion and occupation (he even claimed, dubiously, to have written Haiti's new constitution himself), as president he saw an opportunity to win friends abroad and outflank rivals in Washington.[49] In 1934, as part of his "Good Neighbor Policy" toward Latin America, which also saw the end of the occupation of Nicaragua and the revocation of the Platt Amendment in Cuba, FDR made the first visit by a sitting U.S. president to Haiti. Coming ashore at Cap-Haïtien with the help of his aides and a specially built barge, he shook hands with Haiti's new president, Sténio Vincent, the bespectacled Senate leader whom Butler had threatened at gunpoint seventeen years earlier. There, Roosevelt announced the withdrawal of the Marines, expressing his hope that the Americans "would always be remembered as friends who tried to help Haiti."[50] (*The Crisis,* the NAACP magazine founded by W. E. B. Du Bois, which had opposed the occupation since the beginning noted: "The Marines are gone but the American Financial Advisor is still there."[51])

The long-term achievements of the occupation were relatively minor: a stabilized currency, a pause in military coups, and a temporary reduction in foreign debt—thanks mostly to the prioritization of payments to

American creditors. As with the roads, new infrastructures for water, electricity, and telephones were limited to Port-au-Prince, where they served to "both justify and facilitate nearly two decades of imperial control," as the historian Claire Antone Payton has observed.

Modernization in Port-au-Prince disguised and contributed to the neglect and deterioration of the rest of the country.[52] First there was the sheer loss of life. In late 1918, after the Butlers had left Haiti, another Caco rebellion broke out. It was launched by Charlemagne Péralte, a former Haitian army commander who had been taken prisoner and forced into a labor camp by Butler's Gendarmerie.[53] Péralte's leadership of the revolt did not last long: on Halloween night, 1919, a year into his rebellion, a pair of Marines dressed in blackface snuck into Péralte's base in Grande-Rivière-du-Nord and assassinated him at point-blank range.[54] Having not yet learned the consequences of parading Benjamin Zeledón's body through Nicaragua, the Marines took Péralte's corpse to Cap-Haïtien. It was stripped naked except for a loincloth around his waist, and lashed to a door with the arms splayed out. The Marines took a photograph and made hundreds of copies, which they dropped out of airplanes across the countryside. The image, known today as the "Crucifixion of Charlemagne Péralte," has inspired generations of resistance.

Spurred on by Péralte's martyrdom, the Second Caco War proved longer and more difficult to win for the Americans than the insurgency Butler had crushed at Fort Rivière. But this time the empire had developed more efficient ways of killing as well. While Haitian Gendarmes slaughtered Cacos and suspected Caco sympathizers on the ground, Marines used the newest weapon of war—the biplane—to bomb villages from the sky.[55]

American investors took advantage of the new U.S.-written constitution to snap up land and start large, plantation-style agricultural projects. Dispossession ravaged the peasantry. The Haitian American Sugar Company—whose cane fields were the setting of William Seabrook's landmark zombie story in *The Magic Island*—evicted scores of smallholder farmers and drove small cane producers out of business. (The land around the former Hasco sugar mill is now Cité Soleil, one of Port-au-Prince's largest and most destitute slums.) American capitalists monopolized essential resources, particularly water; the jobs they offered were limited, seasonal, and poorly paid.[56]

Butler's most lasting mark on Haiti was the Gendarmerie. Following the example Trujillo set with the expansion of his Guardia Nacional in the Dominican Republic, near the end of the occupation the Gendarmerie was reorganized into a new national army, the Garde d'Haïti. "We cannot overemphasize the fundamental political difference between the Garde and the army that was dismantled by the Marines," Michel-Rolph Trouillot wrote. While Haiti's original army "saw itself as the offspring of the struggle against slavery and colonialism . . . the Haitian Garde was specifically created to fight against other Haitians. It received its baptism of fire in combat against its countrymen. And the Garde, like the [new] army it was to sire, has indeed never fought against anyone *but* Haitians."[57]

The army continued Butler's legacy of manipulating local politics. In the late 1940s, it kept a close eye on one of Vincent's successors, the nationalist Dumarsais Estimé. Estimé had opposed the occupation and U.S. control. But his critique was not of capitalism, militarism, or the United States itself. Rather, it was rooted in *noirisme,* a philosophy that attributed Haiti's problems to the members of the country's tiny mixed-race minority who had been favored in business and elevated to positions of political authority under the Marines' Jim Crow–style administration. When the Garde saw that Haitian Marxists and independent labor groups were poised to unseat Estimé, they stepped in and overthrew him first. He was replaced by Gen. Paul Magloire, the leader of the Garde, who set out to consolidate a Trujillo- or Somoza-style military rule.[58]

But Haiti's path went in a different direction than its neighbors'. Elites and the public lost faith in Magloire after his failed response to a devastating hurricane. Protesters forced an election in 1957. The army's preferred candidate was a noiriste doctor, François Duvalier, whose mild manner and lack of charisma led them to think he would be easy to control. Duvalier's background as a rural medical worker had also earned him the respect of the Haitian peasantry (they called him "Papa Doc"), a rare accomplishment among politicians vying for power in Port-au-Prince.

Though the Eisenhower administration was not thrilled to see a noiriste take power, it saw Duvalier as preferable to more leftist alternatives. The Defense and State Departments shrugged as the Garde, wearing knapsacks labeled "U.S. Army," massacred supporters of Duvalier's chief rival in Port-au-Prince.[59]

But Papa Doc did not turn out to be as manipulatable as the client army or the Americans had hoped. Duvalier was served by the material and psychic legacies of the American occupation. His Black nationalist ideology appealed to those still wounded by the violence and humiliations of American white-supremacist rule. He took advantage of the central-ized fiscal system to transfer enormous sums into the private accounts of the ruling family and associates—sometimes as much as 40 percent of the country's GDP.[60] A keen student of politics, he recognized the threat the army posed to his power and created his own paramilitary secret police, nicknamed the tonton makout, to counterbalance it.

Those who could not be persuaded or coerced into tolerating him were tortured, exiled, or killed. Whenever it looked like the Americans might challenge his kleptocratic regime, Duvalier simply pointed to nearby Cuba, where Fidel Castro took power in 1959, to remind the Americans what the alternative might be. Some U.S. officials actively supported the regime by "discouraging American journalists from publishing pieces crit-ical of Duvalier and even relayed intelligence to the Haitian government regarding a possible attack from Cuba," as Payton has summarized.[61]

In 1971, Duvalier died of heart failure, leaving the presidency-for-life to his nineteen-year-old son, Jean-Claude. "Baby Doc" further exacer-bated centralization by ignoring agricultural development and investing in assembly plant manufacturing in Port-au-Prince, producing blue jeans, baseballs, and clothes for Cabbage Patch Kids dolls in tax-free "export processing zones" for shipment to the United States. In 1986, Haitians who had had enough of hunger and repression forced the younger Duva-lier to board a U.S. Air Force cargo plane, bound for exile in Paris.

In the aftermath, the army Smedley Butler helped found was once again in charge. The former Garde tried to prevent democracy from tak-ing root by massacring voters in a 1987 election. But in 1990, the first free election since the occupation was held. Jean-Bertrand Aristide, an anti-Duvalierist Catholic priest who promised land and economic redistribu-tion, won—only to be overthrown by the army nine months later. Several of the putschists had been on the CIA's payroll. At least two of the coup's leaders were trained by the U.S. Army.[62]

George H. W. Bush's secretary of state called the junta "illegitimate."[63] But the administration focused far more attention on intercepting Haitian refugees trying to escape to the United States. Tens of thousands were held in the new prison camp, just built by the Marines for that purpose, at Guantánamo Bay.

In the time-honored tradition of caprice and transitions of power in Washington, President Bill Clinton reversed his predecessor's policy and reinstalled Aristide with a 1994 invasion by the Army and Marines. In exchange for U.S. support, Aristide agreed to a "structural adjustment program"—a neoliberal version of "dollar diplomacy," overseen by the International Monetary Fund and the World Bank, in which he lowered trade barriers, slashed deficits, and privatized and deregulated state functions in exchange for controlling loans.

Haiti's economy spiraled. The former slum priest turned to fraud and intimidation to hold on to power. In 2004, with Bush's son in power, a rebel gang and a band of ex-Haitian soldiers—trained in the Dominican Republic and backed by a Republican nonprofit headed by Senator John McCain—overthrew Aristide again.[64]

Between coups, Aristide had disbanded the former Garde, in an effort to keep it from overthrowing him again. That left George W. Bush without a client army to take control. So, for the third time in less than a hundred years, the U.S. military again invaded Haiti, in March 2004, with the support of the Canadians and the French. A few months later, they were replaced by a United Nations peacekeeping force. As a report by the U.S. Government Accountability Office quickly acknowledged, Washington had in effect outsourced a new occupation to the UN.[65]

At the end of a century of upheaval, Haiti was a country unable to grow enough food to support itself, with a crippled government, in which the most powerful institutions were an armed United Nations force and the U.S. embassy. It would not take much to send it all crashing down.

On the afternoon of January 12, 2010, at 4:53 P.M., an earthquake erupted on Haiti's southern peninsula, fifteen miles west of Port-au-Prince. I was in my house in the hills above the capital when the shaking started. When it stopped, I clambered over the fallen walls of my living room to find that the neighborhood that had previously stood behind my house was gone. The air was filled with cries of anguish and pain. A choking cloud of dust hung above the earth. By the most modest casualty estimates, it was the deadliest earthquake ever recorded in the Western Hemisphere. In its upper ranges, with upward of 230,000 dead, it rivals the deadliest in human history.[66]

Among the hundreds of thousands of buildings torn to pieces by the quake were the halls of power built during the U.S. occupation, including the National Palace, finance ministry, and supreme court. The Port-au-Prince cathedral—where Ethel Butler attended services with Dartiguenave while it was under construction in 1917—was utterly destroyed.

The decimated Haitian government was forced to turn back to the hegemon for help. Again, we sent the military: The U.S. Army's 82nd Airborne Division spilled out of helicopters onto the lawn of the destroyed National Palace. The U.S. Air Force Special Operations Command took over the airport. Nineteen American warships anchored offshore, led by a nuclear aircraft carrier.

The top-down, highly centralized military model of the response left huge parts of the quake zone unaided. Billions of dollars were funneled to military contractors and aid worker expense accounts. The most powerful figures in the response were Hillary and Bill Clinton: she in her role as Barack Obama's secretary of state, he in a panoply of roles including UN special envoy and overseeing a World Bank–managed reconstruction fund.[67] Following in the interventionist steps of her predecessors at State, from Philander Knox to John Foster Dulles, Hillary Clinton disrupted a post-quake election to ensure a pliable, pro-business president would take power. All their efforts made sure the cataclysm would be used above all to further the interests of global markets and the U.S. government.

The ultimate expression of this was the building of the $300 million, U.S.-financed Caracol Industrial Park near Cap-Haïtien. The complex, whose plans had been in the works since before the earthquake, was to become a new economic hub: a complex of garment factories and low-wage assembly plants that would at last achieve the long-unfulfilled promise of export-based prosperity. The clients of the South Korean anchor tenant, Sae-A Trading Co. Ltd., included Target, the Gap, Walmart, and Old Navy. The Clintons headlined the grand opening of the park in 2012, overshadowing the two Haitian presidents in attendance, including the one Hillary had just helped win.*

I last went inside the industrial park in 2015. The garment factory floor was clean and bright. The workers were miserable. Their measly wages, starting around $4.75 a day, did not even cover the cost of food and transport to work. The hours were long, the foreign managers overbearing.

The neighbors were also furious: as with the Hasco sugar mill a century before, hundreds of farmers had been forced off their land to build the complex. Some of the farmers fought back, reaching a settlement with the Inter-American Development Bank in 2019. But in many cases all they would get would be an opportunity for a low-wage job at the factory. It was like a page out of the history of the U.S. occupation.[68]

The factory's managers tried to stifle discord by promising production bonuses and discouraging labor unions. But workers rebelled anyway, forming unofficial unions and staging walkouts and strikes that were put down violently by private security guards and Haitian police.

If the Clintons and the rest of the planners had paid attention to their history, they might have realized why: they had constructed their site on a wellspring of resistance. Back in 1919, after the Marines assassinated and "crucified" Charlemagne Péralte, they took his body to the labor camp at Post Chabert, the main site where Smedley Butler's prison laborers had sewed Gendarmerie uniforms. There, they dumped Péralte's body into a grave, wrapped in a Haitian flag. Apparently unbeknown to the Clintons or the other planners, the former footprint of Post Chabert was where the industrial park was built.[69]

---

* The Haitian president whose rise was aided by the Clintons, Michel "Sweet Micky" Martelly, presided over a wave of massive corruption. At the end of his five-year term, Martelly oversaw the fraud-ridden election of his hand-picked successor, a banana exporter and political unknown named Jovenel Moïse. Moïse shocked many by attempting to become an authoritarian in the mold of Papa Doc Duvalier, overseeing a regime in which critics and protesters were massacred with impunity by police, allied gangs, and elements of his reconstituted Haitian army. On July 7, 2021, Moïse was assassinated in his home—the first Haitian president killed in office since Vilbrun Guillaume Sam in 1915. Once again, the political murder prompted calls by some American commentators—and at least one Haitian political faction—for another U.S. military intervention. The Biden administration demurred. As of this writing, the identities of Moïse's killers and those of the authors of the assassination remain unknown.

On my last visit to Caracol, I snuck away from my factory tour to find Péralte's gravesite.* Some construction workers pointed me to a patch of dirt with what looked like a slab of concrete left over from the new industrial park at its center. As I walked closer, a squat, gray obelisk, tipped over into the dirt, came into view. Green snakewood leaves struggled out of its crevices in the horizontal light.

Because the marker was tipped over, I couldn't read what, if anything, was written on its side. But the workers knew who and what it represented. As they walked past a few raised their fists in salute.

"What are you doing here?" asked one of the construction workers, a young man named Anise Jean-Gilles.

I told him that I was researching the era when people like Smedley Butler and Charlemagne Péralte lived, so that Americans would know about our shared past.

"Americans don't know about the occupation?" Jean-Gilles asked, dumbfounded.

I shook my head.

His friends started laughing, but he didn't think it was so funny.

"I don't believe that!" he shouted. "I don't believe Americans don't know about that! How is that possible?"

Try as Butler would to leave Haiti, Haitians would not quickly forget about him. In 1933, the penultimate year of the occupation, the Haitian state press published a novel titled *Le Nègre Masqué* (The Masked Negro), by the writer Stephen Alexis. Its fictional protagonist, a Haitian lawyer named Roger Sainclair, is driven to join a renewed Caco insurgency when the woman he loves—the white daughter of a French diplomat—is stolen from him by the arch-villain: the "ferocious and pale" Marine major "Smedley Seaton."[70]

The faux-Smedley is murderous and vindictive. He flaunts his wealth and power, driving a flashy luxury car—inspired, no doubt, by memories of the Butlers' "blue bird"—through the poorer quarters of Port-au-Prince.

---

* After the occupation ended in 1934, Sténio Vincent had Péralte's body dug up and reburied with state honors in Cap-Haïtien.

He practically breathes the n-word and demeans all Haitians as "filthy" and "beaten-down." As part of his scheme to win Sainclair's girlfriend, the Marine has the revolutionary arrested. As he is taken away, the faux-Smedley curses the Haitian lawyer: "Goddamn son of a monkey, pariah, cannibal, I will teach you to drool over my race."

The protagonist responds with an explosion of rage:

> What do I care about your lynchings, your electric chairs, your "water cures" and the tortures you have introduced to this country? I am not afraid of anything. Do you believe, you imbecile, that your domination of the weak will last forever? . . . One morning, you mechanical men will be annihilated under the rubble of your skyscrapers and factories. Nothing will remain, *nothing,* of your civilization of iron, cement, and linoleum— for you have built it on nothing but material things![71]

At the end of the book, the Haitian hero kills Smedley Seaton, by plunging a steel dagger, slowly, through his throat.

The fictional Smedley is an amalgam of countless interactions with different Marines. (Ethel would have been particularly amused and horrified to think her husband's actions had been motivated by lust for a French woman.) Butler thought of himself as a great friend of the Haitians, their protector and surrogate father. He even sometimes jokingly referred to himself as a "Haitian"—for instance, declaring that "we Haitians want to get everybody we possibly can on our side of the fence," in a letter asking his father's boss in Congress, Republican Minority Leader James R. Mann, to support Haitian development and the Gendarmerie.[72]

Butler became the symbol par excellence of American imperialism in Haiti. "This officer of endurance and indomitable energy, who in his good moments showed himself to be a sparkling conversationalist, had these mood swings that crossed a line and placed him in the ranks of the most vulgar saber draggers," the historian Georges Corvington would remark. "Butler would leave a lasting impression, one characterized by a unique intermingling of devotion and cruelty."[73] When I asked the sociologist Lewis Clorméus what he knew about Butler, he responded with a single word: "Mechan." Evil.

# FOURTEEN

When Congress declared war on the German Empire on April 6, 1917, Americans dropped what little notice they had been paying to their colonial conflicts and turned their full attention to the carnage in Europe. As Congress outlawed dissent and Wilson's federal investigators drove antiwar voices underground, years of impassioned defenses of pacifism and neutrality were swept away by a patriotic furor not seen since the *Maine* blew up in Havana Harbor.

The Marine Corps command turned its focus from the ongoing deployments in the Pacific and Latin America toward taking advantage of mass mobilization and the first U.S. military draft since the Civil War. The number of Marines swelled sixfold, from under 14,000 officers and enlisted men on the day the U.S. entered the war to 75,001. Like Smedley Butler, nearly every Marine became desperate to prove his worth in what many imagined would be a "war to end war."[1]

Many got their chance in June 1918, in a forest in northeastern France that the Americans called "Belleau Wood." For twenty days, the Fourth Marine Brigade, along with Army infantry and contingents of French colonial troops, held off elements of five German divisions bent on reaching Paris. Over a thousand Marines were killed, thousands more were shot or gassed. Among the battle's survivors were Butler's old friends Fritz Wise, Hiram Bearss, and John Quick, along with Maj. Littleton Waller Jr.— the soon-to-be-retired general's son. The battle would take its place as a keystone in Marine Corps lore. Dan Daly, Butler's sergeant in the Caco ambush, secured his canonization above all the rest when he led his men into a counterattack, shouting: "Come on, you sons of bitches! Do you want to live forever?"[2]

Smedley Butler was not there. As Maud had correctly noted, her son had become a hard-to-replace cog in the occupation of Haiti. Headquarters had refused to approve his transfer in time to make the battle. Smedley seethed with jealousy as his little brother Horace joined the Navy and seemingly all of Bunny's male relatives went to France. Even Ethel's cousin Sam Felton was given a commission as director general of military railways on the Western Front. "Someday," Smedley wrote Maud and Thomas from Port-au-Prince, "my grandchildren will be subjected to the remark, 'Where was *your* grandfather during the Big War?' and they will have to hide their heads in shame and either lie or say, 'He was a policeman in the service of a foreign black republic.'"[3]

Butler could not see the irony: that the imperialism he had helped foster was a direct catalyst of the World War.[4] The conflict erupted in 1914 as a fight between empires: Germany and Austria-Hungary on one side; Britain, France, and Russia on the other. All had spent decades in a complex global struggle for colonies, resources, and prestige—a struggle that the Americans (and Butler personally) had been parties to. The older empires, especially the British, were filled with anxiety over new competitors to their global supremacy. The Germans, as the United States' fellow latecomers to global expansion, were reading Alfred Thayer Mahan's tracts on sea power and empire when they declared: "We demand a place for ourselves in the sun."[5]

Thanks to the reach of the belligerents' empires, it was indeed a worldwide war: fighting erupted in Africa, across the Middle East, and off the coast of South America. The empires threw their colonized peoples into the grinder, including over a million Indian soldiers drafted into the British Army, hundreds of thousands of Algerians and Indochinese by the French, and the German *Schutztruppen* in their African colonies—an equivalent to the client police forces the Americans had set up all over Latin America and the Philippines. Japan rushed into the war, too, taking the chance to join the Allies and seize the German treaty port of Qingdao in China's Shandong Province—a cherry on top of the catastrophic breakdown of the old anti-Boxer alliance.

Though Woodrow Wilson had promised to safeguard America's neutrality (he narrowly won reelection in 1916 with the slogan "He Kept Us Out of War"—a claim the peoples of Veracruz, Haiti, and the Dominican Republic could contest), the reach of the U.S. empire had made that pledge impossible to keep. By 1917, U.S. bankers were financing nearly the entire Allied war effort through billions of dollars in loans to the British and French.[6] The Germans saw the United States as a particularly dangerous foe: in one of the decisive steps that pushed the United States into the war, British spies intercepted a German telegram proposing an alliance with Mexico in exchange for helping the Mexicans reconquer Texas, New Mexico, and Arizona. (Mexican president Venustiano Carranza formed a military commission to consider the offer, but decided against it.)[7]

In short, it was not a fight over any particular colony or sea lane that sparked the cataclysm into which millions of American families were now sending their sons, but imperial arrogance, mistrust, and the accelerating war machines that made those empires run. As W. E. B. Du Bois would explain a few years later: "If you are going to keep the colored world in the position of exploitation in which it is today, then you are going to have war. And not necessarily war between colored and white people, but war between those white people who are fighting for the spoils that come from the exploitation of the colored folk."[8]

The U.S. war effort was accordingly run by veterans of America's imperial conflicts, starting with the supreme commander, Gen. John J. Pershing, who, before pursuing Pancho Villa through northern Mexico, had gotten his start suppressing uprisings of the Apache and Sioux, then risen to the general staff by crushing the Moro Rebellion in the southern Philippines.

Butler was eager to join them. He managed to get detached from the Gendarmerie d'Haïti in the spring of 1918, with the help of his ally and assistant commandant, John Lejeune. In May, he was transferred to the new Marine training facility on the Potomac River at Quantico, Virginia, where he would help Lejeune prepare recruits for deployment to France.

When Lejeune got his orders to head to the Western Front, Butler was left alone at Quantico to manage his new regiment, the Thirteenth Marines. He drilled and rallied them, leading training maneuvers on a re-creation of the trench lines of France during the day, and rousing sing-alongs at night. Finally, he tried a bureaucratic maneuver of his own: Butler took on Secretary Daniels's twenty-four-year-old son, Josephus Jr., as his regimental aide, on the guess that the senior civilian in the Navy wouldn't be able to resist the political pressure to send his son to the war for long.

He was correct. The Thirteenth got its orders to head to Europe in September. As the regiment prepared to set sail across the Atlantic, Butler was breveted to colonel. By November, he would get his first general's star.

Knowing the regiment's number might make some of his recruits nervous, Butler leaned into it. He nicknamed the Thirteenth his "Hoodoo Regiment"—a knowing nod to his now thoroughly Caribbeanized reputation. He broke camp on Friday the thirteenth of September, and brought thirteen black cats aboard their transport ship, all in an effort to lighten the mood.

Something else was brought aboard the ship as well. On the second day at sea, Butler came down with a debilitating case of flu, and, as he told his parents, "could not get up until the day we landed."[9] This was no ordinary flu: Since identified as a variant of H1N1, the disease would kill more people than any since the Black Death, and disrupt life on a scale not seen again until the coronavirus pandemic of 2020. The 1918 pandemic would slay at least fifty million people worldwide and account for nearly half the 115,000 U.S. military deaths during the war.

"We had a 'hell' of a trip over," Smedley confided to his parents, in a letter hand-delivered by a fellow officer to circumvent wartime censors. "Our officers, medical and line, worked like the devil to save the men but were almost powerless to overcome such terrific odds—we had at one time fully 500 cases of influenza and over 90 of pneumonia." At least a hundred men, including the twenty-two-year-old son of one of Thomas's former colleagues in Congress, died before the regiment reached France.[10]*

Things did not get much better from there. Upon landing at Brest, a harbor on the far western edge of Brittany, Butler learned that the Thirteenth was not going to the front. Instead, it would be broken up and

---

* While the Marines were crossing the Atlantic, another major outbreak of the flu had just started in Philadelphia. On September 28, 1918, the city had held a parade to promote the sale of "Liberty Bonds," government debt securities sold to raise money for the war effort. An estimated 200,000 people attended, turning it into a super-spreader event. Over 13,000 Philadelphians would die before the end of the year. Maud, Thomas, Ethel, and the children were all spared.

distributed for guard duty in the ports along the Atlantic coast. "I am not even allowed to go with them but am ordered to command this concentration camp, the least desirable and lowest job in France," he groused to his parents. "However I am in France and will do all in my power to make these poor miserable, wretched sick soldiers who pass by the thousands through here as comfortable and happy as my poor strength will let me."[11]

He did his best. As he stood on the flat-bottomed barge taking his Marines to shore, he looked out at the men from the bridge. "Their white, drawn faces were pitiful," he later recalled. "As we were casting off I called out, 'Do you suppose you could sing?'" The Marines responded with a full-throated chorus of "Sweet Adeline." They roused themselves and hiked the three miles uphill to the mud-filled disembarkation camp of Pontanézen.[12]

In camp, Butler slogged through constant flu outbreaks and one of spinal meningitis. He oversaw a top-to-bottom cleanup of the old Napoleonic-era barracks, often wading waist deep in the muck to pitch in himself. When the Army quartermasters ignored his repeated requests for "duckboard"—wooden slats used to line the bottom of trenches, which he wanted as sidewalks—Smedley marched down to the docks with seven thousand men to break into the warehouse. Butler carried up a slat himself. It was shades of his trip across Subic Bay—breaking the rules to help the common soldier. Except this time, there were thousands of people on hand to witness it, which meant no one could dismiss his defiance of authority as a bout of insanity. The men started calling him "General Duckboard" as a sign of affection.

A little over a month after their arrival, the armistice was announced. Brest became the most important embarkation point for American soldiers returning home. They were processed through Pontanézen with mass feedings and mass delousings, attended to by the camp doctors and sixteen kitchens each capable of feeding five thousand mouths at a time.

Though he never got his chance at the front, Butler was nevertheless an eyewitness to the horrors of the war. The hordes of men passing through his camp had been the victims and perpetrators of some of the most innovative forms of cruelty in human history. The "chlorine gas cannon" the British allegedly unleashed outside Tianjin in 1900 had now been mercilessly employed, along with newer poison agents, by both sides of the European conflict against one another. Many of the hundreds of thousands who came through Pontanézen had been burned or blinded by gas. Others were missing limbs. Most bore the mental scars of what they had seen and done.

Butler had seen and caused enough death to imagine what they were going through. His instinctive identification with and empathy for the rank-and-file soldier—"we roughnecks," he called them—drove him to make the doughboys, nurses, and staff as comfortable as possible.[13] He kept up the sing-alongs at night and ordered military bands to play music in regular shifts. To keep production humming at the canteens, he organized competitions to see who could feed the most men: the griddle cake makers or the donut kitchen.[14] He did everything he could to mitigate the rain and the damp and the seas of mud.

"I get so tired by the time I go to bed at night that I see bright stars jumping in front of my eyes," Smedley wrote Bunny, adding that only "Our Heavenly Father and my own overpowering love for thee" were keeping him afloat. He called it "the most trying period of my life."[15]

On a winter's day, I found myself at the National Museum of the Marine Corps. It is a grandiose complex, built atop a hill across the street from Butler's former training grounds at Quantico. The entrance is a soaring glass-and-steel structure meant to evoke the famous photo of the Marines raising the flag at Iwo Jima in World War II.

It was close to closing time when I arrived, meaning that I was mostly alone in the exhibit halls. As I stopped to examine glass cases of Filipino bolo knives, Caco swords, Marine machine guns, and Butler's field uniform from the Boxer Rebellion, it felt like I had the entire museum to myself.

A life-sized mannequin of a knife-wielding Marine overpowering a German marked the entrance to the exhibit on the First World War. After the preliminaries—some old recruiting posters, Woodrow Wilson's declaration that "the world must be made safe for democracy"—I reached a doorway marked with a blood-red sign that read "Belleau Wood." Inside was a narrow hallway mocked up to look like a forest. The sounds of gunfire and screams echoed from an unseen point just beyond the bend.

Suddenly, I stopped. A familiar sensation of nameless terror came creeping in from behind my eyes. As the panic set in, I took a few deep, steady breaths. Then I turned on my cell phone camera in order to mediate the experience, as I had done during much of the real violence I'd been through in the field, and stepped into the main display. The sounds, I realized, were coming from a movie—a re-creation of Marines advancing under fire.

In Butler's day, no one knew what the condition that produced such feelings was called. There had been stories of soldiers driven to panic by memories of combat since humanity's earliest surviving poem, the Epic of Gilgamesh.[16] In the early 1900s, military doctors reached for whatever diagnoses they could find, such as the "dyspepsia nervosa" that got Butler booted from Subic Bay. Surgeons in World War I dubbed it "shell shock." It would take until the Americans invaded Vietnam for it to be named, and thus treated, as post-traumatic stress disorder, or PTSD.

For veterans in particular, these feelings are sometimes augmented by the separate but related condition of "moral injury"—having done something that violated one's core ethics—which it seems Butler had experienced acutely after the massacre at Haiti's Fort Rivière. By the time he was in France, he had spent nearly twenty years at war, struggling to keep up with orders and bureaucracy, with little time to deal with his internal contradictions. Having joined the Marines to fight against a tyrannical empire and live out his parents' Quaker ideals, he had spent two decades invading other people's homes and sacking their lands. "The poor common people are the only sufferers, as is always the case, and their blood will be on our heads," Butler had written his parents from Nicaragua in 1912. And yet, he had kept on going.

I tried to imagine how those conflicts deepened for Butler during the World War. Before coming to France, Butler had continually called the war in Europe "the show"—"this thing of being left out of the show is really more than I can stand," he had written his parents from Port-au-Prince.[17] Such letters seem callous. Did the killing only matter if an audience was watching? Was the suffering he had caused in places like Haiti not enough for him to feel fulfilled?

But surrounded by the echoes and flashing lights of the Belleau Wood exhibit, I realized what Butler was getting at, cynical and unreflective as his point was. He understood that his society saw Europe as the center of civilization, humanity, and war. He had spent his life consigned to the margins, fighting wars for wealth and influence that his superiors thought better to downplay or lie about, against peoples a majority of Americans did not see as fully human. He sensed that those wars, and by extension the Marines who fought them, would be excluded from the public memory of the United States; that of the wars fought in his lifetime, only the maximally murderous one fought in a white man's country would be considered worthy of popular culture or multimedia spectaculars in the big Marine Corps museum. Fighting in Europe must have seemed like the last chance he would have to write a new narrative for himself.

But he missed the show. He arrived near the center of the action just in time to be responsible for a giant bureaucratic headache—and just to be confronted once again with the reality that, once the battles were over and the objectives secured, even his beloved military did not care if the soldiers who fought its wars lived or died, much less got sick or face-planted in the mud.

In that cauldron of traumas, under the stress of running an overtaxed "concentration camp," as he called it, something reached a breaking point in Butler's psyche. He would come back from France changed.

The most senior officials in the United States came through Pontanézen during Butler's ten months in charge. Secretary Daniels came to visit his son. Franklin Roosevelt came to settle some official postwar Navy business and took Smedley out to dinner. President Wilson, on his way to the postwar treaty negotiations in Paris, stopped to shake Butler's hand.[18]

The brass was so pleased with Butler's administrative skill that they awarded him both the Army and Navy Distinguished Service Medals—the former pinned on him personally by General Pershing.[19] The French government awarded him the Order of the Black Star, Commander Grade. That last one may have been a Frenchman's idea of a wry joke. The medal—a gold-backed Maltese cross in white, overlaid by a black-enameled star—was most commonly awarded to those who could prove a "stay of at least three years overseas in the territories of French West Africa" or had otherwise "rendered services to colonial expansion."[20]*

Butler could not help but notice that he was being showered with more official respect and acclaim—promoted in a space of a few months from lieutenant colonel to full colonel to brigadier general—for running a muddy camp on the far point of France than he had been given in decades risking his life in colonial jungles.

Yet he had never felt less worthy. Not even his first, "puffed up" Medal of Honor for the invasion of Veracruz made him feel such a distance between the exemplary figure he wanted to be and the flawed man he was. "For over twenty years I worked hard to fit myself to take part in this war which has just closed, and when the supreme test came my country did not want me," he lamented in a note to his father. He began to mull for the first time the possibility of quitting the Marines, on the basis of a faulty prediction: "Can see no reason for continuing in the regular service as there will be no more wars in our time."[21]

As the demobilization wound down, the tensions at Pontanézen ratcheted up. A Black regiment, the 369th Infantry, arrived at the camp in early 1919. Nicknamed the "Harlem Hellfighters," the regiment had spent months under enemy fire. They fought at Belleau Wood under French colonial command because the white American units refused to fight alongside them.

The all-white military police at Pontanézen, embarrassed about their time at the rear, greeted the Hellfighters with racist epithets, harassment, and constant threats to delay the regiment's return. "It seems as if we at last had struck something worse than the Germans," a member of the regiment recorded in his diary.[22]

When the Hellfighters had finally loaded up their tenders to leave,

---

* Adding to the irony, and almost certainly unbeknownst to Butler or the other Americans, Camp Pontanézen had been used early on as a kind of French concentration camp—to house Haitians. In 1802, Napoleon had used it to house fifteen hundred prisoners taken in the last year of the revolution in Saint-Domingue, as well as an uprising in Guadeloupe, before transferring them to a permanent prison in Corsica. It seems Butler had crossed the Atlantic just to end up on another piece of ground hallowed by association with the Haitian Revolution. See "Histoire: L'épisode méconnu des 1,500 Antillais déportés à Brest," *Le Télégramme,* Sep. 13, 2020, and Arzalier Francis, "Les déportés guadeloupéens et haïtiens en Corse," in *Annales historiques de la Révolution française,* Année 1993, 293–294.

one of the battalion's white commanders, Maj. Arthur West Little, was approached by an officer he identified in his memoirs only as the "Chief of Staff of the base."[23]

"Major, I didn't notice before, but you've got your band with you, haven't you?" the officer said.

The Hellfighters' band, led by the famed Harlem bandleader James Reese Europe, had become a sensation in the war, introducing France and many of their fellow soldiers to ragtime and early jazz.

"Yes, sir," Little answered.

The officer asked for a "little tune."

"I'm sure it would be very welcome to us, sir, but I'm not taking any chances of losing our sailing place. If you so direct, sir, I will give the order."

The officer told him their departure was assured.

Little told Europe to strike up the band before sailing away. "That Chief of Staff was a human being," he noted in his memoir.

Smedley told Bunny about the serenade in a letter home. He said it reminded him of Haiti.[24]

# FIFTEEN

## PHILADELPHIA

**W**oodrow Wilson laid out his vision for a new world order in the last year of the World War. His "Fourteen Points" included open commerce on the seas, self-determination for (mostly European) peoples to found their own nation-states, and a ban on secret alliances. This system was to be overseen by a new League of Nations, governed by an executive council whose five permanent members would be the victorious empires of the conflict: the United States, Britain, France, Italy, and Japan.[1]

Americans on the whole wanted nothing to do with it. Exhausted by war and the flu pandemic, dismayed by an economic downturn, their attention—and aggression—turned inward. In the summer of 1919, race riots broke out across the country. Whites attacked returning Black soldiers, laborers, and many of the 1.6 million African Americans fleeing Jim Crow for the uncertain promise of jobs and safety in the North. Hysteria over Eastern and Southern European immigration and the recent revolution in Russia sparked paranoia and persecution of those suspected of Communist or anarchist ties. The Ku Klux Klan remade itself into an anti-immigrant, anti-Catholic, anti-Jewish, and of course anti-Black organization—its numbers swelling thanks to the popularity of D. W. Griffith's *Birth of a Nation*.[2]

In 1920, voters—including, for the first time, white women nationwide—overwhelmingly rejected Wilsonian internationalism and the Democratic nominee James M. Cox. (Cox's running mate, Franklin D. Roosevelt, helped doom the ticket by bragging on the stump about his role in the Haiti occupation.) Instead, they chose the Republican Warren G. Harding and his running mate, Calvin Coolidge, who advertised their anti-internationalist intentions with the slogan "America First."[3]

With no new invasions or occupations on the horizon, there was little for a stateside Marine brigadier general to do. Smedley Butler became commandant of what had now grown into Marine Base Quantico. He organized a football team and personally supervised the construction of a thirteen-thousand-seat stadium, built by his Marines, mostly by hand. (The Quantico stadium is still named for him.)

Butler also staged big publicity stunts with the aim of guaranteeing funding for the Corps. The biggest were his modernized "reenactments" of Civil War battles. Held on location at battlefields including Gettysburg and the Wilderness outside Chancellorsville, Butler's Marines demonstrated how things might have turned out if the Union or Confederacy had airplanes, machine guns, and other modern technologies of the 1920s. Thousands attended the spectacles, including President Harding and elderly Civil War veterans.

But fake battles and football couldn't hold Smedley's attention for long. The Senate rejected his offer to return to Haiti as U.S. high commissioner, likely due to the negative publicity churned up by the chamber's 1921 committee investigation into the corvée and other atrocities.

Then in 1923, Butler got an alternative proposition from the mayor-elect of Philadelphia, W. Freeland Kendrick. His hometown was being overrun by gangsters—"banditry, promiscuous sale of poisonous liquor, the sale of dope, viciousness and lawlessness of all kinds," as city officials informed the White House.[4] If the president granted Butler a leave of absence from the Marines, would he be interested in taking a crack at running the Philadelphia Police Department?

"It's a big job Tommy and the people of Philadelphia are expecting a whole lot of things that neither I nor anyone else can accomplish," Butler wrote a friend stationed at Guantánamo. "However, in Marine Corps style, I will do the best I know how."[5]

Philadelphia's police department was founded in 1854, making it one of the oldest in the United States. Until then, the streets of William Penn's city, like most in the North, had been patrolled by ad hoc committees of night watchmen and private guards, charged at first with keeping Native Americans from venturing into town. (In the South the first organized law enforcement patrols were built on similarly racist grounds: hunters tracking Black people trying to escape slavery.)[6]

The first modern civilian municipal police debuted in London in 1829. London's leaders chose that model over a gendarmerie-style military force, on the theory that their citizens would find being managed by shock troops of the state "odious and repulsive." But as the sociologist Julian Go has written, the London Metropolitan Police nevertheless took cues from empire: its founder, Sir Robert Peel, took core organizational concepts, including ranks like "sergeant" and "superintendent," from Britain's colonial Irish Constabulary, which he had helped found a decade before.[7]

The London model was imported by Boston in 1838, then New York in 1845. These police forces would also be shaped by the political realities of the places in which they operated. Starting in the late nineteenth century, the cities of America's eastern seaboard would be run by single-party organizations known as "machines," which derived their power from finding jobs and interceding on citizens' behalf in the courts, in exchange for party loyalty.

Philadelphia's machine was known simply as the "Republican Organization." One of the Philadelphia police's main jobs was to run a racket on its behalf: collecting protection payments from both legitimate and criminal enterprises.[8] A muckraking journalist observed in 1903 that, on election days, police would stand beside the ballot box "to see that the machine's orders are obeyed." Specifically, they were there to ensure that "repeaters"—voters enlisted to cast multiple ballots on behalf of the Republican Organization—were "permitted to vote without 'intimidation' on the names they, the police, have supplied."[9]

Reformers working in the Roosevelt-Wilson tradition of Progressivism had tried to stamp out police corruption by turning to the closest example of an organized security force available: the military. They adopted the centralized chain of command that had been developed to fight the war in the Philippines and studied the Army and Navy War Colleges as models for professionalized officers' schools. In 1912, a Philadelphia police chief debuted an Army-inspired guidebook for patrolmen and taught them the "correct 'position of attention' and the proper 'salutes.'"[10] These efforts sometimes created friction with the founding ethos of Anglo-American police as civilian organizations, engendering pushback from the community and the ranks.

In 1919, a new policing problem dawned with the ratification of the Eighteenth Amendment, which made the prohibition of alcohol constitutional. The demand for illegal alcohol attracted a new class of criminals and made millionaires out of those willing and able to take advantage. In Philadelphia that class included Charley Schwartz, a former small-time nightclub and gambling impresario who became known for carrying bankrolls of $500 notes. There were also the Lanzetta brothers, whose network cooked "alky" in home stills in the row houses of Italian South Philadelphia. An ex-Philly cop named Charles Haim, and his brother Irving, established a bootlegging operation out of Havana.[11]

Philadelphia's most dangerous gangsters were Mickey Duffy, a.k.a. "Mr. Big," who ran the beer racket out of southern New Jersey and lived in a $1,000-a-week suite at the Ritz-Carlton Hotel; and Max "Boo Boo" Hoff, an erstwhile boxing promoter and nightclub owner whose liquor ring—housed under his innocuously named Franklin Mortgage & Investment Company—was in league with Al Capone.[12]

The racketeers engaged in the Philadelphia pastime of bribing cops and enlisting those who could be bought as security in their bootlegging operations. The sheer amounts of money to be made by flouting Prohibition brought the old problem to unprecedented heights.

By December 1922, there was so much corruption in the city's Prohibition enforcement that the *Philadelphia Inquirer* couldn't help but joke, in response to its own headline about civilians who'd posed as "dry raider" cops to collect $200 in bribes: "They must look like pikers to some of the real ones."[13]

As gangland killings proliferated and stories of police corruption spread, public pressure began mounting for the city to do something. That's why Kendrick had tapped Butler: if merely imitating the military wasn't enough, perhaps bringing in a real live, highly decorated Marine general would calm his backers' nerves.

On January 7, 1924, Mayor Kendrick inducted Smedley Butler as director of the Department of Public Safety of the City of Philadelphia. Wearing his Marine general's uniform, Butler took the oath of office in front of a City Hall Christmas tree. A half hour later he returned in the new paramilitary uniform he had designed for himself: a blue suit with gold trim, and a barracks cap with the city seal of Philadelphia above the band and embroidered Marine officer's quatrefoil on top. The finishing touch was a cape, modified from his Marine mess jacket, with a bright red lining.

The City of Brotherly Love had changed since Smedley was growing up on the Main Line. Its population had more than doubled to almost two million, making it the third-largest city in the United States and one of the ten largest in the world. One in five Philadelphians were immigrants; the most-heard foreign language was now Yiddish, followed by Italian, German, and Polish.[14] The Black population had also swelled, thanks mostly to the displacement from the South that would later become known as the Great Migration. By the mid-1920s, around two hundred thousand Philadelphians were African American.[15]

Many of the newcomers were desperately poor. Housing shortages meant old homes were divided into squalid tenements; a 1921 study of the homes of recent Black arrivals summarized their conditions as "deplorable."[16] Hoping for better lives, many of Philadelphia's poor and working class joined the labor movement, in turn feeding elite fears of Communist infiltration. A string of purported "Bolshevik" bombings of officials' homes had rocked the city in 1919.[17] At the same time, the moneymaking opportunities of bootlegging and organized crime attracted some who lived in the slums.

Adding to the tensions, many white Protestants had been swept up by the trend of "scientific racism": the racist and anti-immigrant writings of the eugenicist Madison Grant, who had been a friend and ally of Theodore Roosevelt; the antisemitic ravings of Henry Ford's newspaper, *The Dearborn Independent*; and the Harvard-educated lawyer Lothrop Stoddard's bestselling book, *The Rising Tide of Color Against White World-Supremacy*. Pennsylvania became a hot spot for the re-founded Ku Klux Klan, some of whose members appointed themselves freelance Prohibition enforcers.[18]

The police often took the side of whites—including the immigrant "white ethnics"—when trouble arose. In the aftermath of an anti-Black riot in South Philadelphia in 1918, two patrolmen arrested Riley Bullock, a thirty-eight-year-old Black man who had allegedly been defending himself with a razor blade from a white mob, only to shoot him inside the station house.[19] On other occasions, the Klan and cops were at odds. The night before Independence Day 1924, two Main Line policemen were shot responding to a large Klan rally and cross burning just outside the grounds of Butler's alma mater, the Haverford School.[20]

Butler decided to use the tactics and strategies he had developed at war and in setting up the Latin American constabularies, especially the Haitian Gendarmerie, to bring order to a fraying city. Dressed in his new uniform at City Hall, he informed the senior officers of the department: "I hold officers responsible for what goes on in their districts. They must please me or I will reduce the offenders on sight. That goes from the lieutenant straight down the line. . . . You have forty-eight hours to clean up."[21] (This was more merciful than his policy in Haiti, where abusive Gendarmes were executed.)

That evening, he gathered two thousand rank-and-file cops at the Metropolitan Opera House. His "fellow policemen," he said, could forget about all their past misdeeds. From that point on, they would start with a clean slate.

Then Butler gave his final order of the day: to hunt down the bandits. The first officer who killed a gangster in the commission of a crime would receive an immediate promotion.[22] "I don't believe there is a single bandit notch on a policeman's gun in this city," he said. "Go out and get some."[23]

Butler's lethal methods did not stop at encouragement. He created a "gunnery squad," and ordered new armored cars with the rear seats turned around "like an artillery limber" so the officers in back could get off a clean shot. He implemented strict new physical requirements—tests of officers' hearts, lungs, vision, hearing, and stamina—and lowered the maximum age for applicants from thirty-eight to thirty. To make sure targets would not get away, he ordered an "iron ring" of "information booths," modeled after Marine observation posts, on each of the twenty-one major roads out of the city and equipped them with squad cars and bandit-chasing motorcycles. He installed four huge searchlights under the statue of William Penn atop City Hall, to illuminate escaping gangsters and flash their license plate numbers in code. He even issued .45-caliber revolvers to the fire department, which also fell under his jurisdiction, which they were to carry even when off duty.[24]

His reliance on killing was surely a product of his training. But as important was *whom* Butler was prepared to kill. As a Marine he had developed a hierarchy of lives worth protecting: his own men's, then "innocents," then a succession of others. The bootleggers were "others," twice over: mostly foreign-born, foreign-seeming, or nonwhite; and, as he deemed them, "bandits." It was the epithet soldiers had used to justify the killing of insurgents from the Philippines to Haiti, as a way of disgracing them in the eyes of those who might look up to them. (Mickey Duffy and Al Capone were no revolutionaries, but the kind of popular bandits the historian Eric Hobsbawm has called "avengers"—"men who prove that even the poor and weak can be terrible."[25]) Even as his feelings changed about war, Butler also felt a responsibility to protect his men and his hometown. As he told his officers: "A policeman who shoots a bandit is serving his city exactly as a soldier when firing at his country's enemies."[26]

For the first few weeks, Butler ordered a series of forty-eight-hour continuous sorties in every part of the city to sniff out and shut down illegally operating bars. He pledged to sleep in his City Hall office until the mission was complete. The *New York Times* declared on its front page: BUTLER BEGINS WAR: UNDESIRABLES FLEE FROM PHILADELPHIA.[27]

In one forty-eight-hour push in late January, 1,045 arrests were made in seven hundred different operations. In two days in early February, another 800 prisoners were taken. Many of the cops took their bandit-hunting instructions seriously: in May, near the Italian Market, a crew of detectives spotted a heavy truck with a canvas cover over its load. When the truck refused to stop, they began a high-speed chase. Somewhere near South Eighth and Fitzwater Streets, one of the officers heard a shot from the crowd and responded with a volley of gunfire. A firefight in the open street ensued.[28]

Some Philadelphians objected to being treated like colonial subjects by a force that increasingly resembled a Guardia Nacional. One man wrote to the secretary of the Navy complaining of "military tactics which might do in Mexico and other places and has no place in the administration of civil affairs." Butler, he said, was acting like a "military dictator."[29]

But no matter how aggressive the raids got, the saloons didn't stay closed for long. No sooner would the cops clear one out than it would reopen again, fully stocked. One of the problems was that Butler's "troops" were arresting the wrong people: In the first six months under his directorship, the Philadelphia police carried out 15,734 arrests. Of those, one-quarter were Black, even though African Americans made up less than 8 percent of the city's population. A third of the Black men hauled in were arrested for "drunkenness"—meaning they had simply consumed, not been distributing, alcohol.[30]

Despite Butler's clear orders to get the kingpins—"bootleggers who can write checks for hundreds of thousands," as he called them—the major gangsters went largely untouched.[31] In June, a patrolman responding to a car crash recognized the driver as Mickey Duffy. The gangster boss got out of his car and knocked down the cop. Once the officer regained his footing, he handed Duffy off to three fellow officers while he went to look for a telephone to call in the arrest. When the patrolman got back, both Duffy and the other officers were gone.

It seemed that for all of Butler's civic posturing, the bootleggers still had friends in high places. Duffy was "said to be enjoying sunshine at Atlantic City," the *Inquirer* reported soon after.[32]

A century later, on May 30, 2020, thousands of protesters were massed across the street from City Hall. A line of Philadelphia police stood behind them, equipped with riot shields and helmets. The young demonstrators were by all appearances unarmed and unarmored, except for the cloth masks most wore to protect each other from the novel coronavirus. They chanted "Black Lives Matter!" and the name of George Floyd, a Black man who had been suffocated under a cop's knee five days earlier in Minneapolis, setting off an international wave of protests against police brutality. When the police put up their shields, in apparent preparation for an assault, the protesters began hurling water bottles.

But the protesters had not come to confront any living cops. They were there to renegotiate the way the city understood its past, by taking down a statue honoring Philadelphia's most notorious police chief turned mayor, Frank Rizzo.

Francis Lazarro Rizzo was born in 1920. His father, Rafael—better known as Ralph—was an Italian immigrant who spent four decades as a cop in South Philly. Ralph was on the force, and likely one of the patrolmen in attendance at the Metropolitan Opera House on that night in 1924 when Smedley Butler told his officers to kill the bandits.[33]

Frank followed his father into the department in 1943. His first precinct command was in West Philadelphia—which, thanks to discrimination and federal guidelines that discouraged issuing mortgages in neighborhoods with large Black populations (a practice known as "redlining"), had turned into a hyper-segregated ghetto.[34] Rizzo quickly developed a reputation for brutality there. Black clergy warned the mayor at the time of widespread sentiment in their community that "Frank Rizzo hates Negroes." Rizzo was transferred to Center City, where he specialized in raiding underground gay and lesbian bars. (Some of his officers would sexually assault the female patrons.)[35]

When he became police commissioner in 1967, Rizzo dismantled community relations efforts and pushed for punitive tactics such as "stop-and-frisk." He also furthered the militarization of the force. In the face of protests for civil rights and against the Vietnam War, Rizzo assembled machine-gun squads and kept "busloads of officers scattered throughout the city, ready to speed to any trouble spot"—a World War I tactic, historians have noted, used by the French to defend Paris from the Germans. He also pushed for the purchase of armored vehicles and set up a citywide intelligence apparatus to monitor left-wing radicals and other suspected troublemakers. Researchers later found that Rizzo's spies kept files on at least eighteen thousand people.[36]

All of this was happening amid deepening cooperation between police and the military. In the 1960s, as the U.S. government taught foreign police to crush suspected Communist insurgencies—training many at the Inter-American Police Academy, whose first campus was in the Panama Canal Zone—the FBI and Army in turn were teaching American cops to use counterinsurgency techniques against radicals, particularly Black would-be revolutionaries, at home. Rizzo bragged before a board of federal agents in 1967 that his officers had arrested several "card-carrying members of the Communist Party."[37]

In 1972, Rizzo was elected mayor. His record as a hard-line blue-collar populist—a defender of Philadelphia's conservative whites against the Black community and other forces of change—won him a national spotlight. He opposed affirmative action for Black hiring and shut down efforts to build public housing. While campaigning for a charter change that would allow him to run for a third term—a campaign opposed by the NAACP—Rizzo told a crowd: "I'm going to say to the people of this city: *Vote White*."[38]

Rizzo had come up in a police force that bore a disturbing resemblance to Somoza's Guardia in Nicaragua or Trujillo's in the Dominican Republic. As the city's leader, he kept the impression going. As a Pulitzer Prize–winning investigation by the *Philadelphia Inquirer* uncovered in the late 1970s, under Rizzo's mayorship, police coerced confessions by savagely beating suspects, twisting their testicles, and other tactics tantamount to torture.[39] His favorite targets were leftist revolutionary groups, especially those centered on communities of color, such as the Black Panthers. (W. E. B. Du Bois, who died in 1963, would have recognized Rizzo's tactics. As he wrote of his time living in Philadelphia's Black Seventh Ward: "Police were our government."[40])

Rizzo's most infamous target was MOVE, a mostly Black radical commune that staged frequent protests against police brutality and mass incarceration and preached self-liberation for colonized peoples. A series of escalating confrontations, including the alleged police murder of a MOVE member's newborn baby, culminated in Rizzo ordering MOVE's eviction from their West Philadelphia house in 1978. In a predawn raid, hundreds of cops fired thousands of rounds and tear gas, then flooded the Victorian home with high-capacity water jets. One officer was killed in the crossfire. Twelve adult MOVE members were beaten and arrested.[41]

By 1985, MOVE had a new house, and Philadelphia had its first Black mayor, Woodrow Wilson Goode. The son of North Carolina sharecroppers, Goode had grown up under the weight of Philadelphia's systemic racism and informal segregation.[42] But as in the places Americans had conquered overseas, the system of militarized control Butler and Rizzo had each fostered in their own ways was durable enough to keep thriving under a coopted member of the colonized class. As residents of MOVE's new middle-class neighborhood accused the group of harassing and beating them, the mayor called the commune "terrorists" and promised to take action.[43] A renewed standoff ensued. On the late afternoon of May 13, 1985, Police Lt. Frank Powell dropped a bomb of C-4 plastic explosive and Tovex out of a helicopter. It exploded on impact, igniting drums of gasoline the commune stored on the roof. Police commissioner Gregore J. Sambor—a former Army Reserve major who had risen to power under Rizzo—gave the order: "Let the bunker burn." Veterans compared the inferno to scenes they had witnessed in Korea and Vietnam. By morning, two city blocks were destroyed. Six adults and five children were found charred to death in the wreckage of the home.[44]

Rizzo died in 1991, in the middle of a campaign to once again become mayor. A ten-foot-tall bronze statue of him was unveiled in front of the Municipal Services Building in 1999.

In the mid-2010s, young Black activists began organizing weekly protests calling for the statue's removal under the social-media slogan "#FrankRizzoDown." "It represents nothing but white supremacy," one of the organizers, Megan Malachi, explained.[45] Their efforts drew fierce opposition from police and Rizzo's still-powerful legions of fans. By 2020, the fight over runaway police militarization, the disproportionate police killing of Black people, and racist memorials had blown up into a world-wide struggle.

Donald Trump made opposition to the Black Lives Matter movement a centerpiece of his reelection campaign that year. His rallies made prominent use of the "Thin Blue Line" flag—a rendering of the U.S. flag in black and white, with a single blue stripe down the middle, representing the "colonial mythology," as one scholar put it, that police forces are "a thin blue line of defense" against a savage "invasion from within."[46] The day before the protest around the Rizzo statue, Trump had called for protesters to be shot, tweeting: "When the looting starts, the shooting starts." Trump said he had learned the saying from the "very tough" Frank Rizzo.[47]

The police were already believers in that philosophy. Like Butler—who saw himself as a bulwark against the foreign invasion of Jewish, Polish, and German bootleggers—and Rizzo, the self-appointed guardian of Philly's "white ethnics," they spent the summer of 2020 allying with and sometimes fighting alongside the white supremacist and neofascist heirs of the KKK: the Proud Boys, "Patriot," and militia movements. During the George Floyd protests, Philadelphia police permitted white vigilantes armed with baseball bats and hatchets to roam free, threatening protesters.[48]

In the plaza across from City Hall, tensions neared a boiling point. Police watched as protesters tried futilely to push the Rizzo statue down from behind, then to pull it over with a bungee cord. At one point, a man wearing a backward Phillies cap and black bandanna over his face climbed the statue and began smashing a hammer against its head.[49] But Rizzo was too deeply embedded. Rebar and concrete overwhelmed all efforts to tear the statue down. As protesters gave up and left, police rushed into the thinning crowd. A sergeant with the transit police began assaulting protesters with his baton, leaving two with head injuries that landed them in the hospital.[50]

After days more of police cars burning, stores being looted, and cops firing tear gas and rubber bullets, the chaos subsided. The police occupation of poor Black neighborhoods continued: months later, Philadelphia police would shoot and kill a twenty-seven-year-old Black man named Walter Wallace Jr.[51] But the weeks of protest turned out to be a watershed in the United States, fostering new public pressure to grapple with white supremacy and police repression, at least in its symbolic forms. Around midnight on June 3, 2020, city workers removed the statue of Frank Rizzo and hauled it away.

Butler's influence on the militarization of policing, both at home and abroad, would endure. His actual time on the force was briefer. Though his door-busting, guns-blazing raids significantly juiced the arrest numbers, few convictions stuck. Some of that was the fault of sloppy policework, and the fact that the police were mostly focused on the wrong, small-time, disproportionately Black targets.

But Butler focused on another, equally important piece of the puzzle: that many of the magistrates who were letting his prisoners off, as well as many of his cops, were in the pockets of the city's most powerful men. After a string of raids temporarily shuttered a group of well-connected bars, the Philadelphia *North American* reported that the city treasurer had been overheard remarking at the Twenty-Fourth Ward Republican Club, "This country, as well as the Republican Organization, would be a hell of a sight better off without Butler."[52]

Butler had long bristled against the strictures of the military chain of command. On his own, as a civilian, his rejection of authority was unbridled. Realizing that his ideas about order and the role of the police were different than the machine's, he began to strike back against his political superiors. In the summer of 1924, Butler cut the number of police precincts in half, redrawing the new ones' boundaries so they would no longer conform to—and thus no longer be under the influence of—the city's powerful ward bosses. Then, in September, his police raided two machine hangouts that were illegally serving alcohol.[53]

It was at this point that Mayor Kendrick began to second-guess his decision to hire the Marine. Rumors of Butler's imminent firing prompted a letter-writing campaign from fans of Butler's policing. (Some have aged better than others: the head of the state women's chapter of the Ku Klux Klan wrote President Coolidge* that Butler "made it possible for the women to go out at night in safety on the streets of Philadelphia."[54])

It seems that Butler's job was saved, for the moment, by a coincidence. The hangouts he'd raided were under the protection of a less powerful faction within the machine, loyalists of the late Republican senator Boies Penrose. The real power in the organization, and thus Philadelphia, lay with Thomas Butler's fellow congressman William Scott Vare. The squat, chinless politician had grown up poor in South Philly, rising to power as a trash-hauler, then construction contractor, who bought his way into the machine.

By the time Butler came to town, Vare's faction was firmly in charge. It was Vare who had handpicked Kendrick as mayor. Vare would have claimed the job for himself, but he had his eyes on bigger things, starting with Penrose's vacated seat in the U.S. Senate. (Vare would win that race in 1926, only to have the Senate refuse to seat him due to evidence of rampant election fraud.) When Prohibition hit, he had come to understandings with the crime syndicates who would continue to supply his mostly immigrant constituents with beer, wine, and whiskey.[55]

But Butler's goal was not to keep his job. It was to accomplish his mission. He had earlier identified a South Philadelphia machine politi-

---

* Coolidge succeeded Harding after the president's sudden death in August 1923.

cian and distiller, Henry J. Trainer, as the probable source of much of the alcohol flowing through the Quaker City. Trainer was one of the largest holders of a legal federal permit for so-called industrial alcohol and was therefore permitted to dispense to manufacturers of perfumes and medicines.[56]

It was a racket—"something that is not what it seems to the majority of people," as Butler would later define the term, "conducted for the benefit of the very few, at the expense of the very many."[57] Butler's police estimated that just forty of the five hundred recipients of legal alcohol in the city were bona fide manufacturers. Most worryingly, much of the "permitted" stuff being distributed was isopropyl—rubbing alcohol, unfit for human consumption. One coroner estimated that a dozen Philadelphians died in one day of 1925 from consuming bad liquor.[58]

In early December 1925, Magistrate Edward P. Carney informed Butler that alcohol was flowing freely at a high-society debutante ball he had raided at the Ritz-Carlton. Officers seized a few bottles of wine and champagne and brought them to the police lab, where tests confirmed that they had an alcohol content greater than the legal limit of one-half of one percent. Butler ordered the Ritz-Carlton's manager arrested. The whole hotel was to be shut down and padlocked.

"And I mean the whole hotel," Butler said. "Something must be done to teach these big fellows that they must obey the law as well as the little fellows."[59] He also ordered action against two other posh hotels—the Bellevue-Stratford and the Walton—where similar liquor violations had been reported.

That was the last straw. The 150th anniversary of the signing of the Declaration of Independence was the following year. Mayor Kendrick was not going to let his city's best clubs and hotels get shut down at a moment's notice, on the eve of a tourist bonanza, just because of a few hundred violations of federal law. That Mickey Duffy would have been locked out of his favorite suite at the Ritz surely didn't help matters.

On December 22, Kendrick ordered Butler to resign. As Pennsylvania governor Gifford Pinchot, an old Teddy Roosevelt Progressive, had remarked presciently a year earlier: "Butler had little dangerous opposition before he tried to break up the old-time alliance between the police and the liquor gang politicians."[60]

When Anti-Saloon activists pooled their money for the bronze plaque that would end up in the city hall—with its bitterly accurate tagline, "He proved incorruptible"—Butler called it a "tombstone to a living man" and snapped that he didn't care if they put it up or not.[61] He went back to the Marines, convinced he had been fighting the wrong gangsters all along.

# SIXTEEN

## SHANGHAI

L ike any good dysfunctional family, the Marines welcomed Butler back after his ouster from Philadelphia with open arms and his old rank of brigadier general. John Lejeune, who'd become commandant in 1920, assigned him to the Marine base in San Diego, California.

It was not exactly a coveted command: an out-of-the way assignment on a stretch of coastal desert next to the Mexican border—fueling Butler's anxiety that he was again being sidelined for impulsiveness and his past clashes with the chain of command. But Lejeune promised it was an up-and-coming post, noting "the West Coast is gradually becoming the center of naval activity."[1] Smedley, Ethel, and all three children—Snooks, Smedley Junior, and Tom Dick, now nineteen, sixteen, and twelve—sailed from New York in January 1926, passing through the Panama Canal and waving to their old home at Camp Elliott on the way.

San Diego turned out to be as boring as Butler feared. The most excitement in his first months there was an oral infection that resulted in him having twelve teeth pulled, and then being hospitalized with low blood pressure.[2] Having been inspired by his experiences with the bootleggers to give up alcohol, he tried enforcing Prohibition laws—hitting a former colleague from Haiti with a court-martial for drunkenness—only to be mocked in the national press as "Saint Smedley" and "Meddly Butler." ("As far as I am personally concerned, they can all go to hell," Butler wrote a colleague in the Navy.)[3]

But there was one unexpected feature of the post: its proximity to Hollywood. The Corps had agreed to help Metro-Goldwyn-Mayer make *Tell It to the Marines,* a feature film that would serve as a recruiting tool for them and a star vehicle for the most celebrated character actor of the day,

Lon Chaney. Nicknamed the Man of a Thousand Faces, Chaney had become an international celebrity for his equally terrifying and sympathetic portrayals of the title roles in films like *The Phantom of the Opera* and *The Hunchback of Notre Dame*.

Butler signed on as a consultant, charged with teaching Chaney how to look and act like a Marine. The result was a pitch-perfect imitation of Butler as "Sergeant O'Hara"—complete with Butler's crooked smile, his snappy regimental movements, and even his real-life Marine Corps mascot: an English bulldog named Jiggs, as himself.[4]

Because they were filming in California, the MGM filmmakers had to imagine an adventure for their characters to go on across the Pacific. In the movie, the Marines make their first stop at a Navy fueling station on "Tondo Island," a fictional mosquito-infested waypoint "six miles this side of Hell" that audiences immediately recognized as a stand-in for the Philippines.[5] Then they continue on to Shanghai.

The "Chinese" sets, built on an MGM studio lot and the Iverson Ranch in Simi Valley, bore no resemblance to either the political realities of China at that moment nor the bustle and glitz of mid-1920s Shanghai. Instead, the writers lifted a story from the most recent thing most Americans had heard about China: the Boxer Rebellion. Chaney and his fictional Marines rescue the love interest, a Navy nurse played by Eleanor Boardman, from a mob of bandits in barbarian furs and nineteenth-century peasant garb. (The Boxer types are led in yellowface by Warner Oland, a Swedish American actor who would later become famous for his portrayals of Charlie Chan and Dr. Fu Manchu.)

*Tell It to the Marines* would end up the top-grossing film of Chaney's long career. It also added a new dimension to Butler's already considerable fame. Chaney's impression of Butler—gruff, tough-as-nails, but ultimately lovable—became the model for how generations of future Marine drill instructors would learn to carry themselves, in real life and on film.[6]

The filmmakers turned out to be even more prescient in the short term. While the movie version of Smedley Butler was thrilling audiences across America, a storm was raging that would draw the real one back across the Pacific very soon.

B y 1926, China was in chaos. The Boxer Rebellion had ended a quarter century earlier with the foreign powers in control of more Chinese territory and wealth than ever, and the Qing dynasty on its last legs. In 1911, another rebellion succeeded in turning the army against the ruling family, forcing the last emperor of China—the late Empress Dowager Cixi's great-nephew, six-year-old Puyi—to abdicate a year later. The intellectual architect of Chinese nationalism, Sun Yat-sen, made his way to the city of Nanjing to declare the birth of the Republic of China, with himself as its first president.[7]

Sun's celebration was short-lived. With several leaders claiming power, China entered its version of the Mexican Revolution: protracted conflicts between regional warlords. In the north was the Beiyang government, whose founding leader, the egomaniacal ex-Qing general Yuan Shikai, had tried to place himself on the Dragon Throne. Sun's Guomindang, or Nationalist Party, was contained in the south. In between were a cast of disaffected army officers and petty bandits—men with nicknames like "The Jade Marshal" and "The Dogmeat General"—whose only real ideologies were their personal right to plunder or rule.

This all felt extremely foreign to most Americans. But as Butler knew from his first tour in China, the United States had been involved throughout the unraveling.

Sun Yat-sen admired the United States. He had spent years living in Hawai'i, before and after the annexation. He wore Western suits, sported a cowboy mustache, and converted to Christianity.[8] His governing philosophy, the "Three Principles of the People," self-consciously echoed Abraham Lincoln's formulation, "government of the people, by the people, for the people." He also envisioned a scheme of "cultivation and colonization" that drew explicitly on American ideas of the frontier—and thus, indirectly, on Frederick Jackson Turner's Frontier Thesis—in which landless peasants and soldiers of China's ethnic Han majority would "civilize" those on the periphery, including the Manchus and Tibetans, and Muslim ethnic groups.[9]

Sun's admiration was not blind: He sympathized with the Filipinos during the Philippine-American War, at one point trying to help smuggle weapons to Aguinaldo's forces from Japan.[10] He allied with the reform movement of the exiled journalist Liang Qichao, which condemned the United States for its participation in the Boxer War.[11] But Sun believed that, in the end, the American people would support his revolution to overthrow the Qing monarchy and replace it, eventually, with a U.S.-style republic.

Sun's most important financial backer was a fellow Chinese Christian, Charlie Soong. A child of Hainanese sea merchants, Soong was brought to Boston at a young age. He stowed away to North Carolina, where, through a series of unlikely events, he converted to Methodism and found himself under the wing of one of Josephus Daniels's friends, the Klansman "General" Julian Carr.[12] Carr's white supremacy was overwhelmed by his affection for the unthreatening boy, and what he represented: a chance to personally tutor a Chinese person into Methodism and send him back home as a missionary. (Just as U.S. manufacturers saw China as the world's largest potential market, many American Protestants like Carr saw China as the world's largest collection of savable souls.)

After enrolling Soong in the future Duke and Vanderbilt Universities, Carr set him up in Shanghai as a printer, where he made a fortune selling translated Bibles to missionaries. Drawn to Sun Yat-sen's vision of a democratic republic, it was Soong who encouraged Sun to become the "George Washington or Abraham Lincoln" of China.[13] (Sun later married Charlie's middle daughter, the Wesleyan College–educated Song Qingling.)

Soong had returned to North Carolina to push Sun's vision of a New China to Julian Carr and his deep-pocketed Southern Methodists, who responded with millions for the cause. Sun continued relying on American Christians for support: when word reached him that the Qing dynasty had fallen, he was in Denver on a fundraising trip.[14]

After he declared his republic, however, Sun and the Guomindang's relationship with the United States grew rockier. Woodrow Wilson's administration granted official recognition to Yuan Shikai's northern Beiyang government because it controlled the traditional imperial capital of Beijing. Sun's attempts to win the support of successive State Departments failed.[15]

Chinese revolutionaries were further dismayed when, in the peace talks after the World War, Wilson ignored the Chinese delegation's only real demand: that they, not Japan, be given final sovereignty over the former German concession at the Shandong Province port of Qingdao.* On May 4, 1919, thousands of Chinese students massed in Beijing's Tiananmen Square to decry Wilson, the Japanese, and the Beiyang delegates who they felt had sold them out.[16] Several students were arrested and severely beaten; one died of his injuries. As anger and strikes spread, the students coalesced into the radical "May Fourth Movement." Some Chinese students and social leaders began looking away from the United States and toward the new Soviet Union—whose leader, Vladimir Ilyich Lenin, had identified imperialism as "the highest stage of capitalism."

In 1923, Sun Yat-sen tried to take control of the customs houses in Guangdong Province—which the foreign powers were still using to collect their indemnity per the terms of the treaty that ended the Boxer War. The U.S. Navy dispatched four destroyers to intimidate Sun into submission. Furious and betrayed, Sun wrote an open letter in which he asked the question that had reverberated through Havana and Manila decades before: "When we first started our revolution . . . the United States was our model and inspiration. Now we wonder . . . has the nation of Washington and Lincoln abandoned the ideal of liberty and regressed from a liberator to an oppressor?"[17]

Sun never got his answer. He died unexpectedly from cancer two years later. The leadership of the Guomindang's most powerful military faction was soon seized by Sun's most trusted lieutenant: the thirty-eight-year-old head of the party's Huangpu Military Academy, Gen. Chiang Kai-shek.

By then members of the May Fourth Movement had forged a Chinese Communist Party. Soviet agents convinced Sun before his death to allow some of the Communists into his Guomindang as a condition of receiving Soviet assistance and money.[18] The two wings of the party—the Communist left and Chiang's capitalist, militant Nationalist right—

---

* Wilson needed Japan to sign off on his planned League of Nations. But as ever, Wilson's idealism ran into his racism: his idea of which peoples deserved "self-determination" was restricted mainly to European ethnic groups living on the lands of the now-fallen Ottoman and Austro-Hungarian Empires. He similarly ignored a young Vietnamese activist at the Paris Peace Conference named Nguyen Sinh Cung, who petitioned for independence from the French. Embittered, the young man returned home to pursue revolution instead, eventually adopting the nom de guerre Ho Chi Minh.

coexisted uneasily. But for the moment, Chiang kept his attention on achieving Sun's goals: rooting out the remaining warlords and unseating the Beiyang. Above all, he aimed to establish a government strong enough to revoke "unequal treaties" like the Boxer Protocol and take China out of the hands of the United States, the European powers, and Japan.

Throughout the summer and fall of 1926, Chiang Kai-shek led his fragile coalition of Communist and Nationalist soldiers on a northward expedition to expand the Republic of China's territorial control. Everywhere Chiang's National Revolutionary Army went, it was aided by masses of peasants, tired of suffering under the corruption of their local caudillos.

The army also succeeded in stirring up anti-foreign sentiment. As they had under the Boxer threat, terrified Americans began evacuating from China's interior for the familiar protection of the foreign concessions on the coast, including Tianjin, Hong Kong, and the biggest de facto colony of them all, the International Settlement in Shanghai. Meanwhile, in San Diego, Gen. Smedley Butler and the Marines began preparing for the likelihood of another invasion of China.

Shanghai today is a city of twenty-five million, the most populous in China and one of the largest cities in the world. Forced open by the British and French in the nineteenth-century Opium Wars, it remains China's international financial capital. When I visited in the summer of 2017, the historical layers of opulence were apparent: the gargantuan modern skyscrapers of the new financial district, Pudong, looking down across the river on the art deco masterpieces and neoclassical British banks of Shanghai's previous golden age.

On the poshest shopping street of the former French Concession, Shanghainese hipsters flocked to the shimmering storefronts of Gucci, Cartier, and Dolce & Gabbana. In the 1920s this stretch of the thoroughfare was known as Avenue Joffre, after a French World War I general. It's now called Middle Huaihai Road, after a decisive Communist victory in the last stages of the Chinese Civil War.

I turned down a corner into the historic homes of the old concession. It was scorching hot—107 degrees, according to my overheated phone—

and I was grateful to be walking in the shade, through quiet tunnels of twisting sycamores. But I hadn't come for the scenery. In the 1920s, the French Concession was home to one of China's most powerful organized crime syndicates, the Green Gang—which was both a major player in and beneficiary of the conflict that drew in Butler and the Marines.

To learn more about the mafia, I'd signed up for a "Private Gangster Tour" with a local company run by a British expat. But as soon as my guide—a twentysomething from Manchester named Luke—greeted me animatedly with a toy gun, white fedora, and fake Cockney accent, I suspected I'd made a mistake.

"Sorry," he apologized in his real accent when he noticed my frown. "I usually do group tours. Team-building exercises for companies and the like."

"It's OK," I reassured him. "Do your thing."

The Green Gang, I'd read, traced its origins to a secular Buddhist sect that acted as a mutual aid society for boatmen on China's Grand Canal. Its members had made tidy sums smuggling salt around the Qing's official monopoly, which they then reinvested into gambling and prostitution rackets. But like the gangsters of Philadelphia and the Mexican "cartels," the Green Gang reached the apex of its power and ferocity thanks to the prohibition of a drug—in their case, of opium.[19]

In the aftermath of the Boxer War, the Qing and British officials agreed to crack down on the narcotics trade. (With rampant opium addiction having sparked a backlash from both foreign missionaries and the Chinese public, Western governments were happy to move on to less controversial and more lucrative pursuits.) When the prohibition went fully into effect, Shanghai fell completely under warlord rule. By 1925, the Green Gang had forged enough mutually beneficial agreements with area warlords and senior French officials to make the Shanghai French Concession the heart of China's opium-smuggling network.[20]

One of our first stops was the former mansion of the Green Gang's most notorious leader, "Big-Eared" Du Yuesheng. Du rose from street hoodlum to gunman and, finally, opium kingpin.[21] He would use his racketeering profits, political connections, and a few direct threats to found at least two banks, buy one of Shanghai's largest shipping companies, and become a director of the Bank of China.[22] The four-story neoclassical edifice, with its marble lobby, vintage grand piano, and imperial-style dragon sculptures, was a testament to the extent of Du's wealth. It was now a luxury hotel.

A little less than a mile down the road—after subjecting me to a pretend "mafia hit" involving a balloon and his toy revolver—Luke stopped to show me a former home of Chiang Kai-shek. That house was where Chiang had moved after he married the Bible tycoon Charlie Soong's youngest daughter, Song Meiling—a marriage that brought him closer to the American elite while making him Sun Yat-sen's posthumous brother-in-law. It was bought for them by Soong's son, the Harvard-educated banker Ziwen, or "T.V." Soong—the "J. P. Morgan of China" and one-time finance minister to Chiang—who lived nearby.[23]

The proximity to Big-Eared Du's mansion was no coincidence. Chiang had developed a close relationship with the Green Gang during his play-boy days as a broker on the Shanghai Stock Exchange. Evidence found by the researcher Brian Martin suggests Chiang may have at one point been a formal member of the syndicate. In 1926, as the Americans were trying to figure out what to do with the Nationalist movement, a U.S. consul reported that British officials in Shanghai had issued warrants for Chiang years earlier for armed robbery and murder.[24]

As we reached the last stop on the tour—another former Soong family home, rebuilt to host, of all things, a Mexican-themed bar named "Zapata's"—Luke showed me video footage of what Chiang's partnership with the Green Gang wrought.

After Chiang's troops took Shanghai in the spring of 1927, he moved to wipe out his Communist rivals within the Guomindang, with the help of over fifteen hundred hit men from the Green Gang. The gangsters, tired of Communists trying to organize trade unions at factories under their protection rackets, were convinced by Chiang's apparent promises to Big-Eared Du that he would protect their opium monopoly. Du's hit men traveled across Shanghai in armored cars supplied by the British, armed with Tommy guns bought with $3 million Chiang had raised from, as the author Hannah Pakula summarized, "every important banking, commercial, and industrial group" in Shanghai. Thousands were arrested; hundreds were executed without trial. In one case, victims were "fed alive into the fireboxes of locomotives." "It was raining that day," a worker who survived the purge recalled decades later. "Baoshan Road was a river of blood."[25]

Luke played me documentary footage of some of the death-squad killings on his iPad. "And then they take them in a field—and if you look closely," he said, moving the tablet closer for dramatic effect, "you can see some *brains*."

The tree-lined geographic nexus we were strolling through, in other words, represented a historical one: a triangle of political, financial, and mafia power, grown in a substratum of colonized soil. Removed by a few generations from the horror of the moment, it can now be sold as tourist kitsch. But the consequences of that violence are still with us today. For Butler, it was a force he had to reckon with.

O n January 16, 1927, the chief U.S. envoy in China, John V. A. Mac-Murray, asked the Navy Department to dispatch a warship for the purpose of "evacuating foreign residents should it become necessary." Hours later, he transmitted a confidential warning to Secretary of State Frank B. Kellogg: "In the event of Chiang Kai-shek's appearing before Shanghai with the intention of taking possession of the [International] Settlement, with or without assistance of the mob, any naval landing forces would be entirely inadequate." Ground troops would be necessary—at least twenty thousand.[26]

Kellogg was an unlikely candidate to agree. President Coolidge's top diplomat was an icon of the anti-imperialism trend the Republicans had ridden back to power. Two years later, he would accept the Nobel Peace Prize for a pact, coauthored with France's foreign minister, in which sixty-four countries, including the United States, Soviet Union, Weimar Germany, and Japan, renounced war as an "instrument of national policy."

But decades of American involvement in China had woven a web that even one of history's staunchest anti-interventionists could not escape. By the 1920s, one-fifth of all U.S. oil exports went to China. Standard Oil had invested millions in the Middle Kingdom. American missionary-run universities enrolled one in five Chinese college students; a smaller, more influential cadre of Chinese youth (including all of Charlie Soong's children) attended U.S. colleges, many on scholarships underwritten by the Boxer Indemnity. In Shanghai there were Ford and General Motors dealerships, Hollywood studio offices, and a U.S. consular court for cases involving U.S. citizens. A civilian militia, the Shanghai Volunteer Corps, included a company of American machine gunners with a subordinate Filipino platoon.[27]

All of these interests had their own competing agendas. The missionaries, still dreaming of mass conversion, wanted U.S. support for the Guomindang, which they still saw as the party of the Methodists Sun Yat-sen and Charlie Soong. Their church communities, and the congressmen who represented them, played down the party's Communist elements and moved, for one of the last times in the century, as Barbara Tuchman wrote, "to minimize rather than inflate the Red menace." In February 1927, the House of Representatives called for the renegotiation of what it called the "unequal" treaties with China in a resolution that read as if it had been written by Chiang or Song Meiling themselves.[28]

The hard-line imperialists in Shanghai's International Settlement could not have disagreed more. Their livelihoods were based on the unequal treaties. Armed with the same colonial mentality as their counterparts in the Panama Canal Zone, they wanted a show of force against Chiang's army, which they called (unaware of the fractures within the Guomindang) the "Red Wave on the Yangtze."[29]

Finally, Standard Oil and other major corporations wanted stability, with any Chinese government that would impose a minimum of taxation and interference.

Navigating these crosswinds, Kellogg found a compromise. "If we sent to Shanghai a large force of the Regular Army, it would mean arousing all of China and involve us probably in making war," he wrote MacMurray on January 28, 1927.[30] But a smaller force under the auspices of the Navy, he suggested, would lend plausible deniability against accusations of an invasion or a heavy hand against the Nationalists.

That meant the San Diego Marines. At first, Butler was ordered not to go with them, on the theory "that if a general officer were sent it would unduly magnify the importance" of the mission.[31] But the situation continued to deteriorate. In March, when Chiang's army pushed back the forces of the local warlord, the "Smiling Tiger" Sun Chuanfang, and—with the help of a Communist-organized general strike—took control of Shanghai, Butler got his orders to cross the Pacific.[32]

On March 24, while Butler was en route, Chiang's army reentered the Guomindang's former capital of Nanjing. The soldiers, locals, and members of the retreating warlord armies carried out a wave of violence against the powerful foreigners in their midst. At least six, including the American missionary who was vice president of the University of Nanking, were killed in the resulting riots. The best-connected expats—including representatives of British-American Tobacco and Texaco—fled to "Socony Hill," the eponymous housing development that was home to executives of the Standard Oil Company of New York. The U.S. and British navies sent nineteen destroyers up the Yangtze River to bombard the Nationalist positions targeting the oilmen's neighborhood.[33]

Also in Nanjing that day was Pearl S. Buck, then a thirty-four-year-old missionary and English literature professor living with her husband and children. "Were I a young Chinese, had I been taught only what the white man had done to my country, I too would have wanted to be rid of him forever. I could not blame them," the Nobel Prize–winning author later wrote. "But on the other level, I was thinking of this very moment, and of the children."[34] They, like the VIPs on Socony Hill, were evacuated down the Yangtze to Shanghai.

The next day, Brig. Gen. Smedley Butler disembarked at the Shanghai Bund for his final overseas command. Along with his San Diego regiment, he took charge of a smaller expeditionary battalion of Marines from Guam and Cavite, together forming the Third Brigade. They joined three British brigades, four thousand Japanese troops, and the volunteer colonialist militia in Shanghai.[35]

Lejeune had warned Butler in advance to "avoid talking to newspaper correspondents."[36] Butler immediately disregarded that advice. He knew the arrival of a general who bore the scars of Chinese battles past would provoke panic—or hope, among the treaty-port diehards—that a full-scale U.S. invasion was impending. He also knew how deadly such an invasion could get. Two months earlier, the War Department had revised its War Plan Yellow—its standing contingency plan for an intervention in China. That plan now envisioned sending as many as three Army infantry divisions, two reinforced brigades, and an air observation squadron from the Philippines. (A further revision, a year later, included a provision for the use of chemical weapons.)[37]

The cumulative weight of his past battles and the horrors he had seen at his disembarkation camp in France a decade earlier had all but cured Butler of his appetite for foreign combat. When an American newspaper correspondent asked how many troops would be needed to suppress Chiang's Nationalists, Butler replied, to the irritation of his fellow commanders, "I would not dream of starting an armed invasion in China without a half million troops, and it probably would require a million more before the end of the first year."

In case that was unclear, Butler added that he did not plan on asking for reinforcements.[38]

From his new headquarters inside the International Settlement, Butler did everything possible to avoid confrontation with the Nationalists. He kept the Marines away from the front lines and issued clear, consistent warnings to the Nationalists through the press of how to avoid Washington's point of no return: the killing of more Americans, especially women and children. "We can always overlook damage to property," he told Shanghai's most influential English-language newspaper, the *North-China Herald*. "Property can be paid for but lives can't be brought back."[39]

The anti-Communist purge came eighteen days after Butler's arrival. He had gotten word of it the night before, on April 11, reporting to Lejeune that "Chiang Kai-shek had organized a special 'murder squad' of 3,000 soldiers to do away with all the red laborites in the Chinese part of the city."[40] He ordered his men not to interfere.

Butler chose personally to spend the morning of the massacre, April 12, scouting locations for a new Marine campsite. "All day there has been wholesale murdering within a mile of us, but thank heaven 15,000 British soldiers stand between it and the 40,000 foreigners of this Settlement," he wrote Bunny on the afternoon of the purge. He made clear that he was ready to intervene if any Americans were harmed. "If they can't set up a Republic without killing our women and children then they can't have a Republic," he said.[41]

None, it seems, were harmed. Yet Butler kept wrestling with his decision not to act. The next day, in a lengthy letter to Maud, Butler pitted his instincts to intervene on behalf of those he saw as innocents against his deepening desire to avoid war at all costs. "These devils have a perfect right to set up any kind of government they please but they *must not* kill more women and children in the process," he wrote his mother. He tried to stake out a middle ground, saying: "All of us Marines are boiling to get these fiends—not at the poor coolies who are just tools but at the leaders who use them to commit such unspeakable atrocities." A few pages later he changed that back to: "Let Britain and the rest do the fighting and we can step in and collect the goodwill of the Chinamen." Then he immediately contradicted himself again, saying: "But sometime or other I do wish our country would do its share."[42]

It was a version of the debates that would become a regular feature of American political life over the century to come: to go and kill, on the justification that it might ultimately save more lives? Or to stand aside, even though inaction might prove more dangerous in the long run? Each time, the decision is made more fraught by an ever-accumulating litany of past actions—in Butler's case, the anti-Boxer invasion in which he had taken part, which in turn had fueled the anti-foreign sentiments of both the Chinese Nationalists and the Communists.

Whatever the Americans might have done to stop or add to the killing, the violence quickly spread from Shanghai. Chiang Kai-shek ordered similar massacres across the territories under his control. As many as one million people were murdered across China for the barest hint of Communist or leftist sympathies over the next few years. Some of the most gruesome violence of this "White Terror" was directed at women with bobbed hair and unbound feet, both of which were considered signs of radicalization. Their corpses were hung with their breasts cut off and heads shaved as a warning.[43]

Many of the leading Communists escaped the violence. Zhou Enlai—who had served under Chiang at the military academy and organized the general strike in Shanghai—made his way to the left wing's stronghold at Wuhan. There, he linked up with another rising leader of the Chinese Communists, a former part-time history teacher named Mao Zedong. Weeks before the White Terror began, Mao had predicted that "several hundred million peasants" would soon "rise like a mighty storm" and "sweep all the imperialists, warlords, corrupt officials, local tyrants, and evil gentry into their graves."[44]

The violence that had erupted in Shanghai in April 1927 would make

Mao's prediction inevitable. Though it would take some time for everyone to realize it, the Chinese Civil War had just begun.

Like Butler, I had been to China once before, in what already felt like a bygone era. In the early 2000s, I tramped through rural Guangdong Province with thirteen young Chinese Americans in search of their families' roots.

China at the time was on the precipice of sweeping economic change. We traveled down expressways that were still under construction. Several times, our bus driver had to swerve violently to avoid hitting workers hand-churning asphalt in the middle of the road. Many of the old villages we toured, with Cantonese names like Tong Haa (Shrimp Pond) and Maa Mai Wu (Horsetail Lake), were barely electrified, with little plumbing. Some were being transformed, others demolished. One student was reduced to tears when she learned the mountain that had housed her ancestral cemetery had been dynamited to make way for a factory.

On my return trip in 2017, the transformation had taken place. Over a million rural villages like the ones we visited in the Pearl River Delta had disappeared by the beginning of the new decade.[45] Instead of half-finished highways, I traveled on state-of-the-art bullet trains that reached speeds of over two hundred miles an hour. China was the first place I ever saw people pay for taxis and restaurants using their phones or GPS to rent a bike on the street.

But there were many dark sides to this. Nearly all the phone technology was housed in a single app, WeChat, activity on which is analyzed, tracked, and shared around the Chinese mass surveillance state. In the far western province of Xinjiang—home to the Uyghur, a mostly Muslim ethnic group—Communist authorities have used this technology to take Sun Yat-sen's vision of an American-style frontier project to its darkest conclusion. Using facial scans, voice prints, and other phone data, the Chinese government has embarked on a scheme of forced sterilization, psychological indoctrination, and the imprisonment of as many as one million Uyghurs in concentration camps and prisons. The apparent goal is to destroy Uyghur culture, which Beijing sees as a threat to its goal of a cohesive national identity.[46]

Much of the Communist Party's paranoia can be traced to the Chinese Civil War. In the wake of Chiang Kai-shek's White Terror of 1927, the far-left factions went underground. The purge ensured that only the craftiest and most militant Communist leaders survived, as they set up a new Red Army to fight a guerrilla insurgency.

Among the first Americans to argue that the United States should side with the Nationalists was Smedley Butler. Though just months had passed since the Shanghai massacre and the besieging of foreigners by Chiang's forces in Nanjing, Butler argued the U.S. should "back Shek" (as he mistakenly called him), arguing that he was preferable to both the "'Red' branch" and the other warlords, including the Beiyang. The Soviet Union's permanent break with Chiang in response to the White Terror, Butler wrote in a secret memo to Lejeune, was a "golden opportunity for us to get in on the commercial ground floor of this movement."[47]

That shift happened in stages. The Coolidge administration recognized Chiang's faction in Nanjing in July 1928 as the legitimate government of China. It took the aftermath of World War II—and years of skillful and persistent lobbying by Song Meiling, by then known around the world as "Madame Chiang"—but eventually, in the late 1940s, the Americans supported the Nationalists' war against the Communists with military assistance.

But by then it was too late. The Nationalist government was too corrupt, fractured, and unpopular, and the Communists too well disciplined by decades of hardship and war. On October 1, 1949, Mao Zedong proclaimed the new People's Republic of China in Beijing's Tiananmen Square, forcing the Chiangs to flee with two million Nationalists to the island of Taiwan.

Mao had risen to the unquestioned leadership of the party by surviving violence and using violence against all who stood in his way. Tens of millions of Chinese peasants died in a famine caused by Mao's forced agricultural collectivization. In 1966, Mao launched his "Great Proletarian Cultural Revolution," an attempt at purging critics of his regime that became an orgy of recrimination and murder.[48] A man I met in Beijing told me his father-in-law was locked in a utility room in the family's work unit for a year, for the crime of having worked in theater.

Yet just as the Americans overlooked Chiang's mass murders in the 1920s, a preference for political expediency ultimately meant overlooking Mao's as well. In the middle of the Cultural Revolution, in 1972, President Richard Nixon met on friendly terms with Mao in his official residence, and signed a joint communique with Zhou Enlai at a hotel in Shanghai's former French Concession that said that neither the U.S. nor China "should seek hegemony in the Asia-Pacific region."[49] The agreement began the process of transferring official U.S. recognition from the exiled Nationalists in Taiwan to the Communists in Beijing.

Mao died in 1976 at the age of eighty-two. His successor, Deng Xiaoping, was determined to end the poverty and economic stagnation the old man had left behind. Deng knew the toll of those years personally: he had twice been severely demoted by Mao for his reformist ideas; his eldest son, Deng Pufang, was left a paraplegic after being tortured and forced out of a fourth-story window during the Cultural Revolution. But Deng had also been on the wrong end of U.S. power during the civil war, and survived Chiang's 1927 Shanghai massacre as a twenty-two-year-old activist. So he was not inclined to pivot to U.S.-style democracy or capitalism, either.[50]

Instead, Deng abandoned central planning for a mix of state-owned corporations and private capital, while maintaining mass surveillance and suppressing dissent (most notoriously, massacring pro-democracy protesters in Tiananmen Square in 1989). He designated China's first "Special Economic Zones" in which foreign corporations enjoyed tax breaks and fewer regulations—a new twist on the Qing foreign concessions, except this time with the party in control. To dismiss the inevitable question— Was this just U.S.-style global capitalism in disguise?—Deng trotted out his favorite proverb: "It doesn't matter if a cat is black or white. If it catches mice, it's a good cat."[51]

The resulting explosion of prosperity has made China the only rival to the United States for the title of largest economy in the world. Despite the agreement not to pursue hegemony, the two powers are now in a race for influence and territory across the Pacific. General Secretary Xi Jinping is pushing China's frontiers in Teddy Rooseveltian style: insisting on sovereignty over the South China Sea and Taiwan, making plays for islands claimed by the Philippines, Vietnam, and Japan, challenging land neighbors in South and Southeast Asia, and building artificial archipelagos to hold military airstrips, radar, and antiaircraft guns. Farther-flung bases, like the one China opened in the Horn of Africa in 2017, are likely in the offing as well. At the same time, an influential chorus in Washington pushes for aggression—including military buildups and shows of force off China's coast—while seeing Chinese Communist infiltration in the United States, as former Secretary of State Mike Pompeo alleged, down to the level of "our high schools, our colleges and even into our PTA meetings."[52]

It is a combustible situation, made more fraught by Chinese memories of the "national humiliations" in which the United States took part— memories cultivated and instrumentalized by China's one-party government. It would not be the first time rival empires fell into a Pacific war.

In May 1927, Butler went on a mission to his old stomping grounds in Tianjin. He tied up at Dagu Forts, at almost the exact same point where he had first set foot in China twenty-seven years before. (The area "was much changed since that time and I failed to recognize anything," Butler lamented.[53]) After a few days in the north, he called on an officer of the United States' most dangerous Pacific rival at the time: Japan.

After welcoming Butler with honors and showing off a "very handsome looking company of Japanese infantry," the officer, Lt. Gen. Toyoki Takada, pressed Butler for information about the U.S. military's plans in China.

"I escaped without telling anything worth knowing," Butler reported to Lejeune after the meeting. "We are all very suspicious that the Japanese intend to coerce China and I know our government does not intend us to join in any such movement so I dodged all definite answers."[54]

The late Alfred Thayer Mahan had long warned of the threat Japan posed to U.S. Pacific supremacy. By the summer of 1927, the two empires had divided up much of the region, and their territories were dangerously close. The Japanese colony of Formosa (now Taiwan) was sixty nautical miles from the northernmost point of the Philippines. The closest spot in Japan's South Seas Mandate—the large swath of Micronesia that Tokyo had taken from Germany after the World War—was just over thirty nautical miles from Guam. Butler knew from the 1907 war scare at Subic Bay that Japan had designs on the Philippines, and that interest had only risen since. "The islands are intrinsically valued by Japan," an Army intelligence officer had confirmed in 1919. "In the event of war between the United States and Japan, an attempt at military occupation would follow."[55]*

China could be an even bigger flashpoint. The Japanese were the largest foreign population in China, operated some of its biggest banks, and had billions of yen invested in factories and transportation.[56] Thanks to their victory in the 1905 Russo-Japanese War, Tokyo directly controlled a key Manchurian railway and the port of Dalian. The Japanese had their eye on more of the far northern territory, which bordered both the Soviet Union and their mainland colony of Korea. The United States was, as ever, loath to see any large region of China gobbled up by a rival power—Washington still clung to the right of *all* empires to take from China what they wanted, through the McKinley-era "Open Door." If Japan tried to conquer China, the United States might feel obligated to respond, perhaps sparking another world war.

Japan's hopes for snatching up Manchuria quietly had rested on the Beiyang government in Beijing, which was then controlled by the Manchurian warlord Zhang Zuolin, long a Japanese ally. But by the late spring of 1927 it was plain to see that Zhang's position was not secure: besides Manchuria, his army held only Beijing, Tianjin, and parts of Shandong Province.

As Chiang Kai-shek's Nationalists pushed north across the Yangtze River, swatting out lesser warlords along the way, the militarist Japanese

---

* In 1939, a U.S. Naval Intelligence officer would report that someone, presumably the Japanese government, had brought a group of ten Filipino Muslims from Mindanao to Japan to "receive intensive lessons in the art of propaganda in order to inspire religious hatred in their compatriots in the Philippines and thus furnish Japan an excuse to intervene in their favor." In other words, the informant believed the Japanese were trying to stoke jihad in the southern Philippines as a pretext for an invasion. See "Japanese Propaganda in the Philippines," typescript of attaché's report, May 13, 1939, in RG 38: Records of the Office of Naval Intelligence, C-10-j, Register 12062-C, NARA.

prime minister, Tanaka Giichi, ordered the redeployment of six thousand soldiers from Manchuria to Japanese-controlled Qingdao. Butler personally ran a spy mission to the Shandong Province port, "to see what the Japanese were really doing there." He reported back that the Japanese had about twenty-five hundred troops in the area, but that they were not engaged in fighting, for now.[57]

Noting that the action was nonetheless moving north, Butler ordered part of his Third Marine Brigade to move with him to Tianjin. The U.S. Army Fifteenth Infantry, posted as a diplomatic guard force there under the 1901 Boxer Protocol, watched with jealousy as the Marines unloaded their arsenal of light tanks, field artillery, and machine guns. The Marines also brought up two squadrons of airplanes: one fighter, one surveillance. Butler set up an airfield next to the Standard Oil compound at Xin He. The future ExxonMobil allowed the Marines to use several buildings as winter barracks, in exchange for guarding the compound.

Butler's Marines had no idea what they were supposed to be doing with all that firepower. Smedley's orders were just clear enough to add to their confusion: "If we cannot protect our Americans in [Tianjin] they must be rapidly evacuated, and safely, to Shanghai or some point in Japan, but we must not get into a war with China."[58]

As the months wore on, the U.S. envoy in Beijing, MacMurray, insisted the Marines be ready to fight their way in and evacuate his staff if the old imperial capital fell to the Nationalists. Butler publicly demurred. "I shall consider our expedition to have been entirely successful only if we finally withdraw from China without the spilling of any blood, either American or Chinese," he told a *New York Times* correspondent. "This country belongs to the Chinese, and I tolerate no clashes between my men and the Chinese people. If a man so much as slaps a rickshaw coolie or lays a hand upon a servant, he gets a general court-martial."[59]

In April 1928, after the spring thaw, the Nationalist army resumed its push north into Shandong. Still hoping to bottle up Chiang in the south, the Japanese prime minister rushed several thousand Japanese soldiers to the provincial capital, Jinan. When Chiang dispatched one of his chief diplomats and sixteen staff to broker a peace, the Japanese soldiers tortured and murdered them. Then the Japanese bombed the civilian population, killing thousands, in a failed attempt to stun the Nationalists into submission.[60]

The "Jinan Incident" was the last straw for the Beiyang warlord Zhang Zuolin. He condemned the Japanese aggression and withdrew his troops so that Chiang's forces would have more room to maneuver.[61] A few weeks later, Zhang abandoned Beijing to return to Manchuria, effectively handing over the country to the Guomindang. He would never arrive: On June 4, a group of Japanese officers blew up Zhang's train as it passed through a railway station on his way home, killing him instantly.

The Japanese tried to convince Butler and the other foreign generals to establish a perimeter seven miles outside Tianjin to deter the Nationalists' advance, which would have been legal under the extant treaties. Butler refused. As commander of the largest and best-equipped foreign force in northern China, Butler's decision was decisive: none of the other foreign armies, including Japan, made any aggressive moves. The result was ten tense days in which the Nationalist army passed by the barricaded city without incident.[62]

Butler was convinced he had prevented the outbreak of a Sino-Japanese War. And he may have, for the moment.

On one of my last days in Shanghai, I paid a visit to the old Nationalist capital of Nanjing. (Though the cities are 190 miles apart, the trip took just over an hour on the high-speed rail.) Under an overcast sky, I entered the gray complex built in memory of the victims of the mass slaughter and rape that was visited on that city when the Japanese finally tried to conquer all of China, in 1937.

The memorial complex is vast and varied: at turns museum, meditation space, sculpture garden, and open-pit mausoleum. Construction started under Deng Xiaoping in the mid-1980s; the full complex was completed in 2007. (By contrast, during his decades in power, Mao downplayed the atrocities of World War II—preferring a heroic narrative of the victory he helped achieve against the Japanese, and perhaps not wanting to draw uncomfortable parallels to his own record of mass murder.[63]) I shuffled with the other visitors, mainly students on field trips, down a set path meticulously curated to evoke awareness, then horror, and finally a sense of national redemption.

In a darkened space, past a sign ordering "solemn silence," I walked into the mass grave. Laid out like an exposed archeological dig were the crushed and broken skeletons of victims found near the memorial site. They represented some of the uncountable victims of the Japanese mass killings of late 1937 and early 1938—a number that scholars estimate from the tens of thousands to more than two hundred thousand.[64] In an effort, perhaps, to give some precision to the unimaginable, the most visible skeletons were numbered. No. 1 lay on its back, hands and feet severed, a single bullet hole in the forehead. No. 8 lay on her side, skull facing down, mandibles pried open—a placard said it was an old woman who had been choked to death. No. 5 was in pieces: the bones of a six-year-old whose head was severed while he was alive.

They were, in other words, some of the deaths that those who tried to stop the war—a group that included Butler—had hoped to prevent.

Who knows what would have happened had they succeeded; what other paths history might have taken had the wars that combined into the worldwide conflagration never broken out. Yet, looking into the sunken eyes of the victims in Nanjing, I was filled with a sense of what their lives could have been, had the cycles of hatred, exploitation, and violence somehow been halted in time.

Smedley Butler's last overseas mission ended without his Marines firing a shot in battle. The lack of action left his younger Marines confused. "We didn't know what the mission was," David M. Shoup, a future Marine commandant, later recalled thinking as a twenty-three-year-old lieutenant in China. "But we landed at the Standard Oil docks and lived in Standard Oil compounds and were ready to protect Standard Oil's investment. I wondered at the time if our government would put all these Marines in a position of danger, where they might sacrifice their lives in defense of Standard Oil. Later I discovered that of course it would, and did. It was only some years later that I learned that General Butler had been thinking the same way. I thought I had been alone in suspecting it."[65]

Indeed, the Marines' most dangerous action in China was done in service of the future ExxonMobil: on Christmas Eve 1927, two warehouses erupted into flames at the Standard Oil compound where the Marines were staying outside Tianjin. Butler was photographed standing on a barrel, giving orders through the haze with a swagger stick as his Marines built a firewall out of scrap metal and rushed tins of gasoline out of a third warehouse by hand. Butler was personally credited with saving the oil giant's $25 million plant.[66]

Over the course of Smedley's nearly two years in China, Ethel came to visit several times. On one trip, he greeted her by splashing down in a seaplane next to her arriving ship. On another, the couple visited the Great Wall. ("I never had enjoyed Bunny as much," Smedley effused in a letter to Maud.)[67]

On a visit in November 1928, Ethel asked Smedley to show her the places in Beijing that, as she put it in a letter to the children, "he'd known as a little boy Marine: where he was first shot . . . then the march around the walls . . . and where he slept for several weeks in one of the enormous 'parks'"—namely Tiananmen Square. "We hadn't done that the other time and I'd felt very badly about it," she added.[68]

In his last months in China, Butler was accorded an unusual honor. On two different occasions, in two different villages, he was honored with the presentation of a *wan min san,* or Ten Thousand People's Umbrella. (Butler, for whatever reason, called them Umbrellas of Ten Thousand Blessings.) The enormous satin parasols had formerly been given to show a population's gratitude to a retiring official during the Qing dynasty. With the monarchy gone, villagers now felt free to give them to whoever they felt deserved one. The village of Beicang awarded Butler the red umbrella in gratitude for his Marines' replacing a bridge on the Tianjing-Beijing highway. That was the town where, twenty-eight years before, the allied column had come under heavy fire from Boxers and Qing regulars, and the British allegedly fired their "chlorine gas cannon."

An earlier, even grander ceremony had been convened by the people of Dazhigu—a district of Tianjin, whose elders credited Butler with having peacefully prevented the Nationalist army from entering and likely looting their village. "Fifty of the old notables of the town marched up the street to Headquarters with a Chinese band and presented this unique gift to me," Butler wrote Lejeune. "It is very unusual and quite a distinction, I am told, and no one has ever heard of such a thing occurring before in the case of anyone not of Chinese birth." That umbrella bore silk ribbons with the names of hundreds of the townspeople, and the blessing: "Protect this place."[69]

Butler recognized the district the men honoring him came from. He knew it as the "Boxer Village." It was a place where he had killed more people than he cared to remember, and near where he and several of his men had gotten shot. Being honored by people whom he had tried to kill and who had tried to kill him decades before—people with whom he had now developed a mutual respect—touched him profoundly. He resolved that, when he got back to America, he would give the red satin umbrellas the place of honor they deserved.

# SEVENTEEN

## AMERICA

In early 1929, Smedley Butler returned to his home country for good. He and Ethel crossed the Pacific aboard the ocean liner *President McKinley*, aptly named for the leader who first sent Smedley to war back in 1898. From San Francisco they went to Pasadena, California, to see Smedley Junior, now a sophomore at Caltech; then to Eastland, Texas, to visit Smedley's younger brothers, Sam and Horace, who had gone into the oil drilling business. A week later the Butlers pulled up to the family home in West Chester. Maud greeted them, alone. Thomas Butler had died nine months earlier, after suffering a heart attack in his office at the Capitol.[1]

News of his father's death had reached Smedley in China and hit him hard. Thomas was not just a parent and confidant, he was a patron—chairman of the Naval Affairs Committee and champion of funding the Marines. Commandant Lejeune had traveled to West Chester to represent the branch at the burial. "I just don't know how the old Corps will get along without your dear father," he had written Smedley.[2]

Thomas's death was one of a string of misfortunes that doubled as professional setbacks for Butler. Littleton Waller had died of pneumonia in 1926. Lejeune, having lost his most important contact on Capitol Hill, was forced out of his post as commandant in 1929. The death of Butler's comrade from Haiti, Eli K. Cole, cleared space on the promotions list to elevate Smedley to major general. That made him, at just forty-eight, the second-highest ranking Marine, which could have put him next in line to be commandant.[3] But Butler's lack of academy credentials, reputation for insubordination, and thinning network of support put those prospects in doubt.

Butler's burnout was also reaching critical levels. "Though it is simply killing me I must go on and on trying to do the Nation's work—oh I don't care anymore but must pretend I do—just hate it all," he'd written his mother from China, "but Father drove himself to death for the Navy and I must do the same I suppose."[4]

Butler went back to running Quantico. With most of the dwindling Marine command off occupying Haiti and Nicaragua, there was little to do there, so Butler took some time to tend to some much overdue book-keeping and check on his family's financial situation.

It was not good. In decades at war, while Butler had been off making money for bankers and captains of industry, Ethel and the kids had lived off his modest Corps salaries and gifts from their parents. Smedley Junior's tuition at Caltech (he would soon transfer to MIT) and Tom Dick's at Swarthmore totaled $3,000 a year, roughly $45,000 today. Their daughter, Snooks, had gone to finishing school in Paris, embarking on spending sprees to keep up with her wealthy classmates. ("I must say I thank my stars and everything else that we have never been swamped in money like that," Snooks once wrote Ethel, "I don't really believe that one of these girls could do a thing if their fathers suddenly lost their money."[5])

The tax and life insurance bills alone ate up the raise from his promotion to major general. And the bills kept piling up: on returning from China, he and Bunny had bought a custom-made Stutz LeBaron sedan and were looking for a new home on the Main Line.

Butler struggled to find a financial lifeline. An offer to work on another feature film fell through. He tried serializing stories of his adventures overseas, as well as investing in stocks and in his brothers' oil company.[6] But in the summer of 1929, the empire-fueled U.S. economy began to sputter, and opportunities dried up.

The one area in which Butler made consistent money was public speaking. His blunt, sarcastic style was a hit with civilians. On weekends and leaves, Smedley would rush off to American Legion affairs and Rotary Clubs around the Mid-Atlantic. Each event drummed up free publicity, especially when Butler made an especially bold or controversial claim.

On December 5, 1929, Butler was invited to speak at the annual dinner of the Pittsburgh Builders' Exchange. He flew to the Steel City on a new Ford Trimotor plane piloted by Maj. Christian F. Schilt, who'd recently won a Medal of Honor flying rescue missions in the fight against Sandino's guerrillas in Nicaragua.

At the luxe downtown William Penn Hotel, Butler took one of the building's twenty-three new elevators up to a grand ballroom, ostentatiously placed on the seventeenth floor. After dinner and some dance music, Butler was introduced. Staring out at a crowd of seven hundred wealthy Pittsburghers, he opened with a few good lines about corruption in Philadelphia, which elicited some knowing laughs from the in-state crowd.

Feeling bolder, he moved on to a funny story about the "fine free" election his Marines had overseen in Nicaragua in 1912. "The fellow we had in there nobody liked," Butler explained. "But he was a useful fellow—to us—so we had to keep him in. How to keep him in was the problem." The solution, he explained, was to declare all the real opposition candidates "bandits," then keep the polls open just long enough for a few hundred handpicked voters to cast their ballots for the Americans' man.[7]

The banquet crowd, astonished though they may have been, applauded. It was similar to the kinds of stories they'd learned to love about backward, weak-minded natives in faraway lands—like the Chinese bandits Lon Chaney had saved Eleanor Boardman from in *Tell It to the Marines*. The more perceptive listeners might have noticed that, in this case, the Americans were the villains. But Butler had told the story well. He'd also been careful not to mention the candidate's name—Adolfo Díaz—nor the reason that he'd been "useful": his employment with the mining syndicate from right there in Pittsburgh. No use alienating a paying audience.

The applause continued until he got back up for an encore. So he told another story: about the time in Haiti he'd dissolved the National Assembly at gunpoint. This was also apparently a winner. The Builders' Exchange sent Butler a thank-you note a few days later, saying they had been told "by everyone who was present that evening" that "it was the best banquet we have ever held."[8]

But the next day, local coverage of Butler's talk caught the attention of Sinclair Lewis, who happened to be in town doing research for a novel on the labor movement. The soon-to-be Nobel laureate contacted Senator William Borah, a leading critic of the occupation of Haiti, who turned the dinner speech into a national scandal.

The thing was that, while Butler seemed to think he was telling stories from the remote past, the imperial projects in which he had been involved were still going on. The same day as his Pittsburgh talk, Marines in Haiti had committed one of the worst massacres of the occupation, shooting at, bombing, and bayoneting hundreds of protesters in the city of Les Cayes. Meanwhile in Nicaragua, the Marines had just overseen yet another rigged election to succeed Adolfo Díaz with another pro-occupation president.[9]

This meant that Butler's speech came at an extremely inconvenient time for the new U.S. president: his fellow Quaker and old "friend" from the Boxer Rebellion, Herbert Hoover. The former mining executive had risen to fame on his reputation as a humanitarian, overseeing aid to Europe after the World War. Like Harding and Coolidge before him, Hoover seemed to hope that the corrupt and antidemocratic occupations he was now overseeing in Haiti and Nicaragua would just fade into the background. Butler's dinner talk shined an unwelcome floodlight on both. Anonymous State Department sources characterized Butler's speech to the *New York Times* as "loose talk." A syndicated editorial asked: DID HE SPILL THE BEANS?[10]

Forced to defend himself, Butler insisted he'd been misquoted and, anyway, that he was not referring to recent events. "In no speech have I ever criticized the policy of our government," he added, which was, up to that point, true.[11] He had not been denouncing anything. He mostly thought the stories were funny. It was news to him that Americans would be so scandalized by a frank discussion about what their government and military had really been doing overseas.

The national scandal after Pittsburgh torpedoed any hopes Butler may have still harbored about becoming Marine Corps commandant. When Lejeune's successor suffered a debilitating stroke in July 1930, Hoover and Navy Secretary Charles Adams ignored thousands of telegrams supporting Butler for the job.[12] (It did not help Smedley's case when he introduced Adams during a testy inspection of Quantico by saying, "Gentlemen, I want you to meet the Secretary of the goddamn Navy."[13])

With his hopes for career advancement over, Butler's patience permanently ran out. In January 1931, he was giving a speech to a literary and social club in Philadelphia on one of his new favorite topics—"how to prevent war"—when he blurted out a story he'd heard about the Fascist dictator Benito Mussolini. Mussolini had been driving through northern Italy with a friend of Butler's when he ran over a child. "My friend screamed as the child's body was crushed under the wheels of the machine," Butler recounted for the club. "Mussolini put a hand on my friend's knee. 'It was only one life,' he told my friend. 'What is one life in the affairs of a state?'"[14]

When word reached Mussolini's ambassador in Washington, he lodged an official complaint with the State Department. The Hoover administration was, once again, mortified. It had good relations with Fascist Italy. Il Duce himself was popular with many Americans, especially wealthy ones, who saw the bald-headed strongman as a modernizer who was tough on Communists and, as his propagandists falsely insisted, "made the trains run on time."[15] As the Depression deepened, Republican senator David Aiken Reed, cosponsor of the racist 1924 Johnson-Reed Immigration Act, would declare: "I do not often envy other countries their governments, but I say that if this country ever needed a Mussolini it needs one now."[16]

Secretary Adams ordered Butler court-martialed and put under house arrest at Quantico.[17] Incensed, Butler trolled the president by hiring as counsel Maj. Henry Leonard, who had lost his arm rescuing Smedley in China in 1900, when Hoover got them both shot by leading them incompetently into the Battle of Tianjin.

The problem for the Navy Department was that Butler's story was substantially true.* So was his underlying point: that fascists are duplicitous murderers. Mussolini was in the news at that moment arguing in favor of an international disarmament conference to be overseen by the League of Nations. Butler prefaced the story about the child and Il Duce's car by saying there were "mad dog nations" in Europe whose real goal was

---

* Butler's friend was Cornelius Vanderbilt IV, a travel writer and the great-great-grandson of "Commodore" Vanderbilt, of Nicaragua fame. Vanderbilt initially denied the story when reporters sussed him out as the source. But he eventually gave a fuller account of his drive with Mussolini in his 1959 memoir, *Man of the World*: "A small child standing on the right tried to beat the Fiat across the road. The car shuddered, and I felt the car wheels go up, then come down. I turned quickly to look. I can still see the little crumpled-up body lying in the road. Then I felt a hand on my right knee and I heard a voice saying, 'Never look back, Mr. Vanderbilt, never look back in life.'"

war. He concluded it: "How can you talk disarmament with a man like that?"[18]

In that sense, compared with the Pittsburgh speech, Butler was thinking more deeply about what his public addresses might achieve. He was also, thirteen years after the last world war, starting to talk seriously about the possibility of another. At a time when many Americans in power saw fascists as acceptable, even admirable, politicians, Butler was warning the public, in headline-grabbing fashion, that they were not to be trusted. (By comparison, later in 1931, the *New York Times* would publish a friendly interview with "Herr Hitler," in which the Nazi leader was described as a "born orator" and allowed to sidestep the question of whether antisemitism was a fundamental plank in his party.[19])

At the same time, judging by his letters and the memoir he would soon write with the swashbuckling publicist Lowell Thomas, Butler was not yet trying to square his insight into fascism's threat with the memory of his own antidemocratic past, including measures—forced labor, executions, election-rigging, the dismantling of a parliament—that could be described as protofascist, at the very least.

For the moment, Butler's scorn of Mussolini won him praise from enough liberal-minded Americans to create an upswell of support and force the Navy Department to settle the case. Harry Leonard got the charges dropped in exchange for a Butler apology to Secretary Adams— but, crucially, not to Mussolini. (The State Department, on the other hand, had formally apologized to Il Duce for the "discourteous and unwarranted utterances by a commissioned officer of this government.")[20]

That was it. The Fighting Quaker stayed at Quantico long enough to be fully restored as base commander in good standing, then asked President Hoover to let him retire. On September 30, 1931, Maj. Gen. Smedley D. Butler gave his final order: "You may haul down my flag, sir."[21]

At the beginning of 2020, just before the coronavirus pandemic ground life to a halt, I made a pilgrimage to Butler's last home, in Newtown Square, Pennsylvania.

Smedley and Ethel bought the old farmhouse in 1931, between the court-martial and his retirement, and started renovating it right away. They liked it for two reasons: It was close to West Chester, where Maud lived. As important, it had a grand hall down the middle, with a split staircase rising to wraparound balconies on either side. The vaulted ceiling was perfect for displaying his red satin Ten Thousand People's Umbrellas from China. Butler had them mounted on fifteen-foot poles at opposite sides of the hall.

The house stayed in the Butler family until Bunny and Smedley's granddaughter Edith Wehle died in 2013. I'd gotten in touch with the new owners through the local historical society; they greeted me with muffins and a brief tour.

The property had undergone an extensive makeover since the Butlers left: a grander front entrance (the Butlers always entered through the pantry door on the side, Edith's surviving sister, Philippa Wehle, told me), a much smaller dining room, and enlarged kitchen. (Ethel hated to cook but loved to entertain.) The new owners also repainted the whole stucco exterior from Bunny's favorite color, blue, to bright yellow.

Some original touches remained. A cozy fire burned beneath the old mantel, where the Butlers used to gather during the winters. A servants' bell bore markings for "Mrs. Butler's Room" and "Miss Butler's Room"—presumably Bunny and Snooks, in the years after Smedley died. The new family showed me Smedley's old room, with its big sunny windows. It belonged to their teenage daughter, who had a plush Eeyore on the bed and a poster in the window that read: "Real Feminism is Intersectional."[22]

All of Butler's homes on the Main Line had been similarly repurposed. His childhood home in West Chester was subdivided into apartments. The first floor of his birthplace on High Street is now a cat hospital. Unlike other famous generals of his generation—MacArthur, Pershing, Patton—Smedley Butler did not have important sites of his life converted into memorials, nor has he been honored with a museum.

That might seem reasonable: those generals all led fighting forces in the World Wars, after all, a brand of glory that Butler had aspired to and failed to reach. But that raises several questions. Why do we expend so much time and money preserving the memory of the short-duration wars in which European powers were involved; and so little, relatively speaking, remembering the kind of wars Butler fought—protracted, decades-long conflicts in the Americas, Asia, and Africa that have been the most common mode of warfare throughout U.S. history? And why does America celebrate its generals who oversaw death and destruction on a massive scale, while forgetting the exceptional few who spent their later years trying to stop them?

In 1932, Butler tried following in his father's political footsteps, running for U.S. Senate from Pennsylvania. His campaign was doomed from the start: running as a "Dry" on the eve of Prohibition's repeal, he was blown out by the Republican machine candidate nearly two to one.[23]

Butler's focus on alcohol overshadowed his proposals on helping ordinary people weather the Depression. He called for major public works spending and a federal jobs guarantee, pledged to back unions and raise wages, and argued for a federal old-age pension—anticipating Social Security, which would not be proposed for another three years. He also took a strong antiwar position, writing that he was "opposed to sending American boys to be killed abroad in defense of the investments of international bankers."[24]

The cause that brought all those issues together—government spending to get out of the Depression, support for the poor, and veterans' rights—was known as the "bonus." Veterans' benefits had been minimal during and after the World War. Many had come home from Europe to find their savings drained and jobs gone. Various proposals for government assistance were floated and rejected until, in 1924, Congress finally passed a bonus bill over President Coolidge's veto.[25]

Under the law, most who served in the armed forces during the mobilization would get $1 of back pay for each day of home service and $1.25 for each day abroad. But there was a catch: if the sum was more than $50 ($770 today), it would only be paid to the veteran's survivors after they died or in 1945, whichever came first.

When the Great Depression hit, many veterans looked hungrily at their green-bordered bonus certificates and realized they were their only asset that still held any value. In 1931, an Army veteran named Joseph T. Angelo had walked four days from his home in Camden, New Jersey, to Washington, D.C., to demand the bonus be paid immediately. Angelo wore his medals on his ill-fitting suit, including the Distinguished Service Cross he'd gotten for dragging Maj. George S. Patton to safety under machine-gun fire in the Meuse-Argonne.

In response, Congress passed a bill allowing veterans to cash in part of their IOUs as loans. President Hoover vetoed it, warning it would set a dangerous precedent by breaking "the barriers of self-reliance and self-support in our people."[26]

Over the spring of 1932, veterans from every corner of the country began making their way to the capital. They stowed away in boxcars, hitched rides on trucks, or followed Joe Angelo's example and walked. Calling themselves the Bonus Expeditionary Force, they set up encampments—"Hoovervilles," in the parlance of the time—across Washington. By July, there were some forty-five thousand veteran protesters, wives, and children living in shacks and tents in the shadow of the Capitol dome.[27]

Many Washingtonians were sympathetic to the BEF. Some donated food. The Smithsonian Arts and Industries Building let marchers use its bathroom. A D.C. police captain named Sidney Marks, sent to evict the largest encampment—on the mudflats across the Anacostia River—instead told the protesters they had his support. The marchers renamed the site Camp Marks in his honor.[28]

But the federal and military establishments were not as pleased. They denounced the occupiers as Communists and radicals.* Most alarming to some, veterans of all skin colors were living in the bonus camps side by side at a time when both the District of Columbia and military were strictly segregated by race.

The bonus marchers successfully pressured the House into approving a bill, sponsored by Wright Patman, a Democrat from Texas, that would have provided for an immediate cash payment of $2.4 billion ($46 billion today) to be distributed among all certificate-holding veterans. But on July 16, the Senate adjourned without taking it up, effectively killing the measure. Senators left just before midnight, fleeing through the

---

* Indeed, the Communist International would have liked that to be the case: Earl Browder, a Soviet agent and head of the Communist Party of the United States, briefly visited Camp Marks to report back to Moscow on the potential for using the marchers to kick off a revolution. The BEF leader Walter Waters, on the other hand, was attracted to fascism: as the summer wore on, he organized a troop of uniformed enforcers he dubbed the "Khaki Shirts," in an intentional allusion to Mussolini's Black Shirts and the Brown Shirts of Hitler's Sturmabteilung. But try as anyone might, no revolutionary or violent reactionary ideology took hold among the marchers. Their collective goal was not to overthrow the government, but to get help from it. See Dickson and Allen, *Bonus Army,* 134.

underground tunnels beneath the Capitol to avoid confronting marchers. Hoover headed to his Shenandoah summer retreat.[29] As dejected marchers began to take federal agents' offers for train tickets home, the organizer of the BEF, Walter W. Waters, sent an urgent invitation to the one senior military man who had taken a public position in support of the veterans—the one officer whom he knew the veterans would listen to.

Butler arrived at Camp Marks on July 19, accompanied by Smedley Junior, on summer break from MIT. They strolled around the shantytown, greeting men Butler had last seen shuffling through his mudhole camp in France. Word spread, and soon thousands converged around a wooden stage to hear what Old Gimlet Eye had to say.

Smedley took off his sport coat, rolled up his sleeves, and tucked his polka dot tie between two shirt buttons so it wouldn't flop around. A line of sun-worn U.S. flags waved behind him. Waters introduced Butler as "a real soldier, a real man, a real gentleman, and a real comrade"—noting, in case anyone had forgotten, the two Medals of Honor.

Butler looked over the crowd, now totaling about sixteen thousand stalwarts. He told the marchers what an honor it was to be among fellow soldiers; how it made him "so damn mad" to hear people calling them tramps. "By God, they didn't speak of you as tramps in 1917 and '18!" he said to applause. "I mean just what I say. I don't want anything," he assured them, his tie now loose and arms flying wildly through the air. "Nobody can kick me anymore. I'll say what I please."

His thinning hair was now thoroughly mussed, his throat hoarse, but his lungs were filled with anger—at how the veterans were being treated, at the state of the country, at the ruins of his own career. "This is the greatest demonstration of Americanism *we have ever had*! Pure Americanism. Willing to take this beating as you've taken it, stand right steady. You keep every law! And why in the hell shouldn't you? Who in the hell has done all the bleeding for this country, and for this law, and this Constitution anyhow, but you fellas?" The veterans roared back in reply.

"But don't—*don't!*—take a step backward," he warned. "Remember that as soon as you haul down your camp flag here and clear out—every one of you clears out—this evaporates in thin air. And all this struggle will have been no good."[30]

Unable to bear the thought of leaving, Smedley and Smedley Junior stayed the night at Camp Marks, trading war stories with the protesters late into the night. The next morning, they shared a breakfast of potatoes, black coffee, and hard bread with them before departing.

Inspired by Butler, thousands of marchers stayed on. Gen. Douglas MacArthur, then the U.S. Army chief of staff, instructed his adjutants to begin drawing up plans to evict the veterans by force. MacArthur also secretly began moving several combat vehicles, .30- and .50-caliber machine guns, and tanks to Fort Myer, just outside Washington.[31]

On July 28, nine days after Butler's speech at Camp Marks, policemen fatally shot two marchers in an attempt to evict the BEF from an abandoned Ford Motor Co. building next to the Capitol. MacArthur ordered his aide—forty-one-year-old Maj. Dwight Eisenhower—to put on his uniform and join him in the streets to oversee the final maneuver in person.[32]

Around 4:30 P.M., a reporter atop the Ford building spotted four hundred Army infantrymen fixing bayonets and putting on gas masks. Army grenades exploded on the National Mall, releasing gas laced with Adamsite—a chemical weapon that can cause vomiting, asphyxiation, and, under certain circumstances, death. Cavalry, led in the saddle by George Patton, charged into a crowd of spectators. Tear gas and smoke from hundreds of burning shacks blotted out the view of the Capitol dome.[33]

At 9:00 P.M., MacArthur announced that Camp Marks was to be destroyed. Gen. George Van Horn Moseley rushed a message from Hoover, ordering the chief of staff not to cross the Anacostia River. MacArthur ignored the president.[34] He positioned tanks on the bridge to cut off the camp from the city, then ordered the camp burned to the ground. Scores were injured. A twelve-week-old baby whose impoverished parents had brought him to Camp Marks choked on Adamsite and died soon after.[35]

At a press conference, MacArthur defended his assault by asserting that he had prevented a Communist revolution. "I think as a military maneuver, if you can call a thing of this kind a military maneuver, that it was unique. I have been in many riots, but I think this is the first riot I ever was in or ever saw in which there was no real bloodshed."[36] MacArthur was likely thinking of his experiences in the Philippines and Veracruz, though he could have been talking about the U.S. military's experience suppressing uprisings and dissent around the world.

Those who watched it could not believe that scenes they associated with the imperial periphery had taken place in the nation's capital. A reporter who witnessed the violence commented: "God, that I should see such things in the United States."[37]

The "Battle of Washington," as MacArthur's assault on the Bonus March became known, was a clarifying moment for some. For Butler, it hardened a growing conviction that the key fault line in American life was class: Wall Street and those who carried out its wishes against the "little guy." That fall, he tried out a version of the idea he'd been mulling since Nicaragua: that America's wars were started by capitalists at the expense of the soldiers sent to fight them. "When the war is over," Butler told an election-season crowd in Queens, New York, "the soldier comes back, is given a march up Fifth Avenue, and as soon as he is disbanded at the end of the march the capitalists say, 'To hell with him' and start all over again."[38]

Franklin Delano Roosevelt read about the burning of Camp Marks in the *New York Times*, in his bedroom at the governor's mansion in Albany. He could not believe that Hoover had turned the army loose on U.S. citizens, nor how far MacArthur had gone. It was a wonder, Roosevelt told his close friend and economic adviser Rexford Tugwell, that there hadn't been "more resentment, more radicalism, when people are treated that way."[39]

FDR was in a unique position to do something about it. Four weeks before MacArthur's assault, he had accepted the Democratic nomination for president, promising "a new deal for the American people." Motivated by the images of gas and bayonets deployed in Washington, Butler crossed party lines to campaign for his old Haiti ally, calling himself a "Hoover-for-Ex-President Republican."[40] Roosevelt won in a landslide that November.

Though the Roosevelt who moved into the White House in March 1933 was older, grayer, and now mostly paralyzed from the waist down, he was still the ex-Navy official who had helped plan the invasion of Veracruz, supervise the brutal occupations of Haiti and the Dominican Republic, and oversee the colonial district around his "Uncle Ted's vast public work" in Panama. He was still the man who, as his ally Tugwell would later write with maximal charity, had been "perilously close . . . to being an imperialist."[41]

Yet Roosevelt was horrified by the approval with which his empire-building peers greeted MacArthur's assault on American citizens—veterans who had just been asking for their government's help in a crisis. The president told Tugwell that he sensed in the United States "an impulse among a good many 'strong' men, men used to having their way, mostly industrialists who directed affairs without being questioned, a feeling that democracy had run its course and that the totalitarians had grasped the necessities of the time. People wanted strong leadership; they were sick of uncertainty, anxious for security, and willing to trade liberty for it."[42]

Millions of Americans were turning to populist demagogues like Father Charles Coughlin, the antisemitic Catholic priest who used his nationally syndicated radio show to defend Hitler and spread conspiracy theories of a worldwide "Judeo-Bolshevik" plot. But the "Nazi-minded among American leaders," as Tugwell summarized Roosevelt's view, were more fond of the dictatorial MacArthur. His greater "charm, tradition, and majestic appearance" put a high-class and distinctively American shine on the naked repression he had unleashed against the Bonus Marchers on the Anacostia Flats.[43]

Indeed, the divide between outright fascism and the American elite was paper thin at the depths of the Depression. U.S. corporations had not only remained in Germany after Hitler became chancellor in early 1933, but courted Nazi approval. There was money in it: Coca-Cola, General Motors, and IBM all saw their German profits surge in the wake of the Nazi ascent. The most influential of all U.S. businessmen, Henry Ford, had long since entered into a mutual admiration society with the soon-to-be führer. Hitler had heaped praise on Ford's antisemitic writings, and had told a U.S. reporter a decade earlier: "We look on Heinrich Ford as the leader of the growing Fascisti movement in America."[44]

The Nazis had looked elsewhere in the United States for inspiration as well: studying American eugenicists like Madison Grant and Lothrop Stoddard, and writing racial codes based in part on America's own system of legalistic racial authoritarianism: Jim Crow. Pre-Nazi German scholars had praised the system of *Schutzbürger zweiter Klasse*—second-class citizenship—that the United States had foisted upon Filipinos, Puerto Ricans, and others in its formally annexed territories. The word the Nazis used to justify their planned colonization of Eastern Europe, *Lebensraum*, or living space, was an analogue to Frederick Jackson Turner's "free land," coined by Turner's German colleague and mutual admirer Friedrich Ratzel. Hitler had approvingly noted that white settlers and the U.S. Army had "gunned down the millions of redskins to a few hundred thousand, and now keep the modest remnant under observation in a cage."[45] In 1933, the Nazis put those words into action by opening their first concentration camp, at Dachau, modeled on the form pioneered by the Spanish in Cuba, the British in South Africa, and the United States in the Philippines. It would take eight years of growth and war before the Nazi camps took on their final, exterminationist form.

These resemblances were no surprise. Germany and the United States were in many ways sister empires, who had risen at roughly the same time to challenge the older powers of Europe. It was not for nothing that Roosevelt's "Uncle Ted" spent part of his retirement tour gleefully chatting and reviewing Prussian troops with Kaiser Wilhelm, a mere four years before the outbreak of the Great War.[46] Now Germany, defeated and humiliated, was turning its imperialism inward in the form of fascism, as it prepared once again to embark on a war of expansion. Hitler, a former soldier who had survived the wiping out of nearly his entire infantry unit at the First Battle of Ypres in 1914, was thus an indirect product of a process that the Afro-Caribbean writer Aimé Césaire would later describe: of "how colonization works to *decivilize* the colonizer, to *brutalize* him in the true sense of the word, to degrade him, to awaken him to buried instincts, to covetousness, violence, race hatred, and moral relativism." Or, as Frantz Fanon would ask more directly: "What is fascism but colonialism in the heart of a traditionally colonialist country?"[47]

The question for all Americans in the early 1930s was if they would do the same. MacArthur's answer in the burning of the bonus camps seemed, in Roosevelt's eyes, to be a resounding *yes*. Roosevelt, despite his similar background and experience, chose otherwise. He resolved to show "that democracy in the United States—limited and flawed though it remained—was better kept than abandoned, in the hope of strengthening and extending it," as the historian Eric Rauchway has written.[48]

Roosevelt would do so by remaking the relationship between government, business, and the people through his New Deal. His program as president would include massive spending on public works; social insurance against old age, unemployment, and disability; and support for labor unions. With his "Good Neighbor" policy for Latin America, he would reshape, if symbolically, some of the old imperial arrangements he had helped foster. As Rauchway wrote: "The New Deal would show ordinary Americans that their government could work for them, albeit imperfectly."

FDR did so knowing that, if he failed, he could be ushered unceremoniously from office in an election—and, even more dangerously, that a fascist turn could happen in the United States. All that was missing, as the president told Tugwell, was a leader: "the familiar symbolic figure—the man on horseback—to give it realism."[49]

On November 20, 1934, readers of the *New York Post* were startled by a headline:

## GEN. BUTLER ACCUSES N.Y. BROKERS
## OF PLOTTING DICTATORSHIP IN U.S.

### $3,000,000 Bid for Fascist Army Bared
### Says He Was Asked to Lead 500,000 for Capital 'Putsch'
#### U.S. PROBING CHARGE[50]

Smedley Butler revealed the Business Plot before a two-man panel of the Special House Committee on Un-American Activities. The executive session was held in the supper room of the New York City Bar Association on West Forty-Fourth Street. Present were the committee chairman, John W. McCormack of Massachusetts, and vice-chairman, Samuel Dickstein of New York.

Butler stood and was sworn in.

"Without my asking you any further questions, will you just go ahead and tell in your own way all that you know about an attempted fascist movement in this country?" Chairman McCormack asked.

"May I preface my remarks by saying, sir, that I have one interest in all of this, and that is to try to do my best to see that a democracy is maintained in this country?"

"Nobody who has either read about or known about General Butler would have anything but that understanding."

"It is nice of you to say that, sir," Butler replied. "But that is my only interest."[51]

For thirty minutes, Butler told the story, starting with the first visit of the bond salesman Gerald C. MacGuire to his house in Newtown Square in 1933. He took them through the offers to sneak him into the American Legion convention in Chicago, MacGuire's glowing postcards from Fascist Europe, and the roll of $18,000 thrown onto the hotel bed in Newark. Butler named the backers MacGuire had revealed, including the bond salesman's boss, Grayson M.-P. Murphy.

Finally, Butler told the congressmen about his last meeting with Mac-Guire, three months earlier, in August 1934, where the businessman told him: "The time has come to get the soldiers together." It was at that meeting where MacGuire described the model he'd found in Paris for the army of half a million veterans that would carry out the coup: the veterans' "super-organization" Croix de Feu.[52]

It is not clear if Butler was aware of the fact that, months earlier, on February 6, 1934, the Croix de Feu had played a leading role in the assault on the French National Assembly, in which a mob consisting mostly of far-right and fascist groups viciously battled police and forced the resignation of a social democrat prime minister. But MacGuire certainly knew all about Butler's highly publicized rabble-rousing before thousands of rapt veterans at the Bonus March, and seemed eager for a repeat performance.

MacGuire had told Butler to expect to see another, more powerful organization forming to back the putsch from behind the scenes. As Butler testified, "He says: 'You watch. In two or three weeks you will see it come out in the paper. There will be big fellows in it. This is to be the background of it. These are to be the villagers in the opera.'" The bond salesman told the Marine this group would advertise itself as a "society to maintain the Constitution."[53]

"And in about two weeks," Butler told the congressmen, "the American Liberty League appeared, which was just about what he described it to be."[54]

The Liberty League was announced on August 23, 1934, on the front page of the *New York Times*. The article quoted its founders' claim that it was a "nonpartisan group" whose aim was to "combat radicalism, preserve property rights, uphold and preserve the Constitution."[55] Its real goal, other observers told the *Times*, was to oppose the New Deal and the taxes and controls it promised to impose on their fortunes.

Among the Liberty League's principal founders was the multimillionaire Irénée du Pont, former president of the explosives and chemical manufacturing giant that bore his family's name. Other financial backers included the head of General Motors, Alfred P. Sloan, as well as executives of Phillips Petroleum, Sun Oil, General Foods, and the McCann Erickson ad agency.[56] The former Democratic presidential candidates Al Smith and John W. Davis—both of them foes of FDR, the latter counsel to J. P. Morgan & Co.—were among the League's members as well.* Its treasurer was MacGuire's boss, Grayson Murphy.[57]

Sitting beside Butler in the hearing room was the journalist who wrote the *Post* article, Paul Comly French. Knowing the committee might find his story hard to swallow—or easy to suppress—Butler had called on the reporter, whom he knew from his time running the Philadelphia police, to conduct his own independent investigation. French told the congressmen what MacGuire had told him: "We need a Fascist Government in this country, he insisted, to save the nation from the Communists who want to tear it down and wreck all that we have built in America. The only men who have the patriotism to do it are the soldiers and Smedley Butler is the ideal leader. He could organize a million men overnight."[58]

MacGuire, the journalist added, had "continually discussed the need of a man on a white horse, as he called it, a dictator who would come galloping in on his white horse. He said that was the only way . . . to save the capitalistic system."

Butler added one more enticing detail. MacGuire had told him that his group in the plot—presumably a clique headed by Grayson Murphy—was

---

* In the early 2000s, a popular misconception arose that Prescott Bush—the father and grandfather of presidents George H. W. and George W. Bush—came up in association with the Business Plot. That seems to be the result of confusion: Bush did extensive business with Nazi Germany in his role as a partner at Brown Brothers Harriman. A shipping company he and the bank were involved with, the Hamburg America Line, came up in a *separate* investigation by the McCormack-Dickstein committee. The alleged plot to overthrow FDR, by contrast, appeared to be entirely homegrown. Neither Butler nor seemingly anyone else in 1934 made allegations of Bush's involvement in the scheme represented by MacGuire, nor does Bush's name appear in the materials I reviewed from the American Liberty League. On Bush's Nazi ties, see Ben Aris and Duncan Campbell, "How Bush's Grandfather Helped Hitler's Rise to Power," *Guardian*, Sept. 25, 2004, www.theguardian.com/world/2004/sep/25/usa.secondworldwar.

eager to have Butler lead the coup, but that "the Morgan interests"—that is, bankers or businessmen connected to J. P. Morgan & Co.—were against him. "The Morgan interests say you cannot be trusted, that you are too radical and so forth, that you are too much on the side of the little fellow," he said the bond salesman had explained. As Roosevelt intuited, they preferred a more authoritarian general: Douglas MacArthur.[59]

All of these were, in essence, merely leads. The committee would have to investigate to make the case in full. What evidence was there to show that anyone beside MacGuire, and likely Murphy, had known about the plot? How far had the planning gone? Was Butler—or whoever would lead the coup—to be the "man on a white horse," or were they simply to pave the way for the dictator who would "save the capitalistic system"?

But the committee's investigation would be brief and conducted in an atmosphere of overweening incredulity. As soon as Butler's allegations became public, the most powerful men in media did everything they could to cast doubt on them and the Marine. The *New York Times* fronted its story with the denials of the accused: Grayson M.-P. Murphy called it "a fantasy." "Perfect moonshine! Too unutterably ridiculous to comment upon!" exclaimed Thomas W. Lamont, the senior partner at J. P. Morgan & Co. "He'd better be damn careful," said the ex-Army general and ex-FDR administration official Hugh S. Johnson, whom Butler said was mooted as a potential "secretary of general affairs." "Nobody said a word to me about anything of the kind, and if they did I'd throw them out the window."[60]

Douglas MacArthur called it "the best laugh story of the year."[61]

*Time* magazine—published by Henry Luce, the millionaire son of missionaries to China—lampooned the allegations in a satire headlined "Plot Without Plotters." His writer imagined Butler on horseback, spurs clinking, as he led a column of half a million men and bankers up Pennsylvania Avenue. In an unsigned editorial, Adolph Ochs's *New York Times* likened Butler to an early-twentieth-century Prussian con man.[62]

There would only be one other witness of note before the committee. Gerald C. MacGuire spent three days testifying before McCormack and Dickstein, contradicting, then likely perjuring himself.[63] He admitted having met the Croix de Feu in Paris, though he claimed it was in passing at a mass at Notre-Dame. The bond salesman also admitted having met many times with Butler—but insisted, implausibly, that it was *Butler* who told *him* he was involved with "some vigilante committee somewhere," and that the bond salesman had tried to talk him out of it.[64]

There was no further inquiry. The committee was disbanded, as scheduled, at the end of 1934. McCormack argued, unpersuasively, that it was not necessary to subpoena Grayson Murphy because the committee already had "cold evidence linking him with this movement."[65] "We did not want," the future Speaker of the House added, "to give him a chance to pose as an innocent victim."

The committee's final report was both complimentary to Butler and exceptionally vague:

> In the last few weeks of the committee's official life it received evidence showing that certain persons had made an attempt to establish a fascist organization in this country. . . . There is no question but that these attempts were discussed, were planned, and might have been placed in execution when and if the financial backers deemed it expedient.[66]

The committee said it had verified "all the pertinent statements made by General Butler." But it named no one directly in connection with the alleged coup.

Was there a Business Plot? In the absence of a full investigation, it is difficult to say. It seems MacGuire was convinced he was a front man for one. (He would not live long enough to reveal more: four months after the hearings, the bond salesman died at the age of thirty-seven.)[67]

It seems possible that at least some of the alleged principals' denials were honest. MacGuire's claim that all the members of the Liberty League were planning to back a coup against Roosevelt does not make it so. The incredulity with which men like Thomas Lamont and Douglas MacArthur greeted the story could be explained by the possibility that they had not heard of such a plan before Butler blew the whistle.

But it is equally plausible that, had Smedley Butler not come forward, or had MacGuire approached someone else, the coup or something like it might have been attempted. Several alleged in connection with the plot were avid fans of fascism. Lamont described himself as "something like a missionary" for Mussolini as he made J. P. Morgan one of Fascist Italy's main overseas banking partners.[68] The American Legion, an alleged source of manpower for the putsch, featured yearly convention greetings from "a wounded soldier in the Great War . . . his excellency, Benito Mussolini." The *capo del governo* himself was invited to speak at the 1930 convention, until the invitation was rescinded amid protests from organized labor.[69]

Hugh S. Johnson, *Time*'s 1933 Man of the Year, had lavishly praised the "shining name" of Mussolini and the Fascist *stato corporativo* as models of anti-labor collectivism while running the New Deal's short-lived National Recovery Administration. Johnson's firing by FDR from the NRA in September 1934 was predicted by MacGuire, who told Butler the former Army general had "talked too damn much." (Johnson would later help launch the Nazi-sympathizing America First Committee, though he soon took pains to distance himself from the hard-core antisemites in the group.[70])

Nothing lends more plausibility to the idea that a coup to sideline Roosevelt was at least discussed—and that Butler's name was floated to lead it—than the likely involvement of Grayson Mallet-Prevost Murphy. The financier's biography reads like a shadow version of Butler's. Born in Philadelphia, educated for two years at Haverford College, he transferred to West Point during the war against Spain. Murphy then joined the Military Intelligence Division, running spy missions in the Philippines in 1902 and Panama in 1903. Murphy returned to Washington to personally brief Theodore Roosevelt on October 16, 1903—eighteen days before the Marines landed in support of the Panamanian conspiracy organized by the founder of Sullivan & Cromwell.[71]

Murphy later became senior vice president for the Guaranty Trust Company, the fiscal agent for the Dominican Republic's "receivership" and the Morgan loan to Honduras. He served on the board of the Cuba Cane Sugar Corporation alongside fellow Morgan associates and Sullivan & Cromwell representatives. Murphy's uncle, Severo Mallet-Prevost, was the lawyer who informed Brown Brothers of the State Department's plan to take over Nicaragua's banks, with Butler's Marines as collection agents, in 1911. Murphy was the American Red Cross commissioner to Europe during World War I, when the aid group helped run Butler's embarkation camp in France, and had been a member of General Pershing's staff. In 1920, Murphy toured war-ravaged Europe to make "intelligence estimates and establish a private intelligence network" with his fellow soldier, William J. "Wild Bill" Donovan—who would later lead the Office of Strategic Services, the forerunner to the CIA. This was the résumé of someone who, at the very least, knew his way around the planning of a coup.[72]

Again, all of that is circumstantial evidence; none of it points definitively to a plan to overthrow the U.S. government. But it was enough to warrant further investigation. So why did no one—not the committee, nor the press corps writ large—look deeper at the time? Why was the idea that a president could be overthrown by a conspiracy of well-connected businessmen—and a few armed divisions led by a rabble-rousing general—considered so ridiculous that the mere suggestion was met with peals of laughter across America?

It was because, for decades, Americans had been trained to react in just that way: by excusing, covering up, or simply laughing away all evidence that showed how many of those same people had been behind similar schemes all over the world. Smedley Butler had led troops on the bankers' behalf to overthrow presidents in Nicaragua and Honduras, and gone on a spy run to investigate regime change on behalf of the oil companies in Mexico. He had risked his Marines' lives for Standard Oil in China and worked with Murphy's customs agents in an invasion that helped lead to a far-right dictatorship in the Dominican Republic. In Haiti, Butler had done what even the Croix de Feu and its French fascist allies could not: shut down a national assembly at gunpoint.

In his own country, in his own time, Butler drew a line. "My interest, my one hobby, is maintaining a democracy," he told the bond salesman. Butler clung to an idea of America as a place where the whole of the people chose their leaders, the "little guy" got a fair shot against the powerful, and everyone could live free from tyranny. It was an idea that had never existed in practice for all, and seldom for most. As long as Americans refused to grasp the reality of what their country actually was—of what their soldiers and emissaries did with their money and in their name all over the world—the idea would remain a self-defeating fairy tale. Still, as long as that idea of America survived, there was a chance its promise might be realized.

The real danger, Butler knew, lay in that idea's negation. If a faction gained power that exemplified the worst of America's history and instincts—with a leader willing to use his capital and influence to destroy what semblance of democracy existed for his own ends—that faction could overwhelm the nation's fragile institutions and send one of the most powerful empires the world had ever seen tumbling irretrievably into darkness.

Twenty-one U.S. presidential elections later, on January 6, 2021, Donald Trump stood before an angry crowd on the White House Ellipse. For weeks, Trump had urged supporters to join him in an action against the joint session of Congress slated to recognize his opponent, Joe Biden, as the next president that day.[73] Among the thousands who heeded his call were white supremacists, neo-Nazis, devotees of the antisemitic QAnon conspiracy theory, far-right militias, and elements of his most loyal neo-fascist street gang, the Proud Boys. "It is time for war," a speaker at a warm-up rally the night before had declared.[74]

On the rally stage, the defeated president spoke with the everyman style and bluntness of a Smedley Butler. He mirrored the Marine's rhetoric, too, saying his purpose was to "save our democracy."[75] But that was not really his goal. Trump, and his faction, wanted to destroy the election—to dismantle democracy rather than cede power to a multiethnic, cross-class majority who had chosen someone else.[76] Trump lied to the thousands in winter coats and "Make America Great Again" hats by claiming he still had a legitimate path to victory. His solution: to intimidate his vice president and Congress into ignoring the Constitution and refusing to certify the election, opening the door for a critical mass of loyal state governments to reverse their constituents' votes and declare him the winner instead. In this, Trump echoed the French fascists of 1934, who claimed their attack on parliament would defend the popular will against "Socialist influence" and "give the nation the leaders it deserves."[77]

Trump then did what the Bonus Marchers had refused to do, and the Business Plotters—however many there were—could not. He sent his mob, his version of Mussolini's Black Shirts and the Croix de Feu, to storm the Capitol. "We fight like hell," the forty-fifth president instructed them. "And if you don't fight like hell, you're not going to have a country anymore."

Though Trump had telegraphed his intention to overturn the election for weeks, the Capitol police and millions watching around the country were caught wholly unprepared.[78] For nearly five hours, the Trumpist mob attacked the seat of the federal legislature from all sides, armed with flagpoles, chemical sprays, and a handful of firearms. They bowled over barricades, battled and assaulted overwhelmed police, smashed windows and doors, entered the Senate chamber, and tried to force their way into the House. Four rioters and a Capitol police officer died during or immediately after the melee; at least 138 D.C. and Capitol police were injured, some severely. At least four officers present at the attack committed suicide in the months that followed.[79]

But it was not just Trump's personal embodiment of fascism and authoritarian populism that should have prepared Americans for the January 6 attack.[80] Over a century of imperial violence had laid the groundwork for the siege at the heart of U.S. democracy.

Many of the putschists, including a thirty-five-year-old California woman shot to death by police as she tried to break into the lobby leading to the House floor, were veterans of the wars in Iraq and Afghanistan. Some wore tactical armor and carried "flex cuffs"—nylon restraints the military and police use for mass arrests of insurgents and dissidents. The QAnon rioters were devotees of a supposed "military intelligence" officer who prophesized, among other things, the imminent detention and execution of liberals at Guantánamo. A *Washington Post* reporter heard some of the rioters chanting for "military tribunals." (In an ironic spin on the idea of "foreign in a domestic sense," the board where the eponymous "Q" posted was operated by a U.S. Army veteran residing in the Philippines. He traveled to Washington and marched to the Capitol complex with the mob on January 6.)[81]

Even many of those opposed to the insurrection struggled to see what was happening: that the boundaries between the center and the periphery were collapsing. "I expected violent assault on democracy as a U.S. Marine in Iraq. I never imagined it as a United States congressman in America," Representative Seth Moulton, a Massachusetts Democrat, wrote as he sheltered in the Capitol complex. George W. Bush, the president who ordered Moulton into Baghdad, observed: "This is how election results are disputed in a banana republic—not our democratic republic."[82] Watching from home, I wished Smedley Butler was around to remind the former president how those "banana republics" came to be.

The attackers did not achieve their immediate goal: Biden's victory was certified at 3:41 A.M. But just as the effects of the thwarted Parisian attack of *six février* took years to be felt—triggering a powerful left-wing backlash yet also helping set the stage for collaboration with the Nazis—the long-term consequences of the January 6 assault on the Capitol are yet to be seen. Eight Republican senators and 139 GOP representatives voted to reject the election mere hours after the siege.[83] Trump was impeached, for a history-making second time, for inciting the insurrection, and a majority of senators voted to convict. But the body fell ten votes short of the two-thirds majority needed, permitting him to run for office again. Republican-run states that Democrats won or came close to winning in 2020 raced to change their laws to prevent as many would-be Democratic voters, especially nonwhites, from participating in the next election.[84] Trump openly talks about being "reinstated as president" before then.[85]

The new president, meanwhile, resorted to the imperial logics of the forever wars. In his first address to Congress, three months after taking office, Biden announced that he intended to keep the U.S. military engaged "against the threats to the United States wherever they come from . . . in Yemen, Syria, Somalia, other places in Africa and the Middle East and beyond." Then, barely pausing for a breath, he transitioned to "what our intelligence agents have determined to be the most lethal terrorist threat to our homeland today: white supremacy is terrorism."[86]

The strategy implied by that framing is worrying. A former top CIA counterterrorism official (who later became chairman of an investment bank) had called weeks earlier in a *New York Times* essay for a "comprehensive counterinsurgency" in the United States.[87] Such a domestic deployment, modeled on the tactics used by U.S. forces from Nicaragua and Haiti to Vietnam and Afghanistan, would not only be dangerous but counterproductive. Branding masses of U.S. citizens as "terrorists"—placing them and their fates outside the law, instead of subject to it—will only perpetuate the cycles of imperial aggression and blowback that led to the assault on democracy in the first place.

A few weeks after the siege, I talked to Smedley Butler's eighty-five-year-old granddaughter, Philippa Wehle. I asked her over Skype what her grandfather would have thought of the events of January 6.

Her hazel eyes narrowed as she pondered. "I think he would have been in there. He would have been in the fray somehow."

For an unsettling moment, I was unsure what she meant. Butler had much in common with both sides of the siege: Like Trump's mob, he had often doubted the validity of democracy when practiced by nonwhites. (The most prominent Trumpist conspiracy theories about purported fraud in the 2020 election centered on cities with large immigrant and Black populations.) Like many of the putschists, Butler saw himself as a warrior for the "little guy" against a vast constellation of elite interests—even though he, also like most of the Capitol attackers, was relatively well-off.[88] Moreover, the greatest proportion of veterans arrested in connection with the attempted putsch were Marines. An active-duty Marine major—a field artillery officer at Quantico—was caught on video pushing open the doors to the East Rotunda and accused by federal prosecutors of allowing other rioters to stream in.[89]

But I knew too that Butler had taken his stand for democracy and against the Business Plot. I would like to think he would have seen through Trump as well. Butler had rejected Father Coughlin's proto-Trumpian brand of red-baiting, antisemetic conspiratorial populism, going so far as to inform FBI director J. Edgar Hoover of an alleged 1936 effort involving the reactionary priest to overthrow the left-leaning government of Mexico.[90] When a reporter for the Marxist magazine *New Masses* asked Butler "just where he stood politically" in the wake of the Business Plot, he name-checked several of the most left-leaning members of Congress, and said the only group he would give his "blanket approval to" was the American Federation of Labor. Butler added that he would not only "die to preserve democracy" but also, crucially, "fight to broaden it."[91]

Perhaps it would have come down to timing: at what point in his life the attack on the government might have taken place.

"Do you think he would have been with the people storming the Capitol?" I asked Philippa, tentatively.

This time she answered immediately. "No! Heavens no. He would have been trying to do something about it." He might have been killed, she added, given that the police were so unprepared. "Which is so disturbing, because of course they should have known. They would have known. They only had to read the papers."

On March 15, 1935, Butler published what would become his most famous work, *War Is a Racket.* The fifty-two-page pamphlet with a tomato-red cover was a distillation of what had become one of his most-requested speeches, as polished by his favorite ghostwriter, the newspaperman E. Z. Dimitman. In direct prose, the book summarizes the hellishness and unfairness of war, with a metaphor lifted from his time fighting the gangsters of Philadelphia. "For a very few, this racket, like bootlegging and other underworld rackets, brings fancy profits," he writes, "but the cost of the operations is always transferred to the people—who do not profit."[92]

It is not a rigorous book. There are oversimplifications and errors. (A claim that the destruction of the battleship *Maine*, and thus the 1898 war with Spain, could have been prevented with a law limiting Navy ships to sailing "within 200 miles of our coastline" is complicated by the fact that Havana is less than ninety nautical miles south of the Florida Keys.)

But Butler (and Dimitman) were writing a jeremiad for a mass audience. The purpose of the book was to stop the next war: to keep Americans from sending their sons to be massacred, maimed, and "destroyed, mentally" once again in Europe or, as Butler was increasingly convinced they would be, in Asia. The story he told was essentially a parable: the bankers and the industrialists were among the racketeers. The American people—the "lads in the trenches," the loved ones worried sick at home—were the dupes and victims. The racket could only be smashed, Butler concluded, "by taking the profit out of war."[93]

Starting that fall, Butler wrote a complementary, yet sharply different, series of articles for the socialist magazine *Common Sense*. Writing for an intellectual and more radical audience (the magazine's contributors included Upton Sinclair and John Dos Passos), Butler broadened the scope of his critique. Now *he* had been the gangster. That series began with an indictment of "military boondoggling" and ended with the castigation of the wealth-protecting proclivities of American police.

It was in the second installment that Butler made his famous confession of crimes committed in Asia and Latin America—that he "helped in the raping of half a dozen Central American republics for the benefit of Wall Street," saw to it "that Standard Oil went its way unmolested" in China, and so on—and where he made the statement:

> I spent 33 years and 4 months in active service as a member of our country's most agile military force—the Marine Corps. I served in all commissioned ranks from a second lieutenant to Major-General. And during that period I

spent most of my time being a high-class muscle man for Big Business, for
Wall Street and for the bankers. In short, I was a racketeer for capitalism.[94]

Butler's radical turn alarmed the military. In January 1936, Marine
Corps informants infiltrated a meeting of the American League Against
War and Fascism at the Cleveland Public Auditorium, where Butler shared
the stage with radical journalists, an antifascist rabbi, official members of
the Communist Party, and the poet Langston Hughes. Reporting that
Butler had called on the crowd to "lay aside all religious and racial feeling
and stand together" against fascism and war, the informants concluded:
"The General appeared to us to be either insane or an out and out traitor."[95]

The spies may have indeed been picking up a rising desperation in
Butler's voice. His fears of a second world war—of a catastrophe made
worse than the first by accelerating technology—were growing by the
day. Hitler had announced the reconstitution of Germany's armed forces.
Fascist Italy had invaded Ethiopia using aerial bombings and mustard
gas. In the summer of 1936, the Spanish Civil War would begin, drawing
Nazi Germany, the Soviet Union, and thousands of volunteers from the
United States, Britain, and elsewhere into proxy combat.

Most worrying to Butler were the developments in Asia. Japan was
now occupying all of Chinese Manchuria, with the deposed last Qing
emperor, Puyi, as the nominal leader of a puppet state. Butler's warnings
about growing U.S. and Japanese imperial rivalry grew more dire. He
had already come out publicly for the independence of the Philippines. In
1938, he wrote an incendiary article calling for the immediate withdrawal
of U.S. forces from China. "Do you want to send your sons to get their
brains spattered all over Manchuria by Oriental air bombs? If you don't,
you had better do something about it—now. Tomorrow may be too late."[96]

By the spring of 1939, many of Butler's warnings were already proving
prophetic. Hitler and Mussolini had announced an alliance, despite
their countries having been on opposite sides of the previous world war.
Japan had launched its reign of terror in China two years earlier and was
now occupying the ruins of Shanghai and Nanjing.

Butler continued his relentless campaign against war. He traveled across the country giving speeches: from cities like Chicago and Portland, Oregon, to towns as small as Texarkana, Texas, and Coffeyville, Kansas. The constant movement and stress put a deep strain on his body; his back and stomach, which had never been quite right, were now giving him no end of trouble.

His iconoclasm and insistence on always speaking his mind had left him with few consistent allies. He had given up on an increasingly war-like Roosevelt, voting for Socialist Party candidate Norman Thomas in the 1936 presidential election.[97] The Marines washed their hands of him. The Nazi-sympathizing America First crowd, soon to be led by the aviator Charles Lindbergh, had little use for his consistent antifascism. Neither did the Communists, whose party leader, Earl Browder, lamented that "he is a simple man . . . [with] no conception of politics. . . . He is just a soldier fighting for the soldiers."[98]

He was also without his lifelong pillar of support. Maud Butler had died in June 1936, at Smedley's brother's house on the oil ranch in East-land, Texas. She was eighty-one. The West Chester newspaper ran one of the last photos ever taken of her, smiling contentedly next to Smedley in Wichita, where she had come to hear him talk.[99]

In April 1939, an ailing Butler accepted an invitation to speak at a "peace meeting" at the University of California in Berkeley. The students who streamed into the sunny gymnasium that day were young and eager, dressed for the San Francisco Bay spring. The men wore rumpled shirts and brown oxfords, the women light sweaters and long skirts, their shiny hair bobbed and rolled. There were thousands, stacked up the bleachers to the big iron rafters. Classes had been canceled across campus for the event.

Butler sat back as the young university president, Robert G. Sproul, announced the first student speaker, Effie Lockhart. She was well dressed, poised, and, in contrast to nearly everyone else in the arena, Black. "The final decision as to whether we have peace or war rests with those who dare to hope for peace," she trumpeted.[100]

Smedley couldn't share her optimism, but he admired it, and firmly shook her hand. He cared less for the next student, one Bernard Shapiro. The young man tempered his plea for peace with a call for collective security—supporting, through other means, nations fighting against fascism. No, Butler thought. That way lay trouble. Entanglement.

He turned the thought over in his mind, as Sproul read his introduction. ("Smedley D. Butler! . . . A dynamic spirit who shocks his listeners into thinking, into violent agreement—or disagreement!") That righteous anger was lit. He stood, staring out at the crowd, digging deep to call up that grit and gunpowder voice that had roared at presidents and sent boys into hell, now buried under the pain of a prematurely aging gut. He downed a glass of cool water, ran his callused fingers through what was left of his hair, and balled them into a fist.

"I'm going to give my ideas in the words of a Marine!" he thundered. He did not need a microphone. The words pinged off the concrete walls. He pointed at poor Shapiro. "I don't agree with a *damn thing* he said." He let the cuss settle. Then he cracked his impish smile. "But I like the way he said it!" The students roared.[101]

Butler could not stop now. He had killed and nearly been killed. He'd seen friends like Pete Wynne survive the battlefield only to die young from drink and disease. He pictured, perhaps, the faces of the men he had killed, including Zeledón's rebels in Nicaragua and the Cacos of Fort Rivière, who had died fighting to fend off the empire he was now struggling to contain. He remembered the men coming back from the front in France, missing limbs and parts of their faces, a ghastly hollowness inside. They were the same age as the students staring back at him now.

"I can't believe that Roosevelt wants to put us into war," he told them. "He has a son who is a lieutenant colonel in the Marines. I'm damn sure he'll go to the front-line trenches if there are any, for I'll take him. I'll resign my commission and take James as a private!" They applauded.

As he always did, in everything, Butler gave all he had. He ranted and pleaded until, as happened often at his fragile, malarial age of fifty-eight, his strength began to give out. "Go on!" he shouted, his voice now starting to fray. "Have your lousy damn war! Our problem at home is to stop talking about war and put twelve million men to work."

But deep in his gut, under the stabbing pain, Butler may have suspected a deeper truth. The students' comfortable cheap cotton clothes, the Packards and Fords lined up outside on College Avenue, the bananas and breakfast cereals in their bellies, owed everything to his sacrifices and his crimes—what he and his Marines had done to millions of others, what they had bled and died for in jungles and drought-stricken fields thousands of miles away. America had risen on his watch from a regional dynamo to the very cusp of becoming the ultimate power in the world. If Americans wanted to defend that power and position, if they were to ensure that the spoils of empire in the Pacific did not fall into the hands of the Japanese, that the prizes of Latin America and the Caribbean were not overrun by the British, the Soviets, or the killers of the Nazi Reich, then their leaders would have to push them into war.

He had foreseen it years before, because he had helped to make it nearly inevitable. Remembering the human cost of everything Americans had done to build their empire, he prayed, might save countless more lives from even more war, from suffering, from death. He looked out at the young people and beseeched them to remember. But America had already forgotten.

# EPILOGUE

In the last frigid day of February, the trees and bushes at the Oaklands Cemetery were bare. My guide from the local historical society walked ahead while I fumbled with my phone looking for a cemetery map. When I looked up, I saw him standing beside the cluster of plain gray headstones we were searching for.

In the back row lay Thomas and Maud, a clutch of pink flowers beside her marker. There were Tom Dick, Smedley Junior, and Smedley's brothers, Horace and Sam.* Bunny lay under her maiden name, Ethel Conway Peters, with an inscription indicating that she was Smedley's wife. Tucked to her left, at the spot where the property gave way to the forest, was Smedley Darlington Butler.

On May 23, 1940, Butler, complaining of stomach pain, weight loss, and exhaustion, checked into the Philadelphia Naval Hospital. The doctors diagnosed him with an unspecified upper abdominal condition affecting the gall bladder and liver, likely a form of cancer. He never left the hospital. He died on June 21, surrounded by Bunny and the children.[1]

They held the funeral in the Newtown Square house, under the "Umbrellas of Ten Thousand Blessings." A contingent of Marines, a few congressmen, and a few dozen Philadelphia police attended, along with many relatives. A mountain of floral tributes sent from all over the world was piled in front of an American flag. The president sent a short note to Ethel: "I grieve to hear of Smedley's passing. I shall always remember the old days in Haiti. My heart goes out to you and the family in this great sorrow. Franklin D. Roosevelt."[2]

---

* Snooks is buried in Arlington National Cemetery with her husband.

The service consisted of two eulogies: one by a Unitarian minister, the other by a member of the Quaker Meeting. Though Quakers had written from across the country in Butler's later years, demanding (politely) to know how an admitted mass killer could call himself a member in good standing, the West Chester Meeting had defended him throughout. "Although General Butler was for thirty years in the military service of his country, he hated war," the Quaker eulogist at his funeral said. "There can be no doubt that his preaching produced results and that he carried his peace message to places and peoples that would not have been reached and influenced otherwise."[3]

Butler was buried without military honors, likely at the family's request. His headstone was marked with a logo in the shape of a Medal of Honor, his birth and death dates listed in the Quaker style (the months' numbers instead of their names), his final rank, and the Marine motto, *Semper Fidelis*. Over the years, the grave had become a pilgrimage site of sorts. Visitors before me had left an assortment of U.S. and Marine Corps flags, flowers, coins, and an American Legion medallion. Someone had pressed a gold and silver Eagle, Globe, and Anchor into the dirt.

Smedley's "preaching," as it were, did nothing to prevent World War II, which had been raging for months in Europe and three years in Asia when he died. The French surrendered to the Nazis in the Forest of Compiègne the day after he succumbed, shocking American anti-interventionists who had assumed the French army would halt the German advance, as they had in the last war.

A year later, in 1941, Franklin Roosevelt imposed an oil embargo on the Japanese in retaliation for their invasion of the French colonies in Indochina. That gave Emperor Hirohito two choices: give up on his dreams of becoming the dominant empire in East Asia and the Pacific, or seize the oil reserves in the Dutch East Indies, risking war with the United States and Britain. His war cabinet decided to strike first, simultaneously bombing Pearl Harbor, the Philippines, Guam, Wake Island, and the British garrisons in Malaya, Hong Kong, and Singapore on December 7 and 8, 1941.

Roosevelt lifted a bit of Butler's rhetoric in rallying the country to war. "Powerful and resourceful gangsters have banded together to make war upon the whole human race," he said in a fireside chat. "There is no such thing as security for any nation—or any individual—in a world ruled by the principles of gangsterism."[4]

It's impossible to say how Butler would have reacted. Just three years earlier, in 1938, Smedley had said that in case of an attack on Hawai'i the islands should be abandoned and defenses readied closer to the mainland.[5] But he also said during his antiwar years, "Pacifist, hell. I'm a pacifist, but I always have a club behind my back."[6] It is not hard to imagine that Butler might have joined fellow antiwar but non-Nazi-supporting activists, including Norman Thomas, in reluctantly deciding to support the United States' entering the conflict on the side of the Allies.[7]

We do know how the Butler family responded. Smedley Junior joined the Marines. Tom Dick joined the Navy. Snooks's husband, John Wehle, flew missions as a Marine aviator in the Pacific. Snooks was called on to christen the USS *Butler*, a sixteen-hundred-ton destroyer named for her father, which participated in both the Allied invasion of Sicily (the beginning of the end for Mussolini, Smedley would have been pleased to know) and the D-Day invasion of France.[8] In a telling move, in 1944, Bunny refused to allow a pacifist group to publish quotations from *War Is a Racket* until the war was over. "However," she wrote them, "as soon as peace has been established we will do everything possible to help prevent any future development that might lead to war."[9]

After Japan surrendered, the Marine Corps established Camp Smedley D. Butler, a base on the U.S.-occupied Japanese island of Okinawa. It was a tribute-wrapped rebuke of a Marine who died calling on his country to abandon its Pacific colonies in the interest of peace.

Among the many Marines who have passed through Camp Butler over the years was Gen. David M. Shoup, who served under Butler in China in 1927 and 1928, and won a Medal of Honor at the 1943 Battle of Tarawa against the Japanese. He was also Corps commandant from 1960 until 1963. Having learned, perhaps equally belatedly, the same lessons as his former commander, Shoup became one of the most outspoken critics of the escalation in Vietnam, warning Lyndon Johnson's administration to "keep our dirty, bloody, dollar-soaked fingers out of the business of these nations so full of depressed, exploited people."[10]

Shoup was not the last to carry on Butler's tradition of imperfect people trying to speak truth to power from within, or just after leaving, the U.S. military. It's a lineage that includes Col. David "Hack" Hackworth, U.S. Army, who spoke on national television against the Vietnam War, and Lt. Paula Coughlin, who exposed rampant sexual assault in the Navy and Marine Corps in the early 1990s. Scott Ritter, the United Nations weapons inspector who tried to warn the world that George W. Bush was about to make a "historical mistake" by ordering the invasion of Iraq in 2003, was a Marine.[11]

Some have paid with more than their professional relationships. Chelsea Manning, an Army intelligence analyst in Iraq, passed video of a U.S. helicopter gunship killing civilians, as well as hundreds of thousands of classified documents, to the website WikiLeaks.[12] She was court-martialed and sentenced to thirty-five years in prison, though her sentence was commuted after seven. Most recently, Reality Winner, a former Air Force intelligence specialist, was sentenced to over five years for sharing a classified report on Russian interference in the 2016 election that the Trump administration did not want revealed.[13]

Like Butler, each had participated in the destructive system they tried to expose; each was trying to pierce the silences that had made that destruction possible. Those are the kinds of moral conflicts that are perhaps inevitable when trying to do justice from inside an empire. It is something I struggled with in my own way throughout the journey in Butler's footsteps. An empire built on greed and murder may be fraying, but who knows if what comes next will be better or worse. Will it be a world built on justice and equality, restoring what was stolen, and living out the promises that many Americans do believe in? Or one of revanchism and autocracy, of Trumps, Dutertes, and Xis? The possibilities are both liberatory and terrifying. Perhaps it is all we can do to follow the example of Butler and those who came after him, trying to come to grips with the realities of our past, and making the reparations necessary for a better future.

As I meditated on that, standing over Butler's simple grave, two men approached me from another corner of the family plot. One was wearing a beige overcoat. The taller one was in a gray hoodie.

"He says you're writing a biography of Smedley Butler," the one in the gray hoodie said, gesturing toward the historical society guide.

"Close enough," I replied.

He smiled, like we shared a secret code. He told me he had joined the Air Force the year the Iraq War began. Now an E-7, master sergeant, he was about to be deployed again to Iraq. His new mission was to be an adviser in the latest iteration of Americans trying to set up client armies abroad, usually to the detriment of all involved. He was preparing for deployment at Fort Dix, New Jersey. When he found out that Butler was buried within driving distance—about sixty miles—he felt the overwhelming urge to visit with a comrade. He wanted to make a rubbing of the headstone to take with him to Baghdad.

"Personal non-hero," he explained. "I don't want to say hero because I don't think that's what he'd say about himself."

"Too modest?" the historical society guy asked.

"No, that's not it. I don't think he thought he was a hero."

The master sergeant paused, then backtracked, and tried to explain what he meant. But I understood. I knew the look in his eye, a look Butler surely would have recognized: of being proud of what he'd done, and also deeply ashamed, and haunted by it, and also by what he was probably about to go do. He told me he tried to look for soldiers from the past who did their jobs with integrity, and model himself after them. "The military is a sharp instrument in the hands of a blunt man," he said, with a half laugh of resignation.

We stood around for a few minutes more, chatting about Butler's life and times, until he said he had to go. I wished him well. He and his friend walked off toward the road, leaving the graves behind them.

# ACKNOWLEDGMENTS

In his 1932 speech to the Bonus March, Smedley Butler told a joke to explain what it had meant to him to be a member of the military. It went like this: A newcomer to the Old West is riding on a stagecoach when the driver uses his whip to swat a horsefly off a cow. The driver does this so expertly, the cow hardly notices. A little farther down the line, the driver uses his whip to swat a grasshopper off a fence, just as deftly. Finally, they pass a hornets' nest, with one hornet hanging down beneath it. The driver just keeps heading down the road.

"Say, what's the matter with you?" the tenderfoot asks. "You hit the horsefly. And you hit the grasshopper. Why didn't you hit the hornet?"

"Aw," the driver says, "look here, young fella. A grasshopper's a grasshopper, and a horsefly's a horsefly, but a hornet's a *whole damned organization.*"

That is how it often felt to work on this book for the last five years. Its creation and production would not have been possible without the contributions and sacrifices of a huge and varied team, which ultimately grew to encompass individuals scattered across no fewer than seven countries and two hemispheres. There were more people involved than I can possibly name; if I have omitted yours, know it was done without malice.

I was fortunate to spend a year as a fellow at the New America foundation, where my insanely talented colleagues offered their invaluable insights and constructive criticisms that made this project far better than it otherwise would have been. Many thanks especially to Anne-Marie Slaughter, Peter Bergen, and Awista Ayub for that opportunity, along with Arizona State University for sponsoring my fellowship in the Future of War program. I also spent a terrific winter in residency as a Logan

Nonfiction Fellow at the Carey Institute in upstate New York, where an equally exquisitely talented bunch shared meals and drafts, honed our fire-making skills, and did push-ups in the snow. Thanks to Tom Jennings and everyone there.

Duke University, specifically the Franklin Humanities Institute and DeWitt Wallace Center for Media & Democracy, offered me a professional home and support for the first two years I spent working on this project before family and fate stole me away to Charlottesville. Thanks especially to Deborah Jenson and Bill Adair, as well as to my awesome students. And thanks to Duke Library for letting me keep my access as an affiliate. I do not know how I would have researched this otherwise.

Many thanks to the various staffs of the Marine Corps Historical Division archives, starting with J. Michael Miller, James Ginther, Alisa Whitley, and Alyson K. Mazzone. Thanks as well to the tireless archivists at the National Archives and Records Administration, Canal Zone Library and Museum, Ateneo de Manila University, Shanghai Library Bibliotheca Zi-Ka-Wei, and the other archives I depended on for research (see the notes for details).

My travels around the world depended on the help of some amazing people, many of whom I met along the way. Thanks to Rica Concepcion, Rafe Bartholomew, Philbert Dy, Erwin Romulo, and Orlando de Guzman for your help and generosity in the Philippines; to Jason Zheng, James Palmer, Emily Feng, Howard French, Jenny Tang, and Guo Li for the same in China; ditto to Javier Wallace, Anne Gegg, Víctor Peretz, Melva Lowe de Goodin, Marcia Rodriguez, and Ines Sealy in Panama; to Ismael Lopez and Amy Shelton in Nicaragua; and to Arian Terrill and John Presimé in the Dominican Republic. Thanks, as ever, to the man, Evens Sanon, in the Republic of Haiti, *ak mèsi anpil* Lewis Ampidu Clorméus. Many thanks to Douglas Humes of the Newtown Square Historical Preservation Society, and to Melissa and David (and Bunny!) Clark for showing me your (and the general's) home. And for the muffins.

A special thanks to Smedley Butler's granddaughters, Philippa Wehle and Molly Butler Swanton, for your time, good humor, and support. I hope I did your family proud, and have done as little as possible to contribute to any future "pandemonia in the woods."

Elisabeth Dyssegaard at St. Martin's Press believed in my cockamamie vision for this book from the beginning. Thanks to her, as well as to Alex

Brown, Alan Bradshaw, Leah Johnson, Michelle Cashman, and everyone else at SMP. Thanks to my literary agent, the indomitable Gail Ross, and everyone at the Ross Yoon Agency, for shepherding *Gangsters* from a notion to a proposal to a real live book. On my personal production team, thank you to my amazing team of fact-checkers—Rob Liguori, Jamie Fisher, Jane Ackerman, and C.J. Lotz—who told me reliably that this was the "densest" project they ever checked. (I haven't had a chance to confirm that independently.) Rob and C.J. have each now survived checking two of my books, which is surely deserving of some kind of medal. Thank you to Hannah Hallikainen for early research assistance, and to Brendan O'Kane and Marc Opper for translation work. Thanks to Dianna Delling and Johnna Rosenbohm. And many thanks to everyone who supported my work by way of Patreon.com and my newsletter (which you can check out at katz.substack.com), in particular David Henderson and Emma Volk.

Thank you to Christopher Leonard for reassuring me that it would be a fine idea to chase Butler's shadow to the ends of the Earth, and for shaping the idea for a book in its earliest iterations. Thank you as well to Sheri Fink for all your support over the years. Thank you, too, to everyone who took the time to read and in so doing improve my drafts, a list that includes (again, not exhaustively): Emma Beals, Tommy Craggs, Iona Craig, Boris Fishman, Jane Fransson, Masha Gessen, Jennifer Greenburg, Lisa Hamilton, Charles Homans, Daniel Immerwahr, Suki Kim, Adrian LeBlanc, Karen Levy, Larissa MacFarquhar, Pete Mortensen, Samuel Nicholson, Mike Paarlberg, Chase Purdy, Stuart Schrader, Melissa Segura, Christy Thornton, Michael Towne, David Walsh, and Jeffrey Wasserstrom.

I would also like to thank Professor Ken Bain for teaching the most eye-opening class I took as an undergraduate at Northwestern: on the history of U.S. foreign policy during the Cold War. Looking back, I realize your combination of primary documents, analysis, and film were an indirect inspiration for this book.

I can only offer my deepest and most heartfelt appreciation to the Stroke Team and intensive care unit at the University of Virginia Hospital, particularly Dr. Abimbola Sunmonu and Dr. Andrew Southerland. You saved my life and, as important, my brain. I literally could not have finished this book without you.

Thank you to my parents, David and Barbara Myerson Katz, for everything, including your support (and childcare) during the pandemic. Thank you to Teresa Bell Payton for the same.

The list begins and ends with the real historian in the family—my wife, Claire Antone Payton. From our earliest conversations about the Marine with the funny name through the final painstaking edits, she was my most important intellectual collaborator, my toughest editor, my partner, housemate, pandemic officemate, and friend. She taught me the ways of the archives, shared her extensive library and knowledge of the field, and kept me going even when this project seemed hopelessly difficult. In the middle, she somehow found time to write her own doctoral dissertation in Haitian history and publish several academic papers, nurse me back to health in record speed, and give birth to our beautiful Naomi. This book is dedicated, with grateful love and admiration, to her.

# A NOTE ON SOURCES

I was fortunate to discover how many of Smedley Butler's letters, writings, and photos—as well as those of his fellow Marines and family—survive. The Butler family were prolific letter writers; because Smedley became famous as a teenager—especially after his early battlefield heroics in China—his family preserved thousands of documents written by and to him.

Thanks to the dedicated archivists at the Marine Corps History Division, Quantico; the Special Collections Department at the Stanford University Library; and the Chester County (PA) Historical Society—as well as Butler's granddaughter Philippa Wehle, who generously shared previously unseen family letters and other documents with me—I seldom had to guess what was going on inside his head. All of the Butler-related historical material in this book is based on such letters, memoirs (both unpublished and published), contemporaneous press accounts, and other documents.

# SELECTED BIBLIOGRAPHY

## BUTLERNALIA

Butler, Smedley Darlington. *War Is a Racket*. New York: Round Table Press, 1935.

Miller, J. Michael, ed. *My Dear Smedley: Personal Correspondence of John A. Lejeune and Smedley D. Butler, 1927–1928*. Quantico, VA: Marine Corps Research Center, 2002.

Schmidt, Hans. *Maverick Marine: General Smedley D. Butler and the Contradictions of American Military History*. Lexington: University Press of Kentucky, 1998.

Strecker, Mark. *Smedley Butler, U.S.M.C.: A Biography*. Jefferson, NC, and London: McFarland, 2011.

Thomas, Lowell (as told to). *Old Gimlet Eye: The Adventures of Smedley D. Butler*. New York: Farrar & Rinehart, 1933.

Venzon, Anne Cipriano, ed. *General Smedley Darlington Butler: The Letters of a Leatherneck, 1898–1931*. New York: Praeger, 1992.

## THE UNITED STATES, WAR, AND IMPERIALISM

Ackerman, Spencer. *Reign of Terror: How the 9/11 Era Destabilized America and Produced Trump*. New York: Viking, 2021.

Ahamed, Liaquat. *Lords of Finance: The Bankers Who Broke the World*. New York: Penguin Books, 2009.

Anderson, Perry. *American Foreign Policy and Its Thinkers*. London and New York: Verso, 2017.

Baptist, Edward E. *The Half Has Never Been Told: Slavery and the Making of American Capitalism*. New York: Basic Books, 2016.

Bryan, Joe, and Denis Wood. *Weaponizing Maps: Indigenous Peoples and Counterinsurgency in the Americas*. New York: Guilford Press, 2015.

Campbell, James T., Matthew Pratt Guterl, and Robert G. Lee, eds. *Race, Nation, and Empire in American History*. Chapel Hill: University of North Carolina Press, 2017.

Césaire, Aimé. *Discours sur le colonialism* (1955). Translated by Joan Pinkham as *Discourse on Colonialism*. New York and London: Monthly Review Press, 1972.

Challener, Richard D. *Admirals, Generals, and American Foreign Policy, 1898–1914*. Princeton, NJ: Princeton University Press, 1973.

Cooper, John Milton, Jr. *Woodrow Wilson*. New York: Knopf Doubleday, 2009.

Daugherty, Leo J., III. *Counterinsurgency and the United States Marine Corps*, Vol. 1, *The First Counterinsurgency Era, 1899–1945*. Jefferson, NC: McFarland, 2015.

———. *Pioneers of Amphibious Warfare, 1898–1945: Profiles of Fourteen American Military Strategists*. Jefferson, NC: McFarland, 2009.

Dickson, Paul, and Thomas B. Allen. *The Bonus Army: An American Epic*. New York: Walker Books, 2006.

Evans, Stephen S. *U.S. Marines and Irregular Warfare, 1898–2007: Anthology and Selected Bibliography.* Quantico, VA: Marine Corps University, 2008.

Fanon, Frantz. *Les damnés de la terre.* 1961; repr., Paris: Kiyikaat Editions, 2016.

Finchelstein, Federico. *From Fascism to Populism in History.* Oakland: University of California Press, 2019.

Fojas, Camilla. *Islands of Empire: Pop Culture and U.S. Power.* Austin: University of Texas Press, 2014.

Gill, Lesley. *The School of the Americas: Military Training and Political Violence in the Americas.* Durham, NC: Duke University Press, 2004.

Grandin, Greg. *The End of the Myth: From the Frontier to the Border Wall in the Mind of America.* New York: Metropolitan Books, 2019.

Hobsbawm, Eric J. *Bandits.* New York: Pantheon Books, 1981.

Hoganson, Kristin L. *Fighting for American Manhood: How Gender Politics Provoked the Spanish-American and Philippine-American Wars.* New Haven, CT: Yale University Press, 2000.

Hopkins, A. G. *American Empire: A Global History.* Princeton, NJ: Princeton University Press, 2019.

Immerwahr, Daniel. *How to Hide an Empire: A History of the Greater United States.* New York: Farrar, Straus and Giroux, 2019.

Jenkins, Brian, and Chris Millington. *France and Fascism: February 1934 and the Dynamics of Political Crisis.* Milton Park, Abingdon, UK: Routledge, 2015.

Johnson, Chalmers. *Dismantling the Empire: America's Last Best Hope.* New York: Henry Holt, 2010.

Kaplan, Amy, and Donald E. Pease. *Cultures of United States Imperialism.* Durham, NC: Duke University Press, 1993.

Kilcullen, David. *Counterinsurgency.* New York: Oxford University Press, 2010.

Kinzer, Stephen. *Overthrow: America's Century of Regime Change from Hawaii to Iraq.* New York: Henry Holt, 2007.

Lentz-Smith, Adrian. *Freedom Struggles: African Americans and World War I.* Cambridge, MA: Harvard University Press, 2011.

Lisagor, Nancy, and Frank Lipsius. *A Law unto Itself: The Untold Story of the Law Firm Sullivan & Cromwell.* New York: Athena, 1989.

Love, Eric. *Race over Empire: Racism and U.S. Imperialism.* Chapel Hill: University of North Carolina Press, 2004.

Mahan, Alfred Thayer. *The Influence of Sea Power upon History, 1660–1783.* London: Low, Marston, 1890.

———. *The Interest of America in Sea Power, Present and Future.* Boston: Little, Brown, 1897.

———. *The Problem of Asia and Its Effect upon International Policies.* Boston: Little, Brown, 1900.

McCormick, Thomas J. *America's Half-Century: United States Foreign Policy in the Cold War and After.* Baltimore: Johns Hopkins University Press, 1995.

Millett, Allan Reed. *Semper Fidelis: The History of the United States Marine Corps.* New York: Simon and Schuster, 1991.

Morefield, Jeanne. *Empires Without Imperialism: Anglo-American Decline and the Politics of Deflection.* New York: Oxford University Press, 2014.

Morison, Elting E., ed. *The Letters of Theodore Roosevelt.* 8 volumes. Cambridge, MA: Harvard University Press, 1951–1954.

Nagl, John A. *Knife Fights: A Memoir of Modern War in Theory and Practice.* New York: Penguin Books, 2014.

Panitch, Leo, and Sam Gindin. *The Making of Global Capitalism: The Political Economy of American Empire.* New York: Verso, 2012.

Phillips-Fein, Kim. *Invisible Hands: The Businessmen's Crusade against the New Deal*. W. W. Norton, 2010.

Purdy, Jedediah. *After Nature: A Politics for the Anthropocene*. Cambridge, MA: Harvard University Press, 2015.

Rauchway, Eric. *Why the New Deal Matters*. New Haven, CT: Yale University Press, 2021.

Rosenberg, Emily S. *Financial Missionaries to the World: The Politics and Culture of Dollar Diplomacy, 1900–1930*. Durham, NC: Duke University Press, 2004.

Schmitz, David F. *The United States and Fascist Italy, 1922–1940*. New edition. Chapel Hill: University of North Carolina Press, 2009.

Schrader, Stuart. *Badges Without Borders: How Global Counterinsurgency Transformed American Policing*. Oakland: University of California Press, 2019.

Sewall, Sarah, John A. Nagl, David H. Petraeus, and James F. Amos. *The U.S. Army/Marine Corps Counterinsurgency Field Manual*. Chicago: University of Chicago Press, 2007.

Stanley, Jason. *How Fascism Works: The Politics of Us and Them*. New York: Random House, 2018.

Tugwell, Rexford G. *The Brains Trust*. New York: Viking Press, 1968.

———. *The Democratic Roosevelt: A Biography of Franklin D. Roosevelt*. Garden City, NY: Doubleday, 1957.

Wertheim, Stephen. *Tomorrow, the World: The Birth of U.S. Global Supremacy*. Cambridge, MA: Belknap Press of Harvard University Press, 2020.

Whitman, James Q. *Hitler's American Model: The United States and the Making of Nazi Race Law*. Princeton, NJ: Princeton University Press, 2017.

Wise, Frederic May, and Meigs Oliver Frost. *A Marine Tells It to You*. New York: J. H. Sears, 1929.

Wolfskill, George. *The Revolt of the Conservatives; a History of the American Liberty League, 1934–1940*. Westport, CT: Greenwood Press, 1974.

Wood, David. *What Have We Done: The Moral Injury of Our Longest Wars*. New York: Little, Brown Spark, 2016.

Young, Matt. *Eat the Apple*. New York: Bloomsbury USA, 2018.

# CHINA

Barnouin, Barbara, and Changgen Yu. *Zhou Enlai: A Political Life*. Hong Kong: Chinese University Press, 2006.

Biggs, Chester M., Jr. *The United States Marines in North China, 1894–1942*. Jefferson, NC: McFarland, 2010.

Cohen, Paul A. *History in Three Keys: The Boxers as Event, Experience, and Myth*. Revised ed. New York: Columbia University Press, 1998.

Elliott, Jane. *Some Did It for Civilisation; Some Did It for Their Country: A Revised View of the Boxer War*. Hong Kong: Chinese University Press, 2002.

French, Howard W. *Everything under the Heavens: How the Past Helps Shape China's Push for Global Power*. New York: Vintage Books, 2018.

Jordan, Donald A. *The Northern Expedition: China's National Revolution of 1926–1928*. Honolulu: University of Hawai'i Press, 1976.

Karl, Rebecca E. *Mao Zedong and China in the Twentieth-Century World: A Concise History*. Durham, NC: Duke University Press, 2010.

———. *Staging the World: Chinese Nationalism at the Turn of the Twentieth Century*. Durham, NC: Duke University Press, 2002.

Martin, Brian G. *The Shanghai Green Gang: Politics and Organized Crime, 1919–1937*. Berkeley: University of California Press, 1996.

Pakula, Hannah. *The Last Empress: Madame Chiang Kai-Shek and the Birth of Modern China*. New York: Simon & Schuster, 2009.

Palmer, James. *Heaven Cracks, Earth Shakes: The Tangshan Earthquake and the Death of Mao's China*. New York: Basic Books, 2012.

Pomfret, John. *The Beautiful Country and the Middle Kingdom: America and China, 1776 to the Present*. New York: Henry Holt, 2016.

Preston, Diana. *The Boxer Rebellion: The Dramatic Story of China's War on Foreigners That Shook the World in the Summer of 1900*. New York: Berkley Books, 2001.

Silbey, David J. *The Boxer Rebellion and the Great Game in China*. New York: Hill and Wang, 2012.

Tuchman, Barbara W. *Stilwell and the American Experience in China, 1941–1945*. New York: Macmillan, 1971.

Xiang Lanxin. *The Origins of the Boxer War: A Multinational Study*. Psychology Press, 2003.

Yang, Gene Luen. *Boxers*. New York: First Second, 2013.

———. *Saints*. New York: First Second, 2013.

## CUBA

Barnet, Miguel, and Esteban Montejo. *Biography of a Runaway Slave: Fiftieth Anniversary Edition*. Evanston, IL: Curbstone Books/Northwestern University Press, 2016.

Ferrer, Ada. *Insurgent Cuba: Race, Nation, and Revolution, 1868–1898*. Chapel Hill: University of North Carolina Press, 1999.

Foner, Philip S. *The Spanish-Cuban-American War and the Birth of American Imperialism*, Vol. 2, *1898–1902*. New York: New York University Press, 1972.

Hansen, Jonathan M. *Guantánamo: An American History*. New York: Hill and Wang, 2011.

Hulme, Peter. *Cuba's Wild East: A Literary Geography of Oriente*. Liverpool: Liverpool University Press, 2011.

Pérez, Louis A., Jr. *Intervention, Revolution, and Politics in Cuba, 1913–1921*. Pittsburgh: University of Pittsburgh Press, 1979.

———. *Structure of Cuban History: Meanings and Purpose of the Past*. Chapel Hill: University of North Carolina Press, 2013.

Sartorious, David. *Ever Faithful: Race, Loyalty, and the Ends of Empire in Spanish Cuba*. Durham, NC: Duke University Press, 2014.

Smith, Clive Stafford. *Eight O'Clock Ferry to the Windward Side: Seeking Justice in Guantánamo Bay*. New York: Nation Books, 2008.

Tone, John Lawrence. *War and Genocide in Cuba, 1895–1898*. Chapel Hill: University of North Carolina Press, 2006.

## DOMINICAN REPUBLIC

Atkins, G. Pope. *The Dominican Republic and the United States: From Imperialism to Transnationalism*. Athens: University of Georgia Press, 1998.

Calder, Bruce J. *The Impact of Intervention: The Dominican Republic during the U.S. Occupation of 1916–1924*. Austin: University of Texas Press, 1984.

Derby, Lauren H. *The Dictator's Seduction: Politics and the Popular Imagination in the Era of Trujillo*. Durham, NC: Duke University Press, 2009.

Eller, Anne. *We Dream Together: Dominican Independence, Haiti, and the Fight for Caribbean Freedom*. Durham, NC: Duke University Press, 2016.

García-Peña, Lorgia. *The Borders of Dominicanidad: Race, Nation, and Archives of Contradiction*. Durham, NC: Duke University Press, 2016.

Martínez-Vergne, Teresita. *Nation and Citizen in the Dominican Republic, 1880–1916*. Chapel Hill: University of North Carolina Press, 2005.

Paulino, Edward. *Dividing Hispaniola: The Dominican Republic's Border Campaign against Haiti, 1930–1961*. Pittsburgh: University of Pittsburgh Press, 2016.
Peguero, Valentina. *The Militarization of Culture in the Dominican Republic, from the Captains General to General Trujillo*. Lincoln: University of Nebraska Press, 2004.

## HAITI

Byrd, Brandon R. *The Black Republic: African Americans and the Fate of Haiti*. Philadelphia: University of Pennsylvania Press, 2019.
Christie, Deborah, and Sarah Juliet Lauro. *Better Off Dead: The Evolution of the Zombie as Post-Human*. New York: Fordham University Press, 2011.
Corvington, Georges. *Port-au-Prince au cours des ans. Tome III: La capitale d'Haïti sous l'occupation (1915–1934)*. Montreal: Les Éditions du CIDIHCA.
Cussans, John. *Undead Uprising: Haiti, Horror and the Zombie Complex*. London: Strange Attractor Press, 2017.
Dubois, Laurent. *Haiti: The Aftershocks of History*. New York: Henry Holt, 2012.
Gaillard, Roger. *Charlemagne Péralte, le caco*. Port-au-Prince: Le Natal, 1982.
———. *Les blancs débarquent: 1917–1918. Hinche mise en croix*. Port-au-Prince: Le Natal, 1982.
———. *Les blancs débarquent: Premier écrasement du Cacoïsme*. Port-au-Prince: Le Natal, 1981.
Katz, Jonathan M. *The Big Truck That Went By: How the World Came to Save Haiti and Left Behind a Disaster*. New York: Palgrave Macmillan, 2013.
Moreman, Christopher M., and Cory James Rushton. *Race, Oppression and the Zombie: Essays on Cross-Cultural Appropriations of the Caribbean Tradition*. Jefferson, NC: McFarland, 2011.
Ramsey, Kate. *The Spirits and the Law: Vodou and Power in Haiti*. Reprint edition. Chicago: University of Chicago Press, 2014.
Renda, Mary A. *Taking Haiti: Military Occupation and the Culture of U.S. Imperialism, 1915–1940*. Chapel Hill: University of North Carolina Press, 2001.
Schmidt, Hans. *The United States Occupation of Haiti, 1915–1934*. Reprint edition. New Brunswick, NJ: Rutgers University Press, 1995.
Seabrook, William B. *The Magic Island*. Introduction by George A. Romero. 1929; repr. Mineola, NY: Dover, 2016.
Smith, Matthew J. *Red and Black in Haiti: Radicalism, Conflict, and Political Change, 1934–1957*. New edition. Chapel Hill: University of North Carolina Press, 2009.
Trouillot, Michel-Rolph. *Haiti, State against Nation: The Origins and Legacy of Duvalierism*. New York: Monthly Review Press, 1990.
———. *Silencing the Past: Power and the Production of History*. Boston: Beacon Press, 1995.

## HONDURAS

Arce, Alberto. *Honduras a ras de suelo: Crónicas desde el país más violento del mundo*. Mexico City: Ariel México, 2016.
Barahona, Marvin. *Honduras en el siglo XX: Una síntesis histórica*. Tegucigalpa: Editorial Guaymuras, 2005.

## LATIN AMERICA

Bertram, Eva, Morris Blachman, Kenneth Sharpe, and Peter Andreas. *Drug War Politics: The Price of Denial*. Berkeley: University of California Press, 1996.
Colby, Jason M. *The Business of Empire: United Fruit, Race, and U.S. Expansion in Central America*. Ithaca, NY: Cornell University Press, 2011.

Denis, Nelson A. *War against All Puerto Ricans: Revolution and Terror in America's Colony*. New York: Nation Books, 2015.

Hudson, Peter. *Bankers and Empire: How Wall Street Colonized the Caribbean*. Chicago: University of Chicago Press, 2018.

Karnes, Thomas L. *Tropical Enterprise: The Standard Fruit and Steamship Company in Latin America*. Baton Rouge: Louisiana State University Press, 1978.

LaFeber, Walter. *Inevitable Revolutions: The United States in Central America*. New York: W. W. Norton, 1993.

O'Brien, Thomas F. *The Century of U.S. Capitalism in Latin America*. Albuquerque: University of New Mexico Press, 1999.

## MEXICO

Becerra, Ricardo, and José Woldenberg. *Balance temprano: Desde la izquierda democrática*. Mexico City: Grano de Sal, 2020.

Brown, Jonathan C. *Oil and Revolution in Mexico*. Berkeley: University of California Press, 1992.

Hart, John Mason. *Empire and Revolution: The Americans in Mexico since the Civil War*. Berkeley: University of California Press, 2006.

———. *Revolutionary Mexico: The Coming and Process of the Mexican Revolution*. Tenth Anniversary Edition. Berkeley: University of California Press, 1997.

Katz, Friedrich. *The Secret War in Mexico: Europe, the United States, and the Mexican Revolution*. 1981; Reprint edition. Chicago: University of Chicago Press, 1984.

Pasquel, Leonardo. *La invasion de Veracruz en 1914*. Mexico City: Editorial Citlaltepetl, 1976.

———. *Manuel y José Azueta, padre e hijo: Héroes en la gesta de 1914*. Mexico City: Editorial Citlaltepetl, 1967.

Quirk, Robert E. *An Affair of Honor: Woodrow Wilson and the Occupation of Veracruz*. New York: W. W. Norton, 1962.

Thornton, Christy. *Revolution in Development: Mexico and the Governance of the Global Economy*. Oakland: University of California Press, 2021.

## NICARAGUA

Brody, Reed. *Contra Terror in Nicaragua: Report of a Fact-Finding Mission, September 1984–January 1985*. Boston: South End Press, 1985.

Denny, Harold Norman. *Dollars for Bullets: The Story of American Rule in Nicaragua*. New York: L. MacVeagh, 1929.

Ferrero Blanco, Maria Dolores. *La Nicaragua de los Somoza: 1936–1979*. Huelva, Spain: Universidad de Huelva, 2012.

Gobat, Michel. *Confronting the American Dream: Nicaragua under U.S. Imperial Rule*. Durham, NC: Duke University Press, 2005.

*Pensamiento antimperialista en Nicaragua: Antología*. Managua: Editorial Nueva Nicaragua, 1982.

Ramírez, Sergio. *Sandino: The Testimony of a Nicaraguan Patriot, 1921–1934*. Princeton, NJ: Princeton University Press, 1992.

Zimmermann, Matilde. *Sandinista: Carlos Fonseca and the Nicaraguan Revolution*. Durham, NC: Duke University Press, 2001.

## PACIFIC RIM

Asada, Sadao. *From Mahan to Pearl Harbor: The Imperial Japanese Navy and the United States*. 2006; Reprint edition. Annapolis, MD: Naval Institute Press, 2013.

Iriye, Akira. *Across the Pacific: An Inner History of American–East Asian Relations*. New York: Harcourt, Brace & World, 1967.

## PANAMA

Dinges, John. *Our Man in Panama: How General Noriega Used the United States and Made Millions in Drugs and Arms*. New York: Random House, 1990.

Espino, Ovidio Diaz. *How Wall Street Created a Nation: J. P. Morgan, Teddy Roosevelt, and the Panama Canal*. New York: Basic Books, 2003.

Greene, Julie. *The Canal Builders: Making America's Empire at the Panama Canal*. New York: Penguin, 2009.

Lasso, Marixa. *Erased: The Untold Story of the Panama Canal*. Cambridge, MA: Harvard University Press, 2019.

Lindsay-Poland, John. *Emperors in the Jungle: The Hidden History of the U.S. in Panama*. Durham, NC: Duke University Press, 2003.

Major, John. *Prize Possession: The United States Government and the Panama Canal, 1903–1979*. Cambridge and New York: Cambridge University Press, 1993.

McCullough, David. *The Path between the Seas: The Creation of the Panama Canal, 1870–1914*. New York: Simon & Schuster, 2001.

Miner, Dwight Carroll. *The Fight for the Panama Route: The Story of the Spooner Act and the Hay-Herrán Treaty*. New York: Octagon, 1966.

## PHILIPPINES

Capozzola, Christopher. *Bound by War: How the United States and the Philippines Built America's First Pacific Century*. New York: Basic Books, 2020.

Couttie, Bob. *Hang the Dogs: The True History of the Balangiga Massacre*. Quezon City, Philippines: New Day Publishers, 2004.

Jones, Gregg. *Honor in the Dust: Theodore Roosevelt, War in the Philippines, and the Rise and Fall of America's Imperial Dream*. New York: Penguin, 2012.

Karnow, Stanley. *In Our Image: America's Empire in the Philippines*. New York: Random House, 1989.

Kramer, Paul A. *The Blood of Government: Race, Empire, the United States, and the Philippines*. Chapel Hill: University of North Carolina Press, 2006.

Linn, Brian McAllister. *The Philippine War, 1899–1902*. 1989; Reprint edition. Lawrence: University Press of Kansas, 2000.

———. *The U.S. Army and Counterinsurgency in the Philippine War, 1899–1902*. Chapel Hill: University of North Carolina Press, 2000.

Miller, Stuart Creighton. *Benevolent Assimilation: The American Conquest of the Philippines, 1899–1903*. New Haven, CT: Yale University Press, 1984.

Rafael, Vicente L. *Motherless Tongues: The Insurgency of Language amid Wars of Translation*. Durham, NC: Duke University Press, 2016.

———. *White Love and Other Events in Filipino History*. Durham, NC: Duke University Press, 2014.

Silbey, David J. *A War of Frontier and Empire: The Philippine-American War, 1899–1902*. New York: Hill and Wang, 2007.

# NOTES

*Note*: Smedley D. Butler referred to throughout as SDB.

## MAIN ARCHIVES CITED, WITH ABBREVIATIONS:

American Historical Collection, Rizal Library, Ateneo de Manila University, Quezon City, Philippines (Ateneo)

Canal Zone Library and Museum, Balboa Heights, Panama City (CZLM)

Chester County (PA) Historical Society (Chester Co. HS)

Catalogue de la Bibliotheque haitienne des Frères de l'instruction chrétienne, Institution Saint-Louis de Gonzague, Port-au-Prince, Haiti (ISLG)

Marine Corps History Division, Quantico, VA (MCHD)

> Smedley D. Butler Collection, COLL/3124
> Ben Hebard Fuller Collection, COLL/713
> John H. Russell, Jr., Collection, COLL/158
> Joseph Pendleton Collection, COLL/402
> Historical Amphibious Files, COLL/3634
> Littleton W. T. Waller, Sr., Collection, COLL/1784

Museo Afro Antillano de Panama/Afro-Antillean Museum of Panama, Panama City, Panama (MAAP)

National Archives and Research Administration, Washington, DC (NARA)

Shanghai Library Bibliotheca Zi-Ka-Wei/上海图书馆徐家汇藏书楼 (Shanghai ZKW)

Smedley Darlington Butler family correspondence (M1975). Dept. of Special Collections and University Archives, Stanford University Libraries, Stanford, Calif. (Stanford Lib.)

## PROLOGUE: NEWTOWN SQUARE

1   Testimony of Maj. Gen. S. D. Butler (retired), *Investigation of Nazi Propaganda Activities and Investigation of Certain Other Propaganda Activities, Part 1, Before the Special Committee on Un-American Activities*, 73rd Cong. 11 (1934). Source of all dialogue in this section.

2   According to the Congressional Research Service's "Instances of Use of United States Armed Forces Abroad" (updated Jul. 20, 2020), U.S. forces intervened sixty-two times overseas between 1898 and 1934. The vast majority were repeated and overlapping interventions in nine modern-day countries: Cuba, the Philippines, China, Honduras, Panama, Nicaragua, Mexico, the Dominican Republic, and Haiti. Butler personally invaded or participated in occupations of all these, generally in the most intense periods of combat, as well as in both declared wars of the period: the Spanish-Cuban-Filipino-American War of 1898 and World War I. The interventions involving actual combat in which Butler did not participate at any point were the Second Samoan Civil War of 1899 and the U.S. invasion in support of the government of Alexander Kerensky during the Russian Civil War in 1917 and 1918. See Congressional Research Service, "Instances of Use of United States Armed Forces Abroad, 1798–2020," updated Jul. 20, 2020, fas.org/sgp/crs/natsec/R42738.pdf.

3   For example, "Capt. Butler to Wed," *York* (PA) *Daily*, Jun. 29, 1905; "Butler-Peters," *New York Times*, Jul. 1, 1905.

4  Pérez, *Intervention*, 131.
5  Paul Comly French, "Gen. Butler Accuses N.Y. Brokers of Plotting Dictatorship in U.S.," *New York Post*, Nov. 20, 1934.
6  Quote from Irénée du Pont in Phillips-Fein, *Invisible Hands*, loc. 153.
7  SDB, "America's Armed Forces 2. 'In Time of Peace': The Army," *Common Sense*, Nov. 1935, 8.
8  Morison, *Letters of Theodore Roosevelt*, Vol. 7, 32.
9  Quote from Sven Lindqvist, *Exterminate All the Brutes* (London: Granta Books, 1997), 77; Immerwahr, *How to Hide*, 5.
10  William Appleman Williams, "The Frontier Thesis and American Foreign Policy," *Pacific Historical Review*, Nov. 1, 1955, 379.
11  McCormick, *America's Half-Century*, 77; Anderson, *American Foreign Policy*, 42; "The Truman Doctrine, 1947," Office of the Historian, U.S. Department of State, history.state .gov/milestones/1945–1952/truman-doctrine.
12  See Katz, *The Big Truck*.
13  Fanon, *Damnés de la terre*, 216n7.
14  SDB, "America's Armed Forces 2. 'In Time of Peace': The Army," 8.
15  Ibid.
16  Trouillot, *Silencing*, 27, 48.

## ONE: PHILADELPHIA

1  Andrew R. Murphy, *William Penn: A Life* (New York: Oxford University Press, 2018), 140, 184–186; Scott Weidensaul, *The First Frontier: The Forgotten History of Struggle, Savagery, and Endurance in Early America* (Boston: Houghton Mifflin Harcourt, 2012), 265.
2  SDB, "My Service with the Marines," undated, Box 5, Folder 1, Butler Coll., MCHD.
3  "Heard of a Plot to Blow Up the Maine," *The World* (New York), Feb. 17, 1898; "Torpedo Hole Discovered by Government Divers in the Maine," *New York Journal*, Feb. 17, 1898; Kinzer, *Overthrow*, insert.
4  "Report of the Naval Court of Inquiry upon the Destruction of the United States Battle-ship Maine in Havana Harbor, February 15, 1898, 3/21/1898," *Naval History and Heritage Command*, accessed Apr. 2021, www.history.navy.mil/research/publications/documentary -histories/united-states-navy-s/destruction-of-the-m/report-of-the-naval-0.html.
5  Tone, *War and Genocide*, 193–195. For more on the U.S. reaction to *reconcentración*, see Andrea Pitzer, *One Long Night: A Global History of Concentration Camps* (New York: Little, Brown, 2017).
6  "The Spanish War in Cuba," *New York Times*, Jan. 31, 1897.
7  "Red Cross Work in Cuba," *Friends' Intelligencer and Journal*, May 21, 1898, 371.
8  Haverford School, "125 Years for the Boys: Best Practices from the Haverford School," Issuu.com, Dec. 2010, issuu.com/haverfordschool/docs/125yearsbook.
9  Thomas, *Old Gimlet Eye*, 7.
10  Ibid.
11  SDB, "My Service with the Marines," Butler Coll., MCHD.
12  Likely Sgt. Maj. Thomas F. Hayes. See Robert Elmer Barde, *The History of Marine Corps Competitive Marksmanship* (Washington: U.S. Marine Corps, 1961), 8–9.
13  SDB, "My Service with the Marines," Butler Coll., MCHD.

## TWO: GUANTÁNAMO

1  Rex A. Hudson, *Cuba: A Country Study* (Washington: Federal Research Division, Library of Congress, 2002), 309.
2  The U.S. military spells Guantánamo without the accent mark.
3  Hansen, *Guantánamo*, 3.

4   Ibid., 21, 32.

5   "Thomas Jefferson to James Madison, 27 April 1809," *Founders Online*, National Archives, last modified Nov. 26, 2017, founders.archives.gov/documents/Jefferson /03-01-02-0140.

6   Baptist, *Half Has Never Been Told*, 356–358.

7   See, for instance, Millard Fillmore, "December 6, 1852: Third Annual Message," University of Virginia Miller Center, accessed May 2021, millercenter.org/the-presidency/presidential -speeches/december-6-1852-third-annual-message.

8   Ada Ferrer, *Insurgent Cuba* (Chapel Hill: University of North Carolina Press, 1999), 141.

9   Robert J. Gordon, *The Rise and Fall of American Growth* (Princeton, NJ: Princeton University Press, 2017), 39–42.

10  Hopkins, *American Empire*, 388.

11  Ibid., 389; Brian H. Pollitt, "The Rise and Fall of the Cuban Sugar Economy," *Journal of Latin American Studies* 36, no. 2 (2004): 319–348, doi:10.1017/S0022216X04007448.

12  Theodore Roosevelt, *The Winning of the West*, Vol. 1 (New York and London: G. P. Putnam's Sons, 1908), 1; Purdy, *After Nature*, 37–38.

13  "Thurston's Cuban Speech," *New York Times*, Mar. 25, 1898.

14  Letter from José Martí to Manuel Mercado, May 18, 1895, translated by the author from the Spanish as reprinted by *Granma*, accessed Apr. 2021, www.granma.cu/granmad /secciones/26-julio-2011/de-jose-marti/articulo-14.html.

15  SDB, "My Service with the Marines," undated, Box 5, Folder 1, Butler Coll., MCHD.

16  "Journal of the Marine Battalion under Lt. Col. Robert W. Huntington, Apr.–Sept. 1898," Vol. 1, RG 127, NARA.

17  Frank Keeler and Carolyn A. Tyson, *The Journal of Frank Keeler* (Quantico, VA: Marine Corps Museum, 1967), 13.

18  Hulme, *Cuba's Wild East*, 189.

19  José Sánchez Guerra and Wilfredo Campos Cremé, "Los marines yanquis en playa del este (1898)," *Santiago* 84–85 (1998): 225–248, 240.

20  Edward A. Dieckmann Sr., "All Business: The Saga of SgtMaj John Quick," *Marine Corps Gazette* 47, no. 6 (Jun. 1963): 23.

21  Tyson, *Journal of Frank Keeler*, 13.

22  Stephen Crane, *Reports of War* (Charlottesville: University of Virginia Press, 1971), and *Tales of War* (Charlottesville: University of Virginia Press, 1970), in Hulme, *Cuba's Wild East*, 192–194.

23  SDB, "My Service with the Marines," Butler Coll., MCHD.

24  Lentz-Smith, *Freedom Struggles*, 19.

25  Ferrer, *Insurgent Cuba*, 187–192; Foner, *The Spanish-Cuban-American War*, 394–395.

26  "The Future of the 71st," *New York Times*, Aug. 31, 1898.

27  SDB, "My Service with the Marines," Butler Coll., MCHD.

28  Ibid.

29  Vincent J. Cirillo, *Bullets and Bacilli: The Spanish-American War and Military Medicine* (New Brunswick, NJ: Rutgers University Press, 2004), 1, 56.

30  Thomas, *Old Gimlet Eye*, 70.

31  Ibid.

32  Pérez, *Intervention*, 5, 130–131; Simons, *Conquistador to Castro*, 219.

33  Barnet and Montejo, *Biography of a Runaway Slave*, loc. 2983.

34  "Agreement between the United States and Cuba for the Lease of Lands for Coaling and Naval Stations; February 23, 1903," Yale Law School Lillian Goldman Law Library: The Avalon Project: Documents in Law, History and Diplomacy, undated, avalon.law.yale.edu /20th_century/dip_cuba002.asp.

35  Leland L. Johnson, *U.S. Business Interests in Cuba and the Rise of Castro*, typescript, RAND Corporation, Jun. 1964, 3.

36  Nick Miroff, "Castro Town: Fidel Grew Up Here, but He Came Back to Destroy It," *Washington Post*, Dec. 3, 2016.

37  Fidel Castro Ruz, *La historia me absolverá* (Havana: Editorial de Ciencias Sociales, 2007), 13, 54.

38  Pérez, *Structure of Cuban History*, 208–209; Alan Dye and Richard Sicotte, "The U.S. Sugar Program and the Cuban Revolution," *Journal of Economic History* 64, no. 3 (2004): 673–704.

39  Anthony Boadle, "Castro: Cuba Not Cashing US Guantanamo Rent Checks," Reuters, Aug. 17, 2007, www.reuters.com/article/idUSN17200921.

40  The refineries were Texaco and Esso (Standard Oil of New Jersey). John P. Glennon, ed., *Foreign Relations of the United States, 1958–1960*, Vol. 6, *Cuba* (Washington, DC: Government Printing Office, 1991), Document 526, accessed Apr. 27, 2021, history.state.gov /historicaldocuments/frus1958-60v06/d526.

41  "Ramón López Peña," EcuRed, accessed Apr. 27, 2021, www.ecured.cu/Ram%C3%B3n _L%C3%B3pez_Pe%C3%B1a.

42  "Composite Statement: Detention in Afghanistan and Guantanamo Bay, Shafiq Rasul, Asif Iqbal, and Rhuhel Ahmed," Center for the Study of Human Rights in the Americas, University of California Davis, 2004, humanrights.ucdavis.edu/resources/library/documents -and-reports/tipton_report.pdf.

43  Human Rights Watch, "Guantánamo: America's 'Black Hole,'" *The Road to Abu Ghraib*, Jun. 2004, www.hrw.org/reports/2004/usa0604/3.htm; Carol Rosenberg, "What the C.I.A.'s Torture Program Looked Like to the Tortured," *New York Times*, Dec. 4, 2019, www.nytimes.com/2019/12/04/us/politics/cia-torture-drawings.html. For further discussion of black sites, see Ackerman, *Reign of Terror*, 39–46.

44  Karen DeYoung and Adam Goldman, "Islamic State Claims It Executed American Photojournalist James Foley," *Washington Post*, Aug. 20, 2014.

45  Polly Mosendz, "ISIS Used Guantanamo as Model, Former Hostage Says," *Newsweek*, Mar. 16, 2015; Javier Espinosa, "Javier Espinosa, #prisionero43," *El Mundo*, Mar. 15, 2015; Spencer Ackerman, "CIA Photographed Detainees Naked before Sending Them to Be Tortured," *Guardian*, Mar. 28, 2016; Mariano Castillo, "Report: ISIS Waterboarded Captives," CNN, Sep. 1, 2014, www.cnn.com/2014/08/29/world/meast/isis-waterboarding/index .html; Mark Hosenball, "Report Reveals CIA Conducted Mock Executions," *Newsweek*, Aug. 20, 2009.

46  "Composite Statement."

47  SDB to Maud Butler, Aug. 5, 1898, Butler Coll., MCHD.

48  In 1978, Castro's government renamed it Isla de la Juventud, or Island of Youth.

# THREE: LUZON, PHILIPPINES

1  Immerwahr, *How to Hide*, 52; William J. Koenig, *Epic Sea Battles* (London: Peerage Books, 1975), 114–119, archive.org/details/epicseabattles0000koen.

2  Alfred Thayer Mahan, *Letters and Papers of Alfred Thayer Mahan*, ed. Robert Seager and Doris D. Maguire (Annapolis, MD: Naval Institute Press, 1975), 566.

3  Frederick Jackson Turner, "The Significance of the Frontier in American History, July 12, 1893," in *The Frontier in American History* (New York: Henry Holt, 1921), 3; Turner and Fulmer Mood, "Frederick Jackson Turner's Address on Education in a United States without Free Lands," *Agricultural History* 23, no. 4 (Oct. 1949): 256; Grandin, *End of the Myth*, 117; Department of the Interior, Census Office, *Compendium: The Eleventh Census: 1890, Part 1: Population*, ed. Robert P. Porter (Washington, DC: Government Printing Office, 1892).

4  At least seven other uninhabited Pacific islands, including the Midway and Johnston atolls, had been claimed by the Navy decades earlier, under an 1856 law empowering U.S. citizens to claim any uninhabited island that contained guano—nitrogen-rich seabird droppings highly prized as fertilizer for American farms.

5 Linn, *Philippine War*, 19–20.

6 O. D. Corpuz, *The Roots of the Filipino Nation*, Vol. 2 (Manila: University of the Philippines Press, 2005), 320–324.

7 Sulpicio Guevara, trans., "The Act of Declaration of Philippine Independence," Filipino .biz.ph—Philippine Culture, accessed Apr. 27, 2021, filipino.biz.ph/history/declaration .html; "Acta de la proclamación de la independencia del pueblo filipino," *Philippine History Source Materials* (blog), Feb. 9, 2011, philippinehistorysourcematerials.blogspot.com/2011 /02/acta-de-la-proclamacion-de-la.html.

8 Love, *Race over Empire*, 164.

9 "Negritos" was the colonial Spanish term for the darkest-skinned native peoples of Southeast Asia. That archaic grouping included the Aeta peoples of Luzon, whose dark skin and Afro-textured hair makes some superficially resemble African peoples more than they do the islands' Malay majority. Stephen David Kantrowitz, *Ben Tillman and the Reconstruction of White Supremacy* (Chapel Hill: University of North Carolina Press, 2000); United States Congress, *Congressional Record: Proceedings and Debates of the Fifty-Fifth Congress, Second Session*, Vol. 31 (Washington, DC: U.S. Government Printing Office, 1898), 6533.

10 Albert J. Beveridge, *The Meaning of the Times, and Other Speeches* (Indianapolis: Bobbs-Merrill, 1908), 42.

11 Purdy, *After Nature*, 158–163.

12 Lentz-Smith, *Freedom Struggles*, 18; for example, "In the blood of its sons in Cuba and the Philippines the union of North and South has been cemented," in "The South in the War," *Chicago Times-Herald*, Oct. 27, 1899.

13 Downes v. Bidwell, 182 U.S. 244 (1901). The justices rooted the idea in America's first attempts at overseas expansion, as merchants snapped up uninhabited islands rich in guano—bird and bat manure once essential for farming. Congress had declared those glorified rocks a special class of territory "appertaining," or belonging to, the United States, not incorporated into it. Immerwahr, *How to Hide*, 68. See also Christina Burnett, "The Edges of Empire and the Limits of Sovereignty: American Guano Islands," *American Quarterly* 57, no. 3 (2005): 779–803.

14 Silbey, *War of Frontier and Empire*, loc. 677–688.

15 "McKinley's Benevolent Assimilation Proclamation," Filipino.biz.ph—Philippine Culture, accessed Apr. 27, 2021, www.msc.edu.ph/centennial/benevolent.html.

16 Silbey, *War of Frontier and Empire*, loc. 860–862.

17 Willard B. Gates, *"Smoked Yankees" and the Struggle for Empire: Letters from Negro Soldiers, 1898–1902* (Fayetteville: University of Arkansas Press, 1987), 279–281.

18 "Duterte's Philippines Drug War Death Toll Rises above 5,000," *Guardian*, Dec. 19, 2018.

19 Manuel Mogato and Phil Stewart, "U.S. Touts Military Ties in Philippines as Duterte Courts Russia, China," Reuters, Oct. 25, 2017; Martin Petty and Karen Lema, "Philippines' Duterte Lauds China's Help at 'Crucial Moment' in Marawi Battle," Reuters, Nov. 15, 2017; Bong S. Sarmiento, "Rubble, Unexploded Bombs, and More Than 100,000 Displaced: Marawi Two Years On," *New Humanitarian*, May 23, 2019.

20 Adrian Chen, "When a Populist Demagogue Takes Power," *New Yorker*, Nov. 21, 2016; Pia Ranada, "Duterte Curses Pope Francis over Traffic during His Visit," *Rappler*, Nov. 30, 2015, www.rappler.com/nation/elections/rodrigo-duterte-curses-pope-francis; Nestor P. Burgos Jr., "Duterte Calls Daughter Drama Queen," Inquirer.net, Apr. 20, 2016, newsinfo .inquirer.net/780443/duterte-calls-daughter-drama-queen.

21 James Griffiths, "ISIS Claims Manila Casino Attack Despite Police Denial," CNN.com, Jun. 2, 2017, www.cnn.com/2017/06/02/asia/manila-philippines-resort-world-isis/index.html.

22 "President Rodrigo Roa Duterte's Media Interview," Republic of the Philippines Presidential Communications Operations Office, Jul. 21, 2017, pcoo.gov.ph/media-interview /president-rodrigo-roa-duterte-2/.

23 Joseph D. Celeski, *Special Air Warfare and the Secret War in Laos: Air Commandos 1964–1975* (Maxwell Air Force Base, AL: Air University Press, 2019).

24 SDB to Maud Butler, Aug. 8, 1899, Butler Coll., MCHD.

25 Hoganson, *Fighting for American Manhood*, 11.

26 "Theodore Roosevelt, 'Strenuous Life' (10 April 1899)," Voices of Democracy: The U.S. Oratory Project, accessed Apr. 2021, voicesofdemocracy.umd.edu/roosevelt-strenuous-life -1899-speech-text/.

27 SDB to Maud Butler, Apr. 13, 1900, and Maud Butler to SDB, May 4, 1900, Butler Coll., MCHD.

28 Marrion Wilcox, *Harper's History of the War in the Philippines* (New York and London: Harper & Brothers, 1900), 325; United States War Department, Philippines Division, *Report of Major-General E. S. Otis, U.S. Volunteers, on Military Operations and Civil Affairs in the Philippine Islands* (Washington, DC: Government Printing Office, 1899), 17.

29 Thomas, *Old Gimlet Eye*, 34.

30 SDB, Untitled memoir of Philippine insurrection, undated, Butler Coll., MCHD.

31 Ibid.

32 United States Navy Department, *Annual Reports of the Navy Department: Report of the Secretary of the Navy. Miscellaneous Reports* (Washington, DC: Government Printing Office, 1900), 1106–1108; "The Advance from Bacoor Results in Capture of Noveleta and Cavite Viejo," *Los Angeles Herald*, Oct. 9, 1899.

33 "Americans Advance over Rough Ground, Brigade Moves from Racoor Town of Novelita," *Watchman and Southron* (Sumter, SC), Oct. 11, 1899; Newspaper clipping, "A Big Pension for a Blind Hero," in Box 1, Folder 7, Butler Coll., MCHD.

34 Schmidt, *Maverick*, 12.

35 Miguel Perez and Murray Weiss, "Iran Evacuee Tells of Evading Leftist 'Hit Team,'" *Daily News* (New York), Feb. 19, 1979; Associated Press, "Not All the Foreigners Are Leaving," *Ithaca Journal*, Feb. 20, 1979.

36 Navy Department, *Annual Reports*, 1066. Among the cases there were forty-three of gunshot wounds, twenty-five of simple continued fever, thirty-two of malarial diseases, nineteen of dysentery, two of intestinal catarrh, four of simple diarrhea, eleven of typhoid fever, six of dengue, twelve of measles, fifteen of rheumatism, five each of pneumonia and tuberculosis, three of pleurisy, four of bronchitis, eight of heart trouble, and sixty-two of venereal and genitourinary diseases. See Gregg R. Jones, *Honor in the Dust: Theodore Roosevelt, War in the Philippines, and the Rise and Fall of America's Imperial Dream* (New York: Penguin, 2013), 400n5, and Paul A. Kramer, "Colonial Crossings: Prostitution, Disease, and the Boundaries of Empire during the Philippine-American War," in *Body and Nation: The Global Realm of U.S. Body Politics in the Twentieth Century*, ed. Emily S. Rosenberg and Shanon Fitzpatrick (Durham, NC: Duke University Press, 2014).

37 Typescript of narrative essay "Salesmanship," undated, in Ben Hebard Fuller Coll., MCHD. A note attached to the essay suggests the Marine might have been Hiram Bearss.

38 SDB, untitled memoir of Philippine insurrection.

39 Typescript of short story about Littleton Waller, undated, in Ben Hebard Fuller Coll., MCHD.

40 SDB to Maud Butler, Mar. 9, 1900, and SDB to Maud Butler, Jan. 13, 1900, Butler Coll., MCHD.

41 SDB, untitled memoir of Philippine insurrection, undated, Butler Coll., MCHD.

42 Maud Butler to SDB, May 31, 1900, Butler Coll., MCHD.

43 Ibid.; "Boxers Threaten Pekin," *Philadelphia Inquirer*, May 30, 1900.

44 SDB to Maud Butler, Jan. 8, 1900, Butler Coll., MCHD.

45 José B. Capino, *Dream Factories of a Former Colony: American Fantasies, Philippine Cinema* (Minneapolis: University of Minnesota Press, 2010), 3.

46  ABS-CBN News, "'Heneral Luna' Continues Charge, Hits P160M," ABS-CBN News, Sep. 30, 2015, news.abs-cbn.com/entertainment/09/30/15/heneral-luna-continues-charge -hits-p160m.

## FOUR: NORTHERN CHINA

1  Joseph Esherick, *The Origins of the Boxer Uprising* (Berkeley: University of California Press, 1987), 177.

2  *Shandong daxue yihetuan diaocha ziliao huibian* (Shandong University Compilation of Survey Data of the Boxer Regiment) (Jinan: Shandong University Press, 2000), 2.

3  Ibid., 26.

4  Karl, *Staging the World*, 85.

5  Stephen R. Platt, *Autumn in the Heavenly Kingdom: China, the West, and the Epic Story of the Taiping Civil War* (New York: Alfred A. Knopf, 2012), xxiii.

6  Cohen, *Three Keys*, 79.

7  J. Downs, "American Merchants and the China Opium Trade, 1800–1840," *Business History Review* 42, no. 4 (Winter 1968): 418–442, doi:10.2307/3112527; Erin Blakemore, "America's First Multimillionaire Got Rich Smuggling Opium," History.com, Aug. 22, 2018, www.history.com/news/john-jacob-astor-opium-fortune-millionaire; Campbell et al., *Race, Nation, and Empire*, 107; John A. Garraty, *Henry Cabot Lodge: A Biography* (New York: Alfred A. Knopf, 1968), 204.

8  Henry Cabot Lodge, "The Philippine Islands," in *Speeches and Addresses, 1884–1909* (Boston and New York: Houghton Mifflin, 1909), 366–367.

9  Mahan, *Problem of Asia*, 16; Mahan, "Effects of Asiatic Conditions upon International Policies," *North American Review*, Nov. 1900, 616.

10  Walter LaFeber, "Lion in the Path: The U.S. Emergence as a World Power," *Political Science Quarterly* 101, no. 5 (1986): 705–718.

11  SDB to Maud Butler, Jun. 17, 1900, Butler Coll., MCHD.

12  Shubo Li, "Configuring a Threatening Other: Historical Narratives in Chinese School Textbooks," in *The Dispute over the Diaoyu/Senkaku Islands: How Media Narratives Shape Public Opinion and Challenge the Global Order*, ed. Thomas A. Hollihan (New York: Palgrave Macmillan, 2014).

13  Lindsay Maizland, "China's Modernizing Military," Council on Foreign Relations, last updated Feb. 5, 2020, www.cfr.org/backgrounder/chinas-modernizing-military.

14  Chris Buckley, "China Says It Is Building Its Second Aircraft Carrier," *New York Times*, Dec. 31, 2015.

15  Jonathan G. Panter, "Will Americans Die for Freedom of Navigation?," *Foreign Policy*, Apr. 6, 2021.

16  Austin Ramzy, "Crowds in Hong Kong Line Up to See China's First Aircraft Carrier," *New York Times*, Jul. 8, 2017.

17  Silbey, *Boxer Rebellion*, loc. 2428; Vijaya Kumar Tiwary and Vijay Kumar, "The Recruitment of the Gurkhas in the British Army, Their Role in British Empire," *Proceedings of the Indian History Congress* 70 (Indian History Congress: 2009–2010), 802–813; Geoffrey C. Gunn, "'Mort pour la France': Coercion and Co-option of 'Indochinese' Worker-Soldiers in World War," *Social Scientist* 42, no. 7/8 (Jul.–Aug. 2014): 63–84; Le Van Ho Mireille, "Le général Pennequin et le projet d'armée jaune (1911–1915)," *Revue française d'histoire d'outre mer* 75, no. 279 (1988): 145–167, doi:10.3406/ outre.1988.2658.

18  Silbey, *Boxer Rebellion*, loc. 2340.

19  SDB, "Dame Rumor—The Biggest Liar in the World," *American Magazine* 111, no. 6 (Jun. 1931): 24–26, 155–156. It is possible that Butler misremembered the timing of this incident: the annual report of the secretary of war for 1901 records a U.S. service member

committing suicide by gunshot during the China operation, but it places that event as having occurred sometime after Jul. 12.

20 Wise, *A Marine Tells It to You*, 28.

21 Cohen, *Three Keys*, 178–180.

22 SDB, typescript of unpublished memoir of Boxer Rebellion, undated, Butler Coll., MCHD; Thomas, *Old Gimlet Eye*, 47.

23 Thomas, *Old Gimlet Eye*, 48. The four enlisted Marines each received the Medal of Honor. Marine officers were not yet eligible for the award.

24 Xiang, *Origins of the Boxer War*, 301–302.

25 Larry Clinton Thompson, *William Scott Ament and the Boxer Rebellion: Heroism, Hubris and the "Ideal Missionary"* (Jefferson, NC: McFarland, 2009), 101; Robert D. Heinl Jr., "Hell in China" (Marine Corps Association, 1959).

26 "Eighth Grade First Volume, Lesson 5: The Eight-Power Allied Forces Invaded China (Including Courseware)," via Google Translate, People's Education Press, accessed Nov. 2018, www.pep.com.cn/czls/rjbczls/rjczlswd/201008/t20100826_1382755.html.

27 SDB to Maud Butler, Jul. 5, 1900, Butler Coll., MCHD.

28 Heinl, "Hell in China."

29 Herbert Hoover, *The Memoirs of Herbert Hoover: Years of Adventure, 1874–1920* (New York: Macmillan, 1951), 53.

30 SDB, untitled memoir of Philippine insurrection, undated, Butler Coll., MCHD.

31 *Annual Reports of the War Department for the Fiscal Year Ended June 30, 1901* (Washington, DC: Government Printing Office, 1901), 689.

32 Silbey, *Boxer Rebellion*, loc. 2208–2209, 2231.

33 *Papers Relating to the Foreign Relations of the United States, with the Annual Message of the President Transmitted to Congress December 3, 1900* (Washington, DC: Government Printing Office, 1902), 199; Description at 2nd Infantry Division Museum, Uijeongbu, South Korea, accessed May 2021, photo at johnsmilitaryhistory.com/2id3.html.

34 4th Battalion, 9th Infantry Regiment (Manchu), "The Liscum Bowl, an ornate piece of Manchu history, was front and center of the stage and used as part of the grog ceremony. #Manchu #KeepUptheFire #FitInspiredDisciplinedTrained #Ready," Facebook, Apr. 11, 2019, www.facebook.com/ManchuBattalion/posts/2497765740274485.

35 Cohen, *Three Keys*, 123, 174.

36 Paul A. Cohen, *History and Popular Memory* (New York: Columbia University Press, 2014), xiii–xiv.

37 SDB to Maud Butler, Jul. 23, 1900, Butler Coll., MCHD.

38 "All Foreigners in Peking Dead," *New York Times*, Jul. 5, 1900, 3; Michael Brooke, "Attack on a China Mission (1900)," Screenonline, accessed May 2021, www.screenonline.org.uk/film/id/520615/; HuntleyFilmArchives, Dramatic Fake Footage of Boxer Rebellion 'Mission', 1900s - Film 1011080," YouTube, Jul. 2, 2021, www.youtube.com/watch?v=2SjRXaPv-zo, accessed Aug. 2021.

39 SDB to Maud Butler, Aug. 4, 1900, Butler Coll., MCHD.

40 Thomas, *Old Gimlet Eye*, 69.

41 Ibid., 72.

42 Ibid.

43 French, *Everything under the Heavens*, 59.

44 Andrew Jacobs and Jane Perlez, "U.S. Wary of Its New Neighbor in Djibouti: A Chinese Naval Base," *New York Times*, Feb. 25, 2017.

45 SDB, unpublished memoir of Boxer Rebellion; SDB to Maud Butler, Aug. 19, 1900, Butler Coll., MCHD.

46 Silbey, *Boxer Rebellion*, loc. 2877–2878.

47 SDB, unpublished memoir of Boxer Rebellion.

48 Ibid.

49 *Annual Reports of the War Department for the Fiscal Year Ended June 30, 1901*, Part 4 (Washington, DC: Government Printing Office, 1901), 447.

50 Report of Capt. William W. Forsyth, *Annual Reports of the War Department for the Fiscal Year Ended June 30, 1900* (Washington, DC: Government Printing Office, 1900), 139.

51 Mark Twain, "To the Person Sitting in Darkness," *North American Review* 172, no. 531 (1901): 161–176.

52 Jim Zwick, "'Prodigally Endowed with Sympathy for the Cause': Mark Twain's Involvement with the Anti-Imperialist League," *Mark Twain Journal* 32, no. 1 (Spring 1994): 2–25.

53 SDB, unpublished memoir of Boxer Rebellion.

54 Fuller, typescript of "Butler's Bawl," undated, Benjamin Hebard Fuller Coll., MCHD.

55 SDB, unpublished memoir of Boxer Rebellion; Schmidt in *Maverick*, citing Ethel (Snooks) Butler Wehle, Smedley D. Butler Jr., and Thomas R. Butler interview with author, Mar. 1976; Thomas R. Butler to Schmidt, Jun. 28, 1977.

56 Thomas S. Butler to Littleton Waller, Aug. 15, 1900, Waller Correspondence File, MCHD; "Capt. Butler's Mother Tells of When He Was a Baby," *Daily Local News* (West Chester, PA), Aug. 27, 1900, Newspaper Clippings File, Chester Co. HS; "Mrs. Butler Makes a Statement," *Daily Local News* (West Chester, PA), Aug. 28, 1900, Newspaper Clippings File, Chester Co. HS.

57 Michelle Delaney, *Art and Advertising in Buffalo Bill's Wild West* (Norman: University of Oklahoma Press, 2019), 160, Fig. 6.16. Thanks to Jeffrey Wasserstrom for telling me about that staging of the Wild West Show.

58 "A Young Hero of Three Wars," *Republican and Herald* (Pottsville, PA), Jan. 18, 1901.

59 "Final Protocol between the Powers and China, Signed September 7, 1901," *American Journal of International Law* 1, no. 4, Supplement: Official Documents (Oct. 1907): 388–396; Bruce Elleman, *Diplomacy and Deception: Secret History of Sino-Soviet Diplomatic Relations, 1917–1927* (Oxfordshire, UK: Routledge, 1997), 144; Frank H. H. King, "The Boxer Indemnity: 'Nothing but Bad,'" *Modern Asian Studies* 40, no. 3 (Jul. 2006): 663–689.

60 Pomfret, *Beautiful Country*, 116; Paul A. Varg, "The Myth of the China Market, 1890–1914," *American Historical Review* 73, no. 3 (Feb. 1968): 742–758; Theodore Roosevelt, "Address at Mechanics' Pavilion in San Francisco, California," May 13, 1903, American Presidency Project, www.presidency.ucsb.edu/documents/address-mechanics-pavilion-san-francisco-california.

61 "Wang Zhiyuan, 83, Xinnan Village in Renli Commune, Qihe County, December 28, 1965," *Shandong University Compilation of Boxer Survey Data* (Jinan: Shandong University Press, 2000), 751. Translated by Marc Opper.

62 Karl, *Staging the World*, 55, 85.

63 Harold Z. Schiffrin, *Sun Yat-sen and the Origins of the Chinese Revolution* (Berkeley: University of California Press, 2010, reprint edition, orig. pub. 1968), 286.

## FIVE: SAMAR, PHILIPPINES

1 Brian Linn, "We Will Go Heavily Armed: The Marines Small War on Samar, 1901–1902," in Evans, *U.S. Marines and Irregular Warfare, 1898–2007*, 41–53.

2 Kramer, *Blood of Government*, 120. A Google Books Ngram search shows that "boondocks" entered English during the years of the Philippine War, spreading through the armed services. ("We can boast of the best field in the boondocks of Nicaragua," a Marine wrote in a 1930 edition of *Leatherneck* magazine.) It entered wide usage during World War II.

3 United States War Department, *Annual Reports of the War Department*, Vol. 1, Part 7 (Washington, DC: U.S. Government Printing Office, 1900), 15; cited in Linn, *The U.S. Army and Counterinsurgency in the Philippine War*, 98.

4 Linn, *Philippine War*, 176.

5 Ibid.

6  Ibid.

7  Allan R. Millett, Peter Maslowski, and William B. Feis, *For the Common Defense: A Military History of the United States from 1607 to 2012*, 3rd ed. (New York: Free Press, 2012), 307; Thomas Bruno, "Ending an Insurgency Violently: The Samar and Batangas Punitive Campaigns," Strategy Research Paper (Carlisle Barracks, PA: U.S. Army War College, Mar. 1, 2010), 4.

8  Miller, *Benevolent Assimilation*, 134.

9  Bruno, "Ending an Insurgency Violently," 78.

10  Michael V. Bhatia, "Fighting Words: Naming Terrorists, Bandits, Rebels and Other Violent Actors," *Third World Quarterly* 26, no. 1 (2005): 5–22.

11  Letter from Everett C. Bumpus to father, Sep. 6, 1901, republished in Bumpus, *In Memoriam* (Norwood, MA: Norwood Press, 1902), 82–83; Couttie, *Hang the Dogs*, loc. 3187.

12  Testimony of William J. Gibbs, *Affairs in the Philippine Islands, Hearings before the Committee on the Philippines of the United States Senate*, 57th Congress (1902), 2285.

13  Rolando Borrinaga, "The Balangiga Incident: Overview and Update on the Campaign for the Return of the Bells of Balangiga," conference paper presented Sep. 2005; Mark Oswald, "The 'Howling Wilderness' Court-Martial of 1902," Strategy Research Paper (Carlisle Barracks, PA: U.S. Army War College, Mar. 25, 2001); Stephen Bonsal, *Collier's Weekly*, "The War in Samar," *Evening Star* (Washington, DC), May 3, 1902, 10.

14  Filipinos sometimes remember her as Geronima Nacionales, which Couttie says was possibly an alias used in the operation. Couttie, *Hang the Dogs*, loc. 2873.

15  James Arnold, ed., *Americans at War: Eyewitness Accounts from the American Revolution to the 21st Century* (Santa Barbara, CA: ABC-CLIO, 2018), 488.

16  "Forty-Six Heroes Shot by Rebels," *Pittsburgh Press*, Sep. 30, 1901; "Capt. Connell Killed," *Meriden* (CT) *Daily Journal*, Sep. 30, 1901, 1; "Massacre in Samar," *Scranton* (PA) *Republican*, Oct. 1, 1901, 1; "Fully Warned: Americans at Balangiga Knew Attack Was Planned," *Nashville American*, Oct. 7, 1901, 1; "Insurrection Rages in Samar," *Leavenworth* (KS) *Times*, Dec. 18, 1901, 5.

17  In a conversation with fellow anarchist Emil Schilling, Czolgosz lamented that the war in the Philippines "does not harmonize with the teaching in our public schools about our flag." Couttie, *Hang the Dogs*, loc. 2997; Walter Channing, "The Mental Status of Czolgosz, the Assassin of President McKinley," *Journal of Insanity* 59, no. 2 (1902): 223–278.

18  Correspondence from Theodore Roosevelt to Cary Sanger, Oct. 1, 1901, Theodore Roosevelt Papers: Series 2: Letterpress Copybooks, 1897–1916; Vol. 31, 1901, Sep. 20–Nov. 1.

19  Letter from William Cary Sanger to Theodore Roosevelt, Theodore Roosevelt Papers, Library of Congress Manuscript Division, Theodore Roosevelt Digital Library, Dickinson State University, www.theodorerooseveltcenter.org/Research/Digital-Library/Record?libID=o35064.

20  *Affairs in the Philippine Islands, Hearings before the Committee on the Philippines of the United States Senate*, 57th Congress (1902), 1592 (Correspondence between General Chaffee and the War Department); *Affairs in the Philippine Islands. Hearings before the Committee on the Philippines of the United States Senate*, SD 331, 57th Cong., 1st sess.

21  Oswald, "'Howling Wilderness' Court-Martial," 6–7; Linn, "We Will Go Heavily Armed," 44.

22  Among other things, Smith had participated in the ethnic cleansing of Utes from the new state of Colorado in 1880. See Congressional Record, 57th Congress (1902), 5301 (Senator Joseph B. Foraker).

23  Linn, "We Will Go Heavily Armed," 41, 51.

24  Oswald, "'Howling Wilderness' Court-Martial," 8.

25  Littleton Waller, typescript of report on Samar operations, 6 (Oct. 23, 1901), Waller Coll., MCHD.

26  Littleton Waller, typescript of report on Samar operations; "A Howling Wilderness? The

Samar Campaign 1901–1902, as Recorded in the Military Papers of Major Littleton L. T. Waller, U.S.M.C.," *Bulletin of the American Historical Collection* (Manila, Philippines) 29, no. 4 (Oct.–Dec. 2001): 117; Oswald, "'Howling Wilderness' Court-Martial," 8; Harold Kinman to sister, Dec. 23, 1901, in Harold Kinman Papers at MCHD, cited in Linn, "We Will Go Heavily Armed."

27  "Howling Wilderness?," *Bulletin of the American Historical Collection*, 20.

28  Waller, typescript of report on Samar operations, 44–46; Linn, "We Will Go Heavily Armed."

29  Waller, typescript, 50-51.

30  Oswald, "'Howling Wilderness' Court-Martial," 10; Linn, "We Will Go Heavily Armed," 47.

31  ". . . He Served on Samar," *Leatherneck* 31, no. 10 (Oct. 1948).

32  Paterno R. Esmaquel II, "Give Us Back Balangiga Bells, Duterte Tells U.S.," Rappler.com, Jul. 24, 2017, www.rappler.com/nation/sona-2017-philippines-duterte-us-balangiga-bells.

33  Richard Sisk, "Mattis OKs Returning War Trophy 'Balangiga Bells' to Philippines," Military.com, Aug. 13, 2018, www.military.com/dodbuzz/2018/08/13/mattis-oks-returning-war-trophy-balangiga-bells-philippines.html; Joel Funk, "Cheney, Enzi, Barrasso Oppose Return of Bells of Balangiga to Philippines," *Wyoming Tribune Eagle*, Nov. 19, 2017; "Bipartisan Co-Chairs Urge Trump Administration Not to Return Historic Bells to Philippines Due to Human Rights Concerns," Human Rights Commission, U.S. Congress, Jan. 5, 2018.

34  Sec. James Mattis, "Ceremonial Address Marking the Return of the Bells of Balangiga to the Philippines," Nov. 14, 2018, www.americanrhetoric.com/speeches/jamesmattisbellsof balangigareturn.htm.

35  Andrea Pitzer, *One Long Night: A Global History of Concentration Camps* (New York: Little, Brown, 2017), 46–47.

36  SDB to Thomas S. Butler, Mar. 12, 1902, Butler Coll., MCHD.

37  Littleton Waller to Robert John Wynne, Feb. 4, 1902, Theodore Roosevelt Digital Library, Dickinson State University; "Hell Is a Winter Resort Compared with Samar," *Springfield* (MO) *Republican*, Jun. 14, 1902, 1.

38  Theodore Roosevelt, "At Arlington, Memorial Day, May 30, 1902," in *A Compilation of the Messages and Speeches of Theodore Roosevelt, 1901–1905*, Vol. 1, ed. Alfred Henry Lewis (New York: Bureau of National Literature and Art, 1906), 30.

39  Glenn A. May, "Why the United States Won the Philippine-American War, 1899–1902," *Pacific Historical Review* 52, no. 4 (Nov. 1983); John M. Gates, "War-Related Deaths in the Philippines, 1898–1902," *Pacific Historical Review* 53, no. 3 (Aug. 1984); "The Philippine-American War, 1899–1902," Office of the Historian, U.S. State Department, accessed May 2021, history.state.gov/milestones/1899-1913/war. Historian Ken De Bevoise estimates excess mortality in the Philippines due to the American War, including disease, reached 775,000. See his book *Agents of Apocalypse: Epidemic Disease in the Colonial Philippines* (Princeton, NJ: Princeton University Press, 1995), 26.

## SIX: THE ISTHMUS

1  SDB to Maud Butler, Dec. 14, 1902, Butler Coll., MCHD. Other sources for this section include Thomas, *Old Gimlet Eye*, 94–100, and SDB, typescript of unpublished autobiography, Box 74, Folder 25, Butler Coll., MCHD.

2  Robert Seager, *Alfred Thayer Mahan: The Man and His Letters* (Annapolis, MD: Naval Institute Press, 1977), 2; Suzanne Geissler, *God and Sea Power: The Influence of Religion on Alfred Thayer Mahan* (Annapolis, MD: Naval Institute Press, 2015), 11; Ann Haddad, "Ladies of Refinement: The Women Who Educated the Tredwell Daughters," Sep. 27, 2018, Merchant's House Museum; Donald Lankiewicz, "Alfred Thayer Mahan and His Vain Quest to Keep Ships Straight," *Navy Times*, Oct. 14, 2019, www.navytimes.com/news /your-navy/2019/10/14/alfred-thayer-mahan-and-his-vain-quest-to-keep-ships-straight/.

3   Mahan, *Influence of Sea Power upon History*, 25; Rear Admiral Montgomery Sicard, President, Naval War Board, to Secretary of the Navy John D. Long, Aug. 30, 1898, Naval War Board, Naval History and Heritage Command, U.S. Navy, www.history.navy.mil.

4   McCullough, *Path between the Seas*, 35.

5   De Lesseps and his son were convicted of fraud for concealing their bankruptcy. They also had bribed the French parliament, members of the press, and other high officials to continue extending shaky loans, turning, as Hannah Arendt summarized, "a more or less sound private business into a colossal racket." Arendt, "From the Dreyfus Affair to France Today," *Jewish Social Studies* 4, no. 3 (Jul. 1942); McCullough, *Path between the Seas*, 226.

6   "A Letter to Mahan," Theodore Roosevelt: Obstacles to Immediate Expansion, 1897, Papers of Theodore Roosevelt, Manuscript Division, Library of Congress, 225–231, www.mtholyoke.edu/acad/intrel/trmahan.htm.

7   Much was written during the period about a $60,000 donation that Bunau-Varilla said Cromwell had made during the 1900 presidential campaign—further billed, according to McCullough, as an expense to the New Panama Canal Company of France. Miner, McCullough, and others who have examined the evidence argue that this alone would not have been enough to sway Hanna. Regardless, the financial and operational alliance continued between Cromwell and the Republican Party for years. See, for example, Robert E. Mutch, *Buying the Vote: A History of Campaign Finance Reform* (New York: Oxford University Press, 2014), 69; "'Intimate' friend" is from McCullough, *Path between the Seas*, 273.

8   $40 million in 1902 was worth $1.2 billion in 2020. Charles D. Ameringer, "The Panama Canal Lobby of Philippe Bunau-Varilla and William Nelson Cromwell," *American Historical Review* 68, no. 2 (Jan. 1963): 346–363.

9   *The Story of Panama: Hearings on the Rainey Resolution before the Committee on Foreign Affairs of the House of Representatives*, Jan. and Feb. 1912 (Washington, DC: Government Printing Office, 1912), 95.

10   Thomas S. Butler to SDB, Typescript of letter marked "Confidential," Dec. 17, 1902, Butler Coll., MCHD.

11   John Soluri, *Banana Cultures: Agriculture, Consumption, and Environmental Change in Honduras and the United States* (Austin: University of Texas Press, 2005), 20; Dan Koeppel, *Banana: The Fate of the Fruit That Changed the World* (New York: Penguin, 2008), 68.

12   Barahona, *Honduras en el siglo XX*, 52; Karnes, *Tropical Enterprise*, 18.

13   Karnes, *Tropical Enterprise*, 23.

14   SDB to Maud Butler, Mar. 20, 1903, Butler Coll., MCHD.

15   SDB to Maud Butler, Mar. 26, 1903, Butler Coll., MCHD.

16   SDB to Maud Butler, Apr. 14, 1903, Butler Coll., MCHD.

17   "Mr. Combs to Mr. Hay," *Papers Relating to the Foreign Relations of the United States, with the Annual Message of the President Transmitted to Congress December 7, 1903* (Office of the Historian, U.S. Department of State), Guatemala, Document 555.

18   O. Henry, *Cabbages and Kings* (New York: Doubleday, Page, 1904), 132.

19   In 1907, 1911, 1912, 1919, 1924, and 1925. Congressional Research Service, "Instances of Use of United States Armed Forces Abroad, 1798–2020," R42738, updated Jul. 20, 2020, fas.org/sgp/crs/natsec/R42738.pdf; "Honduras (1902–Present)," Political Science, University of Central Arkansas, accessed Apr. 2021, uca.edu/politicalscience/dadm-project/western-hemisphere-region/honduras-1902-present/.

20   Rich Cohen, *The Fish That Ate the Whale: The Life and Times of America's Banana King* (New York: Farrar, Straus and Giroux, 2012), 84–96.

21   Colby, *Business of Empire*, 203–205; Ana Cerdas Albertazzi, "El surgimiento del enclave bananero en el Pacífico Sur," *Revista de Historia* 28 (Jul. 1993): 117–159; Geoffrey Jones and Marcelo Bucheli, "The Octopus and the Generals: The United Fruit Company in Guatemala," Harvard Business School Case 805–146, May 2005; Stephen Kinzer, *The*

*Brothers: John Foster Dulles, Allen Dulles, and Their Secret World War* (New York: Times Books, 2013), 40.

22 Jeff Ernst, "Honduran President Planned to Shove Drugs 'Right up the Noses of the "Gringos,"' According to Witness in New York Drug Case," Univision News, Jan. 9, 2021.

23 For example, Newt Gingrich, interview with Laura Ingraham, transcript in "Gingrich: Caravan Is an Act of Attacking US Sovereignty," Fox News, updated Oct. 22, 2018, www .foxnews.com/transcript/gingrich-caravan-is-an-act-of-attacking-us-sovereignty.

24 Meaning "ape-like." Joseph Bucklin Bishop, *Theodore Roosevelt and His Time Shown in His Own Letters*, Vol. 1 (New York: Charles Scribner's Sons, 1920), 332.

25 "Cullom Talks Boldly," *Baltimore Sun*, Aug. 15, 1903.

26 *Story of Panama: Hearings*, 296–297.

27 See, for example, "Congo Carnival," Picturing Portobelo: A Project of Digital Portobelo, accessed Apr. 2021, PicturingPortobelo.com.

28 Panamanian writers often cite the 1930s American historian William D. McCain's identification of him as "Wong Kong Yee" of "Hong Sang, China" (in *The United States and the Republic of Panama*, Duke University Press, 1937, 16), but I could find no place in China with that name. Other sources in this paragraph: Daugherty, *Counterinsurgency and the United States Marine Corps*, Vol. 1, 33; McCullough, *Path between the Seas*, 368–370; *Story of Panama*, 675; "Mr. Ehrman to Mr. Loomis," Nov. 9, 1903, *Papers Relating to the Foreign Relations of the United States, with the Annual Message of the President Transmitted to Congress December 7, 1903*, Office of the Historian, U.S. Department of State, Colombia, Document 309.

29 *Story of Panama: Hearings*, 387; McCullough, *Path between the Seas*, 376; "Convention for the Construction of a Ship Canal (Hay-Bunau-Varilla Treaty), November 18, 1903," Article III, Avalon Project at the Yale Law School, accessed May 2021, avalon.law.yale .edu/20thcentury/pan001.asp.

30 Gerard Helferich, *An Unlikely Trust: Theodore Roosevelt, J. P. Morgan, and the Improbable Partnership That Remade American Business* (Guilford, CT: Lyons Press, 2018), 122.

31 "Stolen Property," *New York Times*, Dec. 20, 1903, 8; Major, *Prize Possession*, 57.

32 Elihu Root, *The Ethics of the Panama Question: Address by Elihu Root before the Union League Club of Chicago, February 22, 1904* (New York: Burgoyne, Walker, and Centre Sts., 1904); "The Panama Revolution," *Duluth* (MN) *Herald*, Jul. 9, 1914, 8.

33 SDB to Maud Butler, Nov. 20, 1903, and SDB to Maud Butler, Dec. 10, 1903, Butler Coll., MCHD.

34 Lasso, *Erased*, loc. 65.

35 SDB to Maud Butler, Feb. 8, 1904, Butler Coll., MCHD.

36 SDB to Maud Butler, Feb. 16, 1904, in Venzon, *Letters*, 44.

37 Amos E. Clarke, in *Letters from Isthmian Canal Construction Workers*, 1963, MAAP.

## SEVEN: SUBIC BAY, PHILIPPINES

1 Richard Peters had moved to the dusty railroad terminus of Marthasville, Georgia, in the 1840s to oversee the new Georgia railroad. In 1845, Peters decided the town needed a more impressive name; he and his colleague J. Edgar Thompson settled on Atlanta—a riff on the name of the Western and Atlantic Railroad, which ended there. During the Civil War, he made a fortune operating ships that violated the Union blockade. His son, Ethel's father—also named Richard Peters—after being educated at a boarding school in England, moved back to Philadelphia, where he married Ethel's mother and managed an ironworks and streetcar line. "Obituaries," *Iron Trade Review* 68 (Jan. 1–Jun. 30, 1921): 1541; Franklin M. Garrett, *Atlanta and Environs: A Chronicle of Its People and Events, 1820s–1870s* (Athens: University of Georgia Press, 2011), 225; Sara Logue, "Discovering Atlanta: What's in a Name?," Emory Libraries Blog, Emory University, scholarblogs.emory.edu/woodruff/news /discovering-atlanta-whats-in-a-name; John Woolf Jordan, *Colonial Families of Philadelphia*

(New York: Lewis, 1911), 1114; on Ethel's great-great-grandfather (*also* named Richard Peters): "Peters, Richard," Judges, History of the Federal Judiciary, Federal Judicial Center, accessed Apr. 2021, www.fjc.gov/history/judges/peters-richard.

2  "From Brooke Hall to Cuban Palace," *Evening Bulletin* (Philadelphia, PA), dated Apr. 7, 1899, publication date unclear, newspaper clipping in letter from Harriet Parker Felton Peters to Ethel Conway Peters and Edith Macausland Peters, Apr. 25, 1899, Stanford Lib.

3  SDB to Ethel Conway Peters, Sep. 26, 1904, private collection of Philippa Wehle.

4  Interview with Molly Butler Swanton, Jun. 2021.

5  "Capt. Butler Takes a Bride To-Morrow," *Philadelphia Inquirer*, Jun. 29, 1905; "A Week's Society News," *Philadelphia Inquirer*, Jul. 2, 1905; "Capt. Butler to Wed," *York* (PA) *Daily*, Jun. 29, 1905; "Butler–Peters," *New York Times*, Jul. 1, 1905.

6  "Ideal American Soldier Surrenders to Cupid," *Courier-Journal* (Louisville, KY), May 28, 1905; on Roosevelt as one of Butler's "most ardent admirers": "Wedding of a Pennsylvania Soldier," *Pittsburgh Post*, May 28, 1905, 3; "Uncle Sam's Youngest War Captain, Whom Bullets Couldn't Kill, Now Pierced Through and Through by Love's Little Dart," *San Francisco Examiner*, Feb. 26, 1905.

7  About Suez, Smedley wrote his father: "This canal, about which the British bray so much, is nothing more than one of President Roosevelt's irrigation ditches and not worthy to be compared, in any way, to our Panama undertaking." SDB to Thomas S. Butler, Sep. 22, 1905, in Venzon, *Letters*, 49.

8  Gordon had changed his name from Jacob Cohen. "Cohen, Jacob G. alias John J. Gordon," "United States General Index to Pension Files, 1861–1934," database with images, FamilySearch.org, Coggins, Antony-Cole, Robert H. > image 442 of 4373; citing NARA microfilm publication T288, NARA. On Olongapo: Gerald R. Anderson, *Subic Bay: From Magellan to Pinatubo*, 4th ed. (self-pub., CreateSpace, 2009), 55, 62, 196, 268.

9  *Annual Report of the Navy Department for the Year 1900: Report of the Secretary of the Navy* (Washington, DC: Government Printing Office, 1900), 643.

10  SDB to Thomas S. Butler, Oct. 5, 1906, Butler Coll., MCHD.

11  SDB to Thomas S. and Maud Butler, Dec. 30, 1906, Butler Coll., MCHD.

12  Thomas, *Old Gimlet Eye*, 117–118.

13  Letter from SDB to unnamed superior, Nov. 21, 1906, Butler Coll., MCHD, in Strecker, *Biography*.

14  Ethel Butler to Richard Peters (father) and Mary Jane Peters (grandmother), Butler Coll., MCHD.

15  Ibid.

16  Asada, *Mahan to Pearl Harbor*, 16–26.

17  David Brudnoy, "Race and the San Francisco School Board Incident: Contemporary Evaluations," *California Historical Quarterly* 50, no. 3 (Sep. 1971): 295–312; William R. Braisted, "The United States Navy's Dilemma in the Pacific, 1906–1909," *Pacific Historical Review* 26, no. 3 (1957): 235–244; "Japanese-American Relations at the Turn of the Century, 1900–1922," Milestones in the History of U.S. Foreign Relations, Office of the Historian, U.S. Department of State, accessed Apr. 2021, history.state.gov/milestones/1899-1913/japanese-relations.

18  As with anti-Black racism in the U.S. South, the anti-Asian racism in the western United States had a strong psychosexual bent, claiming as its inspiration an impetus to protect the rights of white women. The Asiatic Exclusion League, a white labor group founded by Irish and Norwegian immigrants, argued: "The white taxpayer—millionaire, merchant, or mechanic—does not wish his daughter to associate with Asiatics who regard the status of women as a low one, or with Japanese who believe marriage may be contracted by an

exchange of photographs." It regarded as "a very grave danger" the "enforced association of American girls with males of Asiatic birth and training." Asiatic Exclusion League, *Proceedings of the Asiatic Exclusion League, San Francisco, January 1908* (San Francisco: Organized Labor, 1908), 10.

19 Edward S. Miller, *War Plan Orange: The U.S. Strategy to Defeat Japan, 1897–1945* (Annapolis, MD: Naval Institute Press, 1991).

20 Daugherty, *Pioneers of Amphibious Warfare*, 100–101.

21 Thomas, *Old Gimlet Eye*, 118.

22 Ibid., 119.

23 P. M. Rixey, Surgeon General, U.S. Navy, "Medical Record of Captain Smedley D. Butler, U.S. Marine Corps, Since March 28, 1901," Oct. 10, 1908, RG 125 Records of the Office of the Judge Advocate General, Box 151: Proceedings of Naval and Marine Examining Boards, NARA; Hospital ticket for SDB, Naval Station, Canacao, P.I. (signed by F. S. Nash, Surgeon, U.S.N.), Jun. 19, 1907, RG 125 Records of the Office of the Judge Advocate General, Box 151: Proceedings of Naval and Marine Examining Boards, NARA.

24 "Politics, Pinatubo and the Pentagon: The Closure of Subic Bay," Oral History, Association for Diplomatic Studies and Training, updated May 31, 2016, adst.org/2016/05/politics -pinatubo-pentagon-closure-subic-bay-philippines/.

25 Seth Robson, "Duterte's Deadly Drug War Reaches Former US Bases in the Philippines," *Stars and Stripes*, Oct. 15, 2016.

26 Millett, *Semper Fidelis*, 270–275.

27 United Press, "Gen. Butler Sees Japan Controlling Philippines," *Lancaster* (PA) *New Era*, Jan. 19, 1933, 7.

28 Brian McAllister Linn, *Guardians of Empire: The U.S. Army and the Pacific, 1902–1940* (Chapel Hill: University of North Carolina Press, 1999), 85–87; Millett, *Semper Fidelis*, 270.

## EIGHT: NICARAGUA

1 Benjamin Harrison, "The United States and the 1909 Nicaragua Revolution," *Caribbean Quarterly* 41, no. 3/4 (Sep.–Dec. 1995): 45–63; Michael Gismondi and Jeremy Mouat, "Merchants, Mining and Concessions on Nicaragua's Mosquito Coast: Reassessing the American Presence, 1893–1912," *Journal of Latin American Studies* 34, no. 4 (Nov. 2002): 845–879; John E. Findling, "The United States and Zelaya: A Study in the Diplomacy of Expediency," PhD diss., University of Texas at Austin, 1971.

2 Theodore Roosevelt, *Presidential Addresses and State Papers*, Homeward Bound ed., 8 vols. (New York: Review of Reviews Company, 1910), Vol. 3, 176–177.

3 Serge Ricard, "The Roosevelt Corollary," *Presidential Studies Quarterly* 36, no. 1, Presidential Doctrines (Mar. 2006): 17–26; Walter LaFeber, "The Evolution of the Monroe Doctrine from Monroe to Reagan," in *Redefining the Past: Essays in Diplomatic History in Honor of William Appleman Williams*, ed. Lloyd C. Gardner (Corvallis: Oregon State University Press, 1986), 139–140.

4 Thomas Schoonover, "Max Farrand's Memorandum on the U.S. Role in the Panamanian Revolution of 1903," *Diplomatic History* 12, no. 4 (1988): 501–506.

5 Gismondi and Mouat, "Merchants, Mining and Concessions," 864.

6 Harrison, "The United States and the 1909 Nicaragua Revolution," 55; Gismondi and Mouat, "Merchants, Mining and Concessions," 873.

7 "The Secretary of State to the Nicaraguan Chargé," Dec. 1, 1909, *Papers Relating to the Foreign Relations of the United States with the Annual Message of the President Transmitted to Congress December 7, 1909*, Office of the Historian, U.S. State Department.

8 Typescript of medical report on SDB from John S. Spear, Medical Director, U.S. Navy (ret.), Jan. 6, 1908, RG 125 Records of the Office of the Judge Advocate General, Box 151: Proceedings of Naval and Marine Examining Boards, NARA.

9   Jim Jones, *Made in West Chester: The History of Industry in West Chester, Pennsylvania, 1867 to 1945* (West Chester, PA: Taggart), 33; Venzon, *Letters*, note, 62–63.

10  Thomas, *Old Gimlet Eye*, 121.

11  Ibid., 123.

12  SDB to Maud and Samuel Butler, Oct. 24, 1908, Butler Coll., MCHD.

13  For example, Statement of Brig. Gen. George F. Elliott, Commandant, Feb. 13, 1908, *Hearings before the Committee on Naval Affairs of the House of Representatives* (Washington, DC: U.S. Government Printing Office, 1908), 578–594.

14  SDB to Ethel Butler, Jan., 15, 1910, Butler Coll., MCHD; SDB to Ethel Butler and children, Jan. 22, 1910, Butler Coll., MCHD.

15  SDB to Ethel Butler, Feb. 7, 1910, Butler Coll., MCHD.

16  Likely the ailing Daniel Lacayo Bermúdez, whose then-seventeen-year-old son would serve decades later as a puppet president under the Somoza dictatorship. See: "Daniel Lacayo Bermúdez (1864–1912)," Historical Person Search, Ancestry.com, accessed May 2021, www.ancestry.com/genealogy/records/daniel-lacayo-bermudez-24-t0w0ld.

17  SDB to Ethel Butler, Feb. 7, 1910, Butler Coll., MCHD.

18  SDB to Maud and Thomas S. Butler, Mar. 1, 1910, in Venzon, *Letters*, 75–78.

19  Challener, *Admirals, Generals,* 301.

20  SDB to Maud and Thomas S. Butler, Mar. 1, 1910, in Venzon, *Letters*, 75–78.

21  Laura Blume, "A Tale of Two Dictatorships/Un cuento de dos dictaduras," *North American Congress on Latin America (NACLA)*, Aug. 15, 2018; "Nicaragua, más de 400 muertos en cien días," *La Estrella de Panamá*, Jul. 28, 2018.

22  Carl David Goette-Luciak, "How a Journalist's Death Live on Air Became a Symbol of Nicaragua's Crisis," *Guardian*, May 29, 2018.

23  Juan Carlos Bow, "Brutal represión policial deja 164 detenidos," *Confidencial* (Managua), Mar. 17, 2019, confidencial.com.ni/nacion/brutal-represion-policial-deja-164-detenidos/.

24  Jenny Murray, dir. *¡Las Sandinistas!* Los Angeles: MCRM Productions, 2018; Eduardo Galeano immortalized Baltodano's victory in a poem titled *Las comandantes*.

25  "Ortega y sus serviles traicionaron la revolución para construir una nueva dictadura: Mónica Baltodano, comandante sandinista," *Desinformémonos*, Jul. 20, 2018, desinformemonos.org/ortega-serviles-traicionaron-la-revolucion-construir-una-nueva-dictadura-monica-baltodano-comandante-sandinista/.

26  Augusto Sandino, "Manifesto," Jul. 1, 1927, www.latinamericanstudies.org/sandino/sandino7-1-27.htm.

27  The last U.S. president to deal with Somozas, Jimmy Carter, had the most complex relationship. In keeping with his policy of rhetorical support for human rights, Carter criticized Somoza publicly. But he did not fully terminate military aid for the Guardia Nacional or suspend economic aid until the last months of the Somozas' rule in Jan. 1979, while at the same time actively trying to prevent a Sandinista victory. Martha L. Cottam, "The Carter Administration's Policy toward Nicaragua: Images, Goals, and Tactics," *Political Science Quarterly* 107, no. 1 (Spring 1992): 123–146.

28  One of the most famous apocryphal quotes in U.S. foreign policy, its origins likely date to an unsourced anecdote in a 1948 *Time* magazine story. In a section of the article recounting a 1939 visit by Somoza García to Washington, the author wrote: "To prime President Roosevelt for the visit, [foreign policy adviser] Sumner Welles sent him a long solemn memorandum about Somoza and Nicaragua. According to a story told around Washington, Roosevelt read the memo right through, wisecracked: 'As a Nicaraguan might say, he's a sonofabitch but he's ours.'" FDR was unable to confirm or deny the story, as he had died three years before. There are examples of similar formulations being used by earlier American politicians, which may have inspired FDR's remark, or alternately the quotation

might have been misattributed to him. It is also sometimes said to have referred to other Latin American dictators, such as the Dominican Republic's Rafael Trujillo. Baltodano's version—"*es un hijo de puta pero es nuestro hijo de puta*"—is roughly the most commonly used version of the saying, usually by critics of U.S. foreign policy. See "Nicaragua: I'm the Champ," *Time*, Nov. 15, 1948.

29 "154. Editorial Note," Foreign Relations of the United States, 1950–1955, The Intelligence Community, 1950–1955, Office of the Historian, U.S. State Department.

30 In Honduras, Guatemala, Mexico, Costa Rica, and Venezuela. Baltodano, "De Raudales a la fundación del Frente: Bayardo Altamirano," in *Memorias de la lucha sandinista*, Vol. 1, *De la forja de la Vanguardia a la Montaña*, at memoriasdelaluchasandinista.org, accessed Sep. 2021.

31 Steven Palmer, "Carlos Fonseca and the Construction of Sandinismo in Nicaragua," *Latin American Research Review* 23, no. 1 (1988): 93.

32 Margaret Randall, "The Story of Monica Baltodano and Zulema," *Black Scholar* 14, no. 2, "Nicaragua" (Mar./Apr. 1983): 48–57.

33 Rosenberg, *Financial Missionaries*, 48; Gary Dean Best, "Financing a Foreign War: Jacob H. Schiff and Japan, 1904–05," *American Jewish Historical Quarterly*, Jun. 1, 1972.

34 Rosenberg, *Financial Missionaries*, 41–47; Hudson, *Bankers and Empire*, 45–46.

35 Egypt in particular might have been an example to avoid: Egyptians had rioted against foreign control in 1882, triggering a British bombardment and invasion. One of the lieutenants in the U.S. Marine detachment who came ashore in support was a young Littleton Waller. Harry Alanson Ellsworth, *One Hundred Eighty Landings of United States Marines 1800–1934* (Washington, DC: History and Museums Division, Headquarters, U.S. Marine Corps, 1974), 89. See also Rosenberg, *Financial Missionaries*, 54.

36 Rosenberg, *Financial Missionaries*, 58.

37 "The diplomacy of the present administration has sought to respond to modern ideas of commercial intercourse. This policy has been characterized as substituting dollars for bullets. It is one that appeals alike to idealistic humanitarian sentiments, to the dictates of sound policy and strategy, and to legitimate commercial aims. It is an effort frankly directed to the increase of American trade upon the axiomatic principle that the government of the United States shall extend all proper support to every legitimate and beneficial American enterprise abroad." William Howard Taft, "December 3, 1912: Fourth Annual Message," Miller Center, University of Virginia, millercenter.org/the-presidency/presidential-speeches /december-3-1912-fourth-annual-message.

38 Rosenberg, *Financial Missionaries*, 61.

39 "Message from the President of the United States Transmitting a Loan Convention between the United States and Honduras," Jan. 26, 1911, *Papers Relating to the Foreign Relations of the United States, with the Annual Message of the President Transmitted to Congress December 3, 1912* (Washington, DC: Government Printing Office, 1919), 556.

40 Ibid., 558.

41 Thomas, *Old Gimlet Eye*, 128.

42 Rosenberg, *Financial Missionaries*, 77.

43 Ibid., 67.

44 Brown Brothers made its fortune in securitizing mortgages on enslaved people in the mid-nineteenth century. Seligman, founded by a German Jewish immigrant, had opposed slavery and financed the Union cause before finding a profitable line in expansionism: pioneering U.S. banking in the new state of California, financing the railroad schemes of robber barons like Vanderbilt, and helping finance the Panama Canal. Baptist, *Half Has Never Been Told*, 353; Sources for paragraph: Hudson, *Bankers and Empire*, 154–156; Gobat, *Confronting*, 81; "New Bank Building on Hanover Street," *New York Times*, Sep. 3, 1916, 46.

45   Rosenberg, *Financial Missionaries*, 77.

46   Speech of Dr. Ignacio Suárez in *Speeches Incident to the Visit of Philander Chase Knox, Secretary of State of the United States of America, to the Countries of the Caribbean. February 23 to April 17, 1912* (Washington, DC: Government Printing Office, 1913), 46–52.

47   Ramírez, *Sandino*, 452.

48   Jon Lee Anderson, "The Comandante's Canal," *New Yorker*, Mar. 10, 2014; Rafael Aragón, "Is Ortega's Project Christian? And What Is the Church's Project?," *Revista Envío*, Apr. 2011, www.envio.org.ni/articulo/4328.

49   Larry Rohter, "Nicaragua Rebels Accused of Abuses," *New York Times*, Mar. 7, 1985, 1; Marc Edelman, "Soviet-Nicaraguan Relations and the Contra War," *International Journal on World Peace* 5, no. 3 (1988): 45–67.

50   Jennifer Goett and Courtney Desiree Morris, "Nicaragua's Authoritarian Turn Is Not a Product of Leftist Politics," North American Congress on Latin America (NACLA), Sep. 16, 2016.

51   Gioconda Belli, "How Daniel Ortega Became a Tyrant," *Foreign Affairs*, Aug. 24, 2018.

52   Alejandro Bendana, "Strange Bedfellows: The Aleman-Ortega Pact," North American Congress on Latin America (NACLA), Sep. 25, 2007.

53   Drazen Jorgic and Ismael Lopez, "Special Report: Ortega Media Enrich His Family, Entrench His Hold on Nicaragua," Reuters, Nov. 23, 2020; Hannah Stone, "The Many Political Faces of Daniel Ortega," Council on Hemispheric Affairs, Dec. 21, 2011, www.coha.org/the-many-political-faces-of-daniel-ortega/.

54   Diriangén (d. 1529) was an indigenous sixteenth-century king who resisted Spanish colonialism. Rubén Darió (1867–1916) was a Nicaraguan poet who opposed U.S. imperialism. "Comunicado del Ministerio de Relaciones Exteriores de Nicaragua," *El 19 Digital*, Nov. 12, 2018, www.el19digital.com/articulos/ver/titulo:83831-comunicado-del-ministerio-de-relaciones-exteriores-de-nicaragua-, Google cached version viewed May 2021; Belli, "How Daniel Ortega Became a Tyrant"; Tom Phillips, "Nicaragua President Attacks 'Coup-Mongers' in Speech," *Guardian*, Jul. 8, 2018; "Palabras del presidente comandante Daniel en caminata por la seguridad y la Paz," Barricadaonline.com, Jul. 7, 2018, web.archive.org/web/20180720144304/barricadaonline.com/2018/07/07/palabras-del-presidente-comandante-daniel-en-el-cierre-de-la-caminata-por-la-seguridad-y-la-paz/.

55   Col. Clifford D. Ham, in Rosenberg, *Financial Missionaries*, 74; Gobat, *Confronting*, 95–97.

56   Gobat, *Confronting*, 102.

57   "Nicaragua Goes on Gold Standard with $2,000,000," *Times-Democrat* (New Orleans, LA), Dec. 26, 1913, 5.

58   *Convention between the United States and Nicaragua: Hearing before the Committee on Foreign Relations, United States Senate, Sixty-Third Congress, Second Session* (Washington, DC: Government Printing Office, 1914), 507.

59   SDB to Ethel Butler and children, Aug. 11, 1912, Butler Coll., MCHD.

60   SDB to Ethel Butler and children, Aug. 15, 1912, Butler Coll., MCHD; Daugherty, *Marine Corps and the State Department*, 54–55; Hudson, *Bankers and Empire*, 157.

61   Literally "sin autonomía nacional impera el caos." Benjamín Zeledón, "Orden general del 10 de agosto de 1912 dada en el cuartel general de Tipitapa," *Pensamiento antimperialista*, 144–145. Translation by author.

62   "Keeping the Peace in Nicaragua," *Literary Digest*, Vol. 45, Jul. 1912–Dec. 1912 (Funk & Wagnalls, 1912), 286.

63   SDB, "Camp Weitzel, Managua September 18 [1912]," typescript and handwritten copies of SDB letters from Nicaragua, Butler Coll., MCHD.

64   Thomas, *Old Gimlet Eye*, 153.

65   SDB, "Headquarters 3rd Battalion, Granada, Nicaragua, September 23 [1912]," typescript and handwritten copies of SDB letters from Nicaragua, Butler Coll., MCHD; SDB, "Camp Weitzel, Managua Saturday, September 18 [1912]."

66  SDB, "Camp Weitzel, Managua Saturday, September 18 [1912]."

67  Letter from Gen. Benjamín Zeledón to Col. Joseph H. Pendleton, Sep. 19, 1912, 10 p.m., Joseph Pendleton Collection, MCHD.

68  Zeledón, "Protesta ante el almirante Southerland," Sep. 19, 1912, *Pensamiento antimperialista*, 147–150.

69  SDB, "Camp Weitzel, Managua September 18 [1912]."

70  SDB, ""Headquarters 3rd Battalion, Granada, Nicaragua, September 23 [1912]."

71  Schmidt, *Maverick*, 49.

72  Ibid. Zeledón denied responsibility for the ambush in his letter to Colonel Pendleton, cited above.

73  William Walker, *The War in Nicaragua* (New York: S. H. Goetzel, 1860), 340.

74  Schmidt, *Maverick*, 50.

75  Challener, *Admirals, Generals*, 306.

76  SDB, "Tuesday morning, Sept. 24th [1912]," typescript and handwritten copies of SDB letters from Nicaragua, Butler Coll., MCHD.

77  SDB initially described Mena's malady as "Bright's Disease," then crossed that out and wrote in "rheumatism." SDB, "Headquarters, Dist. of Granada, Granada, Nicaragua, Sept. 30th, 1912," typescript and handwritten copies of SDB letters from Nicaragua, Butler Coll., MCHD.

78  Ibid.

79  *Pensamiento antimperialista*, 153–154.

80  Ibid., 151–152.

81  Typescript of narrative of Battle of Coyotepe, likely by Capt. Edward Greene, Company A, Box 74, Folder 3, Butler Coll., MCHD; SDB, "Saturday Morning, Granada, Nicaragua, Oct. 5th," typescript and handwritten copies of SDB letters from Nicaragua, Butler Coll., MCHD.

82  Thomas, *Old Gimlet Eye*, 167.

83  "Danilo Aguirre y Walter Mendoza mártires que aportaron a la libertad de Nicaragua," Viva Nicaragua Canal 13, Jul. 9, 2019, www.vivanicaragua.com.ni/2019/07/09/sociales/danilo-aguirre-walter-mendoza-martires-asesinados-guardia-somocista/.

84  Vilma Núñez de Escorcia, "Las cárceles reflejan la realidad social y política de un país," *Revista Envío*, Apr. 2018; Candice Hughes, "Sandinistas Free Last Political Prisoners from Somoza Era," Associated Press, Feb. 9, 1990.

85  Gobat, *Confronting*, 119; SDB to Ethel Butler, Oct. 9, 1912, in Schmidt, *Maverick*, 54.

86  SDB to Ethel Butler, Nov. 2, 1912, in Venzon, *Letters*, 129; Election in Dieter Nohlen, ed., *Elections in the Americas: A Data Handbook, Vol. 1: North America, Central America, and the Caribbean* (New York: Oxford University Press, 2005), 489.

87  Hudson, *Bankers and Empire*, 159.

88  Schmidt, *Maverick*, 54.

89  Ibid.

90  SDB, "Wednesday night, Granada, Nic., Oct. 9th, 1912," typescript and handwritten copies of SDB letters from Nicaragua, Butler Coll., MCHD.

91  SDB to Admiral Southerland, telegram, "Copy for Colonel Pendleton," Oct. 4, 1914, Pendleton Coll., MCHD.

92  Ramírez, *Sandino*, 269.

93  Gregorio Selser, "Zeledón y Sandino," *Cuadernos de Marcha*, Jan.–Feb. 1980, 67.

## NINE: THE CANAL ZONE

1  Ethel Butler to Maria Low Felton (grandmother), date partially obscured (likely Apr. 12, 1910), Butler Coll., MCHD; McCullough, *Path between the Seas*, 594.

2  Greene, *Canal Builders*, 231.

3   Ibid., 242.

4   SDB to Ethel Butler, Oct. 23, 1912, in Venzon, *Letters*, 127.

5   Ethel Butler to "Grandma dearest" (presumably Maria Low Felton), Apr. 16, 1910, private collection of Philippa Wehle.

6   The names of the lists were already an anachronism: they harkened to an earlier time, before the Panamanian secession, when American railroad workers in Colombian Panama had been paid in gold-backed dollars and locals in silver-backed Colombian pesos. The new Republic of Panama's official currency, for everyone, was the U.S. dollar.

7   Greene, *Canal Builders*, 62–69, 254–265; Lasso, *Erased*, loc. 160, 1488, 1707, etc.

8   Lasso, *Erased*, loc. 1693–1721.

9   Thomas, *Old Gimlet Eye*, 127; Ethel Butler to SDB, Jul. 30, 1910, Butler Coll., MCHD.

10  "Major Smedley D. Butler Greets President William H. Taft, Panama, 1909," NARA photo, Butler Coll., MCHD; *Army and Navy Register* 48, no. 1618 (Dec. 24, 1910).

11  "Work Force," *Canal de Panamá*, accessed May 2021, www.pancanal.com/eng/history /history/work.html.

12  Greene, *Canal Builders*, 48–51.

13  Alfred S. Mitchell, *Letters from Isthmian Canal Construction Workers*, 1963, MAAP.

14  Joseph Brewster, in ibid.

15  Alfred E. Dottin, in ibid.

16  Joseph Brewster, in ibid.

17  G. Mitchell Berrisford, in ibid.

18  "Europian" and "instantly" in original. Philip McDonald, in ibid.

19  Harrigan Austin, in ibid.

20  Alfred E. Dottin, in ibid.

21  Greene, *Canal Builders*, 52, 159–178.

22  For example, "When Goethals Orders," *Danville* (PA) *Morning News*, Mar. 23, 1909; Jaime Massot, *Panama Canal Construction: Postcards, Tales, and Facts* (self-pub., CreateSpace, 2017), CZLM, 236; *A Trip to the Panama Canal* (souvenir photo set, 1912), Butler Coll., MCHD.

23  SDB, Radio Address, Station WCAU, Philadelphia, Jun. 5, 1935, Butler Coll., MCHD.

24  "Convention for the Construction of a Ship Canal (Hay-Bunau-Varilla Treaty), November 18, 1903," Article III, Avalon Project at the Yale Law School, accessed May 2021, avalon .law.yale.edu/20th_century/pan001.asp; Canal Zone v. Coulson, 1 C.Z. 50 (1907), writ of error dismissed for want of jurisdiction, 212 U.S. 553 (1908); Andrew Kent, "Habeas Corpus, Protection, and Extraterritorial Constitutional Rights," *Iowa Law Review Bulletin* 97, no. 34 (2012).

25  Greene, *Canal Builders*, 88.

26  Major, *Prize Possession*, 160.

27  SDB to Ethel Butler and children, Jul. 5, 1912, Butler Coll., MCHD.

28  *Estrella de Panamá*, Jul. 6, 1912, CZLM; Greene, *Canal Builders*, 326–328.

29  Greene, *Canal Builders*, 328.

30  Major, *Prize Possession*, 127–128; "Ralph Davis" in "Panama: Arbitration of Claims of American Citizens against Panama on Account of Injuries Sustained during the Riot at Panama City on July 4, 1912," file no. 419.11d29, *Papers Relating to the Foreign Relations of the United States, with the Address of the President to Congress, December 5, 1916*, 919; Untitled article, *New York Times*, Jul. 6, 1912, 7.

31  Thomas, *Old Gimlet Eye*, 136; Greene, *Canal Builders*, 328.

32  SDB to Thomas S. Butler, Jul. 9, 1912, Butler Coll., MCHD; Thomas, *Old Gimlet Eye*, 137.

33  Greene, *Canal Builders*, 328.

34  Ibid., 329.

35 Ibid., 331–332.

36 Lasso, *Erased*, loc. 2353 to 2418.

37 *Panama Canal: Hearings before the Committee on Interoceanic Canals, United States Senate, Sixty-Second Congress, Second Session, on H.R. 21969* (Washington, DC: Government Printing Office, 1912).

38 Lasso, *Erased*, loc. 2524.

39 Ibid., loc. 70.

40 Ibid., loc. 2865.

41 Ibid., loc. 57.

42 T. Ambrister, "Panama, Why They Hate US: More Than One Torn Flag," *Saturday Evening Post*, Mar. 7, 1964, 77; Eric Jackson, "The Beginning of the End of the Panama Canal Zone," *Panama News*, Dec. 8, 1999.

43 Miguel Acoca, Philip Hager, and Maynard Parker, "I Guess I Started This Whole Thing," *Life*, Jan. 24, 1964, 30; Jackson, "Beginning of the End."

44 Alan McPherson, "Courts of World Opinion: Trying the Panama Flag Riots of 1964," *Diplomatic History* 28, no. 1 (Jan. 2004), 83–112; Jackson, "Beginning of the End"; interview with Anne Gegg, 2019.

45 Associated Press, "Yanks Flee on Train," *Miami* (FL) *News*, Jan. 12, 1964; Jackson, "Beginning of the End."

46 "Tragedy in Panama," *New York Times*, Jan. 11, 1964.

47 Ronald Reagan, "To Restore America," speech, Mar. 31, 1976, www.reaganlibrary.gov /archives/speech/restore-america, referenced in Rick Perlstein, *Reaganland* (New York: Simon & Schuster, 2020), 143; National Review, *Tear Down This Wall: The Reagan Revolution* (New York: Continuum, 2004), 154.

48 Martin Smith, "Hayakawa . . . He Drives for Center Ground in Race for Senator," *Sacramento Bee*, Sep. 19, 1976.

49 Alan Riding, "Pick One: The Panama Canal Is, Is Not, as Valuable as in the Past," *New York Times*, Aug. 14, 1977; "Transcript of President Carter's Televised Speech on the Panama Canal Treaties," *New York Times*, Feb. 2, 1978; John P. Augelli, "The Panama Canal Treaties of 1977: Impact and Challenges," *Yearbook, Conference of Latin Americanist Geographers* 11 (1985): 75–79.

50 Dieter Nohlen, ed., *Elections in the Americas: A Data Handbook,* Vol. 1, *North America, Central America, and the Caribbean* (New York: Oxford University Press, 2005), 524; Associated Press, "Canal Zone Dies in Peace," *Spokesman-Review* (Spokane, WA), Oct. 2, 1979, 3; Alan Riding, "Panama Takes Control of Canal Zone," *New York Times*, Oct. 2, 1979, A3.

51 McCullough, *Path between the Seas*, 606–607.

52 "Wilson to Blow Up Gamboa Dike To-day," *New-York Tribune*, Oct. 10, 1913, 3; Arnold N. Alexander, in *Letters from Isthmian Canal Construction Workers*, MAAP.

53 SDB to Maud Butler, Oct. 16, 1913, Butler Coll., MCHD.

54 McCullough, *Path between the Seas*, 342.

55 Hudson, *Bankers and Empire*, 70.

56 Gill, *School of the Americas*, 81; David Johnston, "U.S. Admits Payments to Noriega," *New York Times*, Jan. 19, 1991.

57 Dinges, *Our Man in Panama*, 81–82; "Manuel Noriega," U.S. Officials and Major Traffickers, National Security Archive Electronic Briefing Book No. 2, National Security Archive, George Washington University, accessed Apr. 2021, nsarchive2.gwu.edu/NSAEBB /NSAEBB2/index.html#3a; Eytan Gilboa, "The Panama Invasion Revisited: Lessons for the Use of Force in the Post Cold War Era," *Political Science Quarterly* 110, no. 4 (Winter 1995–1996): 539–562; "Manuel Noriega," National Security Archive Electronic Briefing Book No. 2; Kaelyn Forde, "Panamanian Dictator Manuel Noriega's Complex US Ties

Suggest Lessons for Trump Era, Historians Say," ABC News, Jun. 1, 2017, abcnews.go.com /International/panamanian-dictator-manuel-noriegas-complex-us-ties-lessons/story.

58  Seymour M. Hersh, "Panama Strongman Said to Trade in Drugs, Arms and Illicit Money," *New York Times*, Jun. 12, 1986.

59  Dinges, *Our Man in Panama*, 86–87.

60  William Branigin, "Marines' Wrong Turn Set Stage for Invasion," *Washington Post*, Jan. 4, 1990.

61  Ronald H. Cole, *Operation Just Cause: The Planning and Execution of Joint Operations in Panama, February 1988–January 1990* (Washington, DC: Office of the Chairman of the Joint Chiefs of Staff, 1995), 39–40.

62  Gavin Haynes, "How Manuel Noriega Surrendered to the Sanity-Destroying Power of Mallrat Music," *Guardian*, May 30, 2017.

63  Gabriel Zucman, *The Hidden Wealth of Nations: The Scourge of Tax Havens* (Chicago: University of Chicago Press, 2015), 40; Libby Nelson, "A Top Expert on Tax Havens Explains Why the Panama Papers Barely Scratch the Surface," *Vox*, Apr. 8, 2016; Marina Koren, "What Makes Panama a Tax Haven?," *Atlantic*, Apr. 5, 2016.

64  Lisagor and Lipsius, *A Law unto Itself*, 31.

65  Juliette Garside and David Pegg, "Panama Papers Reveal Offshore Secrets of China's Red Nobility," *Guardian*, Apr. 6, 2016; "The International Commercial Bank of China (Panama Branch)," Offshore Leaks Database by the International Consortium of Investigative Journalists, accessed Apr. 2021, offshoreleaks.icij.org/nodes/11003146.

66  Michael Paarlberg, "Enough Collusion Talk. It's Time to Focus on Trump's Corruption," *Guardian*, Mar. 31, 2019; Aggelos Petropoulos and Richard Engel, "A Panama Tower Carries Trump's Name and Ties to Organized Crime," NBC News, Nov. 17, 2017.

67  Gerardo Reyes, "Meet the Drug Trafficker behind a Trump Complex in Panama," Univision News, May 17, 2017, www.univision.com/univision-news/united-states/meet-the-drug -trafficker-behind-a-trump-complex-in-panama; Jeff Horwitz and Juan Zamorano, "Trump Officials Fight Eviction from Panama Hotel They Manage," AP News, Feb. 24, 2018; Ned Parker et al., "Ivanka and the Fugitive from Panama," Reuters, Nov. 17, 2017; John Cassidy, "Panama Papers: Why Aren't There More American Names?," *New Yorker*, Apr. 5, 2016.

68  Associated Press in Panama City, "Panama: Trump Hotel Standoff Ends as President Surrenders Physical Control," *Guardian*, Mar. 5, 2018.

## TEN: VERACRUZ

1  Bertie Charles Forbes, *Men Who Are Making the West* (New York: B. C. Forbes, 1923), 115; Margaret L. Davis, *Dark Side of Fortune: Triumph and Scandal in the Life of Oil Tycoon Edward L. Doheny* (Berkeley: University of California Press, 1998), 35–36; "El chapopote y la expropiación," *Milenio*, Mar. 23, 2014, www.milenio.com/opinion/varios-autores/taller -sie7e/el-chapopote-y-la-expropiacion.

2  Davis, *Dark Side of Fortune*, 9.

3  Daniel Yergin, *The Prize: The Epic Quest for Oil, Money and Power* (New York: Simon & Schuster, 1991), 93–94, 122.

4  Ibid.

5  Davis, *Dark Side of Fortune*, 36.

6  SDB to Maud Butler, Jan. 18, 1914, Butler Coll., MCHD.

7  Hart, *Empire and Revolution*, 224, 260–261.

8  Challener, *Admirals, Generals*, 344.

9  Ibid.

10  A few days after his election, Wilson remarked to Edward Grant Conklin, a colleague at Princeton: "It would be an irony of fate if my administration had to deal chiefly with foreign problems, for all my preparation has been in domestic matters." Cooper, *Woodrow Wilson*, 182.

11  "1912 Democratic Party Platform, June 25, 1912," American Presidency Project, UC Santa

Barbara, accessed Apr. 2021, www.presidency.ucsb.edu/documents/1912-democratic-party
-platform.

12  Kramer, *Blood of Government*, 90.

13  Cooper, *Woodrow Wilson*, 75; Woodrow Wilson, "Democracy and Efficiency," *Atlantic*,
Mar. 1901; Wendell H. Stephenson, "The Influence of Woodrow Wilson on Frederick
Jackson Turner," *Agricultural History* 19, no. 4 (Oct. 1945): 249–253, and Robert Alex-
ander Kraig, "The 1912 Election and the Rhetorical Foundations of the Liberal State,"
*Rhetoric and Public Affairs* 3, no. 3 (2000): 363–395.

14  Jamie Bisher, *The Intelligence War in Latin America, 1914–1922* (Jefferson, NC: McFarland,
2016), 60.

15  Cooper, *Woodrow Wilson*, 183; Hart, *Revolutionary Mexico*, 150–151.

16  Hart, *Empire and Revolution*, 274–275; John Skirius, "Railroad, Oil and Other Foreign
Interests in the Mexican Revolution, 1911–1914," *Journal of Latin American Studies* 35, no.
1 (Feb. 2003): 25–51.

17  "Oil Situation Tampico-Tuxpam Region," no date, RG 38, E-10-c, NARA. Buckley's children included the conservative intellectual godfather William F. Buckley Jr., who founded
the *National Review*, and the conservative senator and Reagan administration official James
L. Buckley. One of his great-grandsons, L. Brent Bozell IV, was charged with storming the
U.S. Capitol with the Trumpist mob on Jan. 6, 2021. Federal prosecutors identified Bozell
as one of the men captured on video on the Senate floor.

18  Hart, *Empire and Revolution*, 306.

19  SDB to Ethel Butler, Feb. 23, 1914, Butler Coll., MCHD.

20  Lind's knowledge of Mexico was limited to his fledgling investments in Mexican real estate.
He reportedly had plagiarized much of a speech he gave that year, titled "The Mexican
People," from the *Encyclopedia Britannica*. Hart, *Revolutionary Mexico*, 285; Larry D. Hill,
"The Progressive Politician as a Diplomat: The Case of John Lind in Mexico," *The Americas*
27, no. 4 (Apr. 1971): 355–372; and Kenneth J. Grieb, "The Lind Mission to Mexico,"
*Caribbean Studies* 7, no. 4 (Jan. 1968): 25–43.

21  "A Memorandum by John Lind," Apr. 30, 1914, The Papers of Woodrow Wilson Digital
Edition, accessed Apr. 2021, rotunda.upress.virginia.edu/founders/WILS.

22  Schmidt, *Maverick*, 64.

23  Thomas, *Old Gimlet Eye*, 171.

24  "Detail of Plans Expeditionary Forces to Mexico City," Mar. 1914, file 6474–356, RG 165
NM-84 296, NARA.

25  Hill, "Progressive Politician."

26  William Randolph Hearst, "The Obligation and Opportunity of the United States in Mexico," *San Francisco Examiner*, May 3, 1916.

27  SDB to Ethel Butler, Feb. 23, 1903, Butler Coll., MCHD.

28  Bertram et al., *Drug War Politics*, 61, 65–68.

29  Gabriela Recio, "Drugs and Alcohol: US Prohibition and the Origins of the Drug Trade in
Mexico, 1910–1930," *Journal of Latin American Studies* 34, no. 1 (Feb. 2002): 21–42.

30  Peter Dale Scott and Jonathan Marshall, *Cocaine Politics: Drugs, Armies, and the CIA in
Central America*, updated ed. (Berkeley: University of California Press, 1998), 34; Carmen
Boullosa and Mike Wallace, *A Narco History: How the United States and Mexico Jointly
Created the "Mexican Drug War"* (New York: OR Books, 2015), 23–36.

31  Luis Astorga, "México, Colombia y las drogas ilegales: Variaciones sobre un mismo tema,"
in *La VIII cátedra anual de historia "Ernesto Restrepo Tirado": Análisis histórico del narcotráfico
en Colombia* (Bogotá: Museo Nacional de Colombia, 2014), 50.

32  Scott and Marshall, *Cocaine Politics*, 23; Boullosa and Wallace, *Narco History*, 37–46.

33  José Luis Pardo Veiras, "Opinión: 13 años y 250 000 muertos: Las lecciones no aprendidas
en Mexico," *Washington Post*, Oct. 28, 2019.

34 "En Veracruz tiran a 40 ejecutados . . . en narcomantas señalan quebmuertos son de Los Zetas," *Blog del Narco*, Sep. 21, 2011.

35 Luis Pablo Beauregard, "Veracruz tiene más fosas clandestinas que municipios," *El País*, Jan. 29, 2018, elpais.com/internacional/2018/01/30/mexico/1517284876_628755.html.

36 Boullosa and Wallace, *Narco History*, 37–46.

37 Robert E. Quirk, *An Affair of Honor: Woodrow Wilson and the Occupation of Veracruz* (New York: W. W. Norton, 1962), 19; "Federal Shells Fire American Oil Plant," *Buffalo Commercial*, Apr. 10, 1914; "Fierce Battle with Fire Rages around Tampico," *Baltimore Sun*, Apr. 10, 1914; Jonathan C. Brown, *Oil and Revolution in Mexico* (Berkeley: University of California Press, 1993), 191.

38 Quirk, *An Affair of Honor*, 22; James C. Bradford, *Admirals of the New Steel Navy: Makers of the American Naval Tradition, 1880–1930* (New York: Naval Institute Press, 2013), 260; H. T. Mayo to Ignacio Morelos Zaragoza, Apr. 9, 1914, RG 38: Records of the Office of Naval Intelligence, C-10-a (4578: Tampico Incident 1914), NARA.

39 51 *Congressional Record* 9096 (1914).

40 Ethel Butler to SDB, Apr. 15, 1914, Butler Coll., MCHD.

41 SDB to Ethel Butler, Apr. 14, 1914, Butler Coll., MCHD.

42 Woodrow Wilson, "The Situation in Our Dealings with General Victorianio [*sic*] Huerta, at Mexico City. Address of the President of the United States, Delivered at a Joint Session of the Two Houses of Congress, April 20, 1914" (Washington, DC: Government Printing Office, 1914).

43 Pasquel, *Manuel y José Azueta*, 53.

44 In fact, the guns were American—manufactured by the Colt company in Hartford, Connecticut. Even the ship was partially American owned: the *Ypiranga* was owned by the Hamburg-America Line, which operated under a profit-sharing agreement with J. P. Morgan. See Michael C. Meyer, "The Arms of the Ypiranga," *Hispanic American Historical Review* 50, no. 3 (Aug. 1970): 543–556.

45 Pasquel, *Manuel y José Azueta*, 55.

46 Pasquel, *Invasion de Veracruz*, 30–33.

47 Berta Ulloa Ortiz, *Veracruz, capital de la nación: 1914–1915* (Veracruz: Colegio de Mexico, Gobierno del Estado de Veracruz, 1986), 20.

48 Enrique Krauze, "The April Invasion of Veracruz," *New York Times*, Apr. 20, 2014.

49 Henry J. Forman of *Collier's* magazine, quoted in R. S. Baker, *Woodrow Wilson, Life and Letters*, Vol. 4, *President: 1913–1914* (Garden City, NY: Doubleday, Doran, 1931), 330.

50 Thomas, *Old Gimlet Eye*, 179.

51 Hart, *Empire and Revolution*, 308; Surgeon General's Report, Apr. 1914, Subject File (WE-Mexico, Vera Cruz), Box 776, RG 45, NARA.

52 SDB to Thomas S. Butler, May 20, 1914, Butler Coll., MCHD.

53 Ethel Butler to SDB, May 20, 1914, Butler Coll., MCHD.

54 Mark Twain, "A Defence of General Funston," *North American Review* 174 (May 1902).

55 Hart, *Empire and Revolution*, 310.

56 Jack London, "Mexico's Army and Ours," *Collier's*, May 30, 1914.

57 Louis Botte, "Les Américains au Mexique," *L'Illustration*, Jun. 13, 1914.

58 Max de Haldevang and Daniel Wolfe, "Mexico Is Illegally Destroying Protected Mangrove Trees to Build an $8 Billion Oil Refinery," *Quartz*, Mar. 5, 2020, qz.com/1807407/mexico-is-illegally -destroying-mangroves-to-build-lopez-obradors-oil-refinery; Jon Lee Anderson, "Why Andrés Manuel López Obrador Went to Dinner with Donald Trump," *New Yorker*, Jul. 9, 2020.

59 Rebecca Watts, "NAFTA in the Time of AMLO," *NACLA Report on the Americas* 51, no. 1 (2019): 10; "Mexico: Evolution of the Mérida Initiative, 2007–2021," In Focus, Congressional Research Service, Jan. 13, 2001, fas.org/sgp/crs/row/IF10578.pdf.

60 "Discurso íntegro de Andrés Manuel López Obrador al rendir protesta como presidente,"

*Animal Político*, Dec. 1, 2018, www.animalpolitico.com/2018/12/discurso-integro-amlo
-protesta-presidente/.

61  Keith Johnson, "Mexico Tries to Turn Back the Clock on Energy," *Foreign Policy*, Oct. 4, 2019,
foreignpolicy.com/2019/10/04/mexico-amlo-lopez-obrador-energy-reform-rollback-pemex/.

62  See, for example, Thomas Palley, "Trump's Neocon Neoliberalism Camouflaged with Anti-
Globalization Circus," *Challenge* 60, no. 4 (Jun. 29, 2017): 368–374, doi.org/10.1080
/05775132.2017.1324190.

63  Krauze, "The April Invasion of Veracruz," *New York Times*, Apr. 20, 2014.

64  SDB, typescript of radio address on oil, war, and foreign trade, undated, folder marked:
"probably 1935," Butler Coll., MCHD.

## ELEVEN: HAITI

1  Hudson, *Bankers and Empire*, 104; "L'incident d'hier à la banque," *Le Matin*, Dec. 18,
1914, Digital Library of the Caribbean, dloc.com/UF00081213/02246/2x.

2  There is no evidence the money was ever returned. Peter Hudson told me: "If it's buried anywhere it would be in the backyards of the country homes of Roger Farnham, Frank Vanderlip,
and Charles Mitchell. But I think you're right . . . I've never seen evidence of its return and
the bankers always saw it as their funds." See also Hudson, *Bankers and Empire*, 106.

3  *Le Matin*, supra.

4  Hudson, *Bankers and Empire*, 90–93.

5  Ibid., 103; "The National Bank of the Republic of Haiti to the Secretary of State," Dec. 8,
1914, file no. 838.516/13, *Papers Relating to the Foreign Relations of the United States, with
the Address of the President to Congress December 8, 1914*, U.S. Department of State, history
.state.gov/historicaldocuments/frus1914/d562.

6  Schmidt, *Occupation*, 52–53.

7  "'D' Confidential Tentative Plans for Employment of Naval Forces Stationed in Haitien
Ports; Port au Prince," 1914, declassified Aug. 2, 1956, RG 45, Box 740, NARA; "Confidential Information. Relative to the City of Port au Prince," declassified Aug. 2, 1956, RG
45, Box 741, NARA; "Shore Liberty and Baseball at Port au Prince," undated, RG 45, Box
741, NARA; "Memorandum, U.S.S. Connecticut, Port au Prince, Haiti, August 3, 1914,"
RG 45, Box 741, NARA.

8  *Le Matin*, supra; Bryan to Menos, Dec. 31, 1914, file no. 838.516/27, *Papers Relating to
the Foreign Relations of the United States* (Washington, DC: Government Printing Office,
1922), 381; Hudson, *Bankers and Empire*, 103.

9  Marvin Chochotte, "The History of Peasants, Tonton Makouts, and the Rise and Fall of the
Duvalier Dictatorship in Haiti," PhD diss., University of Michigan, 2017; Robert Debs Heinl
and Nancy Gordon Heinl, *Written in Blood: The Story of the Haitian People 1492–1995*,
rev. ed. (Lanham, MD: University Press of America, 2005), 367–368; *Papers Relating to the
Foreign Relations of the United States, with the Address of the President to Congress December 5,
1916*, file no. 838.00/1375 (Washington, DC: Government Printing Office, 1925).

10  W. B. Caperton to Secretary of the Navy (Operations), Memorandum, Aug. 4, 1915, "Subject: Report of Operations of Commander, Cruiser Squadron, in Haitien Waters, from 28
July, 1915, to 31 July, 1915," RG 45, Box 746, NARA; Renda, *Taking Haiti*, 80–82.

11  "Administration of Haiti: Finances and Economic Development," treaty signed at Port-au-
Prince, Sep. 16, 1915, Department of State Treaty Series No. 623; 39 Stat. 1654, www.loc
.gov/law/help/us-treaties/bevans/b-ht-ust000008–0660.pdf.

12  SDB to Thomas S. Butler, Oct. 5, 1915, Butler Coll., MCHD.

13  Haley, *Roots: The Saga of an American Family* (1976; repr., New York: Hachette, 2016),
375. Historians now doubt Haley's claim, noting that "Toby" was on the Waller plantation before the ship Haley identifies as bringing Kunta Kinte arrived in Virginia. But
the historical Waller family are nonetheless major characters in *Roots*. See Gary B. and

Elizabeth Shown Mills, "*Roots* and the New 'Faction': A Legitimate Tool for Clio?," *Virginia Magazine of History and Biography* 89, no. 1 (Jan. 1981).

14 Thomas C. Parramore, *Norfolk: The First Four Centuries* (Charlottesville: University Press of Virginia, 1994), 165; Richard Francis, Southampton (VA) Circuit Court Clerk, emails with the author, Jul. 2020.

15 Glenn M. Harned, *Marine Corps Generals 1899–1936*, 2nd ed. (self-pub., CreateSpace, 2017), 49; Marvin Chochotte, "The Twilight of Popular Revolutions: The Suppression of Peasant Armed Struggles and Freedom in Rural Haiti during the US Occupation, 1915–1934," *Journal of African American History* 103, no. 3 (Summer 2018): 277–308; Brianna E. Kirk, "'No Safety for Union Men': The Norfolk Race Riot of 1866 and Military Occupation," master's thesis, Gettysburg College, 2015; quote in Schmidt, *Maverick*, 84.

16 "Extract from Thomas Jefferson to St. George Tucker," Aug. 28, 1797, Library of Congress, tjrs.monticello.org/letter/1748.

17 Sinha, *The Slave's Cause,* 57; Gwendolyn Midlo Hall, "The 1795 Slave Conspiracy in Pointe Coupée: Impact of the French Revolution," *Proceedings of the Meeting of the French Colonial Historical Society* 15 (1992): 130–141.

18 Henry L. Benning, speech, Feb. 18, 1861, "Virginia Secession Convention," *Secession: Virginia and the Crisis of Union, 1861*, University of Richmond, accessed Jun. 2021, searchable database at secession.richmond.edu.

19 Matthew J. Clavin, *Toussaint Louverture and the American Civil War: The Promise and Peril of a Second Haitian Revolution* (Philadelphia: University of Pennsylvania Press, 2012), 52–53.

20 Cooper, *Woodrow Wilson*, 36–37; Tom Shoop, "When Woodrow Wilson Segregated the Federal Workforce: An Inconvenient Truth about a Former President," *Government Executive*, Nov. 20, 2015, www.govexec.com/federal-news/2015/11/when-woodrow-wilson -segregated-federal-workforce/123913; Samuel J. Leistedt and Paul Linkowski, "Psychopathy and the Cinema: Fact or Fiction?," *Journal of Forensic Sciences* 59, no. 1 (Jan. 2014): 167–174; Mark E. Benbow, "Birth of a Quotation: Woodrow Wilson and 'Like Writing History with Lightning,'" *Journal of the Gilded Age and Progressive Era* 9, no. 4 (Oct. 2010): 509–533.

21 Aaron Randle, "America's Only Successful Coup d'Etat Overthrew a Biracial Government in 1898," History.com, Oct. 7, 2000, www.history.com/news/wilmington-massacre-1898 -coup.

22 Carr, "I Was a Ku-Klux and I Am Not Ashamed of It," in "Old Veterans Meet in Annual Session," *News and Observer* (Raleigh, NC), Oct. 15, 1908, 2; "Gen. Carr's Letter to Ex-Confederates," *News and Observer* (Raleigh, NC), May 20, 1900.

23 Carey Olmstead Shellman, "'One of the Lord's Democrats': Nellie Peters Black and the Practical Application of the Social Gospel in the New South, 1870–1919," PhD diss., University of Florida, 2007, 41.

24 W. E. B. Du Bois, *The Philadelphia Negro: A Social Study* (Philadelphia: University of Pennsylvania, 1899), 322. Du Bois added: "Color prejudice makes it difficult for groups to find suitable places to move to—one Negro family would be tolerated where six would be objected to; thus we have here a very decisive hindrance to emigration to the suburbs," 297.

25 SDB to Ethel Butler, Oct. 4, 1915, Stanford Lib.

26 Thomas, *Old Gimlet Eye*, 183–184; Capt. Robert O. Underwood, Report of Operations, Saint-Marc, Haiti, Sep. 28, 1915, RG 127, NARA; Gaillard, *Premier écrasement*, 124.

27 Expeditionary Commander to Major General Commandant, Report of Operations at Gonaives and Vicinity, Oct. 7, 1915, RG 127, NARA.

28 Kilcullen, *Counterinsurgency*, 1.

29 U.S. Senate, *Inquiry into Occupation and Administration of Haiti and Santo Domingo: Hear-*

*ings before a Select Committee on Haiti and Santo Domingo, Sixty-Seventh Congress* (Washington, DC: Government Printing Office, 1921), (Statement of SDB, Oct. 27, 1921), 516.

30  Renda, *Taking Haiti*, 15.

31  Jennifer Greenburg, "'Going Back to History': Haiti and US Military Humanitarian Knowledge Production," *Critical Military Studies* 4, no. 2 (2018): 121–139.

32  Nicholas J. Schlosser, "The Marine Corps Small Wars Manual: An Old Solution to a New Challenge?," *Fortitudine* 35 (2010).

33  U.S. Marine Corps, *Small Wars Manual*, Vol. 6 (Washington, DC: U.S. Government Printing Office, 1940), sec. 1, 4.

34  Greenburg, "Going Back to History," 8.

35  SDB to Thomas S. Butler, Oct. 5, 1915, Butler Coll., MCHD.

36  SDB to Thomas R. Butler (son), Oct. 9, 1915, Stanford Lib.

37  Butler recommended Daly for his second Medal of Honor for the action. He had won his first shooting Boxers in China as a legation guard in 1900. David T. Zabecki, "Paths to Glory: Medal of Honor Recipients Smedley Butler and Dan Daly," *Military History*, Jan./ Feb. 2008; Thomas, *Old Gimlet Eye*, 209.

38  SDB to Ethel Butler and children, Nov. 3, 1915, Stanford Lib.

39  *Inquiry*, 1688.

40  David N. Buckner, *A Brief History of the 10th Marines* (Washington, DC: History and Museums Division, U.S. Marine Corps, 1981), 10; Thomas, *Old Gimlet Eye*, 204.

41  Thomas, *Old Gimlet Eye*, 205; Gaillard, *Premier écrasement*, 186–187.

42  "Haitian Says Gen. Butler Got Medal for Capturing Fort That Doesn't Exist," Associated Press, Apr. 25, 1931.

43  SDB to Ethel Butler, Nov. 30, 1915, Butler Coll., MCHD.

44  Lewis Ampidu Clorméus, "La démonstration durkheimienne de Jean Price-Mars: Faire du vodou haïtien une religion," *Archives de Sciences Sociales des Religions* 57, no. 159 (Jul.–Sep. 2012): 152–170.

45  *Inquiry* (SDB statement), 517.

46  *Inquiry* (Statement of Brig. Gen. Eli K. Cole, USMC), 673.

47  Ramsey, *Spirits and the Law*, 55; Milo Rigaud and Odette Mennesson-Rigaud, *La tradition voudoo et le voudoo haïtien: Son temple, ses mystères, sa magie* (Paris: Niclaus, 1953), 57, ufdc .ufl.edu/AA00002240/00001/59x.

48  John Locke, *The Thing's Incredible! The Secret Origins of Weird Tales* (Elkhorn, CA: Off-Trail, 2018), 189–190.

49  "Book Advertisements," *My Library Journey*, accessed Apr. 2021, ricketiki.weebly.com/book -advertisements.html.

50  Seabrook, *Magic Island*, 93.

51  Ibid., 96.

52  Ann Kordas, "New South, New Immigrants, New Women, New Zombies: The Historical Development of the Zombie in American Popular Culture," in *Race, Oppression and the Zombie: Essays on Cross-Cultural Appropriations of the Caribbean Tradition*, ed. Christopher Moreman and Cory James Rushton (Jefferson, NC: McFarland, 2011).

53  George Romero, introduction to Seabrook, *Magic Island*, 10.

54  "Zombie Preparedness for Educators," Center for Preparedness and Response, Centers for Disease Control and Prevention, accessed Apr. 2021, www.cdc.gov/cpr/zombie/educate .htm.

55  SDB, "America's Armed Forces: In Time of Peace," *Common Sense* 4, no. 11 (Nov. 1935): 8–12.

56  SDB to Thomas S. Butler, Dec. 23, 1915, Butler Coll., MCHD; Schmidt, *Occupation*, 103.

57  Schmidt, *Occupation*, 86, 88.

58 SDB to Ethel Butler, Nov. 27, 1915, Stanford Lib.; SDB to Ethel Butler, Nov. 30, 1915, Butler Coll., MCHD.

59 Wood, *What Have We Done*, 9, 11.

60 SDB to Maud Butler, Feb. 21, 1916, Stanford Lib.

61 Schmidt, *Maverick*, 73.

62 SDB to Ethel Butler and children, Mar. 12, 1916, Butler Coll., MCHD; SDB to Ethel Butler and children, Mar. 13, 1916, Butler Coll., MCHD; example of signature in SDB to Ethel Butler and children, Jun. 30, 1916, Butler Coll., MCHD.

## TWELVE: DOMINICAN REPUBLIC

1 Rosenberg, *Financial Missionaries*, 83; Peter James Hudson, "The National City Bank of New York and Haiti, 1909–1922," *Radical History Review* 115 (2013): 91–114, doi.org /10.1215/01636545-1724733; Gaillard, *Premier écrasement*, 143–147; Report of District Commander, Fort Liberte and Ouanaminthe, RG 127, Gendarmerie d'Haiti 1915–1926, General Correspondence, NARA; U.S. Senate, *Inquiry into Occupation and Administration of Haiti and Santo Domingo: Hearings before a Select Committee on Haiti and Santo Domingo, Sixty-Seventh Congress* (Washington, DC: Government Printing Office, 1921) (Statement of Admiral William B. Caperton), 376.

2 Hudson, *Bankers and Empire*, 46, 160; G. Pope Atkins, *The Dominican Republic and the United States: From Imperialism to Transnationalism* (Athens: University of Georgia Press, 1998), 46–48.

3 Stephen M. Fuller and Graham A. Cosmas, *Marines in the Dominican Republic, 1916–1924* (Washington, DC: History and Museums Division, U.S. Marine Corps, 1974), 9.

4 SDB to Ethel Butler and children, Sep. 5, 1916, Butler Coll., MCHD.

5 Paulino, *Dividing Hispaniola*, 20–35.

6 Casimiro N. De Moya, *Mapa de la Isla de Santo Domingo y Haiti* (London: Rand McNally, 1906). Map, www.loc.gov/item/2009579477/.

7 Venzon, *Letters*, note, 184; SDB to Ethel Butler and children, Jul. 16, 1916, Butler Coll., MCHD.

8 Expeditionary Commander to Commander Cruiser Force, U.S. Atlantic Fleet, Report of operations, Mounted Provisional Company, Major S. D. Butler, Sep. 1 to 26, 1916, RG 127, Gendarmerie correspondence, NARA. Bucá Creol as alternate name of El Cercado in Paulino, *Dividing Hispaniola*, 86.

9 SDB to Ethel Butler, Sep. 13, 1916, Butler Coll., MCHD.

10 Commanding Officer to Expeditionary Commander, Report of operations of Mounted Detachment, 2nd Regiment MC from Sep. 1 to Sep. 26, 1916, inclusive, RG 127, Gendarmerie correspondence, NARA; J. Fred Rippy, "The Initiation of the Customs Receivership in the Dominican Republic," *Hispanic American Historical Review* 17, no. 4 (Nov. 1937): 419–457; SDB to Thomas S. Butler, Oct. 1, 1916, Butler Coll., MCHD.

11 SDB to Thomas S. Butler, Oct. 1, 1916, Butler Coll., MCHD.

12 "Proclamation of the Military Occupation of Santo Domingo by the United States," *American Journal of International Law* 11, no. 2, Supplement: *Official Documents* (Apr. 1917): 94–96.

13 Rear Adm. Thomas Snowden to Brig. Gen. A. W. Catlin, USMC, 936–19 S-McG, May 24, 1919, RG 127, Box 4, NARA.

14 Lauren Derby, "Haitians, Magic, and Money: Raza and Society in the Haitian-Dominican Borderlands, 1900 to 1937," *Comparative Studies in Society and History* 36, no. 3 (Jul. 1994): 489.

15 Amelia Hintzen, "A Veil of Legality," *New West Indian Guide* 90, no. 1/2 (2016): 28–54.

16 Eller, *We Dream Together*, 230.

17  Bruce J. Calder, "Caudillos and *Gavilleros* versus the United States Marines: Guerrilla Insurgency during the Dominican Intervention, 1916–1924," *Hispanic American Historical Review* 58, no. 4 (Nov. 1978): 649–675.

18  César J. Ayala, *American Sugar Kingdom: The Plantation Economy of the Spanish Caribbean, 1898–1934* (Chapel Hill: University of North Carolina Press, 2009), 177.

19  Rob Ruck, *The Tropic of Baseball: Baseball in the Dominican Republic* (Lincoln: University of Nebraska Press, 1999), 11.

20  Valentina Peguero, *The Militarization of Culture in the Dominican Republic, from the Captains General to General Trujillo* (Lincoln: University of Nebraska Press, 2004), 44–45; "Antonio José Ignacio Guerra Sánchez, Cápsulas genealógicas Trujillo, descendiente de oligarquía haitiana," Instituto Dominicano de Genealogía, Apr. 24, 2008, www.idg.org.do /capsulas/abril2008/abril200812.htm/.

21  Trujillo was acquitted of the charges after prosecutors argued that a conviction would discredit the Guardia and the U.S. military government. Peguero, *Militarization*, 47, 51–52; Ernesto Vega i Pagán, *Military Biography of Generalissimo Rafael Leónidas Trujillo Molina, Commander in Chief of the Armed Forces* (Ciudad Trujillo, Dominican Republic: Editorial Atenas, 1956), translated by Ida Espaillat, 55.

22  García-Peña, *Borders of Dominicanidad*, 80.

23  Peguero, *Militarization*, 69; "Elections and Events 1924–1944," Dominican Republic, Latin American Elections Statistics, Research and Collections, UC San Diego Library, accessed Apr. 2021, library.ucsd.edu/research-and-collections/collections/notable -collections/latin-american-elections-statistics/Dominican%20Republic/elections-and -events-19241944.html; Raymond H. Pulley, "The United States and the Trujillo Dictatorship, 1933–1940: The High Price of Caribbean," *Caribbean Studies* 5, no. 3 (Oct. 1965): 22–31.

24  Derby, *The Dictator's Seduction*, 2;"Acoso, violaciones y asesinatos: Violencia hacia las mujeres durante el trujillato," *Hoy*, May 30, 2013, hoy.com.do/acoso-violaciones-y-asesinatos -violencia-hacia-las-mujeres-durante-el-trujillato/.

25  Harold Courlander, "Massacre in Santo Domingo," *New Republic*, Nov. 24, 1937.

26  Ambassador R. Henry Norweb to Secretary of State Cordell Hull, 1937, in Paulino, *Dividing Hispaniola*, 56.

27  Derby, *The Dictator's Seduction*, 2.

28  Sheridan Wigginton, "Character of Caricature: Representations of Blackness in Dominican Social Science Textbooks," *Race, Ethnicity and Education* 8, no. 2 (2005): 191–211; Ernesto Sagás, *Race and Politics in the Dominican Republic* (Gainesville: University of Florida Press, 2000), 75–76.

29  Martínez-Vergne, *Nation and Citizen*, 69; Paulino, *Dividing Hispaniola*, 74–75.

30  Paulino, *Dividing Hispaniola*, 129.

31  *Alleged Assassination Plots Involving Foreign Leaders: An Interim Report of the Select Committee to Study Governmental Operations with Respect to Intelligence Activities*, United States Senate, Nov. 20, 1975 (Washington, DC: U.S. Government Printing Office, 1975), 191–215; Nicholas M. Horrock, "C.I.A. Is Reported to Have Helped in Trujillo Death," *New York Times*, Jun. 13, 1975.

32  Amelia Hintzen, "Historical Forgetting and the Dominican Constitutional Tribunal," *Journal of Haitian Studies* 20, no. 1 (Spring 2014): 108–116.

33  I first wrote about Jean and Lamour's experience in the *New York Times Magazine*. See "In Exile," *New York Times Magazine*, Jan. 13, 2016.

34  "Matan Haitiano y lo Cuelgan en Parque Ercilia Pepín de Santiago," YouTube video, 2:29, uploaded by NoticiasRDComDo, Feb. 11, 2015, www.youtube.com/watch?v=ajhh3qwyFzg; Narciso Pérez, "Hallan haitiano colgado de un árbol en parque Ercilia Pepín de Santiago,"

*Diario Libre*, Nov. 2, 2015, www.diariolibre.com/actualidad/hallan-haitiano-colgado-de-un
-rbol-en-parque-ercilia-pepn-de-santiago-IADL1008541.

35  IOM Haiti, "Border Monitoring SITREP," Sep. 28, 2017; Associated Press, "Matan
haitiano en Hatillo Palma por supuesta violación a una dominicana," *El Día*, Aug. 20,
2015, eldia.com.do/matan-haitiano-en-hatillo-palma-por-supuesta-violacion-a-una
-dominicana/.

36  Fanon, *Damnés de la terre*, 3.

37  Todd Miller, *Empire of Borders: The Expansion of the U.S. Border around the World* (New
York: Verso, 2019), 3, 8.

## THIRTEEN: PORT-AU-PRINCE

1  SDB to Ethel Butler and children, Oct. 12, 1916, Stanford Lib.

2  Ethel Butler to "Family (both!)," Mar. 23, 1917, Butler Coll., MCHD.

3  Ibid.

4  The Hudson River branch of the Roosevelt family had been Democrats since before the
Civil War. See Jean Edward Smith, *FDR* (New York: Random House, 2008), 7.

5  Franklin D. Roosevelt, "Trip to Haiti and Santo Domingo, 1917," Franklin D. Roosevelt
Presidential Library and Museum, University of Florida, ufdc.ufl.edu/UF00082927/00001.

6  SDB to Maud and Thomas Butler, Feb. 4, 1917, Butler Coll., MCHD.

7  Roosevelt, "Trip to Haiti and Santo Domingo, 1917," 1; Schmidt, *Maverick*, 89.

8  U.S. Senate, *Inquiry into Occupation and Administration of Haiti and Santo Domingo: Hearings before a Select Committee on Haiti and Santo Domingo, Sixty-Seventh Congress* (Washington, DC: Government Printing Office, 1921), 670.

9  Roosevelt, "Trip to Haiti and Santo Domingo, 1917," 5.

10  Schmidt, *Occupation*, 96–97.

11  Conrad Black, *Franklin Delano Roosevelt* (New York: PublicAffairs, 2003), 5–6; John Pomfret, *Beautiful Country*, 20.

12  "Frank at Harvard—Courses List—The Franklin Delano Roosevelt Foundation," Compiled
by research associate Justin Roshak from FDR: *His Personal Letters*, Vol 1, 1947, edited by
Elliott Roosevelt, Franklin Delano Roosevelt Foundation: Suite and Historical Collections,
fdrfoundation.org/the-fdr-suite/frank-at-harvard-courses-list/, last accessed Jul. 2021;
Joseph Sweeney, "Franklin Delano Roosevelt as Lord of the Admiralty 1913–1920,"
*FLASH: The Fordham Law Archive of Scholarship and History* 48, no. 4 (2017): 405.

13  SDB to Maud and Thomas Butler, Feb. 4, 1917, Butler Coll., MCHD. In his undated trip
journal, FDR gives a detailed account of Butler accompanying him on the trip north. But
Butler's letters indicate otherwise.

14  Roosevelt, "Trip to Haiti and Santo Domingo, 1917," 10; "Honoring Major Smedley Butler," National Medal of Honor Museum, mohmuseum.org/medal-monday-honoring-major
-smedley-butler/, accessed Jul. 2021.

15  Schmidt, *Occupation*, 96–97.

16  David P. Geggus, "Sugar and Coffee Cultivation in Saint Domingue and the Shaping of the
Slave Labor Force," in *Cultivation and Culture: Labor and the Shaping of Slave Life in the Americas*, ed. Ira Berlin and Philip D. Morgan (Charlottesville: University of Virginia Press, 1993), 73.

17  Dubois, *Aftershocks of History*, 88.

18  *Inquiry*, 702 (Cole).

19  Thomas, *Old Gimlet Eye*, 214; *Inquiry*, 536 (SDB).

20  *Inquiry*, 702 (Cole).

21  *Inquiry*, 536, 538 (SDB).

22  *Inquiry*, 26 (Ernest Angell, the Haiti-Santo Domingo Independence Society, the National
Association for the Advancement of Colored People, the Union Patriotique d'Haiti).

23  *Inquiry*, 536 (SDB).

24 *Inquiry*, 26 (Angell).

25 Schmidt, *Occupation*, 97.

26 Trouillot, *Silencing*, 48.

27 *Inquiry*, 566–567 (Statement of Lt. Col. Alexander S. Williams, USMC).

28 Titre VIII, Article D & Titre VII, Article special: "Haïti, Constitution de 1918," Digithèque MJP, undated, mjp.univ-perp.fr/constit/ht1918.htm.

29 SDB, "'In Time of Peace': The Army," *Common Sense* 4, no. 11 (Nov. 1935): 8–12.

30 Schmidt, *Occupation*, 48.

31 SDB to Littleton Waller, May 16, 1916, in Venzon, *Letters*, 175; SDB to John A. Lejeune, Jul. 13, 1916, in Venzon, *Letters*, 182.

32 SDB to Thomas Butler, Dec. 23, 1915, Butler Coll., MCHD.

33 Gendarmerie d'Haiti, *Rural Code of Haiti* (Port-au-Prince: Imprimerie Edmond Chenet, 1916), 26.

34 J. Saint-Amand, *Le code rural d'Haiti publié avec commentaire et formulaires, notes et annexes à l'usage des fonctionnaires, officiers et agents de la police rural*, ed. A. Guyot, 2nd ed. (Port-au-Prince: A. Guyot, 1890).

35 *Inquiry*, 530 (SDB).

36 Gaillard, *Hinche mise en croix*, 224. Also cited in Marvin Chochotte, "The Twilight of Popular Revolutions: The Suppression of Peasant Armed Struggles and Freedom in Rural Haiti during the US Occupation, 1915–1934," *Journal of African American History* 103, no. 3 (2018): 277–308.

37 *Inquiry*, 165 (L. Ton Evans, Wyoming, PA).

38 *Inquiry*, 508 (T. C. Turner, Major, USMC).

39 SDB to Franklin D. Roosevelt, Dec. 28, 1917, in Venzon, *Letters*, 198.

40 *Inquiry*, 517 (SDB).

41 Schmidt, *Occupation*, 101.

42 Georges Anglade, *Espace et liberté en Haïti* (Montreal: ERCE & CRC, 1982), 25.

43 *Inquiry*, 517 (Roger Farnham, Vice President, National City Bank).

44 SDB to Maud and Thomas Butler, Oct. 6, 1917, Butler Coll., MCHD.

45 Schmidt, *Maverick*, 90–91.

46 SDB to Roger Farnham, Feb. 11, 1918; SDB to John A. McIlhenny, Jan. 29, 1918, cited in *Maverick*, 90–91; "Should not be tolerated for an instant longer than is necessary," SDB to McIlhenny, Jan. 29, 1918, cited in *Maverick*, 90–91; "Haiti Declares War against Germany," *New York Times*, Jul. 16, 1918, 5.

47 Schmidt, *Occupation*, 112.

48 Maud Butler to SDB, Dec. 25, 1917, Butler Coll., MCHD.

49 Schmidt, *Occupation*, 111, fn 1.

50 Associated Press, "Roosevelt Visits Cap Haitien, Haiti," *Evening Star* (Washington, DC), Jul. 5, 1934, 1.

51 William Pickens, "Will Vincent Imitate Machado?," *The Crisis*, Jun. 1935.

52 Trouillot, *State against Nation*, 102–108; Claire Antone Payton, "City of Water: Port-Au-Prince, Inequality, and the Social Meaning of Rain," *Journal of Urban History* (Feb. 2021): 1–22; Suzy Castor, "Veneer of Modernization," in *The Haiti Reader: History, Culture, Politics*, ed. Laurent Dubois et al. (Durham, NC: Duke University Press, 2020), 245.

53 Dubois, *Aftershocks of History*, 248.

54 Gaillard, *Charlemagne Péralte, le caco*, 222–223, 333.

55 Edward C. Johnson, *Marine Corps Aviation: The Early Years 1912–1940*, ed. Graham A. Cosmas (Washington, DC: History and Museums Division, Headquarters, U.S. Marine Corps, 1977), 53; Trouillot, *State against Nation*, 106.

56 Dubois, *Aftershocks of History*, 268–270.

57 Trouillot, *State against Nation*, 105–106.

58  Ibid., 136-153; Matthew J. Smith, *Red and Black in Haiti: Radicalism, Conflict, and Political Change, 1934–1957* (Chapel Hill: University of North Carolina Press, 2009), 103–148, 136–148, 150–153, 151.

59  Smith, *Red and Black in Haiti*, 180–182; Carleton Beals, "Haiti under the Gun," *The Nation*, Jul. 6, 1957.

60  Claire Antone Payton, "Building Corruption in Haiti," *NACLA Report on the Americas* 51, no. 2 (Apr. 3, 2019): 185.

61  Claire Antone Payton, "The City and the State: Construction and the Politics of Dictatorship in Haiti, 1957–1986," PhD diss., Duke University, 2018, 139.

62  Stephen Engelberg, Howard W. French, and Tim Weiner, "C.I.A. Formed Haitian Unit Later Tied to Narcotics Trade," *New York Times*, Nov. 14, 1993, 1, 12; Joshua E. Keating, "Foreign Policy: Trained in the U.S.A.," NPR, Mar. 29, 2012, www.npr.org/2012/03/29/149605074/foreign-policy-trained-in-the-u-s-a.

63  Thomas L. Friedman, "Haiti's Coup: Test Case for Bush's New World Order," *New York Times*, Oct. 4, 1991, 1, 8.

64  Walt Bogdanich and Jenny Nordberg, "Mixed U.S. Signals Helped Tilt Haiti toward Chaos," *New York Times*, Jan. 29, 2006.

65  "Peacekeeping: Cost Comparison of Actual UN and Hypothetical U.S. Operations in Haiti," Government Accountability Office, Feb. 21, 2006, www.gao.gov/assets/a249050.html.

66  See Katz, *The Big Truck*, 13–33. The lowest credible estimate of the earthquake's death toll was roughly 85,000, according to a report sponsored by USAID. The Haitian government's final official total was 316,000. For discussion see Katz, *The Big Truck*, 70. For comparison to other seismic events in history see, for example Katy Stoddard, "All the Deadliest and Strongest Earthquakes since 1900, Including Coordinates," *Guardian: Data Blog*, Jan. 13, 2010, www.theguardian.com/news/datablog/2010/feb/28/deadliest-earthquakes-strongest-data.

67  Jonathan M. Katz, "The King and Queen of Haiti," *Politico*, May 4, 2015, www.politico.com/magazine/story/2015/05/clinton-foundation-haiti-117368.

68  For example, Dubois, *Aftershocks of History*, 270; Teresa Welsh, "IDB Settles Accountability Case in Haiti, Granting Land to Farmers," *devex*, Jan. 11, 2019, www.devex.com/news/idb-settles-accountability-case-in-haiti-granting-land-to-farmers-94129.

69  *Inquiry*, 81 (C. S. Freeman, Captain, United States Navy; Edwin N. McClellan, Maj., USMC); *Inquiry*, 332 (Caperton); Deborah Sontag, "Earthquake Relief Where Haiti Wasn't Broken," *New York Times*, Jul. 5, 2012, www.nytimes.com/2012/07/06/world/americas/earthquake-relief-where-haiti-wasnt-broken.html.

70  Stephen Alexis, *Le nègre masqué: Tranche de vie haitienne* (Port-au-Prince: Imprimerie de l'Etat, 1933), 60.

71  Ibid., 96. Author's translation.

72  SDB to James R. Mann, Apr. 4, 1916, in Venzon, *Letters*, 169; Renda, *Taking Haiti*, 103.

73  Georges Corvington, *Port-au-Prince au cours des ans*, Vol. 3 (Montreal: Les Editions de CIDHICA, 2007), 50, 66.

## FOURTEEN: FRANCE

1  Sometimes misattributed to Woodrow Wilson, the notion of "the war that will end war" was popularized in a series of articles at the outbreak of hostilities and then a 1914 book with that title, both written by H. G. Wells.

2  "Yank Spirit Flashed in Tense, Terse Sentences," *Belvidere* (IL) *Daily Republican*, Jul. 5, 1919, 3.

3  SDB to Maud and Thomas S. Butler, Oct. 6, 1917, Butler Coll., MCHD.

4  James Joll and Gordon Martel, *The Origins of the First World War*, 3rd ed. (Harlow, UK, and New York: Pearson Longman, 2006), 219–248.

5 James Holmes, "Mahan, a 'Place in the Sun,' and Germany's Quest for Sea Power," *Comparative Strategy* 23, no. 1 (Jun. 2010): 27–61, doi:10.1080/01495930490274490.

6 Nicholas Mulder, "War Finance," in *1914–18-online: International Encyclopedia of the First World War*, ed. Ute Daniel et al. (Berlin: Freie Universität Berlin, 2018).

7 F. Katz, *Secret War in Mexico*, 364–367.

8 W. E. B. Du Bois, "Haiti," Dec. 21, 1939, W. E. B. Du Bois Papers (MS 312), Special Collections and University Archives, University of Massachusetts Amherst Libraries, credo.library.umass.edu/view/full/mums312-b197-i009, partially quoted in Byrd, *Black Republic*, 235.

9 SDB to Thomas S. Butler and Maud Butler, Oct. 5, 1918, Butler Coll., MCHD.

10 Ibid.; "Logue's Son Dies at Sea," *Evening Public Ledger* (Philadelphia), Oct. 15, 1918, 13; Thomas, *Old Gimlet Eye*, 244.

11 SDB to Thomas and Maud Butler, Oct. 5, 1918, in Venzon, *Letters*, 207.

12 Thomas, *Old Gimlet Eye*, 245.

13 SDB to Thomas Butler, May 16, 1917, Butler Coll., MCHD.

14 SDB to Ethel Butler, Jan. 15, 1919, in Venzon, *Letters*, 218.

15 SDB to Ethel Butler, Jan. 5, 1919, in Venzon, *Letters*, 213–216.

16 It is also in the Hebrew Bible, Deut. 20:8: "And the overseers shall speak further to the troops and say, 'Whatever man is afraid and faint of heart, let him go and return to his house, that he not shake the heart of his brothers like his own heart.'" Translation by Robert Alter in *The Hebrew Bible: A Translation with Commentary* (New York: W. W. Norton, 2019), 877.

17 SDB to Maud and Thomas S. Butler, Oct. 6, 1917, Butler Coll., MCHD.

18 SDB to Ethel Butler, Mar. 14, 1918, in Venzon, *Letters*, 222.

19 Butler Reference Files, MCHD; SDB to Ethel Butler, Jun. 5, 1919, in Venzon, *Letters*, 227.

20 "Ordre de l'étoile noire," accessed Apr. 2021, www.france-phaleristique.com/ordre_etoile_noire.htm.

21 SDB to Thomas Butler, Mar. 20, 1919, Butler Coll., MCHD.

22 Arthur West Little, *From Harlem to the Rhine: The Story of New York's Colored Volunteers* (New York, c. 1936), 354, hdl.handle.net/2027/mdp.39015005896116.

23 Ibid., 335–356.

24 SDB to Ethel Butler, Jan. 15, 1919, in Venzon, *Letters*, 218–220.

## FIFTEEN: PHILADELPHIA

1 Wilson's vision of "self-determination" did not extend to any of America's de facto or de jure colonies (much to the annoyance of the Haitian delegation to the Paris Peace Conference, among others). But the Senate narrowly refused to ratify the Treaty of Versailles (which would have created the League), arguing that the League would impinge on American sovereignty. "I can never be anything else but an American, and I must think of the United States first," said Teddy Roosevelt's old imperialist ally, Senator Henry Cabot Lodge. See Chelsea Stieber, Twitter post, Jun. 27, 2020, 6:10 p.m., twitter.com/chelseastieber/status/1277001398182445062; "'League of Nations' Speech by Henry Cabot Lodge, 1919," State Historical Society of Iowa: Educational Resources, Jun. 6, 2018, iowaculture.gov/history/education/educator-resources/primary-source-sets/world-war-i-evaluating-americas-role-global/henry-cabot.

2 Cross burnings, which were not a feature of the original Klan, were popularized by the movie. (The leader of the reconstituted Klan credited the film's source novels for the idea.) Griffith's costume department invented the iconic Klan robe for the film. See Tom Rice, *White Robes, Silver Screens: Movies and the Making of the Ku Klux Klan* (Bloomington: Indiana University Press, 2016), 10–11, 16–17.

3 Kristen Newby, "Ohio's Fight for the White House: Warren G. Harding Wins the 1920 Presidential Election," *Ohio Memory*, Nov. 6, 2020, ohiomemory.ohiohistory.org/archives/5227.

4   Schmidt, *Maverick*, 142.

5   SDB to Thomas Holcomb, Dec. 27, 1923, Butler Coll., MCHD, cited in Schmidt, *Maverick*, 142.

6   Victor E. Kappeler, "A Brief History of Slavery and the Origins of American Policing," EKU Police Studies Online, Jan. 4, 2014, plsonline.eku.edu/insidelook/brief-history -slavery-and-origins-american-policing; K. B. Turner, David Giacopassi, and Margaret Vandiver, "Ignoring the Past: Coverage of Slavery and Slave Patrols in Criminal Justice Texts," *Journal of Criminal Justice Education* 17, no. 1 (Apr. 1, 2006): 181–195.

7   Julian Go, "The Imperial Origins of American Policing: Militarization and Imperial Feedback in the Early 20th Century," *American Journal of Sociology* 126, no. 1 (Jul. 1, 2020): 1193–1254; Rachael Griffin, "Detective Policing and the State in Nineteenth-Century England: The Detective Department of the London Metropolitan Police, 1842–1878," PhD diss., University of Western Ontario, 2015, ir.lib.uwo.ca/etd/3427.

8   Patrick Glennon, "In Philly, One of the Nation's Oldest Police Departments," *Philadelphia Inquirer*, Dec. 8, 2017, www.inquirer.com/philly/opinion/commentary/in-philly-one-of -the-nations-oldest-police-departments-20171208.html.

9   Lincoln Steffens, "Excerpts from 'Philadelphia: Corrupt and Contented,' July, 1903," ExplorePAhistory.com, undated, explorepahistory.com/odocument.php.

10  Go, "The Imperial Origins of American Policing," 1205.

11  Sidney Hart and Mark Haller, "Philadelphia Bootlegging and the Report of the Special August Grand Jury," *Pennsylvania Magazine of History and Biography* 109, no. 2 (1985): 215–233; "Man Is Slain as Gang Feud Starts Anew," *Philadelphia Inquirer*, Sep. 20, 1925, 30. The Lanzettas' names (misprinted as Lanzetti) were Leo, Pius, Willie, Ignatius, Lucian, and Teo. Also see Anne Margaret Anderson and John J. Binder, *Philadelphia Organized Crime in the 1920s and 1930s* (Charleston, SC: Arcadia, 2014), 56.

12  Duffy was also an alias. He was Polish, born either William Michael Cusick or Michael Joseph Cusick, depending on the source. See "Mickey Duffy Slain; Riddled While Asleep in Boardwalk Hotel," *Philadelphia Inquirer*, Aug. 30, 1931; "Underworld Menace in Philadelphia," *Daily News* (New York), Sep. 16, 1928, 8; "Philadelphia Rivals Chicago in Gangsters," *Birmingham* (AL) *News*, Sep. 3, 1928, 3.

13  "Editorial Comment," *Philadelphia Inquirer*, Dec. 7, 1922, 12.

14  Half the population was Roman Catholic; about 15 percent were Jewish. See Barbara Klaczynska, "Immigration (1870–1930)," *Encyclopedia of Greater Philadelphia*, accessed Apr. 30, 2021, philadelphiaencyclopedia.org/archive/immigration-1870-1930/; Philip Jenkins, *Hoods and Shirts: The Extreme Right in Pennsylvania, 1925–1950* (Chapel Hill: University of North Carolina Press, 2000), 63.

15  "Historical Overview," The Great Migration: A City Transformed, accessed Apr. 30, 2021, greatmigrationphl.org/node/24.

16  Sadie Tanner Mossell, "The Standard of Living among One Hundred Negro Migrant Families in Philadelphia," *Annals of the American Academy of Political and Social Science* 98 (1921): 175.

17  "Philadelphia Bombers Are Not Captured," *Butler* (PA) *Citizen*, Jan. 1, 1919, 3.

18  Jenkins, *Hoods and Shirts*, 65–66; "Ku Klux Klan Brewing Racial and Religious Hate," *Evening Public Ledger* (Philadelphia, PA), Sep. 12, 1921; Thomas R. Pegram, "Hoodwinked: The Anti-Saloon League and the Ku Klux Klan in 1920s Prohibition Enforcement," *Journal of the Gilded Age and Progressive Era* 7, no. 1 (2008): 89–119.

19  "The Station-House Murder of Riley Bullock," *PhillyHistory Blog*, accessed Apr. 30, 2021, blog.phillyhistory.org/index.php/2016/05/the-station-house-murder-of-riley-bullock/.

20  "Two Policemen Shot by White Hooded Throng," *Philadelphia Inquirer*, Jul. 4, 1924, 1.

21  "Police Get 48 Hours to Rid Philadelphia of Vice or Quit Jobs," *New York Times*, Jan. 8, 1924.

22 Ellen Leichtman, "Smedley D. Butler and the Militarisation of the Philadelphia Police, 1924–1925," *Law, Crime, and History* 4, no. 2 (2014): 48–69.

23 Ibid.

24 "Butler Tightens Philadelphia Grip," *New York Times*, Jan. 13, 1924; Leichtman, "Militarisation of the Philadelphia Police," 66.

25 Hobsbawm, *Bandits*, 58.

26 Leichtman, "Militarisation of the Philadelphia Police," 64.

27 "Butler Begins War; Undesirables Flee from Philadelphia," *New York Times*, Jan. 9, 1924.

28 "Philadelphia Raids Net 1,045 Prisoners; Police Enter 700 Places in 48-Hour Drive and Frustrate Six Hold-Ups," *New York Times*, Jan. 21, 1924; "800 Philadelphians Arrested in 48 Hours," *New York Times*, Feb. 11, 1924; "Fusillade in Street Terminates Pursuit of Liquor 'Convoy,'" *Philadelphia Inquirer*, May 29, 1924.

29 Schmidt, *Maverick*, 149.

30 *Negro Survey of Pennsylvania* (Harrisburg: Commonwealth of Pennsylvania Department of Welfare, 1928), 69–70.

31 "'Get Bootleg Kings,' Butler Thunders," *Philadelphia Inquirer*, Feb. 29, 1924, 2.

32 "Arrested Man Escapes, 3 Policemen Suspended," *Philadelphia Inquirer*, Jun. 10, 1924.

33 Ibid.

34 Kristen B. Crossney, "Redlining," *Encyclopedia of Greater Philadelphia*, 2016, philadelphiaencyclopedia.org/archive/redlining/.

35 Timothy J. Lombardo, *Blue-Collar Conservatism: Frank Rizzo's Philadelphia and Populist Politics* (Philadelphia: University of Pennsylvania Press, 2018), 61–62, 105; Victoria A. Brownworth, "The Rizzo Legacy and the Queer Community," *Philadelphia Gay News*, Jun. 10, 2020, epgn.com/2020/06/10/the-rizzo-legacy-and-the-queer-community/.

36 Gaylord Shaw, "Warning Issued by Johnson's Commission Decried as Senseless by Police Officials," *Hazleton* (PA) *Standard-Speaker*, Mar. 2, 1968, 3; Suzanne Ife Williams, "Police Brutality: Case Study of Philadelphia/MOVE," PhD diss., Atlanta University, 1988, 135; Lombardo, *Blue-Collar Conservatism*, 144–145.

37 Mike Klare, "U.S. Military Operations/Latin America," *NACLA Newsletter* 2, no. 6 (Oct. 1968); Stuart Schrader, *Badges without Borders: How Global Counterinsurgency Transformed American Policing* (Oakland: University of California Press, 2019), 108; "8 Card-Carrying Reds in Group That Defied Tate Ban, Rizzo Says," *Philadelphia Inquirer*, Aug. 16, 1967.

38 "'Vote White,' Rizzo Tells Philly," *Pittsburgh Post-Gazette*, Sep. 23, 1978.

39 Jonathan Neumann and William K. Marimow, "[Interviews with 3 Detectives] . . . on Interrogations by Police," *Philadelphia Inquirer*, Apr. 24, 1977, 13-A.

40 Du Bois, *The Autobiography of W.E.B. Du Bois: A Soliloquy on Viewing My Life from the Last Decade of Its First Century* (New York: Oxford University Press, 2007; reprint edition, orig. pub. New York: International Publishers, 1968), 122.

41 MOVE was the group's full name, not an acronym. Lombardo, *Blue-Collar Conservatism*, 205–214; Tajah Ebram, "Can't Jail the Revolution: Policing, Protest, and the MOVE Organization in Philadelphia's Carceral Landscape," *Pennsylvania Magazine of History and Biography* 143, no. 3 (Oct. 2019): 333–336; Williams, *Police Brutality*, 201–202.

42 W. Wilson Goode with Joann Stevens, *In Goode Faith* (Valley Forge, PA: Judson Press, 1992), 46.

43 Michael Sokolove, "So This Is America: Assaying the Chaos," *Philadelphia Inquirer*, May 17, 1985, 9.

44 Lombardo, *Blue-Collar Conservatism*, 218–219; Sokolove, "So This Is America"; *Guardian* video, "The forgotten police bombing of a Move compound in Philadelphia," 4:22, Jul. 29, 2016, www.youtube.com/watch?v=6RFW9KuL-nk.

45 Phillip Jackson, "Group Demands Mayor Remove Rizzo Statue," *Philadelphia Tribune*,

accessed May 1, 2021, www.phillytrib.com/news/state_and_region/group-demands-mayor
-remove-rizzo-statue/article_ba043fe4-0376-5ef5-91ea-a803a5ababd5.html.

46 Tyler Wall, "The Police Invention of Humanity: Notes on the 'Thin Blue Line,'" *Crime, Media, Culture* 16, no. 3 (Dec. 1, 2020): 319–336, doi.org/10.1177/1741659019873757.

47 Though Rizzo might have agreed with the sentiment, the actual wording—"when the looting starts, the shooting starts"—came from Miami police chief Walter Headley, who made it a personal slogan in the late 1960s, most notably as his cops crushed a protest in a Black neighborhood against the 1968 Republican Convention that nominated Richard Nixon. Rob Tornoe, "Trump Incorrectly Cites Former Philly Mayor Frank Rizzo for Racist Phrase Aimed at Protesters," *Philadelphia Inquirer*, Jun. 12, 2020, www.inquirer.com/news/donald-trump-fox-news-frank-rizzo-protests-philadelphia-looting-shooting-starts-george-floyd-20200612.html.

48 Stella Cooper et al., "'I Am on Your Side': How the Police Gave Armed Groups a Pass in 2020," *New York Times*, Nov. 2, 2020, www.nytimes.com/video/us/100000007424380/police-black-lives-matter-protests.html; "Why Didn't Philly Police Respond to White Men with Bats? Fishtown Neighbors Wait for Answers," *WHYY* (blog), accessed May 2021, whyy.org/articles/why-didnt-philly-police-respond-to-white-men-with-bats-fishtown-neighbors-wait-for-answers/.

49 Over Time Grind, "The Last Day of Frank Rizzo Statue in Philadelphia [Raw Protest Footage BLM Philly George Floyd]," YouTube video, circa 13:30, Jun. 6, 2020, www.youtube.com/watch?v=hdvq3GEQXiI.

50 Patricia Madej, "Video Shows SEPTA Officer Assaulting Protesters with Baton During May Demonstration," *Philadelphia Inquirer*, Oct. 28, 2020, www.inquirer.com/transportation/septa-police-sergeant-assault-video-municipal-services-building-20201028.html.

51 Erin Donaghue, "Philadelphia Officials Release Bodycam Video and 911 Calls in Police Shooting of Walter Wallace Jr.," CBS News, Nov. 5, 2020, www.cbsnews.com/news/walter-wallace-jr-shooting-bodycam-footage-philadelphia-police/.

52 "Butler Raps Damp 'Judges,'" *Daily Local News* (West Chester, PA), Dec. 8, 1925, Newspaper Clippings File, Chester Co. HS; Fred D. Baldwin, "Smedley D. Butler and Prohibition Enforcement in Philadelphia, 1924–1925," *Pennsylvania Magazine of History and Biography* 84, no. 3 (Jul., 1960), 352–368.

53 Ellen C. Leichtman, "The Machine, the Mayor, and the Marine: The Battle over Prohibition in Philadelphia, 1924–1925," *Pennsylvania History: A Journal of Mid-Atlantic Studies* 82, no. 2 (2015): 130.

54 Baldwin, "Butler and Prohibition Enforcement in Philadelphia," 362.

55 "The Election Case of William B. Wilson v. William S. Vare of Pennsylvania (1929)," United States Senate, accessed May 1, 2021, www.senate.gov/about/origins-foundations/electing-appointing-senators/contested-senate-elections/109Wilson_Vare.htm; Leichtman, "Militarisation of the Philadelphia Police," 55.

56 "Butler Scents Huge 'Leak' in Alcohol Outgo," *Philadelphia Inquirer*, Feb. 28, 1924; "Trainer Is Called in Liquor Inquiry," *Philadelphia Inquirer*, Dec. 10, 1924.

57 SDB, *War Is a Racket*, 1–2.

58 "City Chemist Adds Liquor Drive Plea," *Philadelphia Inquirer*, Feb. 10, 1925; Baldwin, "Butler and Prohibition Enforcement in Philadelphia," 359.

59 Baldwin, "Butler and Prohibition Enforcement in Philadelphia," 366.

60 As the criminal justice scholar Ellen C. Leichtman later wrote, it is likely that Carney had set up Butler on behalf of Vare, to get rid of both the mayor and the Marine, who had each outlived their usefulness. Pinchot quote in Leichtman, "The Machine, the Mayor, and the Marine," 133.

61 "Memorial to General Butler," *Daily Local News*, Feb. 2, 1927.

# SIXTEEN: SHANGHAI

1 Lejeune to SDB, Jan. 25, 1926, Butler Coll., MCHD, in Schmidt, *Maverick*, 162.

2 SDB to Maud Butler, Mar. 14, 1926, Butler Coll., MCHD.

3 Schmidt, *Maverick*, 165; Mr. B., "The Extraction of General Butler's Infected Teeth [ . . . ]," letter to the editor, *Sun* (Baltimore), Mar. 18, 1926, 10; SDB to Adm. Philip Andrews, USN, May 24, 1926, Butler Coll., MCHD, in Schmidt, *Maverick*, 167.

4 SDB to Maud Butler, Jun. 29, 1926, Butler Coll., MCHD; "Official Aid Extended in Film Scenes," *Los Angeles Sunday Times*, Dec. 26, 1926, 26.

5 Tondo is the name of a neighborhood of Manila; Martin Dickstein, "The Cinema Circuit," *Brooklyn Daily Eagle*, Dec. 24, 1926, 8A.

6 The cycle would reach its apotheosis in 1987, when R. Lee Ermey, a former Marine staff sergeant, turned his Butler-and-Chaney-inspired bearing back into an iconic portrayal of a Marine drill instructor in Stanley Kubrick's *Full Metal Jacket*. Ermey had in fact been a drill instructor in San Diego before being deployed to Vietnam in 1968. Afterward, he spent two years in Okinawa, at Marine Corps Base Camp Smedley D. Butler.

7 As in Chapter 4, I am generally using the current Pinyin style of Chinese transcription, preferred by scholars and in the People's Republic of China. But for names broadly known to an English-speaking audience as they are rendered in the older modified Wade-Giles style, such as Sun Yat-sen (Sun Yixian, better known in China as Sun Zhongshan) and Chiang Kai-shek (Jiang Jieshi), I have used the more familiar versions.

8 Pomfret, *Beautiful Country*, 126–130.

9 Audrey Wells, *The Political Thought of Sun Yat-Sen: Development and Impact*, repr. (Basingstoke, UK: Palgrave Macmillan, 2001), 34; Bill Hayton, *The Invention of China* (New Haven, CT: Yale University Press, 2020), 147–148.

10 Ma. Luisa T. Camagay, "Mariano Ponce: Emissary to Japan," *Asian and Pacific Migration Journal* 8, no. 1–2 (Mar. 1999): 101–115, doi.org/10.1177/011719689900800106.

11 Karl, *Staging the World*, 64.

12 Sterling Seagrave, *The Soong Dynasty* (London: Corgi, 1996), 28. His given name was Han Jiaozhun.

13 Pakula, *Last Empress*, 48, 758.

14 Pomfret, *Beautiful Country*, 131.

15 Brian T. George, "The State Department and Sun Yat-sen: American Policy and the Revolutionary Disintegration of China, 1920–1924," *Pacific Historical Review* 46, no. 3 (Aug. 1977): 388–389.

16 Jeffrey N. Wasserstrom, "Chinese Students and Anti-Japanese Protests, Past and Present," *World Policy Journal* 22, no. 2 (Summer 2005): 59–65.

17 Charles E. Hughes to Calvin Coolidge, Dec. 5, 1923, *Papers Relating to the Foreign Relations of the United States*, Vol. 1 (1923), history.state.gov/historicaldocuments/frus1923v01/d410; Jing Li, *China's America: The Chinese View the United States, 1900–2000* (Albany: State University of New York Press, 2012), 22.

18 Seagrave, *The Soong Dynasty*, 191; "The Guomindang, the Communist Party and Leninism," *Greater China Journal*, Jun. 1, 2016, china-journal.org/2016/06/01/Guomindang-communist-party-and-leninism/.

19 Martin, *Shanghai Green Gang*, 10–11, 39, 42.

20 Ibid., 46, 71–74.

21 Ibid., 40–43, 78.

22 Ibid., 190–213.

23 Seagrave, *The Soong Dynasty*, 307.

24 Jay Taylor, *The Generalissimo: Chiang Kai-Shek and the Struggle for Modern China* (Boston: Belknap Press of Harvard University Press, 2009), 31; Martin, *Shanghai Green Gang*, 80–81;

Pichon Pei Yung Loh, *The Early Chiang Kai-shek: A Study of His Personality and Politics, 1887–1924* (New York: Columbia University Press, 1971), 133.

25  Pakula, *Last Empress*, 151–152; Martin, *Shanghai Green Gang*, 82–86, 89–90, 106–108; "Shanghai Museum of Public Security," in *Shanghai*, ed. Andrew Forbes and David Butow (Washington, DC: National Geographic Society, 2007), 126; Pakula, *Last Empress*, 151–152; Sue Williams and Kathryn Dietz, "China in Revolution," film (Ambrica Productions, 1990).

26  John V. A. MacMurray to Frank B. Kellogg, Jan. 16, 1927, *Papers Relating to the Foreign Relations of the United States*, Vol. 2 (1927), 893.00/8065: Telegram, history.state.gov /historicaldocuments/frus1927v02/d223; The Minister in China (MacMurray) to the secretary of state, Peking, Jan. 16, 1927, *Papers Relating to the Foreign Relations of the United States*, Vol. 2 (1927), 50, history.state.gov/historicaldocuments/frus1927v02/pg_50.

27  Sherman Cochran, *Encountering Chinese Networks: Western, Japanese, and Chinese Corporations in China, 1880–1937* (Berkeley: University of California Press, 2000), 24, 31–32; Shaw Yu-ming, *An American Missionary in China* (Cambridge, MA: Harvard University Press, 1992), 2; Madeline Y. Hsu, "Chinese and American Collaborations through Educational Exchange during the Era of Exclusion, 1872–1955," in "Conversations on Transpacific History," special issue, *Pacific Historical Review* 83, no. 2 (May 2014): 314–332; Ford Motor Co. advertisement, *Shanghai Volunteer Corps*, archival book, undated, Shanghai ZKW; *Shanghai Directory*, 1928, Shanghai ZKW; "U.S. Court for China, 1906–1943," Courts, Caseloads, and Jurisdiction, History of the Federal Judiciary, Federal Judicial Center, accessed Apr. 2021, www.fjc.gov/history/courts/us-court-china-1906-1943; "American Machine Gun Company, S.V.C," *Shanghai Volunteer Corps*, archival book, undated, Shanghai ZKW.

28  Tuchman, *Stilwell and the American Experience*, 122; "House Concurrent Resolution 45, 69th Congress, 2d Session," *Papers Relating to the Foreign Relations of the United States*, Vol. 2 (1927), 711.93/111, history.state.gov/historicaldocuments/frus1927v02 /d399.

29  Title of series by Putnam Weale in *North China Daily News*, quoted in John B. Powell, *My Twenty-Five Years in China* (New York: Macmillan, 1945), 144, and Tuchman, *Stilwell and the American Experience*, 130.

30  Frank B. Kellogg to John V. A. MacMurray, Jan. 28, 1927, *Papers Relating to the Foreign Relations of the United States*, Vol. 2 (1927), 61, history.state.gov/historicaldocuments /frus1927v02/pg_61.

31  John A. Lejeune to SDB, Feb. 7, 1927, in *My Dear Smedley*, 1.

32  Jordan, *Northern Expedition*, 122–125.

33  The Consul at Nanking (Davis) to the Secretary of State, *Papers Relating to the Foreign Relations of the United States*, Vol. 2 (1927), 155–156, history.state.gov/historicaldocuments /frus1927v02/pg_155; John V. A. MacMurray to Frank B. Kellogg, Mar. 29, 1927, *Papers Relating to the Foreign Relations of the United States*, Vol. 2 (1927), 168, history.state.gov /historicaldocuments/frus1927v02/pg_168; Benjamin R. Beede, *The War of 1898, and U.S. Interventions, 1898–1934: An Encyclopedia* (Hoboken, NJ: Taylor & Francis, 1994), 356–357.

34  Pearl S. Buck, *My Several Worlds: A Personal Record* (New York: John Day, 1954), 208.

35  SDB to John A. Lejeune, Apr. 1, 1927, in *My Dear Smedley*, 12; SDB to John A. Lejeune, Apr. 12, 1927, in *My Dear Smedley*, 39; Tuchman, *Stilwell and the American Experience*, 128.

36  John A. Lejeune to SDB, Mar. 1, 1927, in *My Dear Smedley*, 7.

37  Steven T. Ross, *American War Plans, 1890–1939* (London: Routledge, 2004), 128–130; Top Secret Correspondence Relating to Mobilization Plans, 1922–1942, Yellow

[China], 3479–13, no. 2965865, NARA; Thomas I. Faith, *Behind the Gas Mask: The U.S. Chemical Warfare Service in War and Peace* (Urbana: University of Illinois Press, 2014), 111.

38 Tuchman, *Stilwell and the American Experience*, 129; Powell, *My Twenty-Five Years in China*, 146; Associated Press, "Butler Takes Command of Marines in China, Says He Is Not Asking for Reinforcements," *New York Times*, Mar. 26, 1927.

39 "Interview with American Commander," *North China Herald and Supreme Court & Consular Gazette*, Apr. 9, 1927, Shanghai ZKW.

40 SDB to John A. Lejeune, Apr. 12, 1927, in *My Dear Smedley*, 40.

41 SDB to Ethel Butler and children, Apr. 9, 1927, Butler Coll., MCHD.

42 SDB to Maud Butler, Apr. 13, 1927, Butler Coll., MCHD.

43 Karl, *Mao Zedong and China in the Twentieth-Century World*, 33.

44 Ross Terrill, *Mao: A Biography* (Palo Alto, CA: Stanford University Press, 1999), 69; Mao Tse-tung, "Report on an Investigation of the Peasant Movement in Hunan" (Mar. 1927), in *Selected Works of Mao Tse-tung*, Marxists Internet Archive, www.marxists.org/reference/archive/mao/selected-works/volume-1/mswv1_2.htm.

45 Ian Johnson, "In China, 'Once the Villages Are Gone, the Culture Is Gone,'" *New York Times*, Feb. 1, 2014.

46 Isobel Cockerell, "Inside China's Massive Surveillance Operation," *Wired*, May 9, 2019, www.wired.com/story/inside-chinas-massive-surveillance-operation/; "China Cuts Uighur Births with IUDs, Abortion, Sterilization," Associated Press, Jun. 28, 2020; Stephanie Nebehay, "1.5 Million Muslims Could Be Detained in China's Xinjiang: Academic," Reuters, Mar. 13, 2019; Xinjiang Documentation Project, Institute of Asian Research, School of Public Policy and Global Affairs, University of British Columbia, accessed May 1, 2021, xinjiang.sppga.ubc.ca/.

47 SDB to John A. Lejeune, Jul. 16, 1927, in *My Dear Smedley*, 102.

48 Xizhe Peng, "Demographic Consequences of the Great Leap Forward in China's Provinces," *Population and Development Review* 13, no. 4 (Dec. 1987): 639–670; Thomas Heberer, "The Great Proletarian Cultural Revolution: China's Modern Trauma," *Journal of Modern Chinese History* 3, no. 2 (2009): 165–181, doi:10.1080/17535650903345379.

49 Joint Statement Following Discussions with Leaders of the People's Republic of China, *Foreign Relations of the United States, 1969–1976*, Vol. 17 (China, 1969–1972), history.state.gov/historicaldocuments/frus1969-76v17/d203.

50 Ezra F. Vogel, *Deng Xiaoping and the Transformation of China* (Cambridge, MA: Belknap Press of Harvard University Press, 2013), 25–26.

51 Li Yanzeng, 邓小平同志"黑猫白猫论"背后的故事 [The Story behind Comrade Deng Xiaoping's "Black Cat and White Cat Theory"], *News of the Communist Party of China*, accessed Jun. 2021 via Google Translate, cpc.people.com.cn/GB/85037/8530953.html.

52 Deirdre Shesgreen, "'Painted as Spies': Chinese Students, Scientists Say Trump Administration Has Made Life Hostile amid Battle against COVID-19," *USA Today*, Aug. 23, 2020.

53 SDB to John A. Lejeune, May 31, 1927, in *My Dear Smedley*, 69.

54 SDB to John A. Lejeune, Jun. 25, 1927, in *My Dear Smedley*, 93.

55 Alexander B. Coxe, Colonel, General Staff, Acting Director of Military Intelligence, to W. L. Hurley, Office of the Under Secretary, Department of State, "Japanese Activities in Philippine Islands," Apr. 7, 1920, RG 38: Records of the Office of Naval Intelligence, C-10-j, Register No. 12062, NARA.

56 Roy Hidemichi, "Japan's Economic Relations with China," *Pacific Affairs* 4, no. 6 (Jun. 1931): 488–510.

57 Jordan, *Northern Expedition*, 152; SDB to John A. Lejeune, Jun. 25, 1927, in *My Dear Smedley*, 97.

58 Ibid. letter, in *My Dear Smedley*, 95.

59 Hallett Abend, "Gen. Butler's Marines Win Friends in China," *New York Times*, Apr. 15, 1928, 142.

60 Jordan, *Northern Expedition*, 179; Shuge Wei, "Beyond the Front Line: China's Rivalry with Japan in the English-Language Press over the Jinan Incident, 1928," *Modern Asian Studies* 48, no. 1 (Jan. 2014): 188–224.

61 Zhitian Luo, "The Chinese Rediscovery of the Special Relationship: The Jinan Incident as a Turning Point in Sino-American Relations," *Journal of American-East Asian Relations* 3, no. 4 (Winter 1994): 362–363.

62 SDB to John A. Lejeune, Jul. 23, 1928, in *My Dear Smedley*, 265.

63 See Patrizia Violi, "Educating for Nationhood: A Semiotic Reading of the Memorial Hall for Victims of the Nanjing Massacre by Japanese Invaders," in "Museums and the Educational Turn: History, Memory, Inclusivity," special issue, *Journal of Educational Media, Memory and Society* 4, no. 2 (Autumn 2012): 42.

64 Suping Lu, "The Nanjing Massacre: Primary Source Records and Secondary Interpretations—A Textual Critique of Bob Tadashi Wakabayashi's Review," *China Review International* 20, no. 3/4 (2013): 259–282; Daqing Yang, "The Malleable and the Contested: The Nanjing Massacre in Postwar China and Japan," in *Perilous Memories: The Asia-Pacific War(s)*, ed. T. Fujitani, Geoffrey M. White, and Lisa Yoneyama (Durham, NC: Duke University Press, 2001), 75.

65 Jules Archer, *The Plot to Seize the White House* (New York: Hawthorn Books, 1973), 101.

66 "Gen. Butler Led the United Fire Forces Which Saved Most of Oil Plant at Tien-Tsin," *New York Times*, Dec. 26, 1927.

67 Ethel Peters Butler to Ethel (Snooks) Butler, May 11, 1927, personal collection of Philippa Wehle; SDB to Maud Butler, Feb. 26, 1928, Butler Coll., MCHD.

68 Ethel Butler to children, Nov. 29, 1928, Butler Coll., MCHD.

69 The village's name is Ta Chih Ku in Wade-Giles. SDB to John A. Lejeune, Oct. 2, 1928, in *My Dear Smedley*, 283; SDB, typescript of untitled speech about umbrellas, no date, Box 76, Folder 10, Butler Coll., MCHD; "'Umbrella of Blessings' Conferred on Gen. Butler," *New York Times*, Oct. 21, 1928; Translation of inscription on ribbon from photos provided by Newtown Square Historical Society by Jamie Fisher.

## SEVENTEEN: AMERICA

1 "Smedley Butler, Leader of 'Leathernecks' and Terror of Bootleggers[,] Will Retire," *Honolulu* (HI) *Advertiser*, Feb. 1, 1929, 3; "Gen. Smedley Butler Ends Pasadena Visit," *Pasadena* (CA) *Post*, Feb. 16, 1929, 1; "Gen. Butler Will Stop in Eastland Tomorrow," *Waxahachie* (TX) *Daily Light*, Feb. 15, 1929; "Gen. Smedley Butler Expected Home Today," Feb. 23, 1929, *Evening News* (Wilkes-Barre, PA), 1; "T. S. Butler Dies in Capital Hotel," *New York Times*, May 27, 1928, 3; Schmidt, *Maverick*, 201.

2 John A. Lejeune to SDB, Jun. 13, 1928, in *My Dear Smedley*, 263.

3 Schmidt, *Maverick*, 202.

4 SDB to Maud Butler, Mar. 31, 1928, Butler Coll., MCHD.

5 Ethel (Snooks) Butler to Ethel Peters Butler, Nov. 25, 1925, Stanford Lib.

6 Dubbed the Arab Gasoline Corporation, the company had its headquarters in Philadelphia; it was incorporated in Delaware in 1922. Its incorporators included the Sharples family, whose coal mine Smedley Butler had worked at as a manager in 1909. I don't know where the name "Arab" came from. At the time, oil exploration was just starting in the Arab lands of the former Ottoman Empire. It's possible they intended to eventually branch out there, or just liked the sound of the word. "Oil Field Equipment—Notes of Trade," *National Petroleum News*, May 31, 1922, 24.

7 "Lewis Seeks Senate Quiz of Butler Speech," *Pittsburgh Press*, Dec. 6, 1929, 2.

8 Robert Cochrane Jr., Secretary of Pittsburgh Builders' Exchange, to SDB, Dec. 11, 1929, Butler Coll., MCHD.

9 Schmidt, *Occupation*, 199–200; cf. H. W. Dodds, "American Supervision of the Nicaraguan Election," *Foreign Affairs*, Apr. 1929.

10 "Asks Gen. Butler to Explain Speech," *New York Times*, Dec. 15, 1929, 1, 22; for example, "Did He Spill the Beans?," *York* (PA) *Dispatch*, Dec. 31, 1929.

11 SDB to Maj. Gen. Wendell C. Neville, Dec. 14, 1929, Butler Coll., MCHD.

12 Adams was the great-grandson of John Quincy Adams and great-great-grandson of John Adams, the sixth and second presidents of the United States, respectively.

13 Schmidt, *Maverick*, 207.

14 "Charges by Navy on Butler Bared," *Evening Star* (Washington, DC), Feb. 9, 1931, A-3.

15 This was false. As a journalist who'd been to Fascist Italy later recounted: "The author was employed as a courier by the Franco-Belgique Tours Company in the summer of 1930, the height of Mussolini's heyday, when a fascist guard rode on every train, and is willing to make an affidavit to the effect that *most* Italian trains on which he travelled were not on schedule—or near it. There must be thousands who can support this attestation. It's a trifle, but it's worth nailing down." David Dudley, "The Problem with Mussolini and His Trains," *Bloomberg*, Nov. 15, 2016, www.bloomberg.com/news/articles/2016-11-15/stop-saying -mussolini-made-the-trains-run-on-time.

16 Senator Reed in debate on May 5, 1932, *Congressional Record* 75, Pt. 9, 9644.

17 "United States Apologizes to Mussolini; General Butler to Be Court-Martialed for Slur on Italian Premier in Speech," *New York Times*, Jan. 30, 1931, 1, 2.

18 "Mussolini to Talk over Radio Today," *New York Times*, Jan. 1, 1931, 56; United Press, "Butler Is Called for Speech on Il Duce," *Austin* (TX) *Statesman*, Jan. 27, 1931, 2.

19 Harold Callender, "Herr Hitler Replies to Some Fundamental Questions," *New York Times*, Dec. 20, 1931, 5.

20 Richard V. Oulahan, "Gen. Butler Freed with a Reprimand as He Voices Regret," *New York Times*, Feb. 9, 1931, 1, 2; "Butler's Counsel Wrote Reprimand," *New York Times*, Feb. 15, 1931, 22; "Text of the Formal Apology to Mussolini Given by Stimson to the Italian Ambassador," *New York Times*, Jan. 30, 1931, 1.

21 Associated Press, "Smedley Butler Quits Marines in Simple Ceremony," *Harrisburg* (PA) *Telegraph*, Sep. 30, 1931, 1.

22 The teenager living in it, I was floored to learn, was nicknamed "Bunny."

23 John M. Cummings, "Voters Smash Pinchot; Vare Tightens Grip," *Philadelphia Inquirer*, Apr. 28, 1932, 1.

24 Associated Press, "Butler Pledges to Work for Miners," *Philadelphia Inquirer*, Apr. 6, 1932, 13; SDB, "Republican Candidate for United States Senator Smedley D. Butler: Butler's Pledges to the People," *Perry County* (PA) *Times*, Apr. 21, 1932, 2.

25 Organized veterans groups like the Veterans of Foreign Wars came to reject the term "bonus"—which implied it was a handout, not money they had earned. But the term had been used early on by military publications like *Stars and Stripes*, and stuck even with supporters of the idea. Among other things, "World War adjusted compensation" was much harder to say.

26 Herbert Hoover, "February 26, 1931: Veto Messages Regarding Emergency Adjusted Compensation Act," University of Virginia Miller Center, accessed Apr. 2021, millercenter .org/the-presidency/presidential-speeches/february-26-1931-veto-messages-regarding -emergency-adjusted.

27 Dickson and Allen, *Bonus Army*, front matter.

28 Ibid., 105, 116.

29 Associated Press, "Hoover on Way to Camp Halts His Journey to Let Physician Treat Auto Crash Victim," *New York Times*, Jul. 18, 1932, 2.

30 Butler addresses demonstration—outtakes (Fox Movietone News Story 15–280), Fox Movietone News Collection, Moving Image Research Collections, University of South Carolina.

31 Dickson and Allen, *Bonus Army*, 152–159.

32 Ibid., 170–172.

33 Ibid., 171, 173–176; Dept. of the Army, "Bonus Army Riots in Washington, D.C., July 1932," Historical Films, ca. 1914–ca. 1936, NARA via YouTube, www.youtube.com/watch ?v=hB2kbbRpy5g&feature=youtu.be; Patrick Coffey, *American Arsenal: A Century of Waging War* (New York: Oxford University Press, 2013), 33.

34 Dickson and Allen, *Bonus Army*, 179. MacArthur made disobeying orders a hallmark of his career—a career that would end with him being fired by President Harry Truman during the Korean War for defying orders meant to prevent the outbreak of World War III. MacArthur's last job was as chairman of the board of the Remington Rand company, an early producer of commercial computers.

35 The baby's name was Bernard Myers. Government investigators determined that the baby was already sick and had died of gastroenteritis. But as doctors noted, the "gas certainly didn't do it any good." Ray Tucker, "Senate to Investigate Vets Charges That U.S. Agents Provoked Riots," *Knoxville* (TN) *News-Sentinel*, Aug. 11, 1932.

36 J. F. Essary, "Troops Burn Anacostia," *Baltimore Sun*, Jul. 29, 1932; Transcript of news conference with Sec. Patrick J. Hurley and Gen. Douglas MacArthur, *Public Papers of the Presidents of the United States* (Federal Register Division, National Archives and Records Service, General Services Administration, 1977), 340–342.

37 Dickson and Allen, *Bonus Army*, 174.

38 "Butler Lets Loose Attack on Hoover for Ousting B.E.F.," *Brooklyn Daily Eagle*, Oct. 29, 1932, 7.

39 Tugwell, *The Brains Trust*, 356–359.

40 "Norris Asks Voters to Bolt 'Bosses,' Turn to Roosevelt," *New York Times*, Oct. 18, 1932, 1.

41 Tugwell, *Democratic Roosevelt*, 118.

42 Ibid., 349.

43 Ibid., 350.

44 In 1938, Nazi officials would travel to Dearborn to award Ford the Grand Cross of the German Eagle. Bradley W. Hart, *Hitler's American Friends: The Third Reich's Supporters in the United States* (New York: Thomas Dunne Books, 2018), 121–122; Raymond Frederick, "'Heinrich' Ford Idol of Bavaria Fascisti Chief," *Chicago Tribune*, Mar. 8, 1923, 2.

45 Whitman, *Hitler's American Model*, 7–16, 42–43, etc. ("modest remnant" quote on 9); Peter Bermann, "American Exceptionalism and German 'Sonderweg' in Tandem," *International History Review* 23, no. 3 (Sep. 2001): 505–534; see also Carroll P. Kakel III, *The Holocaust as Colonial Genocide: Hitler's "Indian Wars" in the "Wild East"* (New York: Palgrave Macmillan, 2013).

46 Patricia O'Toole, *When Trumpets Call: Theodore Roosevelt after the White House* (New York: Simon & Schuster, 2005), 87–88.

47 John Keegan, *The Mask of Command* (New York: Viking Penguin, 1987), 248–249; Césaire, *Discours sur le colonialism*, 35–36; Fanon, *Damnés de la terre*, 216n7, translated by author.

48 Rauchway, *Why the New Deal Matters*, 37–38.

49 Tugwell, *Democratic Roosevelt*, 350.

50 Paul Comly French, *New York Post*, Nov. 20, 1934.

51 Testimony of SDB, *Investigation of Nazi Propaganda Activities and Investigation of Certain Other Propaganda Activities, Part 1, Before the Special Committee on Un-American Activities*, 73rd Cong. 11 (1934), 8.

52 Testimony of Charles C. MacGuire, *Investigation of Nazi Propaganda*, 113.

53 SDB, *Investigation of Nazi Propaganda*, 20.

54 John L. Spivak, "Wall Street's Fascist Conspiracy: Testimony That the Dickstein Committee

Suppressed," *New Masses*, Jan. 29, 1935, 11. In 1935, Spivak, a reporter for the Communist Party–affiliated *New Masses*, was given committee documents by Dickstein's staff that included officially redacted parts of Butler's testimony. In response to Butler's criticism over the redactions, Dickstein confirmed in a Feb. 26, 1935, statement on CBS Radio that the committee had indeed "omitted" references to several prominent figures named in his testimony to avoid "dragging [them] into the mud of publicity." Dickstein response to SDB, Butler Coll., MCHD.

55    "League Is Formed to Scan New Deal, 'Protect Rights,'" *New York Times*, Aug. 23, 1934, 1, 4.

56    "Investigation of Lobbying Activities: Hearings before a Special Committee to Investigate Lobbying Activities, United States Senate, Seventy-Fourth Congress, First Session, Pursuant to S. Res. 165, a Resolution Providing for an Investigation of Lobbying Activities in Connection with the So-Called 'Holding Company Bill'" (S. 2796), Jul. 12 to 23, 1935, Part 5 (1935): 1768–1772.

57    Jouett Shouse, *American Liberty League,* pamphlet published by the American Liberty League, 1934, digitized Nov. 20, 2009, 12, 14, www.google.com/books/edition/Document _s/4dlJAAAAYAAJ.

58    Testimony of Paul Comly French, *Investigation of Nazi Propaganda*, 21.

59    Spivak, "Wall Street's Fascist Conspiracy," 7; Tugwell, *Democratic Roosevelt*, 349.

60    "Gen. Butler Bares 'Fascist Plot' to Seize Government by Force," *New York Times*, Nov. 21, 1934, 1.

61    "Butler Charges Draw Laughs in Army Quarters," *Paterson* (NJ) *Evening News*, Nov. 22, 1932, 25.

62    "National Affairs: Plot without Plotters," *Time*, Dec. 3, 1934; "Credulity Unlimited," [editorial], *New York Times*, Nov. 22, 1934, 20.

63    See, for example, "I would say he is in error. He is mistaken." Testimony of Albert G. Christmas, *Investigation of Nazi Propaganda*, 141.

64    Testimony of G. C. MacGuire, ibid., 35.

65    "Butler Attacked by Fascist Prober," *Courier-Post* (Camden, NJ), Feb. 19, 1935, 7.

66    Hearings before the United States House Committee on the Judiciary, Subcommittee No. 2 (Judiciary), Seventy-Fourth Congress, First Session, on H.R. 4313 "A Bill to Make It a Crime to Advocate or Promote the Overthrow of the Government," etc., May 22, 1935, 77.

67    From complications of pneumonia, according to MacGuire's doctor. "G. C. M'Guire Dies; Accused of 'Plot,'" *New York Times*, Mar. 26, 1935, 33.

68    Schmitz, *United States and Fascist Italy*, 67.

69    Address of Nicola Sansanelli, *Proceedings of the Fifteenth National Convention of the American Legion* (Washington, DC: United States Government Printing Office, 1934), 38; Walter Wilson, "American Legion and Civil Liberty," American League Against War and Fascism, Socialist-Labor Collection, Florida Atlantic University, 19, fau.digital.flvc.org /islandora/object/fau%3A5378/datastream/OBJ/view/American_Legion_and_civil_liberty .pdf.

70    James Q. Whitman, "Of Corporatism, Fascism, and the First New Deal," *American Journal of Comparative Law* 39, no. 4 (Autumn 1991): 747; Spivak, "Wall Street's Fascist Conspiracy," 11; John Kennedy Ohl, *Hugh S. Johnson and the New Deal* (DeKalb: Northern Illinois University Press, 1985), 299; "The United States: Isolation-Intervention," *Holocaust Encyclopedia*, United States Holocaust Memorial Museum, accessed Apr. 2021, encyclopedia.ushmm.org/content/en/article/the-united-states-isolation-intervention.

71    Allen C. Thomas, ed., *Biographical Catalogue of the Matriculates of Haverford College, 1833–1900* (Philadelphia: Printed for the Alumni Association, 1900), 258; "G M.-P. Murphy, 58, Financier, Is Dead," *New York Times*, Oct. 19, 1937, 25; George Washington Cullum,

*Biographical Register of the Officers and Graduates of the U.S. Military Academy at West Point, N.Y. Since Its Establishment in 1802: Supplement* (Cambridge, MA: Printed at the Riverside Press, 1910), 695; William R. Corson, *The Armies of Ignorance: The Rise of the American Intelligence Empire* (New York: Dial Press/J. Wade, 1977), 597–598.

72  Hudson, *Bankers and Empire*, 155, 160–161; Pérez, *Intervention*, 131; Corson, *The Armies of Ignorance*, 598; Jay Jakub, *Spies and Saboteurs: Anglo-American Collaboration and Rivalry in Human Intelligence Collection and Special Operations, 1940–45* (London: Palgrave Macmillan, 1999), 1–21.

73  For example, tweet by Donald J. Trump (@realDonaldTrump), "Peter Navarro releases 36-page report alleging election fraud 'more than sufficient' to swing victory to Trump. . . . A great report by Peter. Statistically impossible to have lost the 2020 Election. Big protest in D.C. on January 6th. Be there, will be wild!" on Dec. 19, 2020, archived at trumptwitterarchive.com. Further examples on Dec. 26 and 27, 2020, and Jan. 1 and 3, 2021. "And we're going to fight for president Trump on January 6th. God bless Georgia, God bless America. Let's do this." "Donald Trump Rally Speech Transcript Dalton, Georgia: Senate Runoff Election," Rev.com, Jan. 4, 2021, www.rev.com/blog/transcripts/donald -trump-rally-speech-transcript-dalton-georgia-senate-runoff-election.

74  For example, Francesca Trianni, "Flags, Hate Symbols and QAnon Shirts: Decoding the Capitol Riot," *Time*, Jan. 11, 2021; Dan Barry, Mike McIntire, and Matthew Rosenberg, "'Our President Wants Us Here': The Mob That Stormed the Capitol," *New York Times*, Jan. 9, 2021, updated Apr. 2, 2021.

75  Brian Naylor, "Read Trump's Jan. 6 Speech, a Key Part of Impeachment Trial," NPR, Feb. 10, 2021, www.npr.org/2021/02/10/966396848/read-trumps-jan-6-speech-a-key-part-of -impeachment-trial.

76  Gregory Korte, "Latino Vote Surge Helped Biden in Key States, New Data Suggest," *Bloomberg*, Apr. 30, 2021; Nicholas Carnes and Noam Lupu, "Trump Didn't Bring White Working-Class Voters to the Republican Party. The Data Suggest He Kept Them Away," *Washington Post*, Apr. 14, 2021.

77  Jenkins and Millington, *France and Fascism*, 181–182.

78  See, for example, Hunter Walker, "Trump Falsely Claims Election Win and Says He Wants 'All Voting to Stop' as Biden Calls for 'Patience,'" Yahoo News, Nov. 4, 2020, www.yahoo .com/now/trump-falsely-claims-election-win-and-says-he-wants-all-voting-to-stop-as-biden -calls-for-patience-083101276.html; and "Keystone Koup," *The Long Version*, Nov. 18, 2020, by the author at katz.substack.com/p/keystone-koup.

79  Dmitriy Khavin, et al., "Day of Rage: An In-Depth Look at How a Mob Stormed the Capitol," *New York Times* video, Jun. 30, 2021, www.nytimes.com/video/us/politics /100000007606996/capitol-riot-trump-supporters.html. Jan Wolfe, "Four Officers Who Responded to U.S. Capitol Attack Have Died By Suicide," Reuters, Aug. 2, 2021, www.reuters.com/world/us/officer-who-responded-us-capitol-attack-is-third-die-by-suicide -2021-08-02/.

80  See Robert O. Paxton, "The Five Stages of Fascism," *Journal of Modern History* 70, no. 1 (1998): 1–23, doi:10.1086/235001; Finchelstein, *From Fascism to Populism in History*, ix–xxviii; Stanley, *How Fascism Works*, 15–23.

81  Stephen Losey, "Woman Shot and Killed at Capitol Was Security Forces Airman, QAnon Adherent," *Air Force Times*, Jan. 7, 2021; Ronan Farrow, "An Air Force Combat Veteran Breached the Senate," *New Yorker*, Jan. 8, 2021, www.newyorker.com/news/news-desk/an -air-force-combat-veteran-breached-the-senate; Camila Domonoske, "The QAnon 'Storm' Never Struck. Some Supporters Are Wavering, Others Steadfast," NPR, Jan. 20, 2021, www.npr.org/sections/inauguration-day-live-updates/2021/01/20/958907699/the-qanon -storm-never-struck-some-supporters-are-wavering-others-steadfast; David Wiegel, "The Trailer: Watching the Riot at the Capitol Unfold from the Ground," *Washington Post*, Jan.

7, 2021; *Q: Into the Storm*, directed by Cullen Hoback, United States: HBO Documentary Films, 2021.

82  Seth Moulton, "Seth Moulton: This Is Domestic Terrorism," CNN.com, Jan. 6, 2021; Adela Suliman, "George W. Bush, Others Criticized for Comparing Capitol Unrest to 'Banana Republics,'" NBCNews.com, Jan. 8, 2021.

83  Karen Yourish, Larry Buchanan, and Denise Lu, "The 147 Republicans Who Voted to Overturn Election Results," *New York Times*, Jan. 7, 2021.

84  Nick Corasaniti and Reid J. Epstein, "What Georgia's Voting Law Really Does," *New York Times*, Apr. 2, 2021; Alexa Ura, "Texas Senate Advances Bill Limiting How and When Voters Can Cast Ballots, Receive Mail-in Voting Applications," *Texas Tribune*, Apr. 1, 2021, www.texastribune.org/2021/04/01/texas-voting-restrictions-legislature.

85  Mark Joyella, "Maggie Haberman: Trump Telling People He Expects to Be 'Reinstated' as President by August," Forbes.com, Jun. 1, 2021, www.forbes.com/sites/markjoyella/2021 /06/01/maggie-haberman-trump-telling-people-he-expects-to-be-reinstated-as-president-by -august/.

86  "Biden's Speech to Congress: Full Transcript," *New York Times*, Apr. 29, 2021.

87  Robert Grenier, "How to Defeat America's Homegrown Insurgency," *New York Times*, Jan. 27, 2021; also cited in Spencer Ackerman, *Reign of Terror: How the 9/11 Era Destabilized America and Produced Trump* (New York: Viking, 2021), 354.

88  Rioters arrested or charged in the Jan. 6 siege were "by and large, older and more profes- sional than right-wing protesters we have surveyed in the past . . . 95 percent White and 85 percent male." Robert A. Pape, "Opinion: What an Analysis of 377 Americans Arrested or Charged in the Capitol Insurrection Tells Us," *Washington Post*, Apr. 6, 2021.

89  Gina Harkins and Hope Hodge Seck, "Marines, Infantry Most Highly Represented among Veterans Arrested after Capitol Riot," *Military Times*, Feb. 26, 2021; Andrea Scott, "Quan- tico Marine Major Charged with Assaulting an Officer during Capitol Breach," *Marine Corps Times*, May 13, 2021; Khavin, et al., "Day of Rage," 23:10.

90  J. Edgar Hoover, "Memorandum for the Attorney General," Aug. 8, 1936, Butler file, FBI Records: The Vault, vault.fbi.gov/smedley-butler, accessed Aug. 2017.

91  Walter Wilson, "Where Smedley Butler Stands," *New Masses* 17, no. 7 (Nov. 12, 1935), 17.

92  SDB, *War Is a Racket*, 10.

93  Ibid., 28–29, 37.

94  SDB, "'In Time of Peace': The Army," *Common Sense* 4, no. 11 (Nov. 1935): 8–12.

95  "Butler Controversy" folder, John H. Russell Coll., MCHD.

96  United Press, "Gen. Butler Sees Japan Controlling Philippines," *Lancaster* (PA) *New Era*, Jan. 19, 1933, 7; SDB, "Bring Our Soldiers Home from China," *Liberty Magazine*, Jan. 8, 1938, in Butler Coll., MCHD.

97  Schmidt, *Maverick*, 231.

98  "Butler Controversy" folder, John H. Russell Coll., MCHD.

99  "Obituaries: Mrs. Thomas S. Butler," newspaper unknown, Jun. 22, 1936, Chester Co. HS.

100  Al Degrassi, "'War Is a Lousy Damn Racket' Shouts Butler at Peace Meet; 8000 Hear Fiery Declarations," *Daily Californian* (UC Berkeley), Apr. 17, 1939.

101  Ibid.; "Shout for Peace, Says General Butler at U.C.," *Oakland* (CA) *Tribune*, Apr. 14, 1939.

## EPILOGUE: WEST CHESTER

1  John M. McCullough, "Gen. Butler, 58, Is Dead after Brief Illness," *Philadelphia Inquirer*, Jun. 22, 1940, 1, 9; United Press, "Gen. Smedley Butler, Stormy Petrel of US Marine Corps, Dies," *Honolulu Advertiser*, Jun. 22, 1940, 1.

2  "Gen. Butler Buried in His Native Hills," *Philadelphia Inquirer*, Jun. 25, 1940, 36; "Presi- dent Mourns Passing of Butler," *Philadelphia Inquirer*, Jun. 23, 1940, 10.

3  Letters from Quakers to J. Carroll Hayes, Oct. 28, 1931, and Aug. 27, 1933, Chester Co.

HS; J. Carroll Hayes to Thomas A. Jenkins, Aug. 30, 1933, Butler File, Chester Co. HS; Eulogy of SDB by Dr. William T. Sharpless, Butler File, Chester Co. HS.

4 F. D. Roosevelt, "Fireside Chat," Dec. 9, 1941, American Presidency Project, www.presidency.ucsb.edu/node/210419.

5 United States Congress Senate Committee on Naval Affairs, *Naval Expansion Program: Hearings before the Committee on Naval Affairs, United States Senate, Seventy-Fifth Congress, Third Session, on H.R. 9218, an Act to Establish the Composition of the United States Navy, to Authorize the Construction of Certain Naval Vessels, and for Other Purposes. April 4, 5, 6, 7, 8, 11, 12, and 13, 1938* (Washington, DC: U.S. Government Printing Office, 1938), 152.

6 "National Affairs: Pacifists, Hell!," *Time*, Aug. 31, 1931.

7 Norman Thomas, *A Socialist's Faith* (New York: W. W. Norton, 1951), 313.

8 "USS Butler—Battle of Normandy," D-Day Overlord, accessed Apr. 2021, www.dday-overlord.com/en/material/warships/uss-butler.

9 Ethel Butler to Peace Now Movement, Apr. 21, 1944, Stanford Lib.

10 *Commandants of the Marine Corps* (Annapolis, MD: Naval Institute Press, 2004), 379.

11 "Attack Would Be a Mistake, Says Former UN Inspector," *Irish Times*, Sep. 9, 2002.

12 "Chelsea Manning's Prison Sentence Commuted by Barack Obama," *Guardian*, Jan. 18, 2017.

13 "Reality Winner, Former N.S.A. Translator, Gets More Than 5 Years in Leak of Russian Hacking Report," *New York Times*, Aug. 23, 2018.

# INDEX